Engineering Hydrology
Fundamentals and Applications
Water Resources Engineering Vol II

Subhash C. Verma P. Eng.
Prof. (Retd.) Sault College of Applied Arts and Technology
Sault Ste. Marie, Ontario, Canada

Edited by

Jagdish K. Chawla Ph.D.
Formerly, Director cum Professor
Ludhiana Group of Colleges
Chaukiman, Ludhiana

Preface

This book covers the material for one semester course in engineering hydrology for degree and diploma students in the fields of Civil, Water Resources, Agricultural and Environmental engineering. It is well suited for practicing engineers to refresh their basics in the design of storm drainage systems, measurement of streamflow and precipitation and management of water resources. Material is presented to assist the students grasp basic concepts, and applications in the field of engineering. Although existing references supply total information relevant to water resources engineering, providing a book emphasizing basic concepts, applications, and skills for solving practical problems for undergraduate students and newcomers to this field is a requirement. This book can serve as a foundation to higher level courses in surface hydrology and water resources.

Basic concepts in surface hydrology are explained thoroughly with the help of solved examples and numerous practice problems provided at the end of each chapter. The main topics include water budgeting, precipitation, probability, stream flow measurement, watershed characteristics, flow hydrographs, peak flow, unit hydrograph and flood routing.

Applications of concepts and applicable formulae are illustrated with numerous practical example problems with suitable figures where applicable. In each example problem, a step-by-step solution is shown following the procedure of unit cancellation using SI units. At the end of each unit, practice problems with answers are presented for students to get enough practice in application of theory and use of formulae. For self-evaluation, several review questions of multiple-choice type are presented at the end of each unit. In addition, questions for further discussion are added for students to solidify the concepts and prepare themselves to write tests and competitive examinations.

Based on many years of teaching experience, methodology as presented in this book lays good foundation for engineering students to solve problems without making silly mistakes and avoid the stress of remembering different sets of formulae for different set of units. The application of a formula rather than just cramming it, is emphasized.

Hydrology is not an exact science, therefore, making judicious decisions are emphasized. Since this is an introductory course, more complex theories are avoided. Throughout the entire book, International System of Units (SI) is used.

It is my firm belief that this book will be a useful resource for students, teachers, and practising engineers alike. In the end, author would request students and teachers to provide feedback for further improvements and for any errors and omissions.

- **Author**

Table of Contents

1	INTRODUCTION	1
1.1	Hydrologic Cycle	1
1.2	Quantifying Water Resources	3
1.3	Water Resources of India	5
1.4	Water Management	7
1.5	Hydrologic Data	12
1.6	Water Balance	15
1.7	Applications of Hydrology	19
1.8	Watershed Management	21
2	PRECIPITATION	32
2.1	Forms of Precipitation	32
2.2	Types of Precipitation	34
2.3	Measurement of Precipitation	35
2.4	Snow Surveys	37
2.5	Rainfall Data	39
2.6	Missing Data	42
2.7	Gauge Consistency	46
3	STORM ANALYSIS	58
3.1	Temporal Distribution	58
3.2	Spatial Distribution	62
3.3	Depth and Catchment Area	67
3.1	Depth, Duration, Frequency (DDF)	70
3.2	Intensity-Duration-Frequency (IDF)	71
3.3	Synthetic Storms	78
4	STREAM FLOW MEASUREMENT	93
4.1	Stream flow variation	93
4.2	Measurement of Stage	94
4.3	Measurement of Flow Velocity	97
4.4	Discharge Measurements	98
4.5	Chemical Gauging	102
4.6	Indirect Methods	103
4.7	Flow Measuring Structures	107

4.8	Stage Discharge Relation	107
5	PROBABILITY CONCEPTS	118
5.1	Probability Definition	118
5.2	Rules of Probability	118
5.3	Binomial Process	120
5.4	Probability Distribution	123
5.5	Normal Distribution	125
5.6	Non-Normal Distribution	130
6	WATERSHED CHARACTERISTICS	142
6.1	Classification of Watersheds by Size	142
6.2	Watersheds Classification by Land Use	143
6.3	Watershed Characteristics	146
6.4	Relief Features	148
6.5	Channel Slope/Gradient	151
6.6	Basin Slope	153
7	HYDROLOGIC ABSTRACTIONS	159
7.1	Interception Storage	159
7.2	Depression Storage	159
7.3	Detention Storage	160
7.4	Infiltration	160
7.5	Curve Number (CN) Method	172
7.6	Evaporation and Transpiration	182
8	FLOW HYDROGRAPH	197
8.1	Components of Stream Flow	197
8.2	Hydrograph Shape	199
8.3	Hydrograph Time Characteristics	200
8.4	Stream Flow Recession	206
9	PEAK FLOW RATE	221
9.1	Peak Flow and Watershed Area	221
9.2	Rational Method	222
9.3	Cook's Method	234
9.4	TR-55 Graphical Method	234
9.5	TR-55 Procedure	238

9.6	Triangular Hydrograph	241
10	UNIT HYDROGRAPH	255
10.1	Derivation of UH	256
10.2	UH of Other Durations	259
10.3	Application of UH	264
10.4	Synthetic Unit Hydrograph	269
11	FLOOD ROUTING	291
11.1	Flood Routing Defined	291
11.2	Routing Methods	292
11.3	Hydrologic Storage Routing	293
11.4	Muskingum Method of Routing	304

List of Figures

Figure 1.1 Hydrologic Cycle Components	2
Figure 1.2 Distribution of Water on the Earth	4
Figure 1.3 Hydrologic Budgeting for a Watershed	16
Figure 2.1 Standard and Tipping Bucket Gauge	35
Figure 2.2 Quadrant Method(Ex. Prob. 2.5)	45
Figure 2.3 Double Mass Curve and Consistency	47
Figure 2.4 Adjustment of the Mass Curve	49
Figure 2.5 Tipping Bucket Rain Gauge Graph	52
Figure 2.6 Recording Rain Gauge Chart	53
Figure 3.1 Dimensionless Hyetograph(Ex. 3.1)	59
Figure 3.2 Rainfall Hyetograph (Ex. Prob. 3.2)	61
Figure 3.3 Rainfall Data of a Storm (Ex. Prob. 3.3)	62
Figure 3.4 Isohyetal Method and Polygon Method	64
Figure 3.5 Thiessen Polgon Method (Ex. Prob. 3.5)	66
Figure 3.6 Isohyetal Method (Ex. Prob. 3.5)	67
Figure 3.7 DAD Curve (Ex. Prob. 3.5))	70
Figure 3.8 A Set of IDF Curves	71
Figure 3.9 IDF Curve (Ex. Prob. 3.7)	74
Figure 3.10 IDF Curves (Ex. Prob. 3.8)	76
Figure 3.11 A Semilog Plot	77
Figure 3.12 Fitting an Exponential Equation	77
Figure 3.13 NRCS Synthetic Storms	78
Figure 3.14 Dimensionless Storm (Ex. Prob. 3.10)	80
Figure 3.15 Design of a 6-h Storm(Ex. Prob. 3.11)	82
Figure 3.16 Triangular Shaped Design Storm	83
Figure 3.17 Isohyetal map (Practice Problem 3.7)	86
Figure 4.1 Stage Discharge Relationship	94
Figure 4.2 Staff Gauge and Float Gauge	95
Figure 4.3 Mid-Section Method	100

Table of Contents v

Figure 4.4 Slope Area Method	103
Figure 4.5 Stage Discharge Plot (Ex. Prob. 4.5)	110
Figure 4.6 Fitting Equation (Ex. Prob. 4.5)	110
Figure 5.1 Standard Normal distribution Curve	124
Figure 6.1 Hypsometric Curve (Ex. Prob. 6.2)	149
Figure 6.2 Longitudinal Profile (Ex. Prob. 6.4)	153
Figure 7.1 Plot of Infiltration Curves	164
Figure 7.2 Fitting Exponential Equation	165
Figure 7.3 Fitting Horton Equation	166
Figure 7.4 Infiltration Index(Ex. Prob. 7.4)	169
Figure 7.5 Runoff Rate(Ex. Prob. 7.5)	170
Figure 7.6 Plots of infiltration and rainfall	172
Figure 7.7 Storm Runoff Depths(Ex. Prob. 7.10)	179
Figure 7.8 Rainfall Runoff Histogram	181
Figure 8.1 Components of Stream flow	197
Figure 8.2 Elements of Runoff Hydrograph	199
Figure 8.3 Hydrograph Time Characteristics	201
Figure 8.4 Fitting Equation to Recession Flow Data	209
Figure 8.5 Base Flow Separation	210
Figure 8.6 Base Flow Separation (Ex. Prob. 8.8)	212
Figure 8.7 Base Flow Separation (Ex. Prob. 8.9)	214
Figure 8.8 Storm Flows (Ex. Prob. 8.9)	214
Figure 9.1 Inlet and Travel Time	231
Figure 9.2 Storm Drainage System (Ex. Prob. 9.6)	231
Figure 9.3 Inlet and Travel Time(Ex. Prob. 9.7)	233
Figure 9.4 Triangular Flow Hydrograph	242
Figure 9.5 Drainage Area (Pr. Prob. 9.21)	249
Figure 9.6 Urban Area (Pr. Prob. 8.17)	249
Figure 9.7 Parking Lot (Pr. Prob. 8.20)	250
Figure 10.1 Unit Hydrograph Definition	256

Figure 10.2 Derivation of Unit Hydrograph	258
Figure 10.3 Plot of 3-h UH and Storm Hydrograph	260
Figure 10.4 S-hydrograph (Ex. Prob. 10.3)	262
Figure 10.5 S-Curve Method (Ex. Prob. 10.4)	264
Figure 10.6 Flow Hydrograph (Ex. Prob. 10.6)	267
Figure 10.7 NRCS Dimensionless Flow Hydrograph	272
Figure 10.8 NRCS Triangular Hydrograph	273
Figure 10.9 NRCS Synthetic UH (Ex. Prob. 10.8)	276
Figure 10.10 Unit Hydrograph(Ex. Prob. 10.10	278
Figure 10.11 Flow Hydrograph(Ex. Prob. 10.12)	280
Figure 11.1 Reservoir Outflow versus Elevation	296
Figure 11.2 (S+Δt/2) vs Elevation(Ex.Prob. 11.2)	297
Figure 11.3 Routed Hydrograph (Ex. Prob. 11.2)	298
Figure 11.4 Reservoir Outflow versus Elevation	299
Figure 11.5 (S+QΔt/2) versus Elevation	300
Figure 11.6 Routed Hydrograph (Ex. Prob. 11.3)	301
Figure 11.7 Estimating K of Muskingum Equation	304
Figure 11.8 Routed Hydrograph (Ex. Prob. 11.5)	306

List of Tables

Table 1.1 Water Resources of India 5
Table 2.1 Computations Worksheet (Ex. Prob. 2.3) 41
Table 2.2 Computations Worksheet (Ex. Prob. 2.5) 46
Table 2.3 Table of Data (Ex. Prob. 2.7) 48
Table 2.4 Computations Worksheet (Ex. Prob. 2.6) 49
Table 3.1 Works sheet (Ex. Prob. 3.1) 59
Table 3.2 Computations Worksheet (Ex. Prob. 3.2) 60
Table 3.3 Rainfall data of a storm (Ex. Prob. 3.3) 61
Table 3.4 Table of Computations (Ex. Prob. 3.4) 65
Table 3.5 Thiessen Polygon Method (Ex. Prob. 3.4) 66
Table 3.6 Table of Computations (Ex. Prob. 3.5) 67
Table 3.7 Depth VS Area (Ex. Prob. 3.5) 69
Table 3.8 Worksheet (Ex. Prob. 3.7) 73
Table 3.9 Data for Ex. Prob. 3.8 74
Table 3.10 Computation Worksheet (Ex. Prob. 3.8) 75
Table 3.11 NRCS 24-h Rainfall Distributions 79
Table 3.12 Computation Sheet (Ex.Prob. 3.10) 81
Table 3.13 Storm Rainfall Distributions 81
Table 3.14 Data for Ex. Prob. 3.12 83
Table 4.1 Worksheet of Discharge Computations 101
Table 4.2 Values of Eddy Loss Coefficient, k_m 106
Table 4.3 Worksheet (Example Prob.4.4) 106
Table 4.4 Type of Stage Discharge Equation 108
Table 4.5 Stage Discharge Data (Ex. Prob. 4.5) 109
Table 5.1 Return Periods for a Given Risk 121
Table 6.1 Hypsometric Curve Data (Ex. Prob. 6.2) 150
Table 6.2 Worksheet (Ex. Prob. 6.3) 150
Table 6.3 Excel Worksheet (Ex. Prob. 6.4) 152
Table 7.1 Typical Values of f_l (after 1 hour) 163

Table 7.2 Infiltration Data 164
Table 7.3 Table of Computations (Ex. Prob. 7.2) 165
Table 7.4 ф-Index Calculations 168
Table 7.5 Table of Computations (Ex. Prob. 7.5) 170
Table 7.6 Computations (Ex. Prob. 7.6) 171
Table 7.7 Curve Number and Storm Runoff 174
Table 7.8 Computations Table (Ex. Prob. 7.10) 178
Table 7.9 Computation Ex. Prob. 7.13 182
Table 7.10 Percentage of Annual Daytime Hours 186
Table 7.11 Calculations of Et_o (Ex. Prob. 7.14) 187
Table 8.1 Coefficients n, K in Manning's Equation 205
Table 8.2 Computation Table (Ex. Prob. 8.3) 206
Table 8.3 Flow Hydrograph (Example Prob. 8.7) 212
Table 8.4 Base Flow Separation (Ex. Prob. 8.9) 213
Table 9.1 Typical C Values (Urban Areas) 223
Table 9.2 Runoff Coefficients for Rural Areas 224
Table 9.3 Data Table (Ex. Prob. 9.3) 228
Table 9.4 Table of Computations (Ex. Prob. 9.6) 232
Table 9.5 Excel Worksheet (Ex. Prob. 9.7) 233
Table 9.6 Weighted Curve Number (Ex. Prob. 9.8) 237
Table 9.7 Weighted Curve Number (Ex. Prob. 9.9) 238
Table 9.8 Coefficients for TR-55 Method 240
Table 10.1 Computations of UH Ordinates 259
Table 10.2 Computation Table (Ex. Prob. 10.2) 260
Table 10.3 Excel Worksheet (Ex. Prob. 10.3) 262
Table 10.4 Excel Worksheet (Ex. Prob. 10.3) 263
Table 10.5 Application of UH (Ex. Prob. 10.6) 266
Table 10.6 Stormflow Hydrograph (Ex. Prob. 10.7) 268
Table 10.7 NRCS Dimensionless Hydrograph 271
Table 10.8 NRCS Synthetic Unit Hydrograph 276

Table 10.9 Time of Travel (Ex. Prob. 10.10) 277

Table 10.10 Unit Hydrograph(Ex. Prob. 10.10) 278

Table 10.11 Storm Hydrograph(Ex. Prob. 10.12) 280

Table 11.1 Computations of Term S+QΔt/2 295

Table 11.2 Excel Worksheet (Ex. Prob. 11.2) 296

Table 11.3 Computations of Term (S+QΔt/2) 299

Table 11.4 Excel Worksheet (Ex. Prob. 11.3) 300

Table 11.5 Excel Worksheet (Ex. Prob. 11.4) 304

Table 11.6 Worksheet (Ex. Prob. 11.5) 306

1 Introduction

Water is life and subject of **hydrology** is the science of natural water cycle and its processes. Hydrology can be defined as the science that deals with the quantity, quality, and variation of water. It specifically deals with water occurrence, movement, distribution, circulation, storage, exploitation, development, and management.

Traditionally, hydrology is divided into two main branches: surface-water hydrology and groundwater hydrology. Surface-water hydrology deals mainly with water on the earth's surface whereas groundwater hydrology deals with the water below the earth's surface. It is important to understand, however that the surface water may appear as groundwater or vice versa. This course deals with surface-water hydrology. Other disciplines related to hydrology include agriculture, geography, geology, meteorology, and the basic sciences of physics, chemistry, and biology. For this reason, hydrology is a multi-discipline science.

1.1 Hydrologic Cycle

The endless circulation of water on our planet earth linking oceans, land and atmosphere is called the **hydrologic cycle (Fig.1.1)**. This cycle can be interrupted at any stage, but over time, the cycle repeats itself. Water from oceans, lakes and land evaporates into the atmosphere. Water vapour travels as air mass and precipitates on being cooled. Disposition of the precipitation becomes runoff and is eventually transported to the ocean. The three principal processes involved are evaporation, precipitation, and runoff. Solar energy coupled with gravity causes the circulation of water from the earth to the atmosphere as evapotranspiration, from atmosphere to the earth as precipitation and on the earth as runoff to streams and lakes and then to the oceans. From a global perspective, the hydrologic cycle can be considered comprised of three major systems.
      i)   Hydrosphere - source of water
      ii)   Atmosphere - deliverer of water
      iii)   Lithosphere - user of water

The hydrologic cycle is indeed a natural machine run by solar energy and gravitational forces with water as the material. Hence there is no gain or loss of water. From a global point of view, the hydrologic cycle is a **closed system.** Said differently, the total amount of water on this planet remains the same.

Figure 1.1 Hydrologic Cycle Components

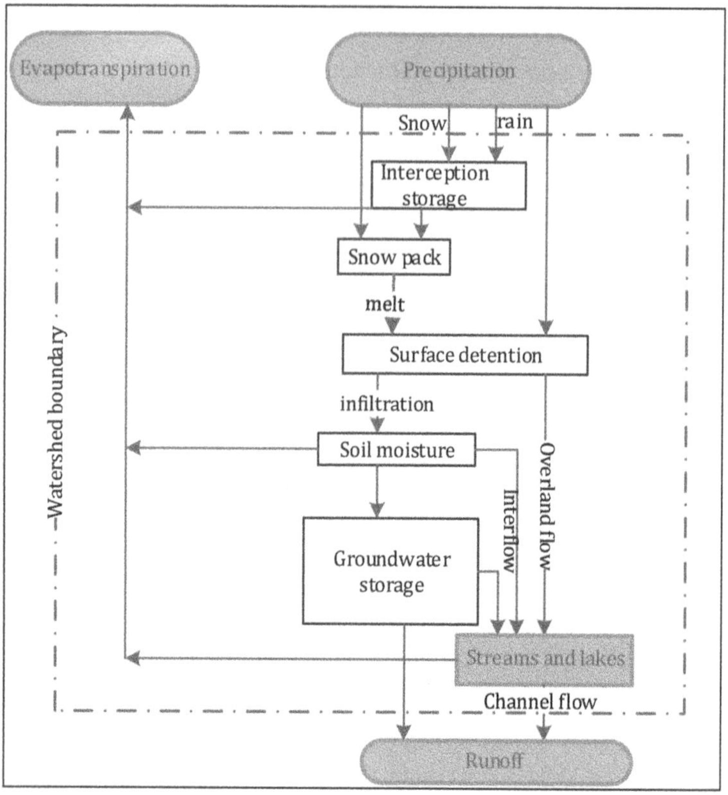

As shown schematically in **Figure 1.1**, the main components of the hydrologic cycle are:
- i. Evaporation, transpiration
- ii. Precipitation (rain, snow, hail, sleet, dew, drizzle, fog, etc.)
- iii. Interception, depression storage, infiltration, percolation, and seepage
- iv. Surface runoff, sub-surface runoff (interflow)
- v. Groundwater runoff (base flow)
- vi. Water storage over and below the land surface.

Water falling on the earth follows different routes on its way back to the ocean. The shortest leg of this journey is the water falling directly in the ocean. The longest leg of the journey is probably the water infiltrating into the land surface and percolating down to join the groundwater reservoir, which eventually flows to streams as spring flow and finds its way back to the ocean.

1.2 Quantifying Water Resources

Water is essential for life. Clean, reliable water supplies are vital for agriculture, industry, domestic use and energy production. Yet the world's water systems face formidable threats. More than a billion people currently live in water-scarce regions, and as many as 3.5 billion could experience water scarcity by 2025. While agriculture and industry withdraw the majority of world's fresh water, demand from households has increased by six times over the last 50 years. Since the beginning of concern over the possible consequences of global warming, it has been widely recognized that changes in the cycling of water (hydrologic cycle) between land, sea, and air could have very significant impacts across many sectors of the economy, society, and the environment. Quantitative estimates of hydrologic effects of climate change are essential for understanding and solving potential water resource problems associated with various uses of water. This section deals with the world water scenario, its demand and supply; water resources of India, water resources potential, and then outlining strategies to effectively manage these water resources.

1.2.1 World Water Resources

Annual turnover of water on the earth is around 580 PL (1000 km^3). This is the amount that evaporates from the oceanic surface (87%) and land (13%). The same amount of water is returned in the form of precipitation; 80% on the ocean and 20% on land. The difference between precipitation and evaporation from the land surface (45 PL/a) represents the total runoff carried by the earth's rivers (96%) and direct groundwater runoff to the ocean (4%).

World oceans have 97% of salty water and cover nearly 75% of the earth's surface. Fresh water is only 2.7 %, of which 75% is stored in glaciers and 23% is available as ground water. Remaining (2.4%) is stored in lakes, rivers and other storages. Two-thirds of global freshwater is found under ground in the form of groundwater. Distribution of water on the earth from different sources is shown in **Fig.1.2**.

1.2.2 Demand and Supply

According to United Nations estimates, total amount of fresh water on the earth is approximately 14 PL. As per the report of Central Water Commission, globally, current withdrawals are about 4.5 PL, which is greater than the availability of 4.2 PL. By the year 2030 estimated demand will increase to 6.7 TL with a slight drop in availability of 4.1 PL - a deficit of nearly 40 per cent. Thus, water demand- supply deficit will ever be increasing in future *(already use of water has increased by more than 35 times over the past three centuries and by over 600 % in the last 50 years)*.

Figure 1.2 Distribution of Water on the Earth

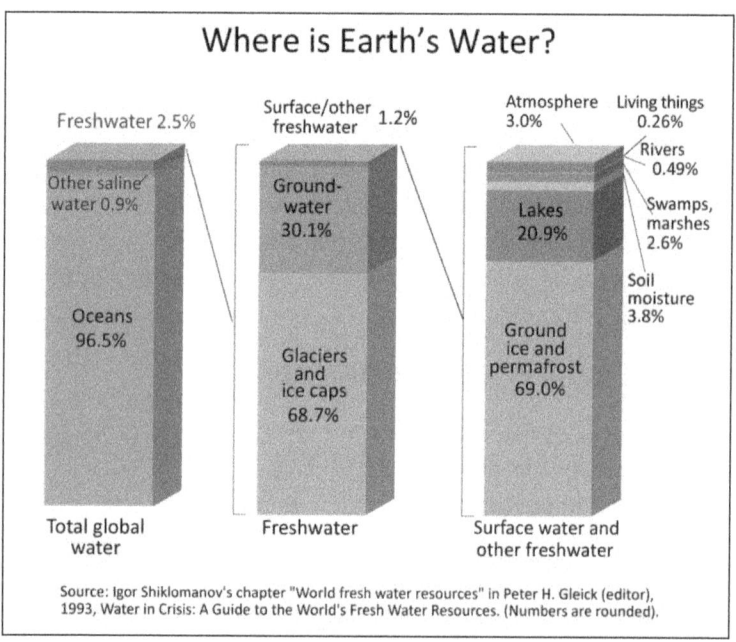

Quantitative estimates of hydrologic effects of climate change are thus essential for understanding and solving potential water resource problems associated with multi uses and it is apprehended that if steps are not taken to conserve and manage water wisely and exploit alternative sources of water, the future wars may be fought for water.

1.3 Water Resources of India

India represents nearly 18% of global population, occupies < 3% of global land area with only 4% of the world's water resources (Food and Agriculture Organization of the United Nations, 2013). As shown in **Table 1.1**, total water available from precipitation in the country in a year is about 4.0 TL. The availability from surface water and replenishable groundwater is 1.9 PL out of which usable extent is only 1.1PL (60%) because of topographic and uneven distribution in various river basins. Out of 1.1 PL/a, the share of surface water and ground water is 690 TL/a, and 430 TL/a, respectively. Leaving aside 35 TL for natural recharge, annual ground water availability for the entire country is roughly about 400 TL.

Table 1.1 Water Resources of India

Item	Volume
Average annual precipitation	4000 TL
Average Precipitation during Monsoon	3000 TL
Natural Runoff	1986 TL
Estimated utilizable surface water resources	690 TL
Total utilizable ground water resources	430 TL
Total annual utilizable water resources	1120 TL
Per capita water availability	17 ML/c

Source: Central Water Commission

1.3.1 Surface Water Resources of India

Four major resources of surface water are rivers, lakes, ponds, and tanks; rivers being the most important source (precipitation being the ultimate source). National Commission for Integrated Water Resources Development (NCIWRD, 1999) has estimated the basin-wise average annual flow in Indian River systems as 2.0 PL. But because of topographical and hydrological constraints, only about 32% of the available surface water can be utilized.

India's water resources comprise of 20 major river basins. Main features of these water resources are as follows:

- i) The flow of Indian rivers constitutes about 6% of discharge of all rivers of the world
- ii) Mean annual flow of Indian rivers is roughly about 2.0 PL out of which only about 1/3rd can be utilized.
- iii) The three main catchment areas of Ganga, Brahmaputra and Barak rivers have 60 % of total surface water resources.

iv) Effective storage capacity of surface waters in India is nearly 150 TL which is 8% of total flow of all the rivers.
v) And 92% of surface water flows into the sea.

1.3.2 Water Resources Management in India

India is not running out of water whereas water is running out of India without its full potential benefits being extracted. In other words, India does not so much face a water crisis as a water management crisis. The apparent abundance of water is deceptive, and we tend to abuse and overuse it leading to water scarcity.

Since there is a declining availability of fresh water, (per capita annual water availability reduced from 1816 m³ in 2001 to 1544 m³ in 2011. This coupled with increasing demand from different sectors, the time has come to conserve it and effectively manage this precious resource for sustainable development. Multi pronged strategy of water resources management needs to be adopted- reduce demand, increase supplies, conserve water and move water across geographies. It is worth mentioning that essence of all the strategies is agriculture sector since this is the major consumer of water.

Reducing demand

Major controlling factor in reducing demand is controlling overall population growth. Limiting growth of population in areas of water shortage, devising more efficient industrial processes with less use of water using efficient methods of irrigation like sprinkler and drip, controlling wastage, crop diversification (replacing water guzzling crops by less water consuming crops) and checking wastage and leakages are other methods of cutting the surging demand.

Increasing supply

It can be achieved through storage in dams and reservoirs, artificially recharging ground water, rainwater harvesting, desalinating sea water, controlling pollution and reclaiming grey water through recycling and cloud seeding. The first one needs a special mention since well established procedures are available in hydrology to design a reservoir of desired capacity based on demand and supply of water.

Conserving Water

Common methods of water conservation are; zero-tillage, raised-bed planting precision farming, crop diversification, organic and nature-based farming. In addition, many more like reducing evaporation and using better drainage in irrigated agriculture to reduce soil salinization

Moving water across geographies

This consists of intercepting, diverting, storing and transferring water among basins, towing icebergs from the Antarctic to water scarcity regions, diverting water from areas having surplus water to water scarce areas through link waterways. Some other approaches of better management of water resources are outlined:
- Overexploitation must not be allowed at any cost.
- Exploitation of groundwater resources should be regulated so that the withdrawals do not exceed recharge.
- Integrated and coordinated development of surface and groundwater resources.
- Conjunctive use of surface and groundwater should be encouraged to the extent possible
- Rooftop rainwater harvesting must be enforced by the local bodies for storing/recharging ground water

1.4 Water Management

Countries like India are likely to face a major challenge in the management of freshwater in view of rapidly rising population and increasing agricultural, industrial and other requirements. As the economy of a country is currently witnessing rapid growth, management of freshwater resources becomes all the more important.

1.4.1 Freshwater Related Problems

To safeguard the economic and social prosperity of the country, it is imperative that enough freshwater is available to meet the requirements of agriculture, industries, and the domestic sector in the coming years. Unfortunately, inadequate water planning, lack of water awareness and non-implementation of desired measures, have created a difficult-to-manage situation. As a result, an alarming scenario of freshwater scarcity is gradually unfolding. The scarcity of water is already evident in many parts of India, varying in scale and intensity at different times of the year. This situation is the result of natural factors and human actions. Intense competition among water users including agriculture, industry and domestic sector, is pushing the groundwater table deeper and deeper. Widespread pollution of surface water and groundwater is degrading the quality of freshwater resources. The major issues related to freshwater problems in India are elaborated in the subsequent sections.

1.4.2 Uneven Distribution of Water

Availability of water in India has large variations– both spatial and temporal. The basin wise per-capita water availability per annum varies between 13 ML/c·a for Brahmaputra-Barak basin to about 0.3 ML/ c·a for Sabarmati basin. As per the international norms, if water availability is less than 1.7 ML/c·a then the country is categorized as water stressed and if is less than 1 ML/c.a then the country is classified as water scarce. Growing water scarcity in India can be gauged from the fact that the available water per capita per year has decreased from 0.60 ML in 1947 to 0.24 ML in 2000. Although India is above the water stressed category, the real situation of per capita availability is more disturbing than what is depicted by the average figures. India receives nearly 75–80% of annual precipitation during the four monsoon months. Of the remaining amount, a large fraction is received during the winter monsoon. Further, out of 8760 hours in a year, most of the precipitation is received in about 100 hours. Instances where 10% of annual rainfalls in just 3 hours are not uncommon. Such a high concentration of precipitation and streamflow makes it imperative to regulate rivers. Moreover, the uneven distribution of rainfall across the country at different times of the year makes several parts of India fall under the water stressed, water scarcity and absolute water scarcity category.

1.4.3 Water Pollution

Water pollution is acquiring serious dimensions in India as almost 70% of its surface water resources and a large proportion of groundwater reserves are already contaminated by biological, toxic organic and inorganic pollutants. Degradation of quality in turn leads to water scarcity as it limits water availability for human use. Sources of water pollution are diverse: untreated sewage, industrial discharges, leaching from municipal waste, and drainage from the residues of agricultural fertilizers and pesticides. With burgeoning cities and increasing industrialization, the quantum of waste dumped into rivers has also increased. Water pollution varies in severity from one region to the other depending on the density of urban development, agricultural and industrial practices, and the systems for collecting and treating wastewater. Most of the polluted stretches exist in and around large urban areas. Some of the agricultural, industrial and domestic sources of water pollution are described below.

Agriculture

The indiscriminate use of agro chemicals has contributed significantly to the pollution of both surface water and groundwater resources. The consumption of pesticides, which rose from less than 1 million tonnes in 1948 to 66 million tonnes during 1994-95, was around 44 million tonnes during 2001-02. Some of the chemicals in these fertilizers and pesticides, which enter water bodies through runoff and leaching, are considered hazardous by the World Health Organization (WHO). Water quality studies on the Ganga River indicate the presence of chemicals such as HCH, DDT, dimethoate, endozoan and malathion in quantities exceeding standards set by international organizations. Severe soil erosion and water quality degradation (in the form of increase in sediment load) due to improper land management practices are particularly noticeable in the mountainous regions in northern and western India.

Industry

Although the industrial sector accounts for about 4% of the annual water withdrawals, its contribution to water pollution, particularly in urban areas, is significant. Wastewater generation from this sector has been estimated at 55 TL per day, out of which 60 GL is discharged into river streams. Of the total pollution load, 40%- 45% is contributed by the processing of industrial chemicals, while nearly 40% of the total organic pollution, arises from the food industries followed by industrial chemicals and the pulp and paper industry.

Domestic

The domestic sector is responsible for majority of the wastewater generation in India. About 50 GL of untreated sewage discharged into rivers has contributed towards pollution of India's fourteen major river systems. The 22 largest cities in the country produce over 7.3 GL of domestic wastewater per day and only about 80% of it is collected for treatment. Inadequate treatment of human and animal wastes adds to the high incidence of water-related diseases.

1.4.4 Excessive Groundwater Exploitation

Large-scale extraction of groundwater has led to overdraft and a drastic fall in water table in some basins. This in turn has created a chaotic situation especially in the water scarce hard rock regions of southern India, where assured sources of surface irrigation are rare and rainfall is non-uniform. Currently, about 32% of the annual utilizable groundwater potential of 430 TL is actually exploited, and only 8% of the groundwater sources have been exploited above 85% of their potential. However, in states like Punjab, Rajasthan and Tamil Nadu, large areas fall under the dark category. In Tamil Nadu and Gujarat, regional decline in water table has resulted in saltwater encroachment in the aquifer systems. Groundwater sources have been classified in three categories depending upon the extent of exploitation. In the 1st category (termed "white"), the level of exploitation is below 65% of the annual utilizable potential. The 2nd category (termed "gray") includes areas and sources in the range of 65% to 85% exploitation levels and the third and the worst category (termed "dark") has the level of exploitation exceeding 85%.

1.4.5 Threat to Biodiversity and Wetlands

About 6.5% and 12.5% of the world's animal and plant species, respectively, can be found in India. Out of these almost 7 000 are endemic to the subcontinent. Unfortunately, habitat destruction in both freshwater and coastal areas has endangered many endemic species. Most vulnerable are the freshwater fish since they are more susceptible to water pollution and environmental change. Other endangered species include freshwater aquatic animals like the Gangetic dolphin and several species of aquatic birds, amphibians, reptiles and insects. Twenty Wetlands in India cover a land area of about 4.1 million hectares. Most of these have become degraded due to pollution and development pressures, like conversion of wetlands for agriculture. This is threatening not only the local fauna but also the livelihood of the people dependent on the wetland ecosystem. In coastal areas, industrial and domestic pollution has severely degraded estuarine and coastal environments. To summarize, the root causes of the freshwater crisis in India are:

1. Rampant pollution of freshwater resources mainly by the agricultural, industrial and municipal activities.
2. Inadequate attention to water conservation, efficiency in water use, water reuse, groundwater recharge, and ecosystem sustainability.

3. Very low water prices which do not discourage wastage.
4. Prevalent system of water rights which gives unlimited ownership of groundwater to the landowner, despite the fact that groundwater is a shared resource from common pool aquifers.
5. Uncontrolled use of the bore-wells that has allowed extraction of groundwater at very high rates, often exceeding recharge.
6. Communities are not partners in managing water resources.

1.4.6 Strategies for Freshwater Management

As per the National Water Policy (2002) of the Government of India, water allocation priorities in the planning and operation of systems should broadly be: drinking water, irrigation, hydropower, ecology, agro-industries non-agricultural industries, and navigation. In view of the current status of freshwater in India and the problems that are likely to arise in future, a well-planned long-term strategy is needed for sustainable water resources management in India. Some key aspects of such a strategy are proposed next.

Water Conservation

Broadly speaking, water conservation implies improving the availability of water through augmentation by means of storage of water in surface reservoirs, tanks, soil, and groundwater zone. It emphasizes the need to modify the space and time availability of water to meet the demands. This concept also highlights the need for judicious use of water. If one looks at utilizable water resources in major river basins, these resources in Indus, Ganga, Brahmaputra, and Godavari basins are 73, 530, 630, and 110 TL (km^3) per annum, respectively. The storages available in these basins, including projects under construction, are 16, 54, 3.5, and 30 TL. Thus, only a small fraction of available water is being regulated in these basins at present. These basins are subject to frequent flooding, making the argument of storage even stronger. Overall, out of 690 TL of utilizable surface water, storage capacity created so far is only 26%, ongoing projects will add another 70 TL and those under planning 130 TL. Thus, even after completing the planned projects, 45% of the potential will remain unutilized. In view of rapidly rising population and demands for water, it will be necessary to conserve adequate quantity of water for later use.

No matter how freshwater is used – whether for agriculture, industry, or domestic purposes – there is a great potential for better conservation and management. On the demand side, a variety of economic, administrative and community-based measures can help conserve water. Side-by-side, it is necessary to control the growth of population since large population is putting massive stress on all natural resources. Since agriculture accounts for about 83% of all water withdrawn, the greatest potential for conservation lies in increasing irrigation efficiencies.

In urban water supply, for example, almost 30% of the water is wasted due to leakage and other losses, while most metro cities face deficit in supply of water. It is, therefore, imperative to prevent wastage.

1.5 Hydrologic Data

To analyse a given hydrologic system, you need data about the system as well as input and output. Hydrologic data is collected by governmental agencies, private companies and individuals engaged in the study of hydrology or its related fields.

1.5.1 Depth and Volume

Some of the hydrologic variables including precipitation, evaporation and infiltration are commonly expressed as depth units. For example, 1 mm of rain or runoff is the volume of water when spread uniformly over the area in question that will produce a depth of one millimetre. Volume, V of water is related to surface area, A and depth of water, d as

Volume and depth
$$V = A \times d \quad \text{or} \quad d = \frac{V}{A}$$

Based on this relationship volume can also be expressed as area multiplied by depth units, for example, km². mm. The most commonly used SI unit of volume is a cubic meter (m³ =1000 L = kL). As indicated by the above relationship, runoff volume from a watershed can be expressed as depth. This is convenient as precipitation and evaporation are commonly expressed in depth units. Runoff depth of 1 mm is the volume of runoff water that is equivalent to 1 mm of water uniformly distributed over the entire drainage area. Following units and their equivalents are commonly used in hydrology.

Area units
$$km^2 = 100 \, ha = 10^6 \, m^2 \quad ha = 10^4 \, m^2 = 1 hm^2$$

Introduction

Volume units

$$\boxed{km^2 \cdot mm = 1000\ m^3 = 1\ dam^3 = 1\ ML}$$

$$\boxed{1\ km^3 = 10^9\ m^3 = 10^{12}\ L = 1\ TL}$$

Example Problem 1.1

Calculate the volume of water in m³ required to produce a depth of 1 mm when spread uniformly over an area of 1 km².

Solution:

$$V = A \times d = 1.0\ mm \times km^2 \times \frac{1000^2\ m^2}{km^2} \times \frac{m}{1000\ mm} = 1000\ m^3$$

1.5.2 Depth Rate

Rate is variation with respect to time. Rainfall rate, more commonly called rainfall intensity, is the depth of rainfall per unit time, for example mm/h. Hour is the more commonly used unit of time in expressing rainfall intensity, but it does not mean rainfall continues at that rate for one hour. Knowing the duration of the storm Δt and average rainfall intensity I, depth of precipitation, P can be determined.

$$I = \frac{\Delta P}{\Delta t} \quad or \quad \Delta P = I \times \Delta t \quad or \quad P = I \times t$$

Runoff discharge rate is volume of runoff, VQ per unit time. The most commonly used units are m³/s and ft³/s.

Runoff rate and Volume

$$\boxed{Q = \frac{V_Q}{t} = \frac{R \times A}{t} \quad or \quad R = \frac{Q \times t}{A}}$$

R = Runoff depth, V_Q = Runoff volume

Example Problem 1.2

Rainfall of intensity 4 mm/h fell on a 2.5 km² drainage area for a period of 20 h. Determine the volume of rainfall.

Solution:

$$P = I \times t = \frac{4.0\ mm}{h} \times 20\ h = 80.0 = \underline{80\ mm}$$

$$V_P = P \times A = 80\ mm \times 2.5\ km^2 \times \frac{10^3 m^3}{km^2 \cdot mm} = \underline{2.0 \times 10^5\ m^3}$$

$$= 2.0 \times 10^5 \ m^3 \times \frac{ML}{1000 \ m^3} = \underline{200 \ ML}$$

Example Problem 1.3

Water for irrigation is to be supplied by a perennial stream with a drainage area of 300 km². The average stream flow is 0.10 m³/km². s. Determine the maximum area that can be irrigated daily with an irrigation depth of 25 mm.

Solution:

$$Q = \frac{0.1 \ m^3}{km^2 \cdot s} \times 300 \ km^2 = 30.0 = 30 \ m^3/s$$

$$V = Q \times t = \frac{30 \ m^3}{s} \times 1d \times \frac{24h}{d} \times \frac{3600 \ s}{h} = 2.59 \times 10^6 \ m^3$$

$$A_{irr} = \frac{V}{d_{irr}} = \frac{2.592 \times 10^6 \ m^3}{25 \ mm} \times \frac{1000 \ mm}{m} \times \frac{km}{10^6 \ m^2}$$

$$= 103.68 = \underline{100 \ km^2}$$

1.5.3 Time and Space Scales

Depending on a given hydrologic situation, the hydrologic cycle or its components can be assumed at different scales of time and space. The global scale is the largest spatial scale, and the watershed is the smallest.

A **watershed** is an area of the earth's surface that concentrates all of the runoff to the same drainage outlet downstream. Depending on the location of the outlet, the catchment area will vary. As the outlet moves downstream, catchment area will increase. The terms catchment, watershed and basin are used interchangeably. Generally, smaller catchments (stream watersheds) are referred to as watersheds and the term drainage basin or simply basin is preferred for large catchments (river basins). Clearly, watershed is the most basic spatial scale. It is important to note that watershed boundaries do not respect territorial boundaries that might be determined by political considerations.

The time scale used in hydrologic studies depends on the nature of the hydrologic problem at hand. Hourly, daily, monthly, seasonal, or annual time scales are common. Sometimes the time interval for collection of data determines the time scale. A hydrologic variable like rainfall varies in space and time. However, depending on the purpose of study, type of hydrologic analysis and more importantly the spatial scale, rainfall can be assumed to be either

    i)   Constant in both space and time,
    ii)   Constant in space but varying in time, or
    iii)   Varying in both space and time.

The spatial scale determines which one of these assumptions is reasonable from a practical point of view. In modelling rainfall-runoff relationships, for small catchments for example, rainfall is assumed constant in both time and space. As the size of the watershed increases to mid-size, rainfall is considered variable in time. However, the areal extent of mid-size watersheds (< 150 km²) justifies the assumption of constant rainfall in space. For accuracy of the analysis, rainfall over large watersheds (> 250 km²) is assumed to vary both in space and time.

1.6 Water Balance

Water balance for a given system is calculated by equating the difference between inflow and outflow to the change of water storage within the system. In the case of a storage reservoir, or a river, applying the principle of **mass conservation**, the water balance equation can be written as

$$\text{Inflow - Outflow = Change in storage} \quad \text{or} \quad I - O = \Delta S$$

Example Problem 1.4

The net evaporation from the surface of a 1460 ha lake is 1200 mm in a given year. At end of the year, the lake level rises by 25 cm. If there is no direct outflow from the lake except evaporation, calculate the average rate of inflow in m³/s that year.

Given:

A = 1460 ha   O = 1200 mm ΔS = 25 cm = 250 mm   I =?

Solution:

$$I = \Delta S + O = 250 \, mm + 1200 \, mm = 1450 \, mm$$

$$\bar{Q} = \frac{Ad}{t} = \frac{1460 \, ha \times 1450 \, mm}{a} \times \frac{a}{365 \, d} \times \frac{d}{24h} \times \frac{h}{3600s}$$

$$= \frac{6.713 \times 10^{-3} \, ha \cdot mm}{s} \times \frac{10 \, m^3}{ha \cdot mm} = 0.671 = \underline{0.67 \, m^3/s}$$

Figure 1.3 Hydrologic Budgeting for a Watershed

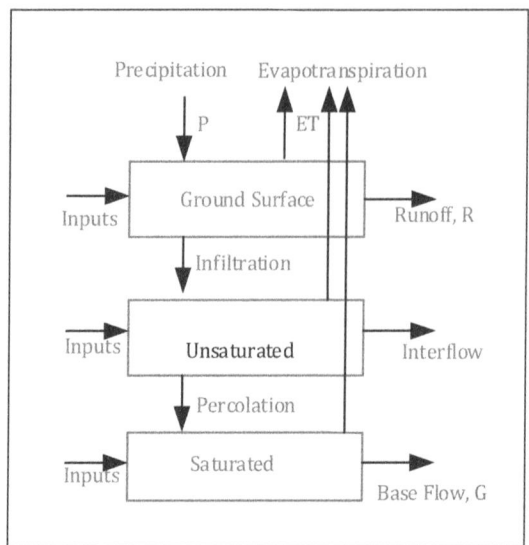

1.6.1 Hydrologic Budget

Hydrologic budget is actually a mathematical statement of the hydrologic cycle. For a drainage basin, it can be calculated by considering the amount of water added, the amount of water removed by various transport processes and equating it to the total change in storage over a specified period of time. A hydrologic system is illustrated in **Figure 1.3**. Applying the principle of mass conservation to the earth system over a long period, following equation can be written.

Hydrologic budget equation
$$P - R - ET - G = \Delta S_s + \Delta S_g$$

ET	=	Evapotranspiration (outflow),
P	=	Precipitation (inflow)
R	=	Runoff (outflow)
G	=	Groundwater (storage)
S	=	Storage
Sub s	=	Surface
Sub g	=	Ground (Sub-surface)

Term ΔS represents change in storage while R and G represent net values for the watershed system.

Modified Budget equation
$$P - R - ET = \Delta S$$

1.6.2 Application of the Hydrologic Equation

Because of the difficulty when measuring or estimating the various components corresponding to the terms in the hydrologic budget equation, care should be exercised when applying it to solve problems. Precipitation is measured by rain or snow gauges, runoff flow can be measured using various devices such as weirs, velocity meters and depth gauges. Soil moisture can be measured using neutron probes and gravimetric methods; infiltration determined locally by **infiltrometers** or estimated through the use of precipitation runoff data. Groundwater flow is exceedingly difficult to estimate. Knowledge about the geology of the area is essential. Most estimates of evapotranspiration are obtained by using **evaporation pans**; energy budgets, heat and mass transfer methods or empirical relationships based on climatic factors.

The simplicity of equation belies its importance. When applied carefully, the budget equation can yield good estimates of the magnitude of hydrologic variables. The estimates will be as good as the data for the known variables in the equations.

1.6.3 Budget equation for larger watersheds

When applied to large watersheds, the assumption that G is zero is quite valid as generally groundwater divide follows surface divide. Also, when working over a large time span, for example a year, ΔS can be assumed to be zero. In situations where groundwater withdrawal is more than recharge or when working with a period shorter than a year this assumption may lead to erroneous results. Hydrology is not an exact science, and reasonable well-founded assumptions are required to solve practical problems. For cases in which both G and ΔS can be assumed to be zero, the hydrologic equation becomes:

$$P - R - ET = 0$$

Estimates based on the hydrologic equation will be as good as the validity of data and assumptions made. The estimates may be crude but can be very useful as first estimates in water resource planning and management.

1.6.4 Budget equation for Individual Storms

For individual storms, the quantities of *ET* and *G* are much smaller and the change in sub-surface storage is due to infiltration, F ($\Delta Sg = F$).

$$P - R - F = \Delta S_S$$

ΔS_s consists of interception and depression storage. When coupled with infiltration it accounts for abstractions $A = F + \Delta S_s$.

$$R = P - A$$

This concept is the basis of many practical methods for runoff computation
- Change in ground water storage is assumed negligible
- Stream flow is one of the components of the hydrologic cycle which can be measured accurately

Example Problem 1.5

A drainage basin area of 22500 km² receives on an average 750 mm of annual precipitation. Evapotranspiration for this basin is estimated to be 455 mm/a. Calculate the mean annual stream flow rate in m³/s?

Given:

A = 22500 km²   P = 750 mm/a   E = 450 mm/a

Solution:

Being a larger watershed, it is fair to assume that net groundwater flow is zero

$$R = P - ET = (750 - 450)\ mm/a = 300\ mm/a$$

$$Q = R \times A = \frac{300\ mm}{a} \times 22500\ km^2 \times \frac{1000\ m^3}{km^2 \cdot mm}$$

$$\times \frac{a}{365d} \times \frac{d}{24h} \times \frac{h}{3600s} = 214 = \underline{210\ m^3/s}$$

Example Problem 1.6

In Southern Ontario province of Canada, the mean annual stream flow is 1.0 L/s for each 1.0 km² of the drainage area. The average annual precipitation in this region is 800 mm. Calculate the percentage loss due to evapotranspiration.

Given:

A = 1.0 km²   Q = 10. L/s   P = 800 mm/a   ET =?

Solution:

$$R = \frac{Q}{A} = \frac{10\,L}{s.km^2} \times \frac{km^2}{(1000\,m)^2} \times \frac{3600\,s}{h} \times \frac{24}{d} \times \frac{365d}{a}$$

$$= \frac{315.36\,L}{m^2.a} \times \frac{m^3}{1000\,L} \times \frac{1000\,mm}{m} = 315.36 = 320\,mm/a$$

$$ET = P - R = 750\,mm - 315\,mm = 435\,mm/a$$

$$\frac{ET}{P} = \frac{435\,mm}{750\,mm} \times 100\% = 58.0 = 58\%$$

1.7 Applications of Hydrology

The most important uses of hydrology are flood control, drought mitigation, water supply, pollution control, urban and industrial development, design of hydraulic works, agricultural production, land conservation, environmental impact assessment, land use change, navigation, recreation and fisheries.

1.7.1 Flood Control

Floods occur when water body is unable to contain the amount of water it receives due to one of the following factors:
1.   There is inadequate drainage provision to drain excess water
2.   Hydraulic structures such dams, levees and dykes have failed.

The hydrologic inputs needed to design flood mitigation and control projects include:
1. Peak discharge and its frequency of occurrence
2. Duration and volume of flood hydrograph and their probability of occurrence,

1.7.2 Drought Mitigation

Drought occurs when demand exceeds supply. Droughts are usually distinguished as agricultural, hydrological and meteorological. The drought is defined by its areal extent, duration, severity, and the onset of next drought. From hydrological perspective, low discharge and its frequency of occurrence, duration and volume of low flow, and the probability of occurrence of the next drought are useful to design drought mitigation projects. Construction of water impoundments, ground water pumpage, inter basin transfer, water conservation, and even augmentation of atmospheric precipitation through cloud seeding are some of the ways to mitigate droughts.

1.7.3 Design of Hydraulic Works

Dams, culverts, spillways, bridge crossings, dikes, levees, diversions, drainage works etc. are typical hydraulic works required for water resources development and management. Design of these works requires an estimate of peak discharge of a given frequency. Applying hydrology concepts, environmental impact of these works are estimated.

1.7.4 Agricultural Production

Agriculture is the largest water user and for sustainable agricultural production efficient water management is essential.

Proper agricultural practices conserve precipitation for crop use, prevent the loss of precious soil, and preserve the quality of stream that drains the land. Crop production involves moisture forecasting, supply of water to farms, management of irrigation water, application of chemical and fertilizers, drainage of excess water and soil conservation. Hydrology is used to determine irrigation scheduling, soil erosion and sediment transport, migration of chemical and their impact on water quality. It also used to design a network of wells for a farm, drainage system to remove excess water, and water conveyance system network (dams, canals, and ditches) based on soil properties, land slope, location of the water table, climate and other factors.

1.7.5 Land Conservation

Careless farming methods, deforestation, over-grazing can speed up runoff, resulting in erosion of soil. This increases the danger of flooding downstream and also increases reservoir sedimentation rate. Loss of fertile lands due to erosion and of coastal areas has been a growing concern.

Hydrology is used to determine the space-time history of erosion and to develop scenarios for prevention of erosion through, soil conservation, appropriate farm practices, vegetation management, water diversion, afforestation, reduced flooding and controlled land use.

1.8 Watershed Management

Watershed management aims to establish a workable and efficient framework for the integrated use, regulation and development of land and water resources in a watershed for socio-economic growth. Typical objectives of watershed development programs include:
1. Raising the productivity of rain-fed agriculture and non-arable lands.
2. Encouraging the sustainable management and optimal use of surface and groundwater.
3. Reducing soil erosion and sediment load.
4. Conserving forests and other natural vegetation.
5. Promoting increased individual and collective responsibility for natural resources management and strengthening the social institutions.

1.8.1 Water Conservation and Environment

To preserve our water and environment, we need to make systematic changes in the way we grow our food, manufacture the goods, and dispose off the waste.

Water quality

In countries like India, agriculture is the biggest user and polluter of water. If pollution by agriculture is reduced, it would improve water quality and would also eliminate cost incurred for treatment of diseases. This would entail learning how to use less chemicals while boosting yields, e.g., eliminating use of fungicides by planting more diverse varieties of grains and switching to organic farming so that fewer chemicals are introduced on the farms. Industries should be required to treat their waste before discharge. Manufacturers may reduce water pollution by reusing materials and chemicals and switching over to less toxic alternatives. Industrial symbiosis, in which the unusable wastes from one product become the input for another, is an attractive solution.

Environment Restoration

Environmental improvement and restoration should be planned and implemented such that the freshwater resources are protected and their quality is maintained. Model efforts in this direction include the capture, storage and safe release of water and the prevention of accelerated soil erosion through hydraulic structures and vegetation. While utilizing water and land resources, their ability to serve other uses is often degraded either inadvertently or due to carelessness. Efforts should be made to restore landscapes and ecosystems to protect water quality aquatic and wildlife more efficiently. On the legislative front, we require laws to check littering as well as to implement "polluter pays" principle.

1.8.2 Inter-basin Water Transfer (IBWT)

The vast variation, both in space and time, in the availability of water in different regions of India has created a food-drought flood syndrome with some areas suffering from flood damages and other areas facing acute water shortage. The drought prone area assessed in the country is of the order of 51 million hectare, while the area susceptible to floods is around 40 million hectares. The States of Karnataka, Tamil Nadu, Rajasthan, Gujarat, Andhra Pradesh and Maharashtra are the worst drought prone states. The States of Uttar Pradesh, Bihar, West Bengal, Orissa and Assam face severe flood problems. Inter basin transfer of water in India is a long-term option to partly overcome the spatial and temporal imbalance of availability and demand of water resources. The transfer of water from surplus areas to deficit areas is not a new concept. Many such schemes have been implemented all over the world. In India too, projects like Periyar –Vaigai system, Indira Gandhi canal, and Telugu Ganga stand as classic examples of inter-basin water transfer. In the seventies, the Garland Canal proposal of Captain Dastur and the Ganga – Cauvery Canal proposal of Rao (1973) were received with considerable attention. A National Perspective Plan for water resources development was formulated by the Government of India in 1980s. The distinctive feature of this plan is the transfer of water essentially by gravity and only in small reaches by lift pumping. This plan comprises of two components:

1. Himalayan Rivers Development, and
2. Peninsular Rivers Development While the second component will be an inter-state venture, the first will involve neighbouring countries too and thus will be an international venture. Some of the major benefits expected from inter linking of the rivers are:
    a. Irrigation potential is to increase from 140 to 175 million ha, drinking water availability is to increase by about 12 km^3,
    b. Peak flood discharge to get reduced by about 30% due to construction of reservoirs,
    c. Generation of 34 GW of electricity, and
    d. Possibilities of inland navigation to provide cheap transport. While planning inter-basin transfer of water,

Water has to be shared between its different uses (energy, cities, food production, environment, etc.), and between users (administrative blocks or states sharing a river basin or aquifer). Many regions and cities rely on upstream users for water flow and any downstream user will be dependent on the action of the upstream users.

Measures used to allocate water between competing uses may include: national strategy and/or legislation on inter-sectoral allocations, tariff disincentives and targeted subsidies, abstraction management, application and enforcement of water-quality objectives, reservoir operating rules, multi-use reservoir management, multi-reservoir system management and reservoir compensation flow releases (UN, 2003).

1.8.3 Groundwater Management

To protect the aquifers from overexploitation, an effective groundwater management policy oriented towards promotion of efficiency, equity, and sustainability is required. The exploitation of groundwater resources should be regulated so as not to exceed the recharging possibilities, as well as to ensure social equity. Integrated and coordinated development of surface water and groundwater resources and their conjunctive use should be envisaged right from the project planning stage and should form an integral part of the project implementation.

Over exploitation of groundwater should be avoided, especially near the coasts to prevent ingress of seawater into freshwater aquifers. The government can initiate a variety of programs and controls for recharge and discharge and implement regulatory measures such as well spacing norms, control drilling of new wells by issuing permits, regulation of water intensive crops, and pricing of electricity for lifting groundwater. To the extent possible, conjunctive use of surface water and groundwater should form an integral part of groundwater management policy. In critically overexploited areas, bore-well drilling should be regulated till the water table attains the desired elevation. Artificial recharge measures need to be urgently implemented in these areas. Amongst the various recharge techniques, percolation tanks are least expensive in terms of initial construction costs. Many such tanks already exist but a vast majority of these structures have silted up. In such cases, cleaning of the bed of tanks will make them reusable.

1.8.4 Rainwater

Rainwater harvesting is the process to capture and store rainfall for its efficient utilization and conservation to control its runoff, evaporation and seepage. Some of the benefits of rainwater harvesting are:
1. It increases water availability,
2. It checks the declining water table,
3. It is environmentally friendly,
    i. It improves the quality of groundwater through dilution, mainly of fluoride, nitrate, and salinity, and
    ii. It prevents soil erosion and flooding.

In many towns and cities, new construction projects including home are legally required to harvest rainwater.

1.8.5 Recycle and Reuse of Water

Another way through which we can improve freshwater availability is by recycle and reuse of water. Use of water of lesser quality, such as reclaimed wastewater, for cooling and fire fighting is an attractive option for large and complex industries to reduce their water costs, increase production and decrease the consumption of energy. This conserves better quality waters for potable uses. Currently, recycling of water is not practiced on a large scale in India and there is considerable scope and incentive to use this alternative. In some towns and cities, effluent from tertiary wastewater treatment plants is used for irrigation of lawns and watering plants.

1.8.6 Desalination of Water

Since 1970, there has been significant commercial development using various desalination technologies, including distillation, reverse osmosis, and electrolysis. This technology is suitable for use in areas where freshwater is scarce, but saline water is available and energy is cheap. Compared to water recycling technologies, desalination presents fewer health risks.

1.8.7 Environmental Flow Requirement

An environmental flow (EFR) is the water regime provided within a river, wetland or coastal zone to maintain ecosystem and their benefits where there are competing water uses and where flows are regulated.

Environmental flows normally include the flow requirements in rivers and estuaries for maintenance of riverine ecology.

1.8.8 Dealing with Climate Change

Climate change is likely to result in hydrologic conditions and extremes of a nature that will be different from those for which the existing projects were designed. Some recommendations to cope up with the problems in a systematic and a planned manner are:

i) A nationwide climate monitoring program should be developed;

ii) While formulating new projects that influence climate, it should be ensured that no action is taken which causes irreversible harmful impact on the climate;

iii) Improved methods for accounting of climate related uncertainty should be developed and made part of decision-making process;

iv) Existing systems should be examined to determine how they will perform under the climate situations that are likely to arise;

v) Water availability and demands in all regions, particularly in water scarce regions should be reassessed in the new climate scenario;

vi) A re-examination of the operating rules should be taken up to see how these need to be updated to handle likely extremes.

Discussion Questions

1. Explain application of hydrologic budget equation when applied to
   a. Individual storm
   b. Large watershed
2. When time period is less than a year, assumption of negligible change in storage may not be valid. Explain?
3. Why infiltration is not a part of the hydrologic budget equation?
4. Referring to hydrologic cycle, list the main pathways and storages?
5. How would you apply mass balance to a river system? In what ways, is it different when applied to larger watersheds?
6. Based on size, describe three types of watersheds and type of input required for rainfall runoff relationship?
7. Compare and contrast evaporation and evapotranspiration?
8. Search and find sources of hydrologic data in your region.
9. What are the instruments or devices commonly used to measure precipitation, evaporation, infiltration, and streamflow?
10. Under what conditions assuming change in storage to be negligible is justified?
11. What strategies would you suggest to better manage water resources in India?
12. Gulf between demand and supply of water is ever increasing. Comment

Practice Problems

Practice Problem 1.1

Rain falls at an average rate of 10 mm/h over a 250-ha area for 40 h. Determine the average rate of rainfall in m^3/s and volume of rainfall in ha.cm. (6.9 m^3/s, 10^4 ha.cm)

Practice Problem 1.2

The average monthly precipitation in a watershed of 5500 km^2 is 86 mm and half of this becomes runoff. Determine the area that can be irrigated per day to provide an irrigation depth of 20 mm. (39 000 ha)

Practice Problem 1.3

The storage in a river reach is 8.5 km^2.mm at a certain time. At this hour, the inflow and outflow are estimated to be 12.5 m^3/s and 12.0 m^3/s respectively. An hour later, the inflow and outflow increased to 15.0 m^3/s and 12.5 m^3/s respectively. Is the storage at the end of the hour greater or less than the initial value? What is the storage at the end of the hour? (Greater, 3.1 km^2.mm)

Practice Problem 1.4

A landfill site is to be designed so that no liquid waste leaves the site. This is to be accomplished by constructing a reservoir to trap and evaporate all of the runoff. Determine the reservoir area required to prevent any discharge downstream. (1.45 km^2)

Practice Problem 1.5

In a given year, a 10000-km^2 watershed received 500 mm of precipitation. The annual rate of flow measured at the outlet of the river draining the area is found to be 68.5 m^3/s. Estimate the depth of water lost due to evapotranspiration.
(284 mm)

Practice Problem 1.6

The average annual stream flow from a drainage area of 100 km^2 in the Algoma District is 2.40 m^3/s. The average annual precipitation for this area is 900 mm. Applying the hydrologic budget equation, determine the percentage of precipitation going back to the atmosphere directly as evapotranspiration. How does this figure compare with that for Southern Ontario? (16%)

Practice Problem 1.7

A watershed has a drainage area of 780 km². Mean annual precipitation for the area is 820 mm. On average, 31% of the precipitation becomes runoff and reaches outlet as streamflow. What is the mean flow rate? (6.3 m³/s)

Practice Problem 1.8

For the month of June, average pan evaporation for an area is 250 mm. A water reservoir with an average surface area of 5100 ha is used to supply water to the city with a population of 21 000 people. Assuming average per capita demand of 400 L/c.d, find how much depth of water is lowered? Assume pan coefficient is 0.75 and water lost due to seepage equals rainfall in the month. (140 mm)

Practice Problem 1.9

The mean annual streamflow from Root river watershed of an area is 2.2 m³/s when the annual mean precipitation is 850 mm. Given that area of the watershed is 280 km², what percentage of precipitation is lost due to evapotranspiration? (71%)

Practice Problem 1.10

During irrigation season of 130 days, 750 mm of irrigation water is needed for total cultivated area of 8500 ha. In addition, groundwater supply of 380 L/c·d is needed to serve population of 98 000 people. Both these demands are met by pumping aquifer with an areal extent 810 km². Assuming no recharge during growing season, determine total depth of water pumped. Further, assuming porosity of the aquifer is 30%, find the depth by which water table will be lowered during cropping season? (85 mm, 280 mm)

Review Questions

1. The land surface is referred to as:
   a) Hydrosphere   b) Lithosphere   c) Atmosphere   d) Troposphere

2. Which of the following terms is commonly used for relatively small drainage areas?
   a) Watershed   b) Basin   c) Catchment   d) Other

3. The assumption of rainfall rate being constant in time and space is valid for
   a) Small catchment   b) Mid-size catchments
   c) Large basins   d) All of the above

4. For many practical purposes, the upper limit for mid-size catchments is
   a) 5 km²   b) 50 km²   c) 150 km²   d) 500 km²

5. How many ha make an area of 10 km²?
   a) 10 ha   b) 100 ha   c) 1000 ha   d) 10 000 ha

6. A volume of one million litres is the same thing as one
   a) km².mm   b) ha.cm   c) ha.mm   d) km².cm

7. Which of the following device can be used to measure evaporation?
   a) infiltrometer   b) Weir   c) Pan   d) Fume

8. Which one of the following elements of the hydrologic cycle is not affected by urbanization?
   a) Rainfall   b) Depression storage
   c) Interception storage   d) Infiltration

9. Which one of the following is considered as part of the hydrologic design?
   a) Spatial variation of rainfall   b) Temporal variation of rainfall
   c) Frequency of rainfall   d) All of these

10. You need to water your lawn to apply a depth of 10 mm. If the sprinkler discharge rate is 10 L/min and areal coverage is 25 m², how long should you run your sprinkler for?
    a) 30 min   b) 25 min   c) 20 min   d) 10 min

11. Average annual global precipitation is about _____ mm.
   a) 700 mm   b) 800 mm   c) 900 mm   d) 960 mm

12. Effective rainfall or storm runoff is rainfall minus
   a) Depression   b) Interception   c) Infiltration   d) All

13. How many litres of water will you need to fill a container of 1 cubic foot capacity?
   a) 28 L   b) 35 L   c) 56 L   d) 70 L

14. Which of the following component of runoff is generated by seepage from the upper layer of saturated soils?
   a) Base flow   b) Groundwater   c) Inter flow   d) Overland flow

15. The downward movement of water through the soil profile is called
   a) Infiltration   b) Percolation   c) Interflow   d) Transpiration

16. The main source of water causing precipitation on the earth's surface is
   a) Evapotranspiration   b) Lake evaporation
   c) Evaporation from sea   d) Land evaporation

17. Which component of the hydrologic cycle will be affected by global warming?
   a) Rainfall   b) Evaporation   c) Runoff   d) All

18. Flow rate of 1-L/s.m², expressed as depth is
   a) 0.1 mm/s   b) 1.0 mm/s   c) 10 mm/s   d) 100 mm/s

19. If the outlet of a watershed is moved upstream, the drainage area contributing to stream flow
   a) Decreases   b) Increases   c) Does not matter   d) a, b

20. Floodwater with an average depth of 15 mm over a parking lot of area 1.0 km² drains into a small river during a storm of 10 minutes duration. The average flow rate in the river during the storm is 15 m³/s. The change in volume is
   a) -6.0 ML   b) +6.0 ML   c) +9.0 ML   d) +12 ML

21. Which of the following is not a part of the hydrologic equation?
   a) Infiltration   b) Precipitation   c) Runoff   d) All are

22. The quantity of ocean water on earth is about
    a) 33%   b) 67%   c) 77%   d) 97%

23. Which of the following are sources of energy causing hydrologic cycle?
    a) Sun, gravity   b)   Sun, capillary
    c) Sun, electric charge   d)   Gravity, Capillary

24. Which of the term in hydrologic budgeting can be dropped when working with large watersheds over longer time periods?
    a) Transpiration   b) Evaporation
    c) Surface runoff   d) Groundwater storage

25. Watershed divide determines the
    a) Catchment boundaries   b) Rainfall water, evaporation
    c) Area with snowfall, rainfall d) Area collecting storm water

26. What percent of total water on the earth is fresh water?
    a) 1.0%   b) 3.0%   c) 13%   d) 99%

27. In India, which of the following is the biggest user of fresh water?
    a) Municipal   b) Agriculture   c) Industry   d) Hard to say

28. Largest amount of fresh water on this planet is in the form of
    a) Groundwater   b) Glaciers   c) Lakes   d) Rivers

29. Fresh water is roughly about _____ of total water on this planet.
    a) 97%   b) 60%   c) 5%   d) 2.5%

30. Which of the following is the largest source of precipitation on the earth?
    a) Ocean   b) Sea   c) Lakes &rivers   d) Reservoirs

2 Precipitation

Precipitation is defined as liquid or solid water that reaches the surface of the earth. Various forms of precipitation include rain, snow, hail, sleet, dew, fog, drizzle, etc.

Precipitation occurs when moist laden air cools sufficiently, it causes part of the water vapour to condense on hydroscopic nuclei. The condensation nuclei might be foreign particles, or, under super cooled conditions, ice crystals. In some cases, clouds are seeded with such nuclei. The droplets coalesce until they are sufficiently large enough to fall down as precipitation.

2.1 Forms of Precipitation

Precipitation is the moisture in the atmosphere that falls on the ground surface in liquid or solid form.

2.1.1 Liquid Form

Precipitation in liquid form include drizzle, rain, mist, dew and fog.

Drizzle

Drizzle is very small droplets and thus precipitation in this form is difficult to measure. Size of drizzle droplets are less than 0.5 mm in diameter. When the drizzle particles coalesce and grow in size, it becomes rainfall. Intensity in this form of precipitation rarely exceeds 1 mm/h. Since the size of droplets is small, settling velocity of droplets is very small. Most of the times, it remains floating in air.

Rain

Rain the most common form of liquid precipitation. Droplets size falls in the range of 0.5 mm to 6 mm. thunderstorms produces very intense rainfall. Most parts of the world receive significant precipitation as rainfall.

Fog , Mist and Dew

Precipitation in these three forms is relatively small. Mist consists of very small droplets floating in air. Fog is kind of mist such that visibility becomes

Precipitation

less than 1 km. Dew falls when temperature of vegetation and other objects is less than dew point temperature of the surrounding air. Under these conditions, water vapours in the atmosphere condenses on to the surface.

Frost and Glaze

When the air temperature near the ground surface is below freezing, liquid rain turns in to ice and stick to ground surface or vegetation as sheet of ice. It is very dangerous form as it can damage the crops and other form vegetation. Glaze is when liquid precipitation turns into ice as it comes in contact with ground surface.

Freezing rain occurs when snowflakes pass through a warmer layer of air and melt completely. As the rain drops fall through another thin layer of sub-freezing temperatures, they do not have enough time to refreeze. Because they are super cooled, they instantly refreeze when they come in contact with anything that is at or below freezing temperature. The freezing rain forms a glaze of ice on the ground, tress, power lines and other objects. Even light accumulations can make driving vary hazardous. Large accumulations can cause power transmission lines snap under the weight of freezing rain.

2.1.2 Solid Form

Most common forms of precipitation in solid form are snow. Include sleet, hail and frost.

Snow

Snow is usually experienced in high altitudes like Himalayan region and high latitudes as in some parts North America and Europe. Though snow particles are relatively large but specific gravity of snow is very low, anywhere from 0.05 to 0.15, hence settling velocities are very low. When solid and liquid precipitation is mixed, it is called wet snow which has SG around 0.5. Wet snow has usually short life and it turns into water as surface temperature is usually above freezing. Snow can fall as flurries which are very light and fluffy or as sand.

Sleet

Sleet is transparent, globular solid grains of ice. Sleet occurs when snowflakes only partially melt when they pass through a shallow layer of warmer air. Sleet is formed when falling rain or slushy snow drops meets sub-freezing layer of air above the ground surface and eventually reach the ground as solid ice. Depending on the intensity and duration, sleet can accumulate on the ground much like snow. This occurs close to the land surface.

Hail

Hail is a solid form which consists of ice balls of size larger than 8 mm. It can be very dangerous and can damage crops and structures.

2.2 Types of Precipitation

Precipitation is classified based on the type of mechanism that produces it. This includes convective, cyclonic, frontal, and orographic.

An unequal heating of the air mass near the earth's surface causes **convective precipitation**. The warmed air lifts and cools. Convective precipitation ranges from moderate rainfall to cloud bursts as in thunderstorms. The size of a convective storm is usually quite small. To summarize the characteristics of a convective storm, it is intense, localized, has a short duration and moves at a speed of about 50 km/h.

Cyclonic precipitation is result of a low-pressure region with circular wind motion. Tropical cyclones are called cyclones in India, hurricane in North America and typhoon in Southeast Asia. The normal areal extent of a cyclone is 100 -200 km in diameter. The **isobars** are closely spaced, and the rotation is anticlockwise in the northern hemisphere. Cyclonic storms are large, have low to medium intensity and are of long duration.

Frontal precipitation results from the lifting of a warm air mass over a cold air mass. If the air masses are moving so that warm air replaces cold air, the front is called a **warm front**. On the other hand, if cold air displaces warm air, the front is said to be a **cold front**. Frontal waves move across a region at varied speeds, usually about 25 km/h in summer and 50 km/h in winter. When normal conditions exist within the air mass, rainfall tends to be steady, extending to within 300 km ahead of a warm front and 40 to 80 km ahead of the cold front.

Orographic precipitation occurs as a result of mechanical lifting of warm moist air over natural barriers such as mountain ranges. The Rocky Mountains in North America and the Himalayas in Southeast Asia are good examples that cause orographic precipitation. It is obvious that precipitation

Precipitation 35

is greater on the windward side than the leeward side. Orographic precipitation is characterized by medium to high intensity, is stationary, medium to long in duration, and has a long and narrow width.

- The visible moisture in a cloud is made up of water droplets or ice crystals about 10 μm in diameter. Raindrop average size is about 1 mm
- Cold fronts move faster than warm fronts and generally produce heavier precipitation with the most intense precipitation falling near the surface front.

2.3 Measurement of Precipitation

Precipitation over a given time is expressed as water depth received. Recording gauges and non-recording gauges are used to observe and record precipitation. Recording gauges produce a continuous record of rain precipitation depth. Non-recording gauges produce only one recording. Snow measurements are reported as depth of snow and as water equivalent.

A **standard gauge** as shown in **Figure 2.1** is a non-recording gauge. It consists of a 203-mm diameter collector having a knife-sharp edge, a receiver, an overflow chamber, and a measuring stick.

Figure 2.1 Standard and Tipping Bucket Gauge

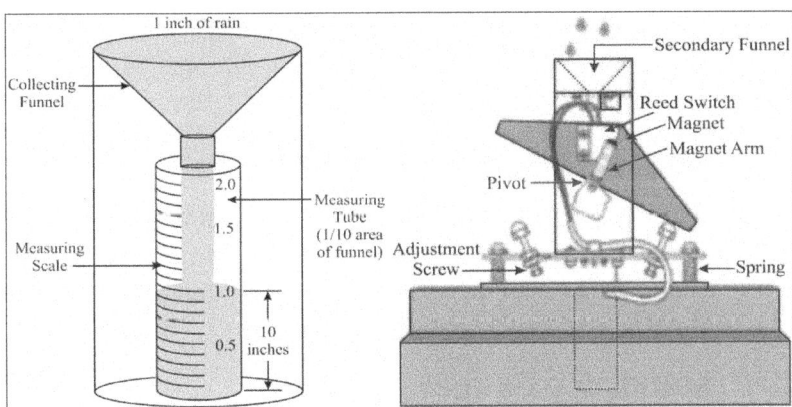

Precipitation is caught in the collector and funnelled into the receiver, which has a cross-sectional area one-tenth of the collector. That is to say, a rainfall depth of 1 mm falling in the collector results in a depth of 1 cm in the receiver. If snow is expected, the collector and receiver are removed, and snowfall accumulates in the overflow chamber. The observer commonly takes the overflow chamber into a warm area to melt the snow and then measures the depth of water as **water equivalent.**

2.3.1 Tipping Bucket Gauge

This gauge provides a continuous record of the rainfall depth and its intensity. A **tipping gauge** as shown in Fig. 2.1, consists of a pair of buckets pivoting under a funnel in such a way that when one bucket receives a fixed amount, usually 0.25 mm of rainfall, bucket tips discharging its contents into a reservoir and bringing the other bucket under the funnel. An electrical pulse is generated on each tip and is transmitted to a recorder. Though the tipping bucket is one of the most used recording gauges, the following limitations should be noted:
- The tipping bucket requires 0.2 s to tip, hence during an intense storm it may cause an error
- Difficult to establish start and end of a light rainfall
- Good for rainfall measurements only
- Graph consists of a series of steps

2.3.2 Weighing-Type Gauge

This gauge is suitable for measuring both rain and snow. The depth of precipitation is sensed by the accumulated weight. In recent models, the data is recorded on the tape or transmitted to a remote data gathering point. They normally have a large holding capacity of about 300 mm to 600 mm of precipitation.

2.3.3 Float-Type Gauge

The typical arrangement of a **float-type** gauge consists of a collector, which leads the rainfall to a chamber in which water level is recorded using a float. To make it more versatile for all types of weather, antifreeze and a bubbler gauge is used to measure the height of water level.

2.3.4 Standpipe Gauge

Standpipe gauge, also known as storage gauge, is used to record snow precipitation particularly in remote locations. The standpipe is erected high enough to extend above the anticipated depth of snow accumulation. To prevent snow from accumulating on the lip of the tube and to minimize the effects of the wind, an **alter shield** is constructed and mounted around the top of the tube. An alter shield is a ring with strips of metal hinged to it. Within the standpipe is antifreeze or a calcium chloride solution to melt the snow so that its water equivalent can be measured. To prevent evaporation of the snowmelt, a thin layer of oil is located on top of the liquid column.

2.3.5 Radar

Radar measurements are used to estimate precipitation intensity. The brightness of the reflected echoes is a measure of the precipitation intensity. The strength of reflected radar pulse depends on the number and size of the raindrops.

2.3.6 Errors in Measurement

Error in precipitation measurement can be caused by instrumental defects and human errors. A large source of error, however, is the wind effect. In one study, it was shown that at an average wind speed of 60 km/h, only 30% of the true rainfall was caught. These errors are much greater for snow. Use of gauge shields and providing natural windbreakers can help to reduce the size of the error. Good judgement is required to interpret observations and reduce inaccuracies caused by poor exposure.

Example Problem 2.1

A bucket with a diameter of 300 mm is used to measure rainfall. At the end of storm, contents of the bucket are transferred to a 100-mm diameter container indicating a water height of 18.0 cm. What is the rainfall depth?

Given:

Diameter: $D_1 = 300$ mm $D_2 = 100$ mm $P_2 = 18.0$ cm $P_1 = ?$

Solution:

$$P_1 = P_2 \times \left(\frac{D_2}{D_1}\right)^2 = 18\ cm \times \left(\frac{100\ mm}{300\ mm}\right)^2 = 2.0\ cm = \underline{20\ mm}$$

2.4 Snow Surveys

The measurement of water equivalent of accumulated snow (**snowpack**) is used as an index of spring runoff. Since snow accumulations vary significantly with slope and aspect, snow surveys are made on permanent courses at fixed measuring sites. **Snow courses** are selected during the winter so that areas subjected to extreme drifting can be avoided.

Measuring points on the courses are selected during summer to avoid drainage channels and seeps. Typically, the elevation difference between courses is 150 to 300 m. North-facing slopes accumulate maximum snow and provide desirable sites. The depth and water equivalent of snow is measured at each sampling site with a snow sampler.

2.4.1 Snow Sampler

A **snow sampler** consists of tubular sections connected by threaded couplings. The tube is pushed into the snow and when it reaches the bottom, the depth of the snowpack is read from graduations on the tube.

Water equivalent of a snowpack is measured by weighing the sampler and its contents. Depending on the diameter of the sampling tube, a relationship between the mass and water equivalent depth can be worked out. For example, if a snow sampler has an inside diameter of 7.5 cm, the mass of the snowpack representing a water equivalent of 1 mm will be:

$$m = V \times \rho = A \times d \times \rho$$

$$\frac{m}{d} = A \times \rho = \frac{\pi}{4} \times (7.5\ cm)^2 \times \frac{1.0\ g}{cm^3} = 44.17 = \underline{44\ g/cm}$$

Each 44 g mass of the snow sample represents a water equivalent of 10 mm or 1 cm. A **Mt. Rose sampler** has a diameter of 1.49 in. so that 1-oz. of snow represents a water equivalent of 1-in.

2.4.2 Specific Gravity of Snow

Specific gravity (SG) or relative density of freshly fallen snow ranges from 0.004 to 0.34 with 0.1 considered a typical value. As the snow ages, the relative density increases due to compaction. Average SG of a snowpack is 0.5. In other words, 10 cm of snowpack has a water equivalent of 5 cm or 50 mm.

$$\boxed{G_S = \frac{depth\ of\ water}{depth\ of\ snow} = \frac{d_w}{d_s}}$$

At a given sampling site, the depth of snowpack is 0.7 m, and the water equivalent is found to be 32 cm, average SG of snow is:

$$G_S = \frac{depth\ of\ water}{depth\ of\ snow} = \frac{d_w}{d_s} = \frac{0.32 m}{0.70\ m} = 0.46 = 46\%$$

2.4.3 Runoff Prediction

The water equivalent information gathered from snow surveys is used to forecast spring runoff from snowmelt. The information is vital to engineers responsible for forecasting and tracking floods on rivers. The expected runoff volume is of great interest to power companies it is used for operation of storage reservoirs.

Example Problem 2.2

A snow sample 20 cm in height melted into 30 mm of water. What is the relative density (SG) of snow?

Given:

d_s = 20 cm d_w = 30 mm   SG =?

Solution:

$$G_s = \frac{d_w}{d_s} = \frac{30mm}{20cm} \times \frac{cm}{10mm} = 0.15 = \underline{0.2}$$

2.5 Rainfall Data

An important piece of information for many hydrologic problems is the quantity of rain that has fallen over a portion of the earth's surface during a specified interval of time. This may be needed as intensity or as depth of rain for the entire storm period or a part of the storm period. In a few areas, weather radar measurements provide patterns of the areal distribution of rain intensity at various times during a storm.

Each rain gauge measures rain over so small an area, compared to the size of areas of concern to hydrologists, that the results from the gauge are called **point rainfalls**. One difficulty in using point rainfall data is the small number of points that must be used to represent patterns of areal variability, which are sometimes very complicated. Another complication arises from the small proportion of recording rain gauges from which detailed information on the timing of rain occurrence and rain intensity can be obtained.

2.5.1 Variation in Rainfall data

There are always some variations in rainfall data, for example annual rainfall varies from year to year. A statistical measure of the variation in a given set of data is called **coefficient of variation**, C_v, which is simply standard deviation divided the mean of data. Standard deviation of a data set can be calculated from the following expression.

Standard deviation

$$S_x = \sqrt{\frac{(x-\bar{x})^2}{n-1}} = \sqrt{\frac{SS}{n-1}} = \sqrt{\frac{n\sum x^2 - (\sum x)^2}{n(n-1)}}$$

Where SS is the sum of squares of deviations from mean value.

$$Coeff. of\ Variation, C_v = \frac{S_x}{\bar{x}}$$

Coefficient of variation is a dimensionless parameter and can be expressed as percentage or decimal fraction. It indicates natural variability in rainfall data for example annual rainfall.

2.5.2 Adequacy of Rainfall Gauge Stations

If there are already some rain auge stations in a watershed, the optimal number(N) of stations that should exist will depend on the acceptable error in the estimation of mean rainfall.

$$Optimal\ number, N = \left(\frac{C_v}{\varepsilon}\right)^2$$

Where ε = allowable degree of error in the estimation of the mean.

Above expression can also be used to find expected error in the estimation of mean for m number of gauges employed to estimate mean of rainfall in the region of interest. In calculating number of optimal gauges, typical value of expectable error is 10%

Example Problem 2.3

A catchment has six rain gauge stations. In a year, the annual rainfall recorded at these gauging stations is tabulated below.

Station	I	II	III	IV	V	VI
Catch, mm	726	929	1703	1003	888	1267

a) Determine the standard error in the estimation of mean rainfall.
b) For acceptable error of 10% in the estimation of mean, work out optimal number of gauging stations required.

Solution:

Sums of the values and square of the values are shown in the **Table 2.1**

Table 2.1 Computations Worksheet (Ex. Prob. 2.3)

ID	A	B	C	D	E	F	Σ
x, mm	726	929	1640	1003	888	1267	6453
$x^2 \times 10^5$	5.27	8.63	26.8	10.0	7.8	16	74

$$\bar{x} = \frac{\Sigma x}{n} = \frac{6453}{6} = 1075.50 = 1075.5 \; mm$$

$$S_x = \sqrt{\frac{n \Sigma x^2 - (\Sigma x)^2}{n(n-1)}} = \sqrt{\frac{6 \times 747559 - (6453)^2}{6 \times 5}}$$

$$= 328.44 = 328.4 \; mm$$

$$C_v = \frac{S_x}{\bar{x}} = \frac{328.44}{1075.50} = 0.30538 = 0.305 = 30.5\%$$

Error in the estimation of mean

$$\varepsilon_{est} = \frac{C_v}{\sqrt{m}} = \frac{0.30538}{\sqrt{6}} = 0.12467 = 0.125 = 12.5\%$$

Optimal number of gauges

$$N = \left(\frac{C_v}{\varepsilon}\right)^2 = \left(\frac{0.30538}{0.12}\right)^2 = 9.325 = 10$$

Thus 4 additional gauges are required to limit the error to 10%

2.5.3 Reading Gauges

Nearly all rain gauges are simple accumulation collectors. The rain depth that is read when the gauge is emptied is the total amount, which has fallen into the gauge since the last time it was emptied. The standard rain gauge procedure in Canada is to read the gauge twice a day at about 9 a.m. and 6 p.m. What is published is a daily rainfall total for each gauge. This is an addition of the 6 p.m. reading and the subsequent 9 a.m. reading with the total listed as the rain depth for the day during which the 6 p.m. reading was taken. This means that the division of rain between the two readings cannot be obtained from the published data. Copies of the report forms from the station can usually be obtained on request and these do contain the two amounts. Gauges at synoptic weather stations are read at six-hour intervals. For the small proportion of stations with recording rain gauges, hourly amounts are published. At a location where both a standard accumulation gauge and a recording gauge are present, the depth of rain published for a given date may differ between the recording and accumulation gauges because the recording gauge data is for the period from midnight to midnight while the standard accumulation gauge data is the total from 9 a.m. on the listed date to 9 a.m. on the subsequent day.

2.6 Missing Data

Filling in missing rain data should be avoided if at all possible. There is usually enough variability of rain from point to point that the estimation is not very accurate. In any case, using the storm pattern to guess the rainfall at a point creates no new information on that particular storm. Nevertheless, there are situations in which it is common practice to fill in occasional bits of missing data. One case is the existence of a long series of rain measurements which are nearly complete, and which would be most useful if they were entirely complete. Another case is the use of a weighted average for a network of rain gauges to determine the mean rainfall over an area. To use the calculated weightings, it is necessary to have data for each gauge in the network.

The technique for estimating missing data depends on the individual situation. In some physical situations - often in mountains or near large water bodies - the ratio of rain at the location where data is missing to the rain at another location where information is available will have been observed to be nearly constant for a long series of past storms where data from both locations was collected. In such a case, this ratio must be considered in making an estimate. In many areas, however, the pattern of rainfall is governed by the weather system creating it and not by the topography of the area. In this case the pattern for each storm will be different and the estimate must be made only from data for the particular storm period in question. A number of methods have been proposed for estimating rainfall data. The station-average method is the simplest method. The normal-ratio and quadrant method provide a weighted mean. Whereas in normal-ratio method weights are based on mean annual rainfall at each gauge, quadrant method weights depend on distance between gauges.

2.6.1 Station-Average Method

The station-average method for estimating missing data uses n number of gauges from a region to estimate the missing rainfall at another gauge.

Precipitation

$$P_x = \frac{1}{n}\sum_{i=1}^{n} P_i = \frac{1}{n}(P_1 + P_2 + \cdots + P_n)$$

Where P_i is the catch at ith gauge and P_x is missing value. Since equal weight is applied to all the gauges, this method yields good results when gauges are uniformly distributed over the watershed.

Normal Ratio Method

The normal ratio method is one of the simplest and most popular methods for estimating the missing data. This procedure is based on selecting m ($\geq$ 3) stations that are near and approximately evenly spaced around the station with the missing record. The missing value is estimated from the following equation.

Missing Value (Normal Ratio method)

$$P_x = \frac{N_x}{n}\left(\frac{P_1}{N_1} + \frac{P_2}{N_2} + \cdots + \frac{P_n}{N_n}\right)$$

N = Normal Precipitation, n = Number of stations, x = missing data station

Example Problem 2.4

In a given river basin, four rain gauges are located in a radius of 50 km. For a given storm, station #4 was not operating. From the rainfall registered from other three stations, estimate the missing storm precipitation at station #4.

Station #	1	2	3	4
Storm precipitation P_i, mm	65.0	77.5	57.5	?
Annual precipitation N_i, mm	1050	1025	975	1030

Solution:

Since the annual catch at all the gauges are relatively close, station-average can be applied to estimate the missing value.

$$P_x = \frac{\Sigma P_i}{n} = \frac{1}{3}(65.0 + 77.5 + 57.5)\ mm = 66.66 = 66.7\ mm$$

To check if estimate is reasonable, let us find missing value by normal ratio method.

$$P_x = \frac{1030\ mm}{3} \times \left(\frac{65.0}{1050} + \frac{77.5}{1025} + \frac{57.5}{975}\right) = 67.46 = \underline{67.5\ mm}$$

This matches closely with the value by the station average method.

Example Problem 2.5

In a given river basin, four rain gauges are located in a radius of 50 km. For a given storm, station #4 was not operating. From the rainfall registered from other three stations, Estimate the missing storm precipitation at station #4.

Station #	1	2	3	4
Storm precipitation P_i, mm	62.3	74.5	59.5	?
Annual precipitation N_i, mm	1510	1680	1375	1290

Solution:

Station-average Method

$$P_x = \frac{\Sigma P}{n} = \frac{1}{3}(62.3 + 74.5 + 59.5) \text{ mm}$$

$$= 64.43 = 64.3 \text{ mm}$$

Normal ratio method

$$P_x = \frac{1290 \text{ mm}}{3} \times \left(\frac{62.3}{1510} + \frac{74.5}{1680} + \frac{59.5}{1375}\right)$$

$$= 55.04 = 55.0 \text{ mm}$$

As is evident, estimate of missing value is significantly different by the two methods.

2.6.2 Quadrant Method

The station average method does not account for either the closeness of the other gauges to the missing data gauge or the density of gauge network. The normal-ratio ratio method requires normal precipitation data in addition to rainfall data.

The quadrant method is an alternative to these methods. Quadrant method provides weighted average of the missing value. The weight applied is the reciprocal of the square of the distance(s) between the gauges and the centre location, that is the location of missing gauge. The closest gauge in each quadrant is chosen. If there is no gauge or it is too far away, no value is chosen from that quadrant. If there is a gauge in each of the four quadrants, then weight applied to the ith gauge is;

$$w_i = \frac{s_i^{-2}}{\Sigma(s_i^{-2})} = \frac{1}{s_i^2} \div \left\{\frac{1}{s_1^2} + \frac{1}{s_2^2} + \frac{1}{s_3^2} + \frac{1}{s_4^2}\right\}$$

Missing value estimate, P_x can be found applying the following formula.

Missing Catch estimate (Quadrant Method)

$$P_x = \frac{1}{\sum_{i=1}^{4}(S_i^{-2})}\left\{\frac{P_1}{S_1^2} + \frac{P_2}{S_2^2} + \frac{P_3}{S_3^2} + \frac{P_4}{S_4^2}\right\}$$

Example Problem 2.6

A network of ten gauges is shown in **Fig. 2.2**. Coordinates of closest gauge to gauge X in each quadrant are shown. Rainfall catches for each of the four gauges (A, H, G, D) is tabulated below. Using Quadrant method, estimate the missing storm rainfall at station X.

Quadrant	I	II	III	IV
Closest Gauge ID	A	H	G	D
Catch, mm	92.5	40.0	75.0	21.4

Solution:

Figure 2.2 Quadrant Method(Ex. Prob. 2.5)

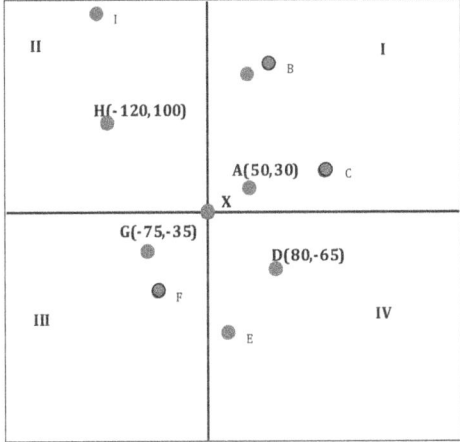

Computations for estimate of the missing value are shown in **Table 2.2**.

Table 2.2 Computations Worksheet (Ex. Prob. 2.5)

Quadrant	Coordinates		s^{-2}	w_i	P_i mm	$w_i \times P_i$ mm
	X	Y				
1	2	3	4	5	6	7
I	50	30	2.94E-04	5.12E-01	92.5	4.73E+01
II	-120	100	4.10E-05	7.13E-02	40.0	2.85E+00
III	-75	-35	1.46E-04	2.54E-01	75.0	1.90E+01
IV	80	-65	9.41E-05	1.64E-01	21.4	3.50E+00
			Σ= 5.75E-04	1.00E+00		7.27E+01

Inverse of square of distance, s (Col. 4) is found by adding squares of X (col. 2) and Y(Col.3) and inversing it. Weight for known value in each quadrant is found by dividing the inverse of square value by the total sum of col. 4. As a check sum of all the weights must be unity as seen in the bottom of col. 5. Each catch value is multiplied by the weight and placed in the last column (Col. 7). Sum of the values in Col. 7 is the estimate of missing value.

Sample of Calculations (Quadrant I)

$$s_1^{-2} = (50^2 + 30^2)^{-1} = 2.9412 \times 10^{-4} = 2.94 \times 10^{-4}$$

$$\Sigma s_1^{-2} = (2.94 + 4.10 + 1.46 + 9.41) \times 10^{-4} = 5.75 \times 10^{-4}$$

$$w_i = \frac{2.941 \times 10^{-4}}{5.75 \times 10^{-4}} = 0.512 = 0.512$$

$$P_i w_i = 92.5 \ mm \times 0.512 = 0.473 \ mm \times 10^{-4}$$

2.7 Gauge Consistency

In addition to the problem of estimating missing value, a hydrologist needs to check if the catch at rain gauges is consistent over a period and if an adjustment is needed. Adjustment of the gauge consistency involves estimation of an effect rather than the missing value. An inconsistent record may occur due to number of factors including, change in observation procedure, changes in exposure of the gauge, or changes in land use that make it impractical to maintain that gauge in the old location. In some cases, vandalism may be the cause of inconsistency.

2.7.1 Doble Mass Curve

Double mass analysis is the method used to check for inconsistency in a gauged record. A **double-mass curve (Fig. 2.3)** is a graph of cumulative

Precipitation

catch at the rain gauge of interest versus the cumulative catch of one or gauges in the region that are known to have consistent record.

Figure 2.3 Double Mass Curve and Consistency

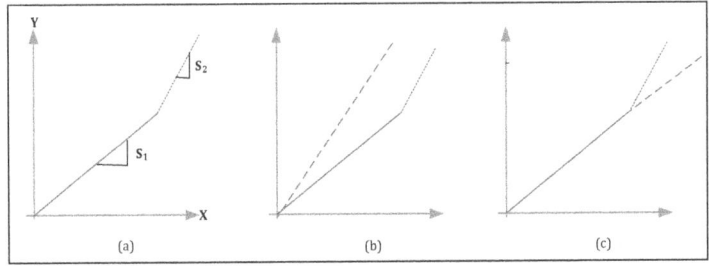

If the mass curve shows a constant slope, it is indicative of consistency. However, a change in the slope of the double-mass curve would suggest that an external factor has come into play. If a change in slope is evident, then the record must be adjusted, with either the early or later part of the record. The section that needs to be adjusted depends on the expected cause of change of slope. Adjustment is done so that resulting curve has constant slope. When double mass curve between cumulative regional catch X and the catch at gauge Y, where the check for consistency is needed, is characterised by two segments 1 and 2 with different slopes, it indicates inconsistency as shown in Fig. 2.3. Slope of the first segment (earlier part of record) and second (later part of the record) is determined as follows:

$$S_1 = \frac{\Delta Y_1}{\Delta X_1} \quad and \quad S_2 = \frac{\Delta Y_2}{\Delta X_2}$$

When the gauge is permanently relocated, it would need to adjust earlier part (segment 1) of the record so that it becomes consistent with the later record that is segment 2 (see Fig.2.3 (a)). Adjustment in an earlier record say Y_i is made and adjusted value is called Y'.

$$Y_i' = \frac{S_2}{S_1} Y_i$$

If the gauge has been relocated for a short period or exposure conditions have affected the catch for a short period, it would need to adjust the later part or segment 2 of the mass curve so that it becomes consistent with the initial part of the record as shown in Fig.2.3(c). Adjustment is made using the expression;

$$Y_i' = \frac{S_1}{S_2}Y_i$$

Example Problem 2.7

Annual rainfall depth data are available (see Table 2.3) for three consistent gauges (A, B and C) and one inconsistent gauge(O). Gauge O was moved and relocated at the end of year 1991; therefore, the annual catches for gauge O for the years 1989-1991 must be adjusted in relation to the catch characteristics at the new location. Find the adjusted values for gauge O before relocation.

Table 2.3 Table of Data (Ex. Prob. 2.7)

Year		1989	1990	1991	1992	1993	1994	1995	1996
Annual rainfall, mm	A	440	420	540	500	380	480	340	420
	B	520	520	620	580	440	500	380	440
	C	460	500	560	580	460	520	400	460
	O	660	760	855	620	480	560	440	520

Computations are shown in Table 2.3 and plot in Fig.2.3

Sample of Calculations (Year 1990)

Annual catches at gauges A, B, C are summed (col.6)
$X_2 = 420 + 520 + 500 = 1440$

Cumulative values of the sums, ΣX_i are found (Col.7)
$\Sigma X_2 = 1420 + 1440 = 2860$

Cumulate the catches for relocated gauge, O (Col.8)
$\Sigma Y_2 = 660 + 760 = 1420$

Compute the slope for the years 1989-1991
$$S_1 = \frac{2275 - 0}{4580 - 0} = 0.4967 = 0.497$$

Compute the slope for the years 1992-1996
$$S_2 = \frac{4895 - 2895}{11460 - 6240} = 0.3831 = 0.383$$

Adjust the values of catch at gauge O (Col.10)
$$Y_2' = Y_2 \times \frac{S_2}{S_1} = 760 \times \frac{0.383}{0.497} = 585.67 = 586$$

Table 2.4 Computations Worksheet (Ex. Prob. 2.6)

Year	Total		Cumulative	Slope		Adjusted	
	O	A+B+C	A+B+C	O			
	Y_i	X_i	ΣX_i	ΣY_i		Y'	$\Sigma Y'$
1	5	6	7	8	9	10	11
1989	660	1420	1420	660	0.497	509	509
1990	760	1440	2860	1420		586	1095
1991	855	1720	4580	2275		659	1755
1992	620	1660	6240	2895	0.383		
1993	480	1280	7520	3375			
1994	560	1500	9020	3935			
1995	440	1120	10140	4375			
1996	520	1320	11460	4895			

Figure 2.4 Adjustment of the Mass Curve

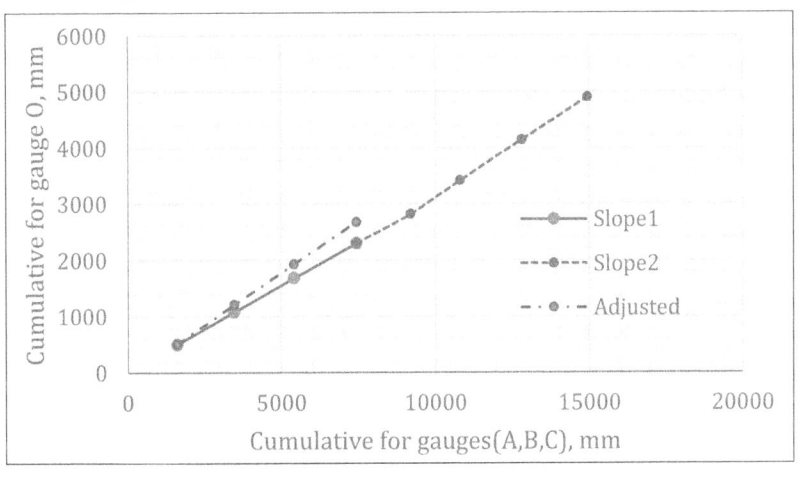

Discussion Questions

1. Briefly describe the mechanism of precipitation.
2. Compare cyclonic precipitation and frontal precipitation.
3. Explain a procedure for estimating missing data
4. What considerations would you have to set up gauge network?
5. What are the limitations of tipping bucket gauge?
6. For doing snow surveys, what things you should keep in mind when selecting snow courses and snow measuring points?
7. Describe the working of a snow sampler.
8. Explain the following terms: water equivalent, snow density, snowpack, point rainfall, orographic precipitation
9. Explain how radar can be used to measure precipitation
10. Describe orographic precipitation and name three natural barriers those are responsible for causing orographic precipitation.

Practice Problems

Practice Problem 2.1

A bucket with a diameter of 300 mm is used to measure rainfall. After the storm, contents of the bucket are transferred to a 2-L capacity graduated cylinder. What should be the reading to indicate rainfall depth of 20 mm? (1.41 L)

Practice Problem 2.2

You have been asked to design a snow sampler, each 1.0 g of snow represents a water equivalent of 1.0 mm. What must be the inside diamter of the snow sampler? (36 mm)

Practice Problem 2.3

What is the water equivalent of a snowpack (SG = 0.5) with a depth of 1.2 m? (600 mm)

Practice Problem 2.4

For the data of Example Problem 2.3, station #1 was not in operation for a given storm, which produced at stations #2, 3, and 4 respectively 25.4 mm, 31.0 mm and 32.1 mm of rainfall. Estimate the missing value. (31.5 mm)

Practice Problem 2.5

The average relative density of 50 cm of snow packed over a catchment area of 10 km^2 is estimated to be 40%. What is the expected volume of runoff assuming 60% of snow melt becomes runoff? (1.2 GL)

Practice Problem 2.6

Before the spring runoff, average snowpack depth is observed to be 1.4 m with water equivalent of 0.45 over a watershed encompassing an area of 85 km^2. Assuming half of the snow becomes runoff, how much runoff volume is expected? (2.7×10^7 m^3)

Practice Problem 2.7

For the tipping bucket recording rain gauge chart shown in **Fig. 2.5**, find the rainfall intensity for the interval 10:00-11:00 and 11:00-12:00, most intense half hour and for the whole duration of the storm? Comment on the correction applied to the tipping bucket data as to yield the same total as standard rain gauge data. (3.0 mm/h, 1.4 mm/h, 2.4 mm/h, 4.0 mm/h)

Figure 2.5 Tipping Bucket Rain Gauge Graph

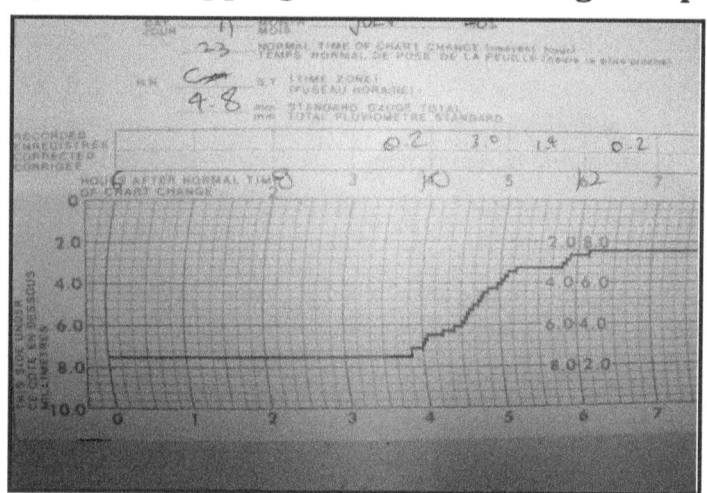

Practice Problem 2.8

A bucket with a diameter of 350 mm is used to measure rainfall. At the end of storm, the contents of the bucket are transferred to a 100-mm diameter container indicating a water height of 16.0 cm. Find rainfall depth. (13 mm)

Practice Problem 2.9

For the tipping bucket gauge graph in **Fig. 2.5**, what is maximum rainfall intensity for durations of 10 min, 30 min, 60 min, and 120 min?
(9.6 mm/h, 4.0 mm/h, 3.2 mm/h, 2.2 mm/h)

Practice Problem 2.10

The normal rainfall at stations A, B, C, D and E respectively are 1250, 1020, 760, 1130 and 1370 mm. During a particular storm, stations A, B, C and D received 122, 92, 68 and 98 mm of rainfall while station E was inoperative. Estimate the missing value. (125 mm)

Practice Problem 2.11

From the chatrt shown in **Fig, 2.6**, tabulate rcumulative values of the rainfall for the period 1000 to 1900 hours and find rainfall for each hour.
    a.   What the total rainfall received? (12 mm)
    b.   In which hour, rainfall intensity was the maximum?(1300-1400)
    c.   What is the maximum rainfall rate (2.2 mm/h)
    d.   Which hour received minmum rainfall?(1500-1600)

Figure 2.6 Recording Rain Gauge Chart

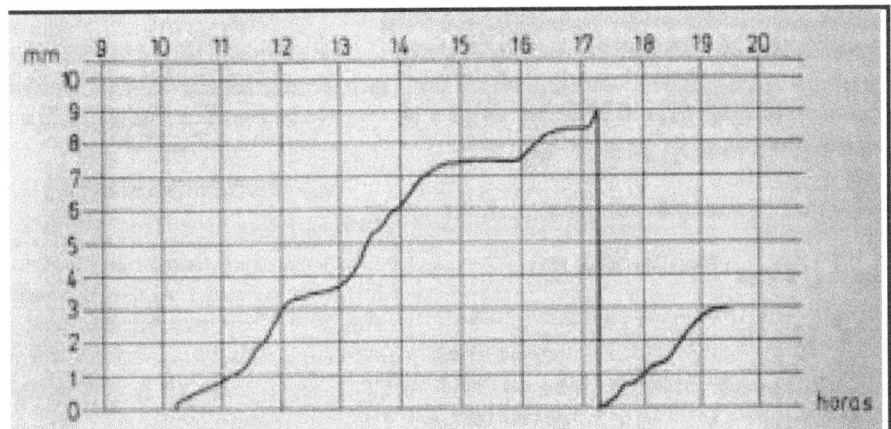

Practice Problem 2.12

The coordinates and rainfall catch of gauge closest to gauge X in each quadrant is tabulated below. Using Quadrant method, estimate the missing storm rainfall at station X. (72.6 mm)

Quadrant	I	II	III	IV
Gauge co-ordinates	35, 32	-86, 110	-55, -30	95, -45
Catch, mm	76.4	55.6	77.5	49.5

Practice Problem 2.13

In a watershed five rain gauges are located within a radius of 75 km. For a given period, station #4 was not operable. Rainfall catch for the period in question are tabulated below. From the rainfall registered from other four stations, estimate the missing storm precipitation at station #4 using station-average and normal-ratio methods. (59.5 mm, 60.7 mm)

Station #	1	2	3	4	5
Storm precipitation P_i, mm	62.0	72.5	55.5	?	48.0
Annual precipitation N_i, mm	1050	1025	975	1030	980

Practice Problem 2.14

Repeat ex. Prob. 2.3 with gauge C value of 1580 mm (N=8)

Practice Problem 2.15

Annual rainfall depth(cm) data are available (see table below) for three consistent gauges (A, B and C) and one inconsistent gauge(D). Gauge D was relocated at the end of year 1987; therefore, data for gauge D for the years

1988-1996 must be adjusted in relation to the catch characteristics at the new location. Find the adjusted values before relocation.
(60.2, 69.8, 72.2, 74.6, 62.6 cm)

Y	83	84	85	86	87	88	89	90	91	92	93	94	95	96
A	54	62	64	68	58	56	64	72	62	56	50	56	66	68
B	50	60	58	66	58	52	68	68	58	54	44	50	62	66
C	56	66	72	68	60	54	68	74	68	58	50	58	68	72
D	50	58	60	62	52	60	72	76	72	62	56	60	74	74

Practice Problem 2.16

A catchment has six rain gauge stations. In a year, the annual rainfalls recorded by the gages are as follows:

Stations: A   B   C   D   E   F
Rainfall (cm):   82.6   102.9   180.3   110.3   98.8   136

For a 10% error in the estimation of mean rainfall, calculate optimum number of stations in the catchment. (9)

Review Questions

Indicate the correct choice.

1. The precipitation occurring as a result of mechanical lifting over natural barrier is
   a) Convective   b) Orographic   c) Frontal   d) Cyclonic

2. Which one of the following is not a form of precipitation?
   a) Rain   b) Snow   c) Dew   d) All are

3. Which one of the following recording rain gauges is more common?
   a) Tipping   b) Weighing   c) Float type   d) None

4. Specific gravity of freshly fallen snow is about
   a) 0.5   b) 1.0   c) 0.1   d) 0.01

5. What is the water equivalent of 70.0 cm of snow packed with a SG of 0.46?
   a) 23 mm   b) 32 mm   c) 23 cm   d) 32 cm

6. A sample of snow 20 cm high melts into 5 cm of water. The relative density of snow is
   a) 4,0   b) 0.4   c) 0.5   d) 0.25

7. Snow measuring points on the snow courses are selected during
   a) Summer   b) Fall   c) Winter   d) Spring

8. Which one of the following is a form of precipitation?
   a) Infiltration   b) Evaporation   c) Sleet   d) Transpiration

9. Which of the following can be used to measure snow as well as rain?
   a) Weighing type   b) Tipping bucket   c) Siphon gauge   d) Standard

10. How much rainfall needs to be collected before tipping bucket gauge tips?
    a) 0.10 mm   b) 0.25 mm   c) 2.5 mm   d) 1.0 mm

11. A non-standard rain gauge has an opening of 15 cm. Rainwater collected is poured into a graduating cylinder reads 1.56 L, Rainfall depth is
    a) 11 mm   b) 22 mm   c) 33 mm   d) 44 mm

12. As the accumulated snow ages, it becomes
    a) Soft b) Wetter c) Denser d) Lighter

13. Specific gravity of aged snow is about
    a) 0.05 b) 0.10 c) 0.20 d) 0.50

14. The normal annual precipitation at stations A, B and C are 1750 mm, 1800 mm, and 1500 mm, respectively. Station B was inoperative in 2005 and stations A and C recorded 150 cm and 135 cm respectively. Annual rainfall for station B is
    a) 1500 mm b) 1430 mm c) 1580 mm d) 1680 mm

15. After a rainfall event, depth of rainwater collected in the receiver of a standard rain gauge was read to be 17 cm. Total rainfall depth is
    a) 17 cm b) 17 mm c) 17 dm d) 17 dam

16. When specific gravity of freshly fallen snow is unknown, it is safe to assume it as
    a) 0.90 b) 0.50 c) 0.30 d) 0.10

17. A frontal storm forms due to
    a) Lifting of Warm air
    b) Lifting of Cold air
    c) Clockwise rotation
    d) Anticlockwise rotation

18. A front is an interface between
    a) Distinct air masses
    b) Earth surface and warm air
    c) Earth surface and cold air
    d) All the above

19. A tropical cyclone is also called
    a) Cyclone b) Typhoon c) Hurricane d) All

20. A tropical storm in the Northern Hemisphere is a zone of____ rotation
    a) Low, clockwise
    b) High, clockwise
    c) Low, anticlockwise
    d) High, anticlockwise

21. Snow water equivalent indicates
    a) Snowpack depth
    b) Snow specific gravity
    c) Equivalent water depth
    d) Area with same snow depth

Precipitation

22. Orographic lifting of air results in
    a) Rainfall on windward side   b) Drop in atmospheric pressure
    c) A warmer climate   d) Possibility of hurricane

23. Rainfall depth observed is more accurate, when using
    a) Tipping bucket   b) Standard   c) Weighing type   d) Float type

24. Snow measurement points are selected in which of the following seasons?
    a) Winter   b) Summer   c) Spring   d) Fall

25. Missing rainfall data is usually estimated using ____method.
    a) Isohyetal   b) Thiessen   c) Arithmetic   d) Normal ratio

26. Snow courses are selected in which of the following season?
    a) Winter   b) Summer   c) Spring   d) Fall

27. Rainfall data from tipping bucket gauge is corrected using data from ___ gauge.
    a) Siphon   b) Standard   c) Weighing   d) Float

28. The data values obtained from reading standard rain gauge indicates _____ rainfall.
    a) Point   b) Areal   c) Average   d) Maximum

29. To prevent the effect of wind, snow gauges are provided with
    a) Lid   b) Cover   c) Umbrella   d) Shield

30. _____ storms are usually of smaller duration and localized.
    a) Orographic   b) Convective   c) Tropical   d) Frontal

3 Storm Analysis

Once storm rainfall has been measured, the search begins for ways in which this information on rain can be put into forms that will be useful for future reference. Some of the most frequently required data are **typical (average)** and **extreme areal mean rainfalls** for a specified watershed (or catchment) with a known shape and area. In addition to the study of the areal variation, the other aspect of storm analysis deals with the **temporal variation** or rainfall rate. In summary, the storm data is analysed to answer the following questions:
- What is the areal average rainfall?
- What is the maximum mean depth for a given area?
- What is the maximum mean intensity for a given duration?
- What is the frequency of a given storm?

The last question on the frequency or return period of a storm is dealt with in Unit 5. Precipitation varies both in space and time. Time variation is very important to consider when working out peak runoff rate. Space variation mainly governs the total volume of runoff.

3.1 Temporal Distribution

The **temporal** rainfall distribution indicates the variation of rainfall depth within storm duration. Rate of rainfall is called **rainfall intensity** is usually expressed in mm/h. It can be expressed in either discrete (histogram) or continuous form (cumulative). A histogram of rainfall depth is called **hyetograph** and is a more common way of expressing the temporal rainfall distribution. As seen in **Figure 3.1**, rainfall rate is generally low in the beginning and end of the storm.

The continuous form is the plot of accumulated depth of rainfall with time. Rainfall duration and rainfall depth can be both expressed in percentage of total value. Such a dimensionless graph can be used to convert a given rainfall depth into a hyetograph. This is illustrated in the following example problem.

Example Problem 3.1

An 8-hour duration storm produced the following rainfall depth (cumulative) recorded every hour. Express the cumulative depth and hourly rainfall intensity as percentage of the total.

Time (h)	1	2	3	4	5	6	7	8
Depth (mm)	2.5	8.4	17.5	45	55	61	66	70

Solution:

Computations and Plot are shown in **Table 3.1** and **Fig. 3.1** respectively.

Table 3.1 Works sheet (Ex. Prob. 3.1)

Time		Cumulative Rainfall		intensity	
h	%	mm	%	mm/h	%
1.0	12.5	2.5	3.6	2.5	3.6
2.0	25.0	8.4	12.0	5.9	8.4
3.0	37.5	17.5	25.3	9.1	13
4.0	50.0	45.0	64.3	27.5	39.2
5.0	62.5	55.0	78.6	10.0	14.2
6.0	75.0	61.0	87.1	6.0	8.6
7.0	87.5	66.0	94.3	5.0	7.1
8.0	100.0	70.0	100.0	4.0	100

Figure 3.1 Dimensionless Hyetograph(Ex. 3.1)

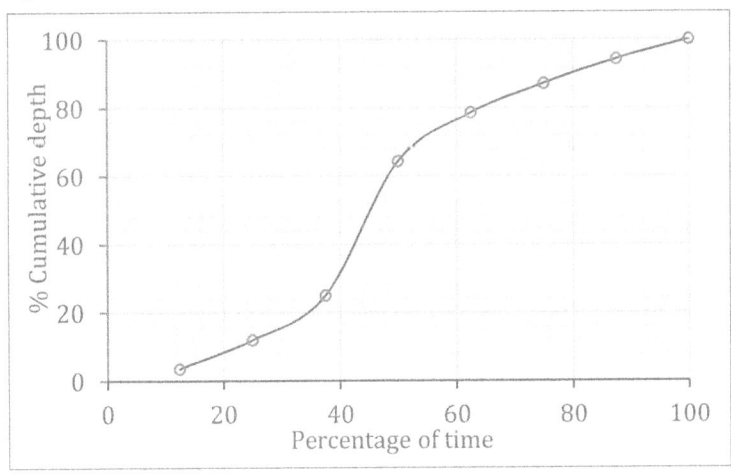

Sample of Calculations (end of third hour)

$$P = \frac{17.5 \text{ mm}}{70 \text{ mm}} \times 100\% = 25.0 = \underline{25\%}$$

$$I = \frac{\Delta P}{\Delta t} = \frac{(17.5 - 8.4) \text{ mm}}{1.0 \text{ h}} = \underline{9.1 \text{ mm/h}}$$

$$= \frac{9.1}{70} \times 100\% = 0.13 = \underline{13\%}$$

$$t = \frac{3h}{8h} \times 100\% = 0.375 = \underline{38\%}$$

Example Problem 3.2

Based on the rainfall distribution of Example Problem 3.1, find the distribution of a storm which produces total rainfall of 150 mm.

Solution:

Based on the rainfall distribution of Example Problem 3.1, rainfall depth of 150 mm is distributed and rainfall intensity in each hour is calculated and is shown in **Table 3.2** and **Fig. 3.2** respectively.

Table 3.2 Computations Worksheet (Ex. Prob. 3.2)

Time		Cumulative depth, mm		Intensity
h	%	%	mm	mm/h
1.0	12.5	3.6	5.4	5.4
2.0	25.0	12.0	18.0	12.6
3.0	37.5	25.0	46.0	28.0
4.0	50.0	64.3	98.0	52.0
5.0	62.5	78.6	117.9	19.9
6.0	75.0	87.1	130.7	12.8
7.0	87.5	94.3	141.5	10.8
8.0	100.0	100.0	150.0	8.6

The dimensionless curve shown in **Fig.3.1** is steepest in the middle hours indicating that rainfall rate was maximum. Whereas dimensionless curve is relatively flat in the beginning and end periods indicative of low rainfall intensity.

Figure 3.2 Rainfall Hyetograph (Ex. Prob. 3.2)

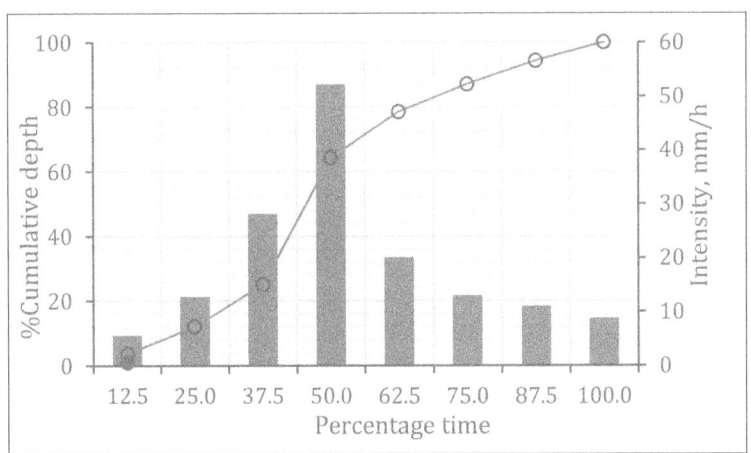

Example Problem 3.3

The incremental rainfall data of a storm is shown below. Present the data as a histogram, hyetograph and a mass curve

min	30	60	90	120	150	180	210	240
mm	17.5	27	73	52	39	34	11	7.5

Solution:

Based on the incremental data, cumulative depth, and intensity for each time interval is calculated and is shown in **Table 3.3**. A plot of histogram, hyetograph and a mass curve is shown in **Fig. 3.3**.

Table 3.3 Rainfall data of a storm (Ex. Prob. 3.3)

Time	Rainfall		
	Incremental	Cumulative	Intensity
min	mm	mm	mm/h
30	17.5	17.5	35.0
60	27.0	44.5	54.0
90	73.0	117.5	146.0
120	52.0	169.5	104.0
150	39.0	208.5	78.0
180	34.0	242.5	68.0
210	11.0	253.5	22.0
240	7.5	261.0	15.0

Figure 3.3 Rainfall Data of a Storm (Ex. Prob. 3.3)

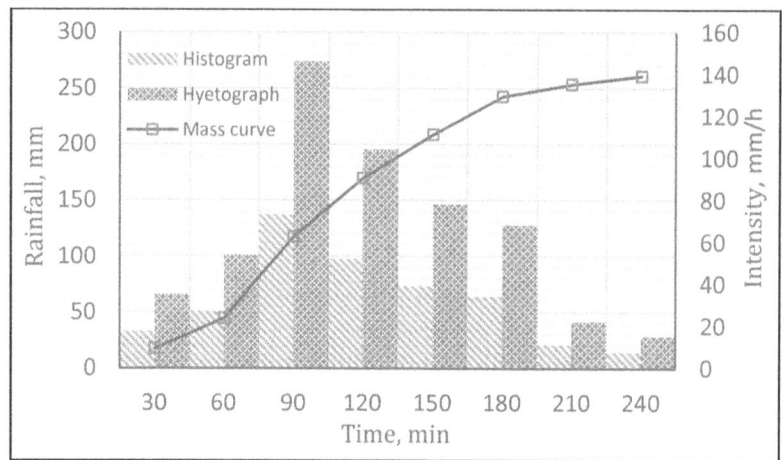

3.2 Spatial Distribution

Rainfall varies from point to point over the catchment. Rainfall intensity is the maximum at the centre of storm. An **isohyetal map** is used to study the areal variation of rainfall. **Isohyet** is a rain depth contour. It is the line joining points receiving equal depth of rainfall. Like a topographic map, the closeness of the isohyets indicates the degree of spatial variation. The widely spaced isohyets indicate a storm with relatively uniform distribution over a given area.

Individual storms may have spatial distributions or patterns of concentric isohyets of elliptic shape. The inner isohyet is called the **storm eye**. Storm eye depicts the area receiving maximum rainfall. As we move away from the eye, the rainfall intensity/depth decreases. In general, storm patterns are not static. They move gradually in the direction of the prevailing winds. **Isopluvial** refers to an isohyet of a regional map. These maps show rain depth contours applicable for a range of storm durations, frequencies, and catchment sizes. More detailed discussion is provided in **Section 3.3**.

3.2.1 Average Areal Precipitation

In hydrologic analysis, it is often necessary to determine a spatial or areal average of the storm depth. Rain gauge networks must be designed to depict the rainfall distribution. In order to get better estimates of areal average, one should search for all rain gauge information that can be found. A bucket survey can provide sufficient rain data for better estimates. The average areal rainfall can be found by either of the three methods: Station Average, Thiessen's polygons and Isohyetal method. In the last two methods, the average areal rainfall P is expressed as a weighted average.

Weighted average

$$P_{avg} = \Sigma(w_i \alpha \times P_i) \quad and \quad \Sigma w_i = 1$$

Where w_i is the weight assigned to the ith gauge recording precipitation P_i.

3.2.2 Station-Average

Station-average is simply the arithmetic mean. In other words, the weight attached to each gauge value is the same, $a_i = 1/N$. The accuracy of this method depends on the density and distribution of gauges. Because of the equal weight, this method may provide poor estimates when the precipitation is highly irregular due to topographic and wind effects. Rain gauges outside the boundary of the watershed should not be used for arithmetic averaging. However, they can be used in other methods as discussed in the following sections. This method is recommended when gauges are densely distributed over the watershed.

3.2.3 Thiessen's Polygon Method

Thiessen's method attempts to define the area representative of each gauge to weigh the effects of non-uniform rainfall distribution. Perpendicular bisectors of the connecting lines between gauges are drawn to form a polygon (**Fig. 3.4A**). The polygon around each gauge is assumed to be the representative area. The polygon area expressed as a fraction of the total area is the weighing factor for a given gauge.

An advantage of polygon method is that for a given layout of gauges, the weighting factors remain the same, thus it becomes quick and easy to compute the average rainfall over the catchment from different storms. The disadvantage is that no allowance is made for topographic influences and storm morphology into the calculation of weights.

The more commonly method used for finding mean precipitation, especially for larger watersheds is the isohyetal method.

Figure 3.4 Isohyetal Method and Polygon Method

A   B

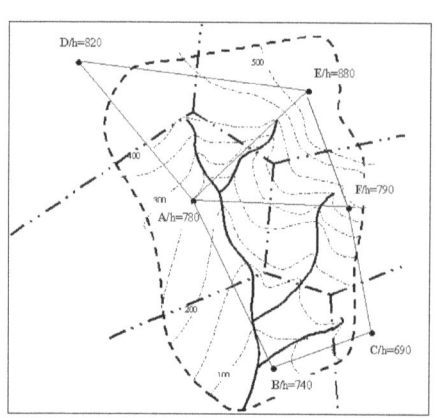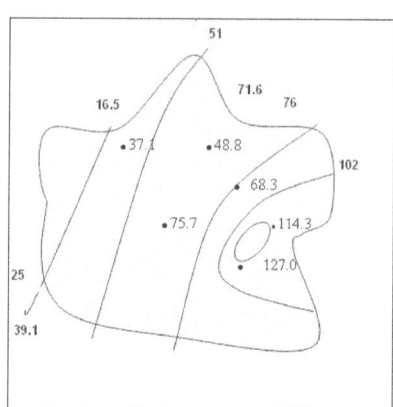

3.2.4 Isohyetal Method

The **isohyetal method** permits an analyst to allow for variation in topography, type of storm - convective versus frontal - or other features like mountain barriers that might affect precipitation. The isohyetal map (**Fig. 3.3B**) is prepared by drawing isohyets using a suitable contour interval. From the isohyetal map, area between adjoining contours and watershed boundary are measured. This becomes the representative area for the mean rainfall (mid-way) between contours. The area becomes the weighting factor to compute the weighted average of rainfall over the catchment area. A disadvantage of this method is that it requires drawing a different map and measurement of area for each storm event. However, this is a more accurate method especially when the storm is highly non-uniform. Areal mean computed by this method is dependent on the skill of the hydrologist and isohyetal map drawn by each person is different.

Example Problem 3.4

An isohyetal map was drawn for a storm that fell on Speed River watershed and computed areas between successive contours are shown in **Table 3.4**. Calculate the areal average rainfall

Solution:

Computations for determining areal average rain depth by **isohyetal method**

Table 3.4 Table of Computations (Ex. Prob. 3.4)

Isohyet mm	Net area A_i, km²	Mean depth P_i, mm	Volume $V_i = A_i \times P_i$ km².mm	Weight Factor $W_i = A_i/A$	Weighted depth $W_i \times P_i$
50 - 60	125	55.0	6875	0.21	11.55
60 - 75	250	67.5	16875	0.42	28.36
75 -100	220	82.5	18150	0.37	30.50
	$\Sigma = 595$		41970	1.0	70.42

$$\bar{P} = \frac{V}{A} = \frac{41970 \; km^2 \cdot mm}{595 \; km^2} = 70.5 = 71 \; mm$$

N.B. Net area refers to the area between the two successive isohyets. If one of the contours lies outside the watershed boundary, net area is the area bound by the contours and the watershed boundary.

Example Problem 3.5

Rainfall depth from a storm that fell on Aryan River watershed was recorded at six gauges shown in **Fig. 3.5**. Each square in map is 400 m×400 m. Three gauges viz. B, C, and D are located within the boundary of the watershed and remaining three, A, E, and F are in the vicinity of the watershed. Determine the areal mean rainfall using station average, polygon and isohyetal methods. Station average method can be applied based on arithmetic mean of the gauges with in the boundary of the watershed and or all gauges including ones close to the boundary.

Gauge ID	A	B	C	D	E	F
Depth, mm	110	78	65	55	51	35

$$\bar{P} = \frac{\Sigma P_i}{n} = \frac{(110 + 78 + 65 + 55 + 51 + 35) \; mm}{6} = \frac{394 \; mm}{6}$$

$$= 65.66 = 65.7 \; mm$$

If only the gauges within the watershed boundary are considered, which is usually the case, average rainfall is;

$$\bar{P} = \frac{\Sigma P_i}{n} = \frac{(78 + 65 + 55) \; mm}{3} = \frac{198 \; mm}{3} = 66.0 = 65.7 \; mm$$

Based on the location of the rain gauges, polygon map is drawn and shown in **Fig. 3.5**. the number of squares lying in each polygon is counted and land area is determined by multiplying number of squares (Col. 2) by 0.64 and shown in Col. 3 of **Table 3.5**. Summation of weighted values = 64.6 mm is the weighted average by the polygon method

Figure 3.5 Thiessen Polgon Method (Ex. Prob. 3.5)

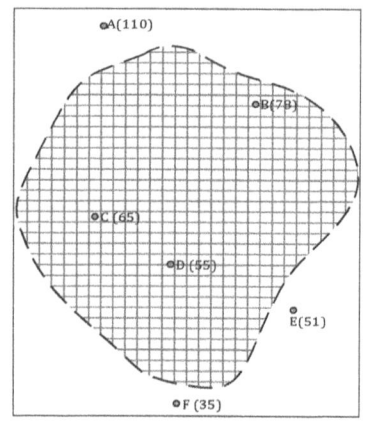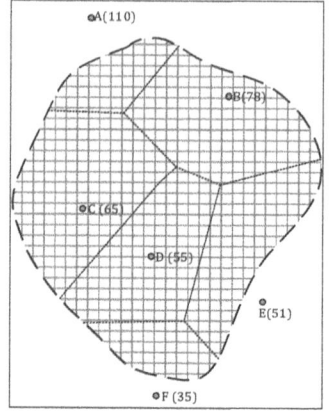

Table 3.5 Thiessen Polygon Method (Ex. Prob. 3.4)

Gauge ID	Squares #	Net Area A_i, km²	Depth P_i, mm	Volume km².mm	Factor A_i/A	Weighted $W_i \times P_i$
A	203	130	110	14291	0.10	10.6
B	420	269	78	20966	0.20	15.6
C	457	292	65	19011	0.22	14.1
D	406	260	55	14291	0.19	10.6
E	437	280	51	14264	0.21	10.6
F	177	113	35	3965	0.08	3.0
	2100	1344		86788	1.00	64.6

$\bar{P} = \Sigma W_i \times P_i = 64.6 \, mm$

Isohyetal Method

Isohyetal map is shown in **Fig. 3.6** and computations of areal average in **Table 3.6**. In the isohyetal map, it can be seen that isohyets are closely spaced indicating large variation in the head end of the watershed. Weight is worked out by the fraction of the area and is shown in Col.6. Weighted value for each interval is shown in Col.7. Summation of weighted values = 68.1 mm is the weighted average.

Figure 3.6 Isohyetal Method (Ex. Prob. 3.5)

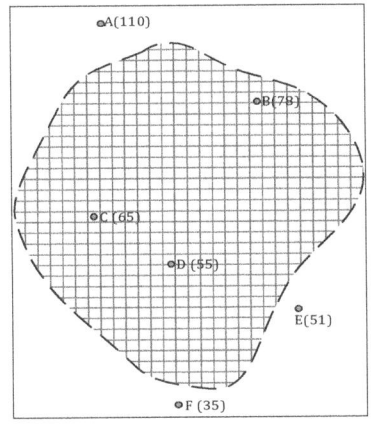 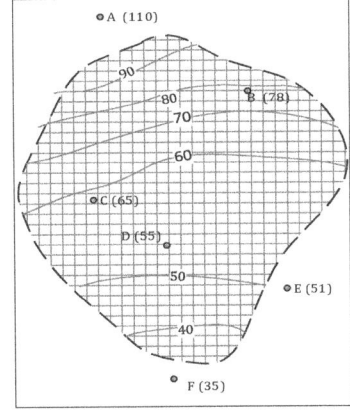

Table 3.6 Table of Computations (Ex. Prob. 3.5)

Isohyet mm	Squares #	Net area A_i, km²	Depth P_i, mm	Volume km².mm	Factor $W_i = A_i/A$	Weighted $W_i \times P_i$
30 - 40	93	60	35	2083	0.04	1.6
40 - 50	216	138	45	6221	0.10	4.6
50-60	222	142	55	7814	0.11	5.8
60 -70	396	253	65	16474	0.19	12.3
70-80	857	548	75	41136	0.41	30.6
80-90	219	140	85	11914	0.10	8.9
90-100	97	62	95	5898	0.05	4.4
	2100	1344		91539	1.00	68.1

3.3 Depth and Catchment Area

As one would expect, larger is the catchment area smaller is the areal average storm depth. This variation of storm depth with catchment area has led to the concept of point depth and point area.

Point depth is the storm depth associated with the point area. **Point area** is the smallest area below which the variation of storm depth is assumed negligible. The accepted value is 25 km². The values of storm depth read from isopluvial maps represent point depth for a given region. For all catchments with areas less than point area, storm depth is equal to the point depth. For areas greater than the point area, a reduction in point depth is made to account for decrease in depth due to spatial spread.

The generalized area depth curves relate the point depth to average depth over areas up to 1000 km². The reduction factor is smaller for large durations. For example, for a catchment area of 200 km², reduction is 26% and 15% for durations of 1-h and 3-h respectively.

3.3.1 Depth-Area-Duration (DAD)

A **depth-area duration curve** is another way of describing the relation between storm depth, duration, and catchment area. DAD analysis is used to study regional storm characteristics. To construct a DAD chart, do the following:
- Prepare an isohyetal map for the selected storm.
- By definition of the isohyet (rain-depth contour), the rain depths outside the contour are smaller than depth inside it.
- The analysis is conducted by calculating the mean depth within the contour and the total area enclosed by the contour.
- Each data point represented by the area enclosed within a contour and the mean depth within the contour is a defining point for the DAD curve.

Since catchments cannot be split up and moved across country to position different parts of them under different parts of storms, it is not permissible to combine areas of separated storm centres.

Example Problem 3.6

The data from an isohyetal map of a 24-h storm area (km²) enclosed by each isohyet drawn at an interval of 10 mm is tabulated below. Assuming storm centre had an enclosed area of 155 km² and rainfall depth of 108 mm, plot depth area duration curve and fit an exponential equation. From the developed equation, find average depth of 24-h rainfall over an area of 5000 km².

Given:

mm	100	90	80	70	60	50	40	30	20
km²	341	1430	2266	2970	3250	3960	4430	5280	6600

Solution:

Computations of mean depth are tabulated in **Table 3.7**. The plot of depth of rainfall versus area is shown in **Fig. 3.7**.

Sample of Calculations (80 mm isohyet)

$Net\ Area, A_i = 2266 - 1430 = 836\ km^2\ (Col.3)$

$Avg.\ isohyet\ value, P_i = \dfrac{1}{2} \times (80 + 90) = 85\ mm\ (Col.4)$

$Net\ Volume, V_i = A_i \times P_i = 836 \times 85 = 71060\ km^2.mm\ (Col.5)$

$Total\ volume\ \Sigma V_i = 139539 + 71060 = 21059\ km^2.mm\ (Col.6)$

$Mean\ Depth, \overline{P} = \dfrac{Col.6}{Col.2} = \dfrac{21059}{2266} = 92.9 = 93\ mm\ (Col.7)$

Table 3.7 Depth VS Area (Ex. Prob. 3.5)

Isohyet	Area Enclosed	Net Area	Isohyet Average	Net Volume	Total Volume	Mean Depth
mm	km²	km²	mm	km².mm	km².mm	mm
1	2	3	4	5	6	7
108	155	155	108	16740	16740	108
100	341	186	104	19344	36084	106
90	1430	1089	95	103455	139539	98
80	2266	836	85	71060	210599	93
70	2970	704	75	52800	263399	89
60	3250	280	65	18200	281599	87
50	3960	710	55	39050	320649	81
40	4430	470	45	21150	341799	77
30	5280	850	35	29750	371549	70
20	6600	1320	25	33000	404549	61

Fitted exponential equation from **Fig. 3.7** is;

$\overline{P} = 112 e^{-9 \times 10^{-5} A}$

For an area of 5000 km^2,

$\overline{P} = 112 e^{-9 \times 10^{-5} \times 5000} = 71.4 = 71\ mm$

Figure 3.7 DAD Curve (Ex. Prob. 3.5))

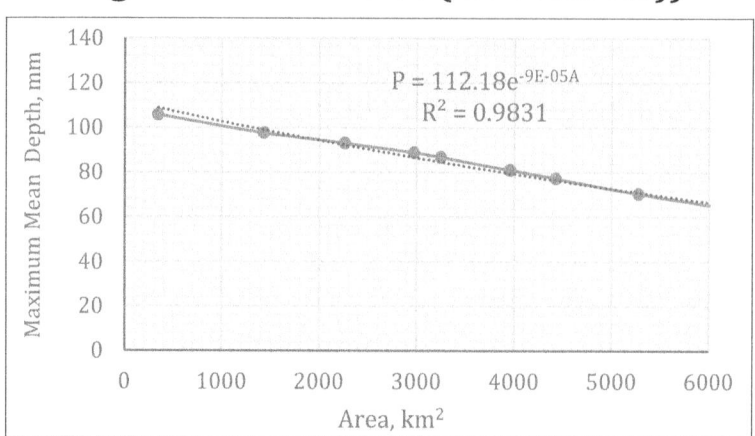

3.1 Depth, Duration, Frequency (DDF)

Rainfall depth increases with storm duration. A 24-h storm produces more rain as compared to a 2-h storm. The relationships between storm depth d and storm duration t, can be expressed by the following equation.

$$d = ct^n \quad c = Coefficient, \quad n = exponent\ (0 < n < 1)$$

Exponent is a positive real number less than one and varies between 0.2 and 0.5. This means storm depth increases at a lesser rate than storm duration. This equation fitted to the world's greatest observed rainfall events is as follows:

$$\boxed{d(mm) = 190\sqrt{D} \qquad D = rainfall\ duration\ in\ h,}$$

For example, rainfall depths for duration of 1-h and 4-h durations respectively are 390 mm and 780 mm. While the storm duration increases four times, storm depth increases by a factor of two. Isopluvial maps show the relationship between storm depth, duration and frequency of occurrence (DDF). These maps show how much rainfall one could expect during a 1-hour storm, every 10 years and every 100 years. Similar maps show how much rainfall to expect every 2, 10, or 100 years for 1-hour duration of the storm, 6 hours, 24 hours, and so on. Isopluvial or DDF maps are used to study rainfall runoff relationships for mid-size catchments.

A professional hydrologist, like all scientists, obviously needs a library of reference material in addition to raw data. While these generalized analyses are useful, though, because each watershed is unique and each storm is unique, hydrologists must also use their own analytical procedures.

3.2 Intensity-Duration-Frequency (IDF)

The intensity versus duration plot is one way in which storm properties are summarized. For any particular storm such a curve represents the maximum average intensity defined as rain depth divided by the time interval (duration) that is obtained from the recording rain gauge data. For shorter periods usually, high intensity bursts are nested within longer periods of higher intensity. This need not be always the case. Thus, the highest 1-h rain interval may not contain all or any of the periods, which produced the maximum rainfall depth over 30-min interval. Storm intensity and duration are inversely related. This relationship for a given region is described by an intensity duration frequency curve or a mathematical function.

Figure 3.8 A Set of IDF Curves

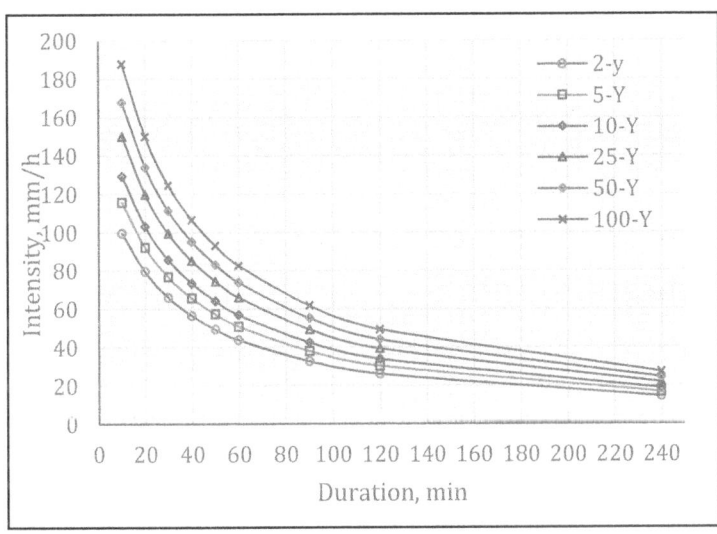

The highest intensities occur over short intervals (durations) and progressively decrease as duration is increased. This is to say, 10-min duration intensity will be smaller than 5-min intensity. This effect is more pronounced when storm duration is less than 1 hour. For durations greater than one hour, the decrease in intensity is relatively small. A set of IDF curves for Northern India is shown in **Figure 3.8**

3.2.1 IDF Function

IDF function represents mathematical form of IDF curve. A typical form of IDF function is as follows:

$$\boxed{\text{IDF function}\quad I = \frac{aT^x}{(b+t_D)^n}}$$

IDF function for Northern India is:

$$I = \frac{3730 T^{0.1623}}{(30+t_D)^{1.013}}$$

I = intensity in mm/h, storm duration t_D in min and return period T in years.

Using the above IDF equations, for 10 min duration and a 10-y storm, the rainfall intensity is 92 mm/h. And if the duration is 30 min, rainfall intensity drops to 65 mm/h. As expected, the intensity for a given duration will be greater for an infrequent storm that is the storm with larger return period.

As seen in **Figure 3.8**, the upper curve refers to the largest return period. A 10-year storm has a frequency of 0.1 or 10%. This corresponds to an average of 10 occurrences over a 100-year period. IDF curves are readily available from government agencies and local municipalities. This information is widely used in the design of drainage facilities for small catchments.

Example Problem 3.7

From the chart of recording gauge data of selected storm average maximum rainfall depths at time intervals are shown in columns 1 and 2 of **Table 3.8**. Find the rainfall intensities for various durations and plot the curve.

Solution:

Spread worksheet is shown in **Table 3.8**. Data values of I versus (t_D+10) are regressed

Sample of Calculations:

At 90 min, rainfall intensity for durations Δt of 10 min and 30 min are shown below:

$$I(10 \text{ min}) = \frac{\Delta P}{\Delta t} = \frac{P(90) - P(80)}{90 \text{ min} - 80 \text{ min}}$$

Storm Analysis

$$= \frac{(105-95)\text{mm}}{10 \text{ min}} \times \frac{60 \text{ min}}{\text{h}} = 60 \ mm/h$$

$$I(30 \text{ min}) = \frac{\Delta P}{\Delta t} = \frac{P(90) - P(60)}{90 \text{ min} - 60 \text{ min}}$$

$$= \frac{(105-70) \text{ mm}}{30 \text{ min}} \times \frac{60 \text{ min}}{\text{h}} = 70 \ mm/h$$

In the last row of **Table 3.8**, maximum value of each duration (Col.3 to Col.9) are shown. The plot is shown in **Fig. 3.9**.

Table 3.8 Worksheet (Ex. Prob. 3.7)

Time	Rainfall	Duration t_D (Δt), min						
min	mm	10	20	30	60	90	120	150
10	8	48						
20	15	42	45					
30	25	60	51	50				
40	34	54	57	52				
50	50	96	75	70				
60	70	120	108	90	70			
70	83	78	99	98	75			
80	95	72	75	90	80			
90	105	60	66	70	80	70		
100	112	42	51	58	78	69		
110	116	24	33	42	66	67		
120	119	18	21	28	49	63	60	
130	121	12	15	18	38	58	57	
140	122	6	9	12	27	48	54	
150	122	0	3	6	17	35	49	49
I, mm/h		120	108	98	80	70	60	49

Figure 3.9 IDF Curve (Ex. Prob. 3.7)

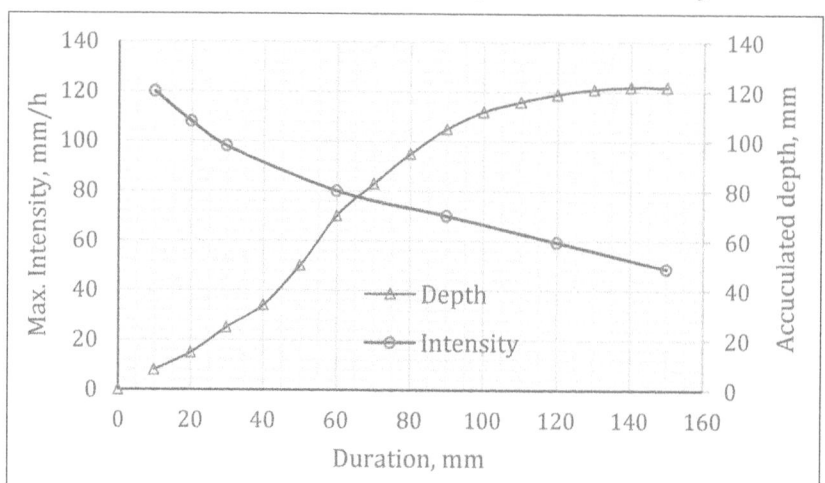

Example Problem 3.8

From the historical data, maximum rainfall for durations of 5 min, 10, min, 15 min, and 120 min in the descending order is presented in **Table 3.9**. compute maximum rainfall intensity for various durations and return periods and plot IDF curves.

Table 3.9 Data for Ex. Prob. 3.8

Rank	Maximum rainfall, mm			
	5 min	15 min	60 min	120 min
1	7.9	13.4	20.9	29.1
2	7.1	11.3	18.7	25.8
3	6.7	10.5	16.4	22.8
4	6.6	9.7	13.9	20.6
5	6.0	9.1	13.4	17.7
6	5.6	8.6	12.7	15.8
7	4.5	8.4	11.9	14.9
8	3.9	7.6	11.4	14.5
9	3.0	6.1	10.8	14.0
10	2.2	5.6	10.5	13.5
11	1.5	4.6	10.3	12.8

Solution:

Calculation of rainfall intensity for the four durations and various return periods are shown in **Table 3.10**.

Sample of Calculations (#2):

Return period, T of a hydrologic event is a reciprocal of probability, p. (More in Chapter 5 on Probability).

$$Return\ Period, T = \frac{1}{p} = \frac{n+1}{m} = \frac{11+1}{2} = 6\ years$$

$$I(15min) = \frac{11.3\ mm}{15\ min} \times \frac{60\ min}{h} = 45.2\ mm/h$$

$$I(120\ min) = \frac{25.8\ mm}{120\ min} \times \frac{60\ min}{h} = 12.9\ mm/h$$

Table 3.10 Computation Worksheet (Ex. Prob. 3.8)

Rank	T= (n+1)/m	Maximum Rainfall Intensity, mm/h			
		5 min	15 min	60 min	120 min
1	12.0	94.8	53.6	20.9	14.6
2	6.0	85.2	45.2	18.7	12.9
3	4.0	80.4	42.0	16.4	11.4
4	3.0	79.2	38.8	13.9	10.3
5	2.4	72.0	36.4	13.4	8.9
6	2.0	67.2	34.4	12.7	7.9
7	1.7	54.0	33.6	11.9	7.5
8	1.5	46.8	30.4	11.4	7.3
9	1.3	36.0	24.4	10.8	7.0
10	1.2	26.4	22.4	10.5	6.8
11	1.1	18.0	18.4	10.3	6.4

Plot of rainfall intensity versus duration for selected Return periods is shown in **Fig. 3.10**

Figure 3.10 IDF Curves (Ex. Prob. 3.8)

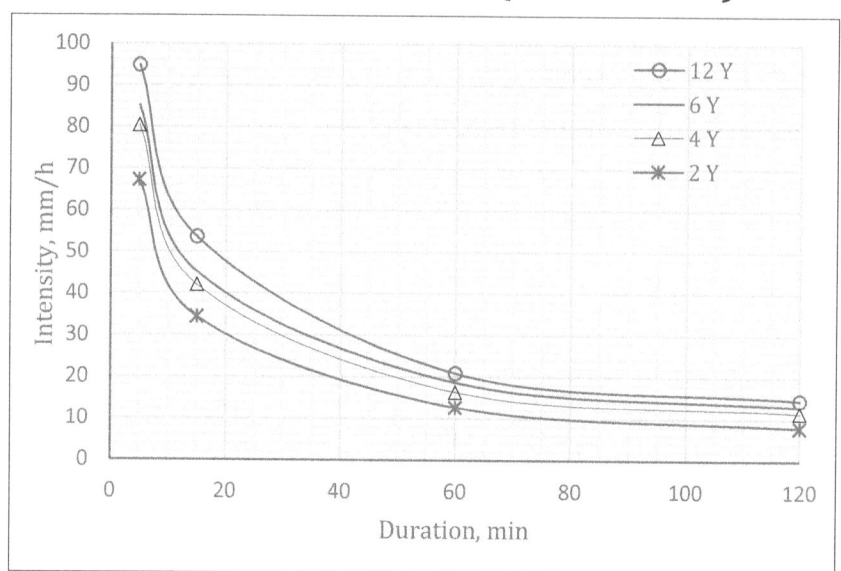

Example Problem 3.9

For the data of Example Prob. 3.7, develop IDF function of maximum intensity versus (D+20).

Solution:

D, min	10	20	30	60	90	120	150
I, mm/h	120	108	98	80	70	60	49
(t_D+20)	30	40	50	80	110	140	170
Log(t_D+20)	1.477	1.602	1.699	1.903	2.041	2.146	2.230
Log(I)	2.079	2.033	1.991	1.903	1.845	1.778	1.690

An exponential equation is fitted to the data of I vs (D+20) as shown in **Fig. 3.10**.

IDF function

$$I = \frac{656}{((t_D + 20)^{0.488}}$$

IDF function can also be developed by fitting linear equation to the data of Log(I) versus Log(t_D+20) as shown in **Fig. 3.10**.

$$Log(I) = 2.817 - 4.885 Log(t_D + 20) \; or$$

$$Log(I) = Log\, 656.1 - 4.885 Log(t_D + 20) \; or \quad I = \frac{656}{(t_D + 20)^{0.488}}$$

Figure 3.11 A Semilog Plot

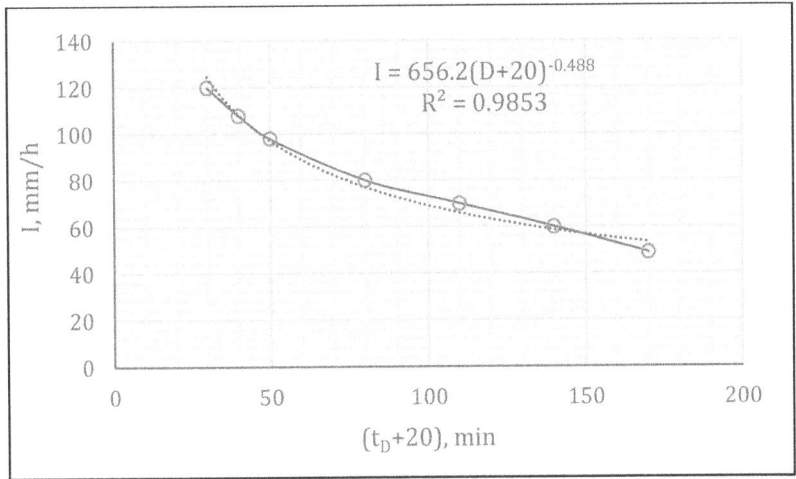

Figure 3.12 Fitting an Exponential Equation

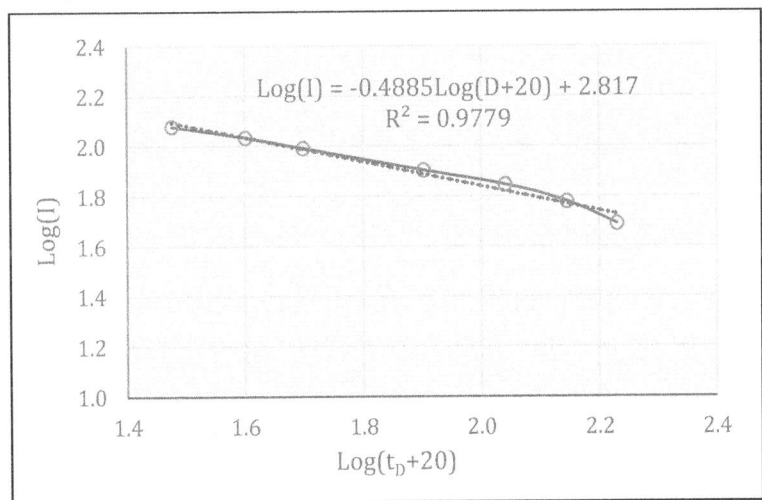

3.3 Synthetic Storms

As demonstrated in previous example problems, storm intensity varies significantly over the duration of the storm. In addition to storm duration, intensity of rainfall also varies considerably from one region to other. To represent various regions of the United States, National Resources Conservation Service (NRCS) developed four synthetic 24-hour rainfall distributions (I, IA, II, and III) as shown in **Fig 3.13 and Table 3.11**.

Figure 3.13 NRCS Synthetic Storms

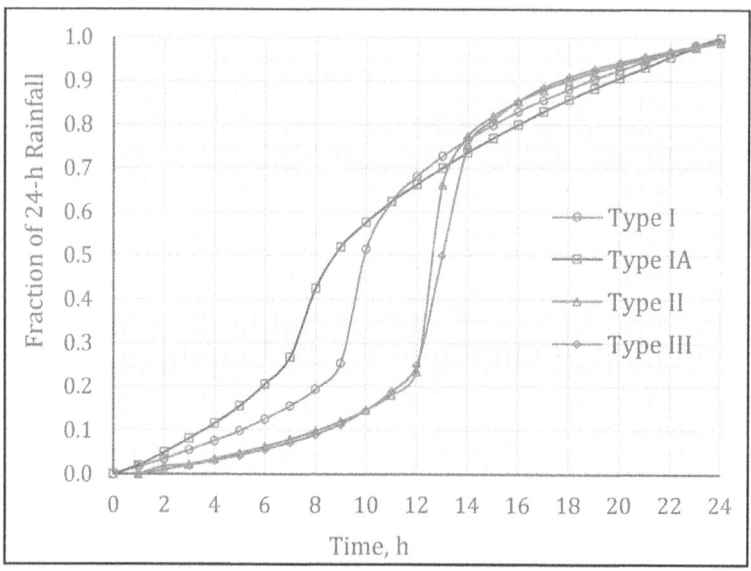

These rainfall distributions are based on long term data and are typical of the region. As seen in **Fig. 3.13**, storm intensity is maximum in the middle of the storm duration. Storm intensity is represented by slope of the curve and seems to be maximum in case of type II storms, which represents significant area of USA.

Types I and IA represent the Pacific maritime climate with wet winters and dry summers. Type III represents Gulf of Mexico and Atlantic coastal areas where tropical storms bring large 24-hour rainfall amounts. Type II represents rest of the country. Type IA is the least intense and type II the most intense short duration rainfall. In addition, type II rainfall storm is the most common to most area of USA.

Table 3.11 NRCS 24-h Rainfall Distributions

Time, h	Type I	Type IA	Type II	Type III
0.0	0.000	0.000	0.000	0.000
1.0	0.017	0.020	0.018	0.010
2.0	0.035	0.050	0.022	0.020
3.0	0.055	0.082	0.035	0.031
4.0	0.076	0.116	0.048	0.043
5.0	0.099	0.156	0.063	0.057
6.0	0.126	0.206	0.080	0.072
7.0	0.156	0.268	0.098	0.091
8.0	0.194	0.425	0.120	0.114
9.0	0.254	0.520	0.147	0.146
10.0	0.515	0.577	0.181	0.189
11.0	0.624	0.624	0.235	0.250
12.0	0.682	0.664	0.663	0.500
13.0	0.728	0.701	0.772	0.750
14.0	0.766	0.736	0.820	0.811
15.0	0.799	0.769	0.854	0.854
16.0	0.830	0.800	0.880	0.886
17.0	0.857	0.830	0.902	0.910
18.0	0.882	0.858	0.921	0.928
19.0	0.905	0.884	0.937	0.943
20.0	0.926	0.908	0.952	0.957
21.0	0.946	0.932	0.965	0.969
22.0	0.965	0.956	0.978	0.981
23.0	0.983	0.978	0.989	0.991
24.0	1.000	1.000	1.000	1.000

Example Problem 3.10

For the 10-y IDF function given below, construct and plot dimensionless 6-h storm with time interval of 30 min.

$$I(mm/h) = \frac{3730 T^{0.1623}}{(30 + t_D)^{1.0127}}$$

Solution:

Calculations are tabulated in **Table 3.12** and plot of dimensionless storm is shown in **Fig. 3.14**. Stepwise computations are explained below.

1. Using the IDF function, for duration shown in Col. 1 of Table 3.12,

rainfall intensities are calculated and are put in Col. 2. For a duration of 90 min, rainfall intensity I is:

$$I = 3730 \times 10^{0.1623} \times \frac{1}{(30+90)^{1.0127}} = 42.50 = 42.5 \; mm/h$$

2. Next rainfall depth is calculated by multiplying rainfall intensity by the duration of the storm and placed in col. 3

$$P = \frac{42.503 \; mm}{h} \times 90 \; min \times \frac{h}{60 \; min} = 63.75 = 63.8 \; mm$$

3. Change in depth is worked out by subtracting previous depth from the current depth and are shown in col.5.

$$\Delta P = 63.8 \; mm - 56.9 \; mm = 6.9 \; mm$$

4. The depths in column 5 are then distributed by placing the maximum at the centre of design storm and then distributing other values in a before-after-before-after sequence (Col.6). the maximum value of 42.9 mm is placed in the row correcting to 180 min, middle of storm.

5. The incremental depths are summed and shown in col. 7 as cumulative depths. The last cumulative value is 77.6 mm for 6-h duration of the storm.

6. Cumulative depths are converted to decimal fraction by dividing each value by the total value and are placed in col.8

Figure 3.14 Dimensionless Storm (Ex. Prob. 3.10)

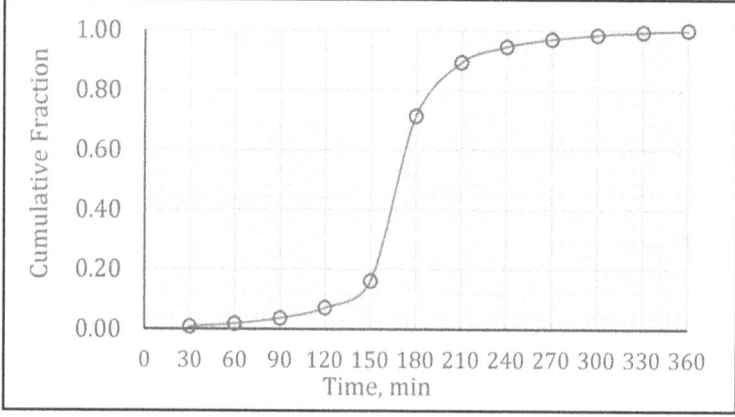

Table 3.12 Computation Sheet (Ex.Prob. 3.10)

t	I	P	ΔP		Cumulative depth	
min	mm/h	mm	mm		mm	Fraction
1	2	3	4	5	6	7
30	85.8	42.9	42.9	0.6	0.6	0.01
60	56.9	56.9	14.0	0.8	1.4	0.02
90	42.5	63.8	6.9	1.4	2.8	0.04
120	33.9	67.8	4.1	2.7	5.5	0.07
150	28.2	70.5	2.7	6.9	12.4	0.16
180	24.1	72.3	1.9	42.9	55.3	0.71
210	21.1	73.7	1.4	14.0	69.3	0.89
240	18.7	74.8	1.1	4.1	73.4	0.95
270	16.8	75.6	0.8	1.9	75.3	0.97
300	15.3	76.3	0.7	1.1	76.4	0.98
330	14.0	76.8	0.6	0.7	77.1	0.99
360	12.9	77.3	0.5	0.5	77.6	1.00

Example Problem 3.11

Based on the rainfall distribution of Ex. Prob. 3.8, construct a 6-h design storm with total depth of 110 mm.

Solution:

In the first two rows of **Table 3.13**, time distribution as found in the previous example is shown.

Table 3.13 Storm Rainfall Distributions

Time, min	30	60	90	120	150	180
Fraction	0.01	0.02	0.04	0.07	0.16	0.71
ΣP, mm	1	2	4	8	18	78
ΔP, mm	1.1	1.1	2.2	3.3	9.9	60.5

Time, min	210	240	270	300	330	360
Fraction	0.89	0.95	0.97	0.98	0.99	1.00
ΣP, mm	98	105	107	108	109	110
ΔP, mm	19.8	6.6	2.2	1.1	1.1	1.1

Figure 3.15 Design of a 6-h Storm (Ex. Prob. 3.11)

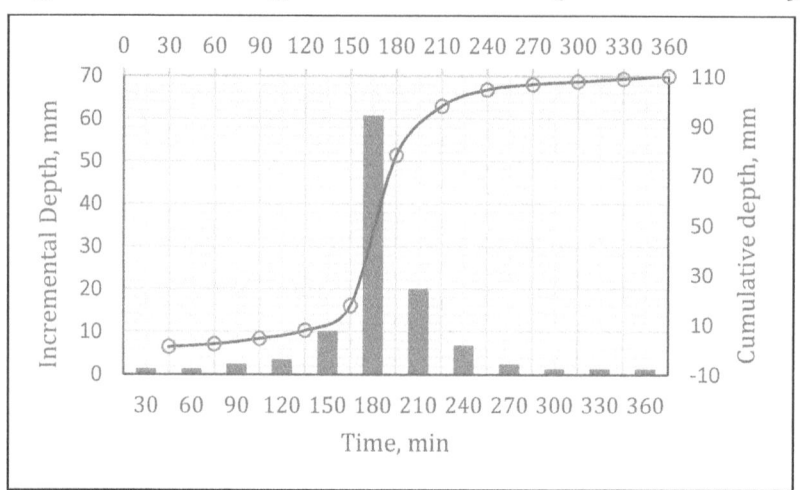

3.3.1 Triangular Shaped Design Storm

In addition to NRCS type of distributions, some authors prefer to use triangular shaped hyetograph for the design storm. In such cases, design storm has a triangular balanced temporal distribution as seen in **Fig. 3.16**. this rainfall distribution is also called the alternating block method. This concept is further illustrated with the following Example Problem 3.12.

Example Problem 3.12

Develop a design storm using balanced triangular distribution for a duration 24 h and using a computational interval of 2.0 h. IDF function for 50-y return period is as follows:

$$I\left(\frac{mm}{h}\right) = \frac{2550}{(t_D, min + 10)^{0.77}}$$

Using this function rainfall intensity and total rainfall for various duration are shown in **Table 3.14**.

Sample of Calculations (4-h duration):

$$I = \frac{2550}{(t_D, min + 10)^{0.77}} = \frac{2550}{(240 + 10)^{0.77}} = 36.31 \; mm/h$$

$$P = I \times D = \frac{36.31 \; mm}{h} \times 4.0 \; h = 145.27 = 145.3 \; mm$$

$$\Delta P = 145.3 - 120.2 = 25.1 \; mm$$

The maximum value is 120.2 which is placed in the centre (ending 12 h) and alternately placing values below and above it as shown in column 6 of the **Table 3. 14**. In the last column, total rainfall values are presented. Rainfall in each 2-h duration is shown in **Fig. 3.16**.

Table 3.14 Data for Ex. Prob. 3.12

Duration, D		Intensity, I	Rainfall, P	Design Storm, mm		
h	min	mm/h	mm	P	ΔP	$\sum$P
2	120	60.1	120.2	120.2	4.9	4.9
4	240	36.3	145.3	25.1	5.8	10.7
6	360	26.9	161.1	15.9	7.2	17.9
8	480	21.6	173.1	11.9	9.7	27.6
10	600	18.3	182.7	9.7	15.9	43.4
12	720	15.9	191.0	8.2	120.2	163.6
14	840	14.2	198.2	7.2	25.1	188.7
16	960	12.8	204.6	6.4	11.9	200.6
18	1080	11.7	210.4	5.8	8.2	208.9
20	1200	10.8	215.7	5.3	6.4	215.3
22	1320	10.0	220.6	4.9	5.3	220.6
24	1440	9.4	225.2	4.6	4.6	225.2

Figure 3.16 Triangular Shaped Design Storm

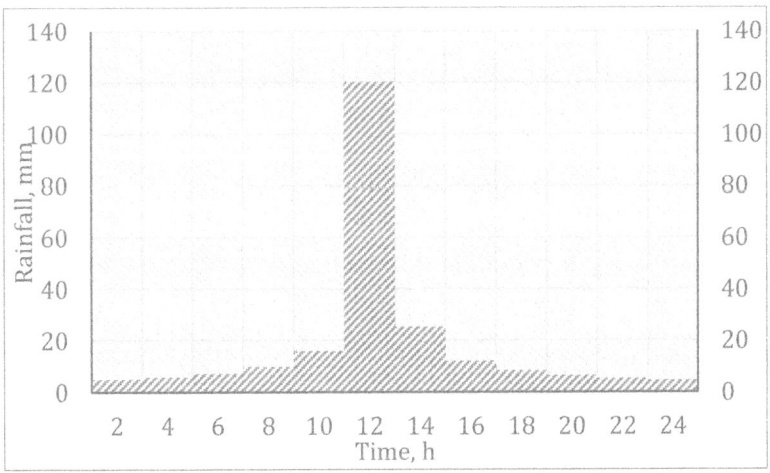

Discussion Questions

1. What is a hyetograph? What type of rainfall gauge data is suitable to prepare a such a graph?
2. Define the terms: isohyet, isopluvial, point rainfall, and point area.
3. Compare DDF and DAD curves.
4. Describe various methods to find average precipitation and suitability of each?
5. How IDF curves for a region are prepared?
6. Discuss the general shape of IDF curves and their relationship with return period?
7. You have sufficient rainfall data pertaining to maximum average rainfall intensity, I and duration, D. How would go to fit an equation $I = \dfrac{a}{(b+D)^n}$
8. Describe various methods of averaging rainfall depth over a watershed. Discuss the suitability of each.
9. Compare isohyetal map and isopluvial map.
10. Compare NRCS design storm withtriangular shaped design storm

Practice Problems

Practice Problem 3.1

Based on the temporal distribution in Example Problem 3.1, calculate and design the hyetograph for a 100 mm, 8-h storm (4, 11, 29, 20, 14, 9, 7, 6 mm/h)

Practice Problem 3.2

A large river basin with a watershed area of 105 000 km² is subdivided into five sub-basins. Annual average precipitation for each sub-basin is shown in the following Table. Find the average annual precipitation for the whole basin? (630 mm)

Sub-basin	1	2	3	4	5
Net area, km²	6100	19500	35400	21800	22200
Precipitation, mm	850	750	640	580	490

Practice Problem 3.3

Rainfall data derived from a drainage basin of area 138 km² is given below. Calculate the average depth of rainfall by the isohyetal method. (50. mm)

Isohyet, mm	10-30	30-50	50-70	70-90	90-110
Net area, km²	43	35	25	20	15

Practice Problem 3.4

Complete calculations for the 100-mm contour in **Figure 3.6**. Plot the set of points on a graph with depth on the y-axis and logarithm of the area on the x-axis. Draw a smooth curve and read the value of maximum mean depth produced by this storm over an area of 600 km². (108 mm, 120 mm)

Practice Problem 3.5

For the data of **Example Problem 3.4**, do the following

i) Express both time and cumulative depth as percentage of the total value and prepare a continuous graph showing the temporal distribution. (19, 65, 10, 6 all in mm)

ii) Using this distribution, calculate a hyetograph for a 100 mm, 4-h storm.

(Duration %   25, 50, 75, 100 cumulative depth % 19, 84, 94, 100)

Practice Problem 3.6

An IDF equation is of the general form: $I\left(\frac{mm}{h}\right) = \frac{KT^a}{(D+b)^n}$ where D in h
For Bangalore, India: Constants are K = 62.75, a = 0.126, b = 0.5, n = 1.128. Determine rainfall intensity for 10-y storm and duration of 1 h and 6 h? (53 mm/h, 10 mm/h)

Practice Problem 3.7

Isohyetal map (cm) of a storm that fell on a drainage basin of area 295 km² is shown in **Fig. 3.17**. Work out the mean depth of rainfall (37 mm)

Figure 3.17 Isohyetal map (Practice Problem 3.7)

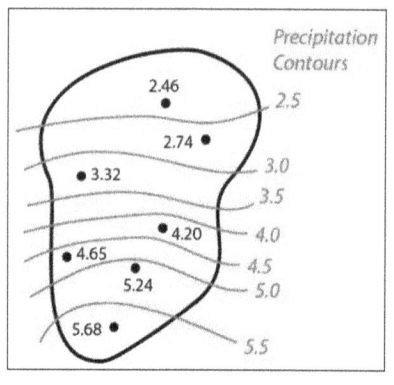
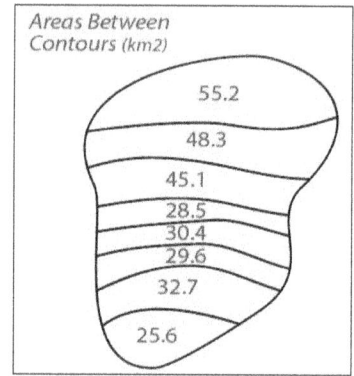

Practice Problem 3.8

For a ceratain region, 25 years of data was analysed and rainfall depths for various durations are shown below. Find the rainfall intensity and plot IDF curve.

Duration, min	5	10	15	20	25	30	60
Depth, mm	25	39	49	57	63	67	86

Practice Problem 3.9

Recording rain gauage data of a 10-year storm was analysed and maximum rainfall depth for various duration are shown below;

Duration, min	15	30	45	60	180
Depth, mm	40	60	75	90	120

For this data, compute rainfall intensities and fit an equation of type: $I = \frac{a}{(t_D+15)^n}$ (a = 2025 and n = 0.738)

Storm Analysis

Practice Problem 3.10

A catchment has an area of 122 km². There are four rainfall gauges located within or close to the boundary of the watershed. Poygons were constructed and percentage of the area for each station is shown below.

Station	A	B	C	D
Depth, mm	25	10.0	5.0	15
Area, %	15	30	35	20

Compute the mean rainfall using by arithmetic mean method and Thiessen's polygon method(13.8 mm, 11.5 mm)

Practice Problem 3.11

For the fitted equation (Practice. Prob. 3.9), predict rainfall intensity for 15 min duration and 60 min duration.(160 mm/h, 84 mm/h)

Practice Problem 3.12

A catchment has an area of 8.5 ha. Snow smpling was done at three points and following information was obtained.

Station	A	B	C
Snow Depth, mm	350	210	280
Water Equivalent, %	0.15	0.20	0.18

Compute the mean water equivalent, runoff depth and volume assuming 75% of this snowpack becomes runoff. (48 mm, 36 mm, 3100 m³)

Practice Problem 3.13

For a watershed of 590 km², based on rainfall depths recorded at various stations within and close to the boundary of the watershed are given below. What the weighted average depth of rainfall produced by this storm over the catchment. (74.2 mm)

Isohyet, mm	10-30	30-60	60-90	90-120	120-150
Net area, km²	82	173	118	126	91

Practice Problem 3.14

Data of a storm is read from the graph of a recording gauge and shown in the Table below. Find maximum rainfall intensities for durations of 10, 30, and 60 min. (198, 168, 133 mm/h)

Time, min	10	20	30	40	50	60	70	80	90	120
Depth, mm	19	41	48	68	91	124	152	160	166	170

Practice Problem 3.15

Data derived from the isohyetal map of annual rainfall over the catchment is shown in the Table below. Caculate the mean annual rainfall over the catchment. If 55% of precipitation becomes runoff, find mean annual discharge? (50 mm, 37 m³/s)

Isohyet, mm	700-750	750-800	800-850	850-900	900-950	950-1000
Net area, km²	220	340	550	770	450	130

Practice Problem 3.16

The data from an isohyetal map of a 24-h storm, area (km²) enclosed by each isohyet drawn at an interval of 20 mm is tabulated below. Assuming storm centre had an enclosed area of 130 km² and rainfall depth of 98 mm, plot depth area duration curve and fit an exponential equation.

$(P(mm) = 91 e^{-\frac{A}{10000}})$

Isohyet, mm	98	80	60	40	20
Enclosed A, km²	130	850	1850	3130	4500

Practice Problem 3.17

Isohyets produced by a 6-h storm of interest are almost circular in shape. The diameter of each of the four circular isohyets on the isohyetal map is given below. Work out ground area under each isohyet given that the map scale is 1:100 000. (17, 71,190, 660 km²)

Isohyet, mm	100	75	50	25
Diameter, mm	46	95	157	290

Storm Analysis

Practice Problem 3.18

Rainfall depths for a 2-h rainstorm are tabulated below. Work out the maximum rainfall intensities for 20 min and 60 min durations.
(108, 80 mm/h)

Time, min	10	20	30	40	50	60	70	80	90	100	110	120
Cum. P, mm	8	15	25	34	50	70	83	95	105	112	116	119

Practice Problem 3.19

For the data of 2-h storm in Practice Problem 3.18, regress maximum intensity versus (t_D+20) and fit a power law function.
($I = 656(t_D + 20)^{-0.488}$)

Practice Problem 3.20

For the IDF function given below, construct and plot dimensionless 50-y, 6-h storm. Use a time interval of 60 min. $I(mm/h) = 4730 T^{0.1623}(t_D + 30)^{-0.90}$

Duration, h	1	2	3	4	5	6
Cum. Fraction	0.04	0.12	0.66	0.90	0.97	1.0

Practice Problem 3.21

Develop a design storm using balanced triangular distribution for a duration of 24 h and using a computational interval of 2.0 h. IDF function for 100-y return period is as follows:

$$I\left(\frac{mm}{h}\right) = \frac{2550}{(t_D, min + 10)^{0.77}}$$

Using this function rainfall intensity and total rainfall for various durations.

Time, h	2	4	6	8	10	12	14	16	18	20	22	24
ΔP, mm	6	7	9	13	25	188	46	17	11	8	6	5
P, mm	6	13	22	35	60	248	294	312	322	330	336	341

Practice Problem 3.22

The IDF curve for a 10-y storm is given by

$$I\left(\frac{mm}{h}\right) = \frac{2500}{(\Delta t, min + 9.3)^{0.8}}$$

Assuming that the peak rainfall rate occurs at 45% of the storm duration, and is twice the average rainfall rate, estimate the peak rainfall rate for a 1-h storm. (27 min, 170 mm/h)

Review Questions

1. What is the area of a watershed if a 99 ha·cm rainfall occurs during a 3-hour storm with a depth of 110 mm?
   a) 9 ha b) 99 ha c) 99.9 ha d) 69 ha

2. The purpose of DAD curves is to correct
   a. Rainfall depth for storm duration
   b. Rainfall depth for watershed size
   c. Rainfall depth for frequency
   d. Point rainfall for storm duration

3. Which one of the following is not a method for computing the average areal rainfall?
   a) Isohyetal method b) Polygon
   c) Station average d) Normal ratio

4. Which of the following methods accounts for storm characteristics in determining areal average rainfall?
   a) Isohyetal method b) Polygon method
   c) Station average d) Quadrant method

5. In which of the following methods of determining areal average rainfall, the weights applied vary from storm to storm?
   a) Isohyetal method b) Polygon method
   c) Station average d) Quadrant method

6. For a 0.5 ha parking lot with 30-minute time of concentration, what is the rainfall intensity of a 10-year storm (Figure 3.8)?
   a) 40 mm/h b) 50 mm/h c) 60 mm/h d) 70 mm/h

7. The purpose of the depth-area adjustment factor decreases with
   a. An increase in storm duration
   b. A reduction in watershed size
   c. An increase in watershed size
   d. Not a function of storm duration

8. A thunder burst dumps 1.5 mm of rainfall over a 2-min time. The rainfall intensity for this period is
   a) 15 mm/h b) 30 mm/h c) 45 mm/h d) 60 mm/h

9. A point rainfall is valid for areas up to
   a) 25 ha b) 25 km² c) 25 acres d) 250 km²

10. For a given frequency, a 12-hour duration storm will produce ___ as much

as a 6-hour duration storm.

a) 2×   b) 4×   c) <2×   d) >2×

11. The area outside an enclosed isohyet receives _____ rainfall than the area within the isohyet.

a) More   b) Less   c) Equal   d) All possible

12. An isohyet is a contour of

a) Infiltration   b) Evaporation   c) Rainfall   d) Elevation

13. For a given location, 24-h rainfall is 100 mm, 12-h rainfall is

a) 50 mm   b) < 50 mm   c) >50 mm   d) 25 mm

14. The general shape of IDF curves is
a) Concave upwards
b) Concave downwards
c) Logarithmic
d) Parabolic

15. Storm rainfall intensity _____ with increase in duration and decreases with _____ decrease in return period.

a) Increases, increases
b) Increases. decreases
c) Decreases, increases
d) Decreases, decreases

16. A plot of rainfall intensity versus time is called

a) Hydrograph   b) IDF curve   c) Isohyet   d) Hyetograph

17. Maximum average rainfall due to 24-h storm is read to be 310 mm from DAD curves for an area of 10 000 km². For the same area, maximum depth for 3-d storm is expected to be

a) <310 mm   b) >310 mm   c) 310 mm   d) Hard to say

18. What abbreviation DAD stands for
a) Drainage area depth
b) Depth area duration
c) Duration area depth
d) Duration and depth

19. A plot of maximum storm intensity versus duration is called

a) Hydrograph   b) IDF curve   c) Mass curve   d) Hyetograph

20. The mass curve of rainfall of a storm is a plot of _____ vs _____
a) Rainfall depth, duration
b) Rainfall depth, time
c) Rainfall intensity, duration
d) Cumulative depth, time

a) <50 mm/h   b) >50 mm/h   c) 100 mm/h   d) 25 mm/h

21. 10-y rainfall intensity for 1h-duration is 50 mm/h. Rainfall intensity of 5-y storm for 1-h duration will be

22. On an isohyet map of a storm, inner isohyet represents
   a) Eye of the storm
   b) Periphery of the storm
   c) Map Area
   d) Area of the catchment

23. For the IDF curve shown in Fig. 3.8, read the 10.y maximum rainfall intensity for a 30-min duration?
   a) 150 mm/h   b) 125 mm/h   c) 100 mm/h   d) 82 mm/h

24. For the IDF curve shown in Fig. 3.8, what is the 25-y maximum rainfall intensity for a 45-min duration?
   a) 150 mm/h   b) 125 mm/h   c) 100 mm/h   d) 82 mm/h

25. Thiessen polygon method is used to
   a) Carry snow survey
   b) Estimate areal rainfall
   c) Estimate missing value
   d) Divide catchment

26. A rainfall hyetograph is a plot of ____versus, ____.
   a) Cumulative depth, time
   b) Rainfall depth, area
   c) Rainfall Intensity, duration
   d) Average intensity, time

27. Which one of the following methods used to compute average areal rainfall assumes that the weights applied to each station value are equal?
   a) Isohyetal   b) Polygon   c) Arithmetic   d) All

28. Which one of the following methods is used to compute missing value of rainfall at a station?
   a) Isohyetal   b) Polygon   c) Normal Ratio   d) Quadrant

29. In which method of finding average areal rainfall, weights applied remain the same from storm to storm?
   a) Isohyetal   b) Polygon   c) Arithmetic   d) All

30. General form of the equation fitting a DDF curve is d= C×D^n. The value of exponent n is
   a) n>1   b) 0<n<1   c) 0<n<2   d) 0<n<0.5

4 Stream Flow Measurement

Stream flow measurement is very important in managing water resources and hydrologic analysis. Whereas hydrologic input; like precipitation is hard to measure exactly, stream flow measurement at a given section of the stream can be measured accurately.

4.1 Stream flow variation

Stream flow measurement is a record of flow measurements versus time called hydrograph. This information, at a given point on the stream where data is collected can be presented as stage or flow rate as described in the following sections.

Stage Hydrograph

Variation in measurement of water level in rivers is the oldest form of hydrological measurement. Elevation of the water surface in the stream is called **stage**. The pattern or graph obtained when water level observations are plotted as a function of time is called a **stage hydrograph.**

Flow Hydrograph

The stage hydrograph is useful for purposes of navigation, and design of flood levels. It is used in siting of water supply intakes, to know the maximum and minimum heights, which a river has reached in the past. For many other purposes such as unit hydrograph derivation, it would be more useful to know the flow rate in a river as a function of time. A curve graph depicting discharge versus time is called a **flow hydrograph** or simply hydrograph.

Rating Curve

Fortunately, at many locations on rivers there is a fairly well defined, approximately single-valued, functional relationship between flow rate and stage called **rating curve** (**Fig. 4.1**). As the water level or stage goes up so does the flow rate and as the water level goes down so does the flow rate. A great deal of skill, and many accurate measurements are needed to pick a site along a river where the relationship between height and flow is nearly without hysteresis, and then to define the exact form of the relationship.

Discharge Hydrograph

Once a stage-discharge relationship or **rating curve** has been established at a location along a river, it is possible to use this relationship to convert a stage hydrograph to a discharge hydrograph. This is done by reading the flow rate which corresponds to the measured stage or water level at various times from a **rating table** for the location and then plotting the flow rates to form a continuous plot of flow rate versus time.

Figure 4.1 Stage Discharge Relationship

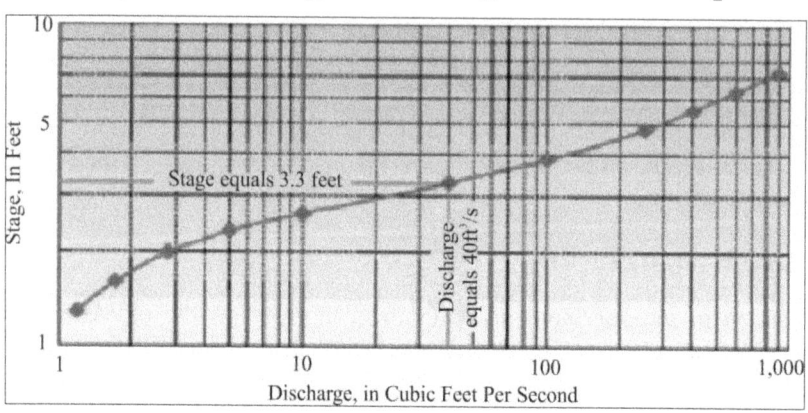

From a discharge or flow hydrograph one can obtain information on the highest and the lowest flow rates which have been observed at a location within a period of record. It is also possible to calculate the integral of flow rate over a period of time. This integral is the total volume of water, which has passed through the specified cross-section during the time interval of integration. In the graphical sense, the area under the flow hydrograph represents the flow volume. It is worth noting that some strange units of volume appear in the hydrological literature. A common measure of flow rate is m^3/s. It is also common to record the flow rate as the mean flow rate per day.

4.2 Measurement of Stage

The term **stage** refers to the elevation of water surface in the channel. The reference level or datum is generally the mean sea level. It is preferred to have the reference level below the streambed so that the stage is always a positive value.

4.2.1 Non-Recording Stream Gauges

A **staff gauge** as seen in **Fig. 4.2** is the simplest gauge and is frequently used as outside reference at stations equipped with recorders. The staff gauge is rigidly attached to a permanent structure such as a bridge pier or an abutment and the graduations are clearly marked.

A **wire gauge** measures the water level from above such as from a bridge. The gauge has a drum with a circumference equal to one unit of length. The number of revolutions of the drum is measured by a mechanical counter, which in turn measures the length of wire to reach the water surface.

Figure 4.2 Staff Gauge and Float Gauge

A **crest gauge** is designed to measure the maximum stage during the flood period. The gauge consists of an iron pipe containing a graduated wooden stick. Powdered cork is placed in a pocket near the lower end of the stick and water enters the pipe through holes in the lower cap. A ring of powdered cork on the stick marks the maximum gauge height.

4.2.2 Recording Stream Gauges

As the name indicates, these gauges continuously record the water stage to produce a stage hydrograph. Two types of gauges in general use are float type and bubbler gauge.

A **float gauge** consists of a tape passing over a pulley with a float attached to one end and a counterweight to the other. The float is in a stilling well connected to the stream by pipes. The purpose of stilling well (**Fig. 4.2**) is to dampen the water level fluctuations. As the float follows the rise and fall of the water level in the stream, the tape turns a pulley that activates a pen.

A **bubbler** gauge eliminates the need for a **stilling well** but requires power and a nitrogen gas cylinder. Nitrogen fed through a tube bubble freely into the stream through an orifice. The gas pressure in the tube is equal to the piezometric head on the bubble orifice. A change of 10 cm in water level corresponds to a change of 1 kPa in pressure. The servo manometer converts changes in pressure in the gas purge system to the height of water and transmits to the recorder. This instrument is attached to a digital recorder and can be remotely monitored by telephone or radio. A bubbler gauge is preferable to the float type for the following reasons:
- Stilling well not required
- Suitable for measuring large changes in stages (up to 30 m)
- The inlet is less likely to be blocked because of the gas pressure
- The recorder assembly can be located far away from the sensing unit

4.2.3 Gauge Site

The type of hydraulic control employed determines the water level or stage at gauging site. The control may be a section or channel reach that determines the stage discharge relationship. The ideal control should be permanent and cause a unique stage discharge relation without any hysteresis.

A **sectional control** as in the case of rock riffle or small waterfall provides a stable control. If natural control does not exist, low weirs or dams are sometimes built to stabilize the stage discharge relationship. Downstream flow conditions do not affect the rate of flow and water depth upstream of the control section for example a weir, completely defines discharge rate.

A **channel control** is employed when the channel bed is stable and sectional control is not available. Sand bed stream reaches or sites where channel instability is obvious should not be selected. Sites just above tributaries are not suitable because tributaries may cause backwater effects. Other desirable characteristics of a good gauging site are:
- A good measuring channel section
- A uniform channel
- Measurable velocities
- Accessibility during flood

- Flow direction is perpendicular to the measuring section
- A suitable structure from which to measure the floods

4.3 Measurement of Flow Velocity

The discharge passing at a given section can be found by knowing the area of water section and the average flow velocity. Velocity distribution in a channel is not uniform over width and depth of the channel. Flow velocity is greatest in the deepest part of the channel and is zero along the boundary of flow. Water flow velocity is maximum just below the water surface and almost zero at the bottom of channel. The velocity distribution in a vertical section is logarithmic in nature. Knowing this relationship, the average velocity can be determined by measuring the point velocity or velocity at certain point in depth. The average velocity in shallow streams with depth of flow less than a metre is taken as velocity at 60% of the depth below the water surface. For larger flow depths, it is recommended to have two measurements at 20% and 80% of depth and average of these two becomes the mean flow velocity for a given vertical.

4.3.1 Float

It is possible to estimate the flow velocity in a channel by timing the distance travelled by a float. Because velocity varies across depth and width of flow stream, a coefficient must be applied to convert **float velocity** to mean flow velocity. The coefficient selected depends on the type of float and average depth. For weighted floats, the coefficient is about 0.90 and for other floats coefficient is in the range of 0.80 to 0.85. This method is quick and simple but limited in accuracy.

4.3.2 Current Meter

A **current meter** is the most commonly used instrument to measure point velocity in streams. Current meters are manufactured with the cups or vanes on either a vertical axis such as a **Price meter** or horizontal axis such as an **Ott meter**. Vertical axis meters operate in lower water velocity. Horizontal axis meters like propellers disturb the flow less because the direction of flow is parallel to the axis. An advantage of the Price current meter is that velocity is measured accurately without being pointed directly in the direction of flow. A current meter is placed at a point in the stream and revolutions of the rotor during a measured interval of time are counted to obtain the velocity of water. These rotations may be counted by means of an audible signal transmitted to earphones. For a current meter, the relation between revolutions per second N and flow velocity, v (m/s), is linear. For a standard 12.5 mm diameter Price current meter, calibration equation is:

$$v\left(\frac{m}{s}\right) = 0.65 + 0.03\ N \left(\frac{rev}{s}\right)$$

Some of the newer meters use ultrasonic signals to measure flow velocity. The transducers receive as well as send signals. The shift in the reflected signal is indicative of flow velocity. Ultrasonic equipment is commercially available and easy to use. This method of gauging is more suitable for automatic recording of data.

4.4 Discharge Measurements

There are four principal methods of measuring stream flow discharge; weir stations, control meter stations, power plants and velocity area stations. Velocity area method is discussed in more detail here.

4.4.1 Velocity-Area Station Method

Stream flow rate determinations are often made by observing velocity v_i and depth d_i at every vertical section of the width of the river. The number of vertical sections usually varies from 10 to 20. The observations along the cross-section are accomplished by wading or using a cableway, bridge, or boat. If the line holding the velocity-measuring device is not vertical, then a correction must be applied to the depth measurement. Following measurements and observations are noted.

> The distance from the bank reference point b_i
> The mean velocity v_i and depth d_i at the ith section/vertical
> The river stage, h that corresponds to the time of measurement at the gauging station

The minimum numbers of vertical sections are usually ten. From the theory of open channel flow, it is known that velocity measured at 60% of depth from the water surface is representative of mean velocity. Likewise, the average of velocity measurements taken at 20% and the 80% depths is representative of mean flow velocity. For depths less than one metre, one measurement of velocity $v_{0.6}$ is sufficient. However, for depths greater than one metre, it is recommended to have two velocity measurements that are at 20% and 80% of depth.

Stream Flow Measurement

Average velocity

$$v_{Avg} = v_{0.6d} \text{ or } \frac{v_{0.2d} + v_{0.8d}}{2}$$

4.4.2 Mean Section Method

Using this method, flow area for a given vertical section is taken as product of the mean of depths and the distance between the verticals (width of section). Similarly, mean of flow velocities at the two verticals forming section is taken as the average velocity for the section.

$$Q_i = A_i \times v_i = w_i \times d_{avg} \times v_{avg}$$

Discharge from the ith flow subsection

$$Q_i = (b_{i+1} - b_i) \times \left(\frac{d_i + d_{i+1}}{2}\right) \times \left(\frac{v_i + v_{i+1}}{2}\right)$$

4.4.3 Mid-Section Method

An improvement over the mean section method was suggested in 1950. An illustration of mid-section method is shown in **Fig. 4.3**. This method differs from the mean section method in the sense that observed depth and velocity at a vertical represents the mean depth and velocity for the panel or subsection having a width equal to distance halfway from the preceding vertical plus one half the distance to the following vertical. Discharge from each subsection is calculated as follows:

Discharge from the ith panel/subsection

$$Q_i = A_i \times v_i = w_i \times d_i \times v_i = \frac{(b_{i+1} - b_{i-1})}{2} \times d_i \times v_i$$

Calculations for the first and last sections of a discharge measurement are handled in much the same manner. However, for these sections, there being no preceding or following vertical, the width becomes one half the distance from the shore or edge to the first vertical or from last vertical to the edge. To make the computational procedure easy, the first and last vertical are kept close to the edge so that the discharges from the end sections becomes small enough to be neglected.

Figure 4.3 Mid-Section Method

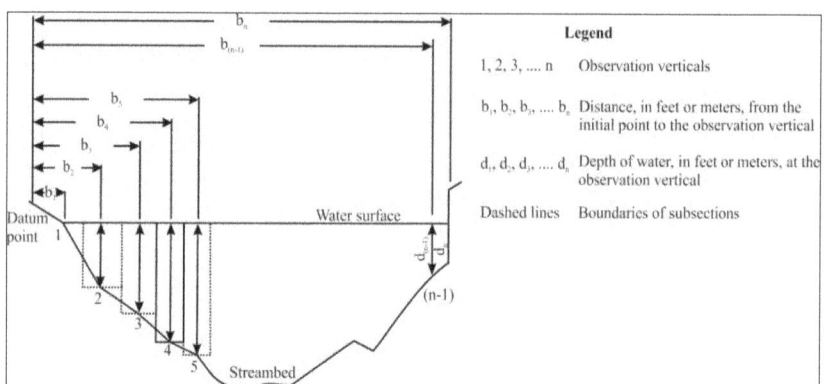

An edge section will also occur when there is a vertical drop at the water's edge such as at a pier or a bridge abutment for a wing wall. In such a case depth at the edge being appreciable, discharge from such a section cannot be neglected without causing error in the total discharge.

When it is not possible to accurately observe the velocity and depth at vertical edge sections, an estimate is made as a percentage of that at the adjacent vertical. Generally, the velocity in such cases is assumed 70% to 80% of the velocity observed in the adjoining section.

First and last vertical

$$w_i = \frac{(b_2 - b_1)}{2} \qquad w_n = \frac{(b_n - b_{n-1})}{2}$$

Example Problem 4.1

The Root River at Sault Ste Marie was waded, and observations of depth and flow velocity were made using a Price current meter as shown in **Table 4.1**. Compute the total discharge rate.

Given:

Current meter rating equation v (m/s) = 0.008 + 0.680 N (rps)
Drainage area = 108 km², Location: Lat. 46° 33' 49" N Long. 84° 16' 55" W

Table 4.1 Worksheet of Discharge Computations

#	Distance b, m	Width W, m	Depth d m	Revs. #	Time t, s	Velocity v m/s	Area A, m²	Flow Q m³/s
1	0.6	0.20	0.00	-	-	0.00	0.00	0.00
2	1.0	0.70	0.28	16	61.6	0.18	0.20	0.04
3	2.0	1.00	0.43	70	69.8	0.69	0.43	0.30
4	3.0	1.00	0.48	70	62.7	0.77	0.48	0.37
5	4.0	1.00	0.56	60	64.9	0.64	0.56	0.36
6	5.0	1.00	0.49	80	67.8	0.81	0.49	0.40
7	6.0	1.00	0.64	80	70	0.79	0.64	0.51
8	7.0	1.00	0.61	80	65.2	0.84	0.61	0.51
9	8.0	1.00	0.56	70	66.8	0.72	0.56	0.40
10	9.0	1.00	0.51	70	67.6	0.71	0.51	0.36
11	10.0	1.00	0.45	80	68.1	0.81	0.45	0.36
12	11.0	1.00	0.41	80	67	0.82	0.41	0.34
13	12.0	1.00	0.38	70	67.1	0.72	0.38	0.27
14	13.0	1.00	0.33	70	66.8	0.72	0.33	0.24
15	14.0	1.50	0.30	70	65.3	0.74	0.45	0.33
16	16.0	1.75	0.18	70	69.5	0.69	0.32	0.22
17	17.5	0.75	0.08	-	-	0.48	0.06	0.03
							Σ	5.03

Sample of Calculations (Observation #10)

$$w_{10} = \frac{(b_{11} - b_9)}{2} = \frac{(10-8)m}{2} = 1.00 = 1.0\ m$$

$$A_{10} = w_{10} \times d_{10} = 1.0\ m \times 0.51 m = 0.51\ m^2$$

$$N_{10} = \frac{70\ rev}{67.57\ s} = 1.036 = 1.04\ rps$$

$$v_{10} = 0.008 + 0.68 N_{10} = 0.008 + 0.68 \times 1.036 = 0.710 = 0.71\ m/s$$

$$Q_{10} = A_{10} \times v_{10} = 0.51 m^2 \times \frac{0.71 m}{s} = 0.363 = \underline{0.36\ m^3/s}$$

Observation #17

The left bank is a vertical wall, and it is not practical to observe the velocity at this point. Velocity at this point is assumed 70% of the neighbouring vertical.

$$v_{17} = 0.7 v_{16} = 0.7 \times \frac{0.69 m}{s} = 0.483 = 0.48 \ m/s$$

$$w_{17} = \frac{(b_{17} - b_{16})}{2} = \frac{(17.5 - 16)m}{2} = 0.750 = 0.75 \ m$$

$$Q_{17} = 0.75 \ m \times 0.08 \ m \times \frac{0.48 m}{s} = 2.88 \times \frac{10^{-3} \ m^3}{s}$$

$$Q_{tot} = \Sigma Q_i = 0 + 0.04 + 0.37 + \cdots 0.03 = 5.03 = \underline{5.0 \ m^3/s}$$

4.5 Chemical Gauging

If a chemical solution is injected into a stream at a constant rate and samples are taken downstream (d/s) at a point where mixing is complete, the steady flow rate in the stream can be found by doing the mass balances of traces.

Flow (Chemical Gauging)
$$\boxed{Q_0 = \frac{C_1 Q_1 - C_2 Q_1}{C_2 - C_0}}$$

Q_1 = Dose rate of tracer, Q_0 = Water flow rate
C_1 = Concentration of tracer solution (upstream and dosing solution)
C_0, C_2 = Concentration of tracer in dosed water (upstream and downstream)

In majority of situations, tracer concentration in stream water before injecting is zero ($C_0 = 0$). Furthermore, **Dilution factor**, C_1/C_2 is relatively a large value as compared to one. In such cases, the formula is modified to:

Chemical Gauging
$$\boxed{Q_0 = \frac{C_1 Q_1 - C_2 Q_1}{C_2} = Q_1 \times \left(\frac{C_1}{C_2} - 1\right) \ or}$$

$$\boxed{Q \sim Q_1 \times \left(\frac{C_1}{C_2}\right) = Dosage \times DF}$$

The stream discharge is equal to the dose rate multiplied by the dilution factor. This procedure is well adapted to boulder-strewn streams where use of a conventional meter is difficult. The tracer may be a salt, non-toxic chemical, or a dye.

Example Problem 4.2

A 400 g/L solution of sodium dichromate is used for gauging a stream. The solution is injected at a constant rate of 48 L/min. Downstream, the equilibrium concentration is measured as 2.4 mg/L. Estimate the discharge in the stream.

Given:

Q_1 = 48 L/min, C_1 = 400 g/L, C_2 = 2.4 mg/L, C_0 = 0.0 mg/L

Solution:

$$DF = \left(\frac{C_1}{C_2}\right) = \frac{400 g}{L} \times \frac{L}{2.4\ mg} \times \frac{1000\ mg}{g} = 1.67 \times 10^5$$

$$Q_0 = Q_1 \times \left(\frac{C_1}{C_2}\right) = \frac{48\ L}{min} \times 1.67 \times 10^5 \times \frac{m^3}{1000\ L} \times \frac{min}{60s} = \underline{134\ m^3/s}$$

4.6 Indirect Methods

Measuring stream discharge with a current meter is impossible during floods. Consequently, peak discharges must be determined by indirect methods including slope area method and flow measuring structures.

Figure 4.4 Slope Area Method

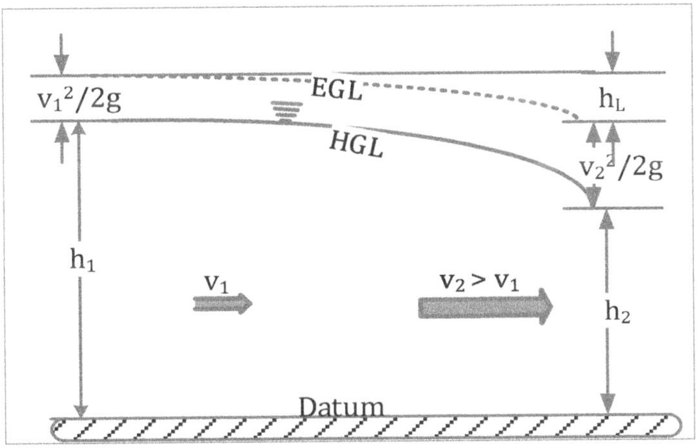

4.6.1 Slope Area Method

This method is particularly useful for estimating flood flows. A field survey is made after the flood to determine the location and elevation of high-water marks and characteristics of the channel. Based on this data, the slope of the energy gradient is determined. Knowing the energy gradient, the flow can be calculated from Manning's flow equation. Refer to **Figure 4.4**, applying the energy equation between points 1 (upstream) and 2 (downstream) energy gradient in terms of drop in water surface can be determined.

$$\frac{p_1}{\gamma} + Z_1 + \frac{v_1^2}{2g} = \frac{p_2}{\gamma} + Z_2 + \frac{v_2^2}{2g} + h_l$$

$$h_1 + h_{v1} = h_2 + h_{v2} + h_m + h_f$$

$$h_f = h_1 - h_2 - h_m + h_{v1} - h_{v2}$$

h_f = head loss due to friction, h_m = minor losses due to abrupt changes
h = hydraulic head (height of water surface), h_v = velocity head

$$\text{Minor losses}, h_m = k_m(h_{v1} - h_{v2}) = \mp k_m \Delta h_v$$

Where k_m = minor head loss coefficient

Head loss due to friction

$$h_f = h_1 - h_2 + h_{v1} - h_{v2} - h_m = \Delta h + \Delta h_v(1 \mp k_m)$$

v_1> v_2; Expansion $h_f = \Delta h + \Delta h_v(1 - k_m)$

v_1< v_2; Contraction $h_f = \Delta h + \Delta h_v(1 + k_m)$

Slope area method

$$\boxed{Q = k\sqrt{S_f} = \frac{k\sqrt{h_f}}{L} \qquad h_f = \Delta h + \Delta h_v(1 \pm k_m)}$$

Uniformity of channel section:

If the length of channel over which head drop is measured is relatively uniform, then head loss, h_f equals the drop in water surface elevation, Δh. To account for the non-uniformity of flow, geometrical average of the conveyance factors is taken, and effects of contracting or expanding flow are considered to calculate friction slope. $k = \sqrt{k_1 \times k_2}$

Further, for a contracting section, k_m is usually assumed zero, and for an expanding section, assume k_m = 0.5 unless otherwise stated.
v_1> v_2; Expansion $h_f = \Delta h + \Delta h_v(1 - 0.5) = \Delta h + 0.5\Delta h_v$
v_1< v_2; Contraction $h_f = \Delta h + \Delta h_v(1 + 0) = \Delta h + \Delta h_v$

Example Problem 4.3

The water surface of a river drops 12 mm over a length of 9.5 m. The channel is straight, and the average section area and wetted perimeter are 2.78 m² and 6.25 m, respectively. Assuming n = 0.035, determine the flow passing through the river.

Section	n	A, m²	V, m/s	h_v, m	Δh_v
1	0.03	3.1	1.35	0.093	
2	0.03	2.7	1.55	0.123	-0.030

Given:

Δh = 12 mm = 0.012 m, L = 9.5 m A = 2.78 m², P_w = 6.25 m, n = 0.035

Solution

$$k = \frac{AR_h^{2/3}}{n} = \frac{2.78}{0.035} \times \left(\frac{2.78}{6.25}\right)^{2/3} = 46.27 = \underline{46.3}$$

$$Q = k\sqrt{h_f/L} = 46.3\sqrt{\frac{0.012\ m}{9.5\ m}} = 1.644 = \underline{1.64\ m^3/s}$$

Example Problem 4.4

Use the slope area method to calculate stream discharge. Length of the reach is 9.45 m and drop in water surface is measured as 6.86 cm.

Section	n	A, m²	R_h, m	k = $AR_h^{2/3}/n$, m³/s
1 = u/s	0.038	3.17	0.534	54.8
2 = d/s	0.035	2.76	0.446	46.0

Given:

Δh = 0.0686 m   L = 9.45 m   Q = ?

Solution:

$$k_{mean} = \sqrt{k_1 k_2} = \sqrt{54.8 \times 46} = 50.2\ m^3/s, ignoring\ \Delta h_v$$

$$Q = k\sqrt{S_f} = k\sqrt{\frac{h_f}{L}} = 50.2\sqrt{\frac{0.0686\ m}{9.45\ m}} = 4.28\ m^3/s$$

Δh_v is -ve since flow is accelerating as section is contracting

Table 4.2 Values of Eddy Loss Coefficient, k_m

Change	Expansion	Contraction
Gradual	- 0.3	0.1
Abrupt	- 0.8	0.6

$$h_f = \Delta h + \Delta h_v(1 + k_m) = 0.0686 - 0.03(1 + 0.1) = 0.0356 \, m$$

$$Q = k\sqrt{S_f} = k\sqrt{h_f/L} = 50.2\sqrt{\frac{0.0356}{9.45m}} = 3.081 = 3.1 \, m^3/s$$

Table 4.3 Worksheet (Example Prob.4.4)

$h_{f,}$ cm	S_f	Q, m³/s	h_{v1}, cm	h_{v2}, cm	Δh_v, cm	h_{f}, cm
6.86	7.26E-03	4.28	9.28	12.2	-2.96	3.60
3.60	3.81E-03	3.10	4.87	6.42	-1.55	5.15
5.15	5.45E-03	3.71	6.97	9.19	-2.22	4.41
4.41	4.67E-03	3.43	4.35	7.87	-3.51	2.99
3.70	3.92E-03	3.14	3.65	6.60	-2.95	3.62
3.65	3.86E-03	3.12	3.60	6.51	-2.91	3.66
3.66	3.87E-03	3.12	3.61	6.53	-2.92	3.65

4.6.2 Ultrasonic Method

In this method, ultrasonic signals are used to measure flow velocity. Two transducers are installed at the same elevation from the bed on both sides of the stream. The path connecting the transducers makes an angle with the direction of flow. The transducers receive as well as transmit ultrasonic signals. Time taken by a signal from one transducer to the other is recorded. The average velocity of flow along the path is then obtained by knowing the path length and its angle with the flow direction. This method of gauging is suitable for automatic recording of data. It is accurate, efficient, and can accommodate rapid changes in the magnitude and direction of flow. However, unstable cross-sections, large loads of sediment in suspension, steep temperature changes, changing weed growth, air entrapment, changes in salinity, etc., can reduce accuracy of this method.

4.6.3 Electromagnetic Method

The electromagnetic method is based on the Faraday's principle that an emf is induced in the conductor (water in the present case) when it cuts a normal magnetic field. Large coils buried at the bottom of the channel carry a current to produce a controlled vertical magnetic field. Electrodes provided at the sides of the channel section measure the small voltage produced due to flow of water in the channel. It has been found that the signal output E will be of the order of millivolts and is related to the discharge Q as

$$Q = K_1 \left(\frac{Ed}{I} + K_2\right)^n$$

Where d is depth of flow, I is current, and n, K_1 and K_2 are system constants

Present day commercially available electromagnetic flowmeters can measure the discharge to an accuracy of ±3%, the maximum channel width that can be accommodated being 100 m. The minimum detectable velocity is 0.005 m/s.

4.7 Flow Measuring Structures

Different types of flow measuring structures include contracted opening, weir dam, culvert, flumes, and v-notch weirs. When a flow measuring structure is installed in a stream, it produces a unique control section in the flow. The discharge Q through the structure is related to the water surface elevation upstream of the weirs. For weirs, the general flow equation is: $Q = kH^n$. The value of k considers the channel geometry, the frictional loss due to weir, flow contraction, type of the weir and the units.

Triangular Weir
$$\boxed{Q = 1.42 \tan\left(\frac{\theta}{2}\right) H^{2.5} \ (SI)}$$

θ *is angle of the triangular weir and H is the head over the weir*

Rectangular Weir
$$\boxed{Q = 1.84 \ LH^{1.5} \ (SI)}$$

L is the length of rectangular weir.

4.8 Stage Discharge Relation

A **stage discharge** relation for a gauging section is obtained by plotting measured stage on the ordinate and measured discharge on the abscissa as discussed earlier. This relationship is also called the **rating curve** and is unique for every **control section**. If this relationship does not change with time, the control is called permanent; otherwise, it is called shifting control.

Using this relationship, stage hydrograph is converted to stream flow hydrograph as discussed earlier.

4.8.1 Rating Curve/Equation

A simple stage discharge relationship is a parabolic curve given by:

$$Q = C(h - h_0)^n$$

Q = discharge rate   h = gauge height
h_0 = gauge height (zero flow)   C, n = rating curve constants for a station

Traditionally gauge heights are plotted against discharge rates and a curve is fitted by eye. Two different controls coming into effect at different stages result in a compound curve. A parabolic curve, when plotted on a log-log scale will produce a straight line. Mathematically, taking logarithms of the stage discharge equation shown above, it becomes:

$$log\, Q = log\, C + n\, log(h - h_0)$$

This indicates a linear relationship between log Q and log (h-h_0). To develop the mathematical equation, constants c, n, and h_0 need to be evaluated. Noting that the relationship is linear between log Q and log (h-h_0), the determination of the stage of zero flow is to be performed first. The constant h_0 is zero, when data of stage versus discharge plots a straight line on a log-log scale. Zero discharge corresponds to zero stage. From a log-log plot of stage and discharge, it can be determined if the value of h_0 is zero or not. In case, h_0 is not zero, it can be evaluated as described in the next section.

Table 4.4 Type of Stage Discharge Equation

Plot of log h vs log Q	Type of equation	Comments
Straight line	$Q = Ch^n$	Q = 0 when h = 0
Concave up h > 0	$Q = C(h - h_0)^n$	Q = 0, h = h_0
Concave down h < 0	$Q = C(h + h_0)^n$	Q = 0 h = h_0

4.8.2 Computation of h_0

When fitting an equation to the rating curve, first thing is to find parameter h_0. This can be done as described below:
i) From the stage discharge data, select two points (Q_1, h_1) and (Q_2, h_2).
ii) Compute Q_3 as geometric mean of Q_1 and Q_2. $Q_3 = \sqrt{Q_1 \times Q_2}$
iii) From the plot, read h_3 corresponding to Q_3.
iv) Calculate h_0, using the following equation

Rating curve parameter

$$h_0 = \frac{h_1 h_2 - h_3^2}{h_1 + h_2 - 2h_3}$$

4.8.3 Determination of C, n

After h_0 is evaluated, next step is to find constant C and exponent n of the rating equation. This is done as follows:

i) Subtract h_0 from h and produce a data set of (h - h_0).

ii) Create a new data set by taking logarithms of Q and (h - h_0).

iii) Run a linear regression of log Q vs. log (h - h_0) to obtain a linear equation of the form y = a + bx, where a is the intercept and b is the slope of straight line

iv) Constant a and b can also be found using graph

v) The exponent n is equal to slope of the regressed line, b

vi) Constant C is equal to the inverse log of intercept a.

Example Problem 4.5

For the stage discharge data shown below, find the rating equation.

#	1	2	3	4	5	6	7	8
Q, m³/s	1.1	1.8	4.0	4.6	11	19	26	28
h, m	0.56	0.61	0.69	0.75	0.92	1.1	1.2	1.23

Solution:

$$Q_3 = \sqrt{Q_1 \times Q_2} = \sqrt{1.1 \times 19} = 4.57 \ m^3/s$$

From **Figure 4.5**, corresponding to Q = 4.57 m³/s, Stage h is 0.74 m

$$h_0 = \frac{h_1 h_2 - h_3^2}{h_1 + h_2 - 2h_3} = \frac{0.56 \times 1.1 - 0.74^2}{0.56 + 1.1 - 2 \times 0.74} = 0.38 \ m$$

Table 4.5 Stage Discharge Data (Ex. Prob. 4.5)

h, m	Q, m³/s	h-ho	Log(h-ho)	Log(Q)
0.56	1.1	0.18	-0.745	0.04
0.61	1.8	0.23	-0.638	0.26
0.69	4.0	0.31	-0.509	0.60
0.75	4.6	0.37	-0.432	0.66
0.92	11.0	0.54	-0.268	1.04

1.10	19.0	0.72	-0.143	1.28
1.20	26.0	0.82	-0.086	1.41
1.23	28.0	0.85	-0.071	1.45

Figure 4.5 Stage Discharge Plot (Ex. Prob. 4.5)

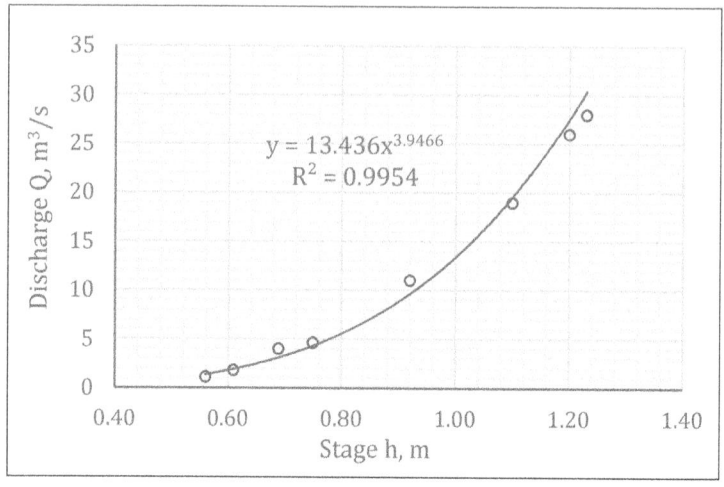

Linear Regression of log Q versus log (h-h_0) ((**Fig. 4.6**)

$\log Q = 1.5909 + 2.07 \log(h - 0.38)$

$n = slope = 2.07 \quad C = 10^{1.5894} = 38.85$

Rating equation

$Q = 39(h - 0.38)^{2.07}$

Figure 4.6 Fitting Equation (Ex. Prob. 4.5)

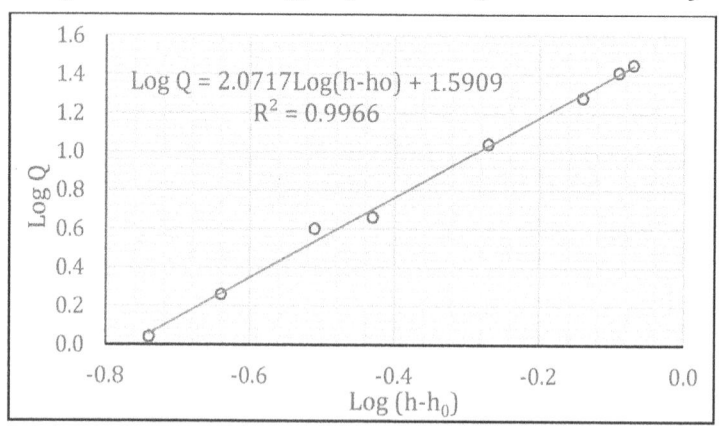

Discussion Questions

1. What factors should be considered when selecting a gauging station and a measuring section?
2. Define stage and describe commonly used methods to measure it.
3. Explain the procedure for obtaining a stage discharge relationship for a stream.
4. Compare price current meter and Ott meter
5. Explain a procedure for slope area method for estimating the flood flow.
6. Explain the stream flow measurement by velocity area method and discuss mid-section method in detail?
7. Briefly describe the dilution method of stream flow measurement and the qualities of a good tracer.
8. Explain the following graphs: flow hydrograph, stage hydrograph, rating curve
9. Explain why triangular weir as a flow measuring structure is preferred when measuring relatively small flows?
10. Applying Manning's equation, develop the relationship for discharge rate in terms of flow depth and slope of water surface. Applying this relationship prove that when depth of flow increases by 50% and water surface slope is half of original value, discharge rate increases by 39%?

Practice Problems

Practice Problem 4.1

Given the following stream gauging data, calculate the stream discharge using the mid-section method. (73 m³/s)

Vertical #	1	2	3	4	5	6	7	8	9	10	11
Distance, m	15	20	25	30	35	40	45	50	55	60	65
Depth, m	0.0	0.5	0.8	1.2	1.5	2.5	3.0	2.0	1.2	0.8	0.0
Velocity, 0.2	-	0.5	0.7	0.9	1.2	1.4	1.7.	1.3	0.9	0.7	-
Velocity, 0.8	-	0.4	0.6	0.7	0.8	1.1	1.3	1.0	0.7	0.6	-

Practice Problem 4.2

Compute discharge in the stream based on the current meter measurements shown in the following table using mid-section method.
(16.5 m³/s)

Vertical #	1	2	3	4	5	6	7	8	9	10
Distance, m	0	2	4	6	8	10	12	14	16	18
Depth, m	0.0	0.95	1.84	2.54	3.20	3.50	2.65	1.56	0.50	0.0
Velocity, 0.2 d	-	0.35	0.49	0.51	0.56	0.64	0.57	0.45	0.32	-
Velocity, 0.8 d	-	0.34	0.36	0.48	0.45	0.51	0.53	0.36	0.28	-

Practice Problem 4.3

For stream discharge of 100 m³/s, calculate the dose rate of tracer to cause a million times dilution. (6.0 L/min)

Practice Problem 4.4

Rework **Ex. Prob. 4-4** treating it as uniform section with K = 50 m³/s.
(4.3 m³/s)

Practice Problem 4.5

Using the slope area method estimate the flood discharge for the following observations after the passing of flood wave.
$L = 500$ m $A_1 = 1050\ m^2$ $\Delta h = 50.0$ cm $K = 4.90 \times 10^4\ m^3/s$
(1550 m³/s)

Stream Flow Measurement

Practice Problem 4.6

Determine the rating equation for stream flow data collected by Water Survey of Canada for Big Carp River at Sault Ste. Marie. Assume $h_0 = 1.8$. ($Q = 3.21 (h - 1.8)^{1.98}$)

Date	Nov 78	Nov 81	Jul 79	Apr 81	Apr 82	Apr 80
Stage, m	2.27	2.36	2.61	2.85	3.17	3.42
Discharge, m³/s	0.75	1.01	1.95	3.50	6.25	8.25

Practice Problem 4.7

Based on current meter velocity measurements in the stream given in the table below, compute the stream discharge for that day? (4.8 m³/s)

Vertical #	1	2	3	4	5	6	7	8	9	10
Distance,	0	1	2	3	4	5	6	7	8	8.6
Depth, m	0.0	0.40	1.20	1.60	2.80	2.51	2.10	1.60	0.71	0.0
m/s	-	0.20	0.26	0.40	0.52	0.48	0.32	0.23	0.14	-

Practice Problem 4.8

Sodium dichromate solution of strength of 500 g/L was used as a chemical tracer. Tracer was dosed at the rate of 3.5 L/s and downstream concentration of 4.5 mg/L was observed. Estimate the stream flow rate? (390 m³/s)

Practice Problem 4.9

During a high flow event, water levels in a small stream were observed at two points 5.5 km apart. Using n = 0.020 and loss coefficient, 0.30, work out stream discharge? (51 m³/s)

Section	h, m	A, m²	R_h, m
u/s	98.77	73.3	2.61
d/s	98.50	93.4	1.95

Practice Problem 4.10

Rework Example Problem 4.4 assuming the mean value of the conveyance factor K of 42 m³/s. (2.61 m³/s)

Review Questions

1. For an average flow of 1.0 m³/s, the volume of flow in passing over a day is
   a) 3600 ML   b) 86 ML   c) 86000 ML   d) 36 ML

2. In a bubbler gauge arrangement, 1 kPa change in pressure represents ___ mm change in stage.
   a) 1.0 mm   b) 10 mm   c) 100 mm   d) 1000 mm

3. Mean velocity is typically ___ % of the float velocity.
   a) 85%   b) 60%   c) 40%   d) 100%

4. The current meter rating equation is v (m/s) = 0.03 + 0.65 N (rev/s). At 60% of the depth, it takes 28 s to complete 30 revolutions. Mean flow velocity in the stream is
   a) 0.68 m/s   b) 0.65 m/s   c) 0.62 m/s   d) 0.73 m/s

5. At a given section of the stream, the average depth and width are 0.56 m and 11.4 m respectively. What is the discharge rate assuming an average flow velocity of 0.55 m/s?
   a) 3.51 m³/s   b) 0.35 m³/s   c) 350 m³/s   d) 3500 m³/s

6. A tracer injected at the rate of 1 L/min in a stream is diluted by a factor of 1200 when completely mixed. The estimated flow is
   a) 1.2 L/s   b) 12 L/s   c) 120 L/s   d) 20 L/s

7. In a uniform channel, a 50 cm drop in water surface is measured over a 15 m length. The energy slope is
   a) 0.33   b) 0.033   c) 33%   d) 0.33%

8. A channel with an average conveyance factor of 152 m³/s produces a friction slope of 4.5% during a flood. The estimated flow is
   a) 32 m³/s   b) 23 m³/s   c) 12 m³/s   d) 25 m³/s

9. Rating curve of a given station is Q (m³/s) = 0.45(h - 0.22)$^{2.2}$. The flow corresponding to a stage, h of 3.1 m is
   a) 2.6 m³/s   b) 3.5 m³/s   c) 4.6 m³/s   d) 33 m³/s

10. For the station with the rating, Q (m³/s) = 0.45 (h - 0.22)$^{2.2}$ described in Question (9), what is the stage corresponding to a flow of 3.0 m³/s?
    a) 1.6 m   b) 0.88 m   c) 2.6 m   d) 1.6 m

Stream Flow Measurement

11. The following is an indirect method of stream flow measurement.
    a) Slope area   b) Ultrasonic   c) Velocity area   d) Dilution

12. A stilling well is required when the stage is measured by _____ gauge.
    a) Bubbler   b) Staff   c) Float   d) Snow

13. The following device is not related to streamflow measurement.
    a) Sounding Wt.   b) Current meter   c) Wading Rod   d) Hydrometer

14. The float velocity or surface flow velocity is _____ flow velocity
    a) = maximum   b) = Mean   c) <Mean   d) >Mean

15. The slope area method is better suited to
    a) Develop a rating curve   b) Estimating flood flow
    c) Produce flow hydrograph   d) Low flow measurement

16. If the applicable rating curve for a control section is available, you can predict the discharge by knowing
    a) Stage   b) max. velocity   c) Float velocity   d) Water marks

17. In a rectangular channel section, the top width and depth of flow respectively are 2.0 m and 0.90 m. Current meter readings at 60% and 80% depths indicate flow velocities of 0.60 and 0.40 m/s. Discharge in the channel is
    a) 0.25 m³/s   b) 0.45 m³/s   c) 0.90 m³/s   d) 1.8 m³/s

18. A servo manometer is required when the stage measurement is made by employing a _____ gauge.
    a) Staff   b) Crest   c) Float   d) Bubbler

19. A 40 g/L strength solution of common salt was injected into stream at a constant rate of 15 L/s. At a downstream section where the salt solution is known to have completely mixed, the equilibrium concentration was found to be 80 mg/L. Given that background concentration is 15 mg/L, the discharge rate in the stream is
    a) 2.5 m³/s   b) 4.5 m³/s   c) 9.2 m³/s   d) 18 m³/s

20. During a flood in a wide channel, for the same stage, water surface slope doubles of the original value. What is the approximate change in discharge rate in the channel?
   a) 39%↓   b) 100%↑   c) 100%↓   d) 41%↑

21. In a triangular channel, the top width and depth of flow respectively are 2.0 m and 0.90 m. If the mean flow velocity is observed to be 0.60 m/s, the discharge in the channel is
   a) 0.45 m³/s   b) 0.54 m³/s   c) 0.90 m³/s   d) 1.8 m³/s

22. A rectangular channel laid on a slope of 0.10% carries 14 m³/s of water flowing full. What is the conveyance factor of this channel?
   a) 110 m³/s   b) 220 m³/s   c) 330 m³/s   d) 440 m³/s

23. Which of the following is not used in stream flow measurement?
   a) Tipping bucket gauge
   b) Depth sounder
   c) Current meter
   d) Bubbler gauge

24. During a flood in a wide rectangular channel, at a section the depth of flow increases by 40% and slope of the water surface reduces to half of its original value. This indicates a _____ change in the discharge rate?
   a) 11%↑   b) 24%↑   c) 11%↓   d) 24%↓

25. Mean flow velocity in an open channel is assumed to be equal to point flow velocity at _____ of depth.
   a) 20%   b) 40%   c) 60%   d) 80%

26. In a small creek, a 120° triangular weir is installed for flow measurement. What is the flow rate when head over the weir is 0.56 m?
   a) 18 L/s   b) 42 L/s   c) 34 L/s   d) 58 L/s

27. In case of V-notch weir, if 10% error is made in reading the head over the weir, this would cause the flow rate to be in error by
   a) 10%   b) 15%   c) 27%   d) 34%

28. In slope area method, friction slope is less than observed value slope of water surface as found from flood marks when the channel section is
   a) Contracting   b) Expanding   c) Uniform   d) All

29. In fitting a rating equation, values of log Q were regressed with log(h-0.38) data values to yield linear equation: $\log Q = 1.60 + 2.07 \log(h - 0.38)$.
Rating equation is;
a) $Q = 13(h - 0.38)^{2.07}$
b) $40(h - 0.38)^{2.07}$
c) $Q = 49(h - 0.38)^{2.07}$
d) $53(h - 0.38)^{2.07}$

30. For a river, rating curve is available. To determine the flow rate, which of the following data is required?
a) Velocity measurement in the middle of section
b) Manning's coefficient of roughness
c) Stage and area of section
d) Water stage

5 Probability Concepts

Probability concepts are applied to hydrologic studies to make the best possible forecast of events to formulate decisions to control and manage water resources. A short description of probability concepts follows.

5.1 Probability Definition

Probability is the equivalent of relative frequency of an event A of happening, In the familiar coin tossing experiment, the probability of getting a head or a tail can be found intuitively. Knowing that there are only two outcomes in a single trial, P(H) = P(T) = ½ or 0.50, that does not mean that if you toss the coin ten times you will always get five heads. However, as the number of trials become larger and larger, the number of heads and tails will be close. Of course, this will not apply to a loaded coin.

5.1.1 Return Period (T)

Return period also called **recurrence interval** is the reciprocal of probability of occurrence in any given year.

$$P = \frac{1}{T} \quad or \quad T = \frac{1}{P}$$

A flood probability of 1/25 or 0.04 is referred to as 25-y flood. Other way to say the same thing is that flood of this or greater magnitude will occur on an average of four times in a 100-year period. However, during any selected period of 25 consecutive years, it may not occur at all or may occur more than once. In many of the hydrologic events, a year represents a single trial. Thus a 10-y storm will occur on an average of 10 times in a century. *One thing we cannot answer is the exact timing of this storm.* It may not happen in the first 10 years or may happen more than once.

5.2 Rules of Probability

1. The probability of an event is non-negative and never exceeds one. The probability of 1.0 indicates an event is certain and the probability of an impossible event is 0.
2. The sum of probabilities of all possible outcomes in a single trial is unity. In a single toss of a coin, there are two outcomes, hence:

    $P(H) + P(T) = 1$

In an experiment when there are only two possible outcomes, for example success and failure, flood and no flood, the probability of failure becomes the complementary probability of success. The probability of a 10-y flood to occur in any given year is 1/10 = 0.10 and the complementary probability is 1 - 0.1 = 0.90.

5.2.1 Addition Rule

The probability of several independent and mutually exclusive events is the sum of probabilities of separate events.

Addition rule (exclusive events)
$$P(A \text{ or } B) = P(A) + P(B)$$

For example, probability of drawing a king or an ace from a deck of cards is 2/13. If A and B are inclusive events, then the additional rule is modified. *P(A and B)* is the probability when *A* and *B* occur together. For exclusive and independent events, joint probability *P(A and B)* = 0.

Addition rule (inclusive events)
$$P(A \text{ or } B) = P(A) + P(B) - P(AB)$$

For example, probability of drawing an ace or a card of spade is

$$P(A \text{ or } B) = \frac{4}{52} + \frac{13}{52} - \frac{1}{52} = \frac{16}{52}$$

5.2.2 Multiplication Rule

The probability of two independent events occurring simultaneously or in succession is the product of individual probabilities.

Multiplication rule (independent events)
$$P(A \text{ and } B) = P(A) \times P(B)$$

The multiplication rule can be applied to find the probability of getting three heads in succession. Outcome of every trial is independent of the previous trial. For example, probability of getting three heads in succession is: 0.5×0.5×0.5=0.125 = 1/8

5.2.3 Conditional Probability

When A and *B* are dependent events, the multiplication rule needs to be modified.

Multiplication rule (dependent events)

$$P(A \text{ and } B) = P(A/B) \times P(B)$$

Where P(A/B) signifies the conditional probability, the chances of occurrence of event A provided B has already occurred. For example, probability of a rainy day following a dry day is not the same as a rainy day following a rainy day.

Example Problem 5.1

An urban drainage channel reaches flood stage each spring with a relative frequency of 0.1. Power failure in the industry along the channel occurs with the probability of 0.20. Based on experience, it can be said that when there is a flood, the chances of power failure are raised to 0.4. Determine the probability of having either flood or power failure in each year?
Event of river reaching flood stage = A   Event of power failure = B

Solution:

$$P(A \text{ and } B) = P(B|A)P(A) = 0.4 \times 0.1 = 0.04$$

$$P(A \text{ or } B) = P(A) + P(B) - P(AB)$$

$$= 0.1 + 0.2 - 0.04 = 0.26 = 26\%$$

5.3 Binomial Process

Binomial process involves two possible outcomes in a single trial. The trials are dependent, and probability of success or failure remains constant in an experiment of n trials. The outcome is either a success or a failure. If the probability of success in a single trial is p then the probability of failure, q = (1 - p), because total probability of all the outcomes must be one. The general formulation of the probability of exactly x number of occurrences in n number of trials:

Binomial Probability Distribution

$$P(n,x) = {}^n_xC \times p^x \times q^{n-x}, \quad {}^n_xC = \frac{n!}{x!\,(n-x)!}$$

5.3.1 Risk and reliability

Risk is when an event like flood happens at least once in the design period of a structure. Probability of having zero happening of an event is known as **reliability** and is given by the following expression. It should be noted that at least once includes all other possibilities except zero or no occurrence.

Watershed Characteristics

Probability of zero occurrence over n years

$$P(n, 0) = {}^n_0C \times p^0 \times q^n = q^n = (1-p)^n$$

Reliability

$$P(n, 0) = (1-p)^n = \left(1 - \frac{1}{T}\right)^n$$

This expression yields the probability of zero successes (not a single occurrence) in *n* trials. When applied to flood events this probability is called reliability. Since risk is the probability of occurrence of a flood at least once (*x* > 0) over a period of *n* years (trials), expression for risk becomes.

Risk of T-year flood over n years period

$$P(n, > 0) = 1 - (1-p)^n = 1 - q^n = 1 - \left(1 - \frac{1}{T}\right)^n$$

Since sum of probabilities of all the possible outcomes equals unity, it follows:

Risk + Reliability = 1 or Risk = $P(x > 0) = 1-(1 - p)^n$

For example, the chances that a 25-year flood (*p* = 0.04) will occur at least once in a 25-year period (*n* = 25) is.

$$P(n, > 0) = 1 - (1 - 0.04)^{25} = 0.639 = \underline{64\%}$$

Naturally, if a given structure with a life span of 25 years is designed based on the 25-year flood, chances are great that it will be flooded during its useful lifespan. Thus, to reduce the risk of flooding, you need to *select the return period of the design flood greater than the lifespan of the structure.* For an accepted risk, design return periods are shown in **Table 5.1**.

Table 5.1 Return Periods for a Given Risk

%Risk	Expected Life, n Years							
	2	5	10	15	20	25	50	100
50	3.4	7.7	15	22	29	37	73	145
25	7.5	18	35	53	70	87	174	348
10	20	4	95	143	190	238	475	950
5	40	98	196	293	390	488	976	1949
1	98	498	996	1492	1990	2488	4975	9950

Example Problem 5.2

What is the probability of a 25-year flood occurring exactly twice in a 25-year period?

Given:

T = 25   x = 2   n = 25   p = 1/25 = 0.04

Solution:

$${}^{25}_{2}C = \frac{25!}{2!(25-2)!} = \frac{25 \times 24}{2 \times 1} = 300$$

$P(25,2) = {}^n_xC \times p^x \times q^{n-x} = 300 \times 0.04^2 \times 0.96^{23} = 0.187 = \underline{19\%}$

$P(25,1) = {}^n_xC \times p^x \times q^{n-x} = 25 \times 0.04 \times 0.96^{24} = 0.187 = \underline{38\%}$

$P(25,0) = {}^n_xC \times p^x \times q^{n-x} = 1 \times 0.96^{25} = 0.187 = \underline{36\%}$

Example Problem 5.3

A cofferdam has been built to protect homes in a flood plain until a major channel project can be completed. The coffer dam was built for a 20-y flood. The channel project will require 3 years to complete. Find the probability that:

a) The dam will *not be overtopped* during the three-year period.
b) The dam will be *overtopped only once* during the three-year period.

Given:

n = 3   T = 20   p = 1/20 = 0.05

Solution:

$P(3,0) = q^n = (1 - 0.05)^3 = 0.86 = \underline{86\%}$

$P(3,1) = {}^n_xC \times p^x \times q^{n-x} = 3 \times 0.05^2 \times 0.95^2 = 0.135 = \underline{14\%}$

Example Problem 5.4

What return period an engineer should use to design a structure if we want to be 90% sure that the structure will not be flooded during its lifespan of 25 years?

Given:

Reliability = 90% = 0.90   n = 25   T = ?

Solution:

$$Rel = (1 - 1/T)^n \text{ or } T = \frac{1}{1 - Rel^{1/n}} = \frac{1}{1 - 0.90^{1/25}}$$

$$= 237 = \underline{240 \text{ y}}$$

Example Problem 5.5

In the month of June in Toronto, the chance of rainfall on any given day of the month is 25%. A convention is being planned during this month that may last about 5 days. What is the probability of having?
 a. No rainfall over the 5-day period?
 b. One rainy day over the 5-day period?
 c. More than one rainy day over the 5-day period
 d. At least one rainy day

Given:

p = 0.25   q = 1 - 0.25 = 0.75   n = 5

Solution:

$$P(5,0) = q^n = 0.75^5 = 0.237 = \underline{24\%}$$

$$P(5,1) = {}^n_xC \times p^x \times q^{n-x} = 1 \times 0.25 \times 0.75^4 = 0.395 = \underline{40\%}$$

$$P(5, > 1) = 1 - P(5,0) - P(5,1) = 1 - 0.237 - 0.395 = 0.36 = \underline{36\%}$$

$$P(5, > 0) = 1 - P(5,0) = 1 - 0.237 = 0.76 = \underline{76\%}$$

5.4 Probability Distribution

A probability distribution is a function that expresses in mathematical terms the probability of each of all possible outcomes of the random variable, X. A random variable is **discrete** if it assumes whole number values and is described by discrete probability distribution like Binomial discussed earlier. The variable like rainfall is a **continuous** variable because it can take any value.

A distribution is an attribute of a statistical population. If each element of a population has a value of x, then the population describes the constitution of the population through its x-values.

Figure 5.1 Standard Normal distribution Curve

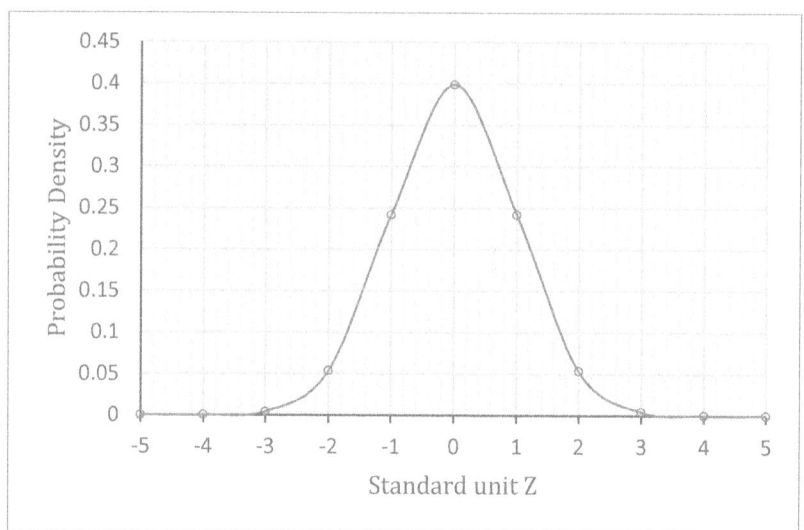

5.4.1 Probability Function

When a population is sufficiently large, the relative frequency plot of a random variable becomes a smooth curve like a bell curve shown in **Fig. 5.1**. Bell curve represents the probability distribution of a Normal or Gaussian distribution. The curve describing the distribution is called a **probability density function** (PDF) whose cumulative function (area under the curve) is known as **cumulative distribution function** (CDF). The bell curve shown in **Fig. 5.1**, is the PDF of a standard normal distribution. The area enclosed by any two verticals, yields the relative frequency or probability. Area under the curve, which would yield an exponential curve, as area would increase with increase in interval, will be the CDF of the distribution.

Properties of statistical distributions are described by the descriptive statistics like mean and standard deviation.

5.4.2 Central Tendency

Central tendency indicates the point value of the centre of the distribution of a data set. In layman terms it is the average value. Mean, mode and median describe the central tendency of a distribution of data; however arithmetic mean is the one commonly used. *Mean is also the most expected value.*

5.4.3 Dispersion

Dispersion refers to the variation in data and is described by measures including range, variation, standard deviation and absolute deviation. Most commonly used measure of dispersion is Standard deviation. Standard deviation is square root of the variance, which describes the spread of the random variable around the mean. Standard deviation of a sample of random variable can be calculated using the following formula.

Mean and Standard deviation

$$\bar{x} = \frac{\sum x}{n} \quad s = \sqrt{\frac{\sum (x - \bar{x})^2}{n - 1}}$$

Mean and standard deviation of a population is represented by Greek letters, μ and σ respectively.

Coefficient of variation is simply standard deviation divided by mean. **Variance** is square of standard deviation. Both mean and standard deviation have the same units as of the random variable, X.

5.4.4 Symmetry

Symmetry of the distribution is measured by the coefficient of skewness. It is a measure of separation of the mean, median and mode. *For symmetrical distributions, the coefficient of skewness is zero*. Pearson skewness is defined as the difference between the mean and median divided by one third of standard deviation. For an asymmetrical distribution with tail to the right (mean > median), the **coefficient of skewness** is positive. When median is greater than mean, the coefficient of skewness is less than zero.
Kurtosis is a measure of the peakedness of a distribution.

5.5 Normal Distribution

Normal distribution is one of the most common probability distributions in the field of statistics. It is a symmetrical distribution and is popularly known as **bell curve**. It has two parameters: mean and standard deviation. Knowing the two for a given population, probability of random variable exceeding a certain value can be found. By using a simple transformation, the normal distribution is converted into one parameter (Z) distribution known as **standardized distribution**. *The mean of standard normal distribution is zero* and standard deviation is one unit. Standard unit, Z is also equal to **frequency factor K** and has no units (**Fig. 5.1**)

Probability density function
$$f(z) = \frac{1}{\sqrt{2\pi}} e^{-\left(\frac{z^2}{2}\right)}$$

Cumulative distribution function
$$F(z) = \int_{-\infty}^{z} \frac{1}{\sqrt{2\pi}} e^{-\left(\frac{z^2}{2}\right)} dz$$

Probability density function, PDF of a standardised normal distribution is used to find probability of random variable falling in a given interval. To do that random variable X is expressed in standard units, Z. Standard unit or Z of the population is estimated from a sample drawn from that population.

Population and Sample variate, z
$$Z = \frac{(X - \mu)}{\sigma} \qquad z = \frac{(x - \bar{x})}{S_x}$$

Since probability of getting a specific value of a continuous variable is zero (area under a point value is zero), probability of exceeding or equal to is the same as probability of exceedance.

A **standardized distribution** curve can be used to analyze any hydrologic variable that follow normal distribution. For a known value of z, value of the integral is found by reading area under the curve in a given interval. Area under the curve is read from Tables available in any statistics text. Thus, probability of the variable falling in a given interval, $P(z_1 < Z < z_2)$ can be found.

Probability of falling a random variable in an interval
$$P(x_1 \leq X \leq x_2) = P(z_1 < Z < z_2) = F(z_2) - F(z_1)$$

In events like floods, we are interested in finding probability of exceeding a certain value, or area to the right of standard unit on the standard normal curve.

Probability of exceedance
$$P(X > x = 1 - F(z) \text{ or } 0.5 - F(z)$$

Note: in the above equation, 1 is used when z is measured from left and 0.5 when z is measured from left.

Watershed Characteristics

In extreme events like droughts, you may be interested in finding probability of getting annual precipitation less than a certain value. This is found by reading area under the curve to the left of standard variate.

Probability of less than
$$P(X < x) = F(z) \text{ or } 0.5 - F(z)$$

5.5.1 Characteristics of a standard Normal Curve

- Area under the normal distribution of a curve is the probability of an occurrence and equals 1.0.
- The mean divides the curve in exactly two halves and that is equivalent to saying the curve is symmetrical about the mean.
- The dispersion about the mean is measured in standard deviation units of z. The normal curve has a point of inflection at a point $z = 1$.
- From the normal probability density curve, it is possible to find the probability of less than or exceeding a given value by noting the area under the curve on the left-hand side or the right-hand side of a particular point defined by the z value. Cumulative area under the normal curve gives the probability of less than to a given value of x or z.
- Area under the curve is represented by F(z) and its value is always less than or equal to unity. The value of z represents the point in question. When z is zero, x is equal to the mean. Left of the centre ($z < 0$) represents values less than the mean and points lying on the right of centre ($z > 0$) represent values greater than the mean. For continuous variables, the probability refers to an area in a given interval ($x_1 < X < x_2$). Because an area under a point is zero, thus $P(x = x_1) = P(x = x_2) = 0$
- Measuring with respect to mean position, the centre is ($z = 0$), extreme right ($z = 4$) and extreme left ($z = -4$).
- When table of F(z) is measured from the left ($z = -4$), probability of exceedances or other probabilities can be found.
- Probability of non-exceedance (area to the left)

Z	Area F(z) measured from		
	Left	Centre	Right
0	0.5	0	0.5
1	0.8413	0.3413	0.1587
2	0.9772	0.4772	0.0228
3	0.9987	0.4987	0.0013

- Probability of exceedance (area to the right)

$$P(X > x) = P(Z > z) = 1 - F(z_1) \text{ or } 0.5 - F(z_1)$$

  Use 1 if measured from left and 0.5 if measured from the centre
- Probability of a random variable lying in a given interval:

$$P(x_1 \leq X \leq x_2) = P(z_1 < Z < z_2) = F(z_2) - F(z_1)$$

- The curve approaches the abscissa asymptotically on either side of the mean ($Z = 0$). In other words, the normal curve touches the axis at infinity. However, from a practical point of view, area under the curve beyond $Z = \pm 4$ is negligibly small.
- Area under the curve for a given value of Z can be approximated by a formula proposed by Swamee and Rathie (2007).

$$F(Z \leq z) = \left[e^{(-1.7255z|z|^{0.12})} + 1\right]^{-1}$$

- Probability that continuous variable assumes a certain value is zero.
- A given variable follows normal distribution, the probability of getting a value in between an interval of one standard deviation ($z = 1$) on both sides of mean ($z=0$) is 68%
- Area under the curve in the interval of two standard deviations ($z \pm 2$) is about 95% and three standard deviations 99.7%.
- The mean and standard deviation of a distribution are rarely known for certainty. This is because we are often working with a sample and do not have the access to all values of the population. The mean and standard deviation of the sample are used to estimate population mean and standard deviation. Thus, to have reliable predictions, minimum sample size ($n > 20$) is recommended.
- Mean and standard deviation are called the location and scale parameters.

Example Problem 5.6

Based on 30 years of annual precipitation data at Sault Ste. Marie, the mean and standard deviation are 708 mm and 166 mm, respectively. Calculate the probabilities of receiving more than 956 mm (wet year) and less than 500 mm (dry year) of precipitation in a given year.

Solution:

$$z = \frac{(x - \bar{x})}{s} = \frac{(956 - 708) \, mm}{166 \, mm} = 1.494 = 1.50$$

$$P(X > 956) = P(z > 1.5) = 0.50 - F(1.5)$$
$$= 1.0 - 0.9332 = 0.0668 = \underline{6.7\%}$$

$$z = \frac{(x - \bar{x})}{s} = \frac{(500 - 708)\ mm}{166\ mm} = -1.253$$

$$P(X < 500\ mm) = F(Z < -0.035)$$

$$F(-0.035) = \left[e^{(-1.7255(-1.253)|1.253|^{0.12})} + 1\right]^{-1} = 0.0978$$

$$T = \frac{1}{P} = \frac{1}{0.0978} = 10.2 = 10\ y$$

Return period of a dry year for the city of Sault Ste. Marie is about 10 y.

Example Problem 5.7

A normal variable has a mean of 4.0 units and standard deviation of 1.0 unit. What is the value of variable when the probability of exceedances is 67%?

Given:

Mean = 4.0 units   Std. Dev. = 1.0 unit   P(>x) = 67% = 0.67

Solution:

$$F(\leq z) = 0.5 - F(\geq z) = 0.50 - 0.67 = -0.17\ (x<\ mean)$$

From Table (Appendix E),
    When F = 0.67, Z = -0.44

$$x = \bar{x} + Zs = 4.0 - 0.44 \times 1 = 3.56 = \underline{3.6\ units}$$

Example Problem 5.8

The mean and standard deviation of annual precipitation at a gauging station are 1410 mm and 280 mm respectively. Assuming that the annual rainfall is normally distributed, estimate the annual precipitations of having 10% and 1% chances of being exceeded.

Given:

Mean = 1410 mm   Std. Dev. = 280 mm   P(>x) = 10% = 0.10, 0.01

Solution:

For P(>x) = 0.10, Z = 1.282 and P(>x) = 0.01, Z = 2.326

$$x = \bar{x} + 1.28s = 1410 \, mm + 1.282 \times 280 \, mm$$

$$= 1768.9 = 1770 \, mm$$

$$x = \bar{x} + 2.326 = 1410 \, mm + 1.282 \times 280 \, mm$$

$$= 2061.2 = 2060 \, mm$$

Example Problem 5.9

Based on the data of 10-year and 25-year floods given below, estimate the flow of a 100-year flood. Assume flood flow data follows normal distribution.

Parameter	Flood 1	Flood 2	Flood3
T, years	10	25	100
x, (m³/s)	73	84	?
F (> z)	0.10	0.04	0.01
F (z)	0.9	0.96	0.99
z	1.28	1.75	2.327

Solution:

$$73 = \bar{x} + 1.28s \quad 84 = \bar{x} + 1.75s \ or$$

Solving the above two equations simultaneously

$$84 = 73 - 1.28s + 1.75 \, s \ or \ s = \frac{1100}{47} = 23.4$$

$$\bar{x} = x - zs = 73 - 1.28 \times 23.4 = 43.048 = \underline{43 \, m^3/s}$$

$$x = \bar{x} + zs = 43 + 2.327 \times 23.4 = 97.45 = \underline{97 \, m^3/s}$$

5.6 Non-Normal Distribution

The probability distribution of many hydrologic variables, for example floods, is not normal. The distribution of data should be checked for normalcy. Plotting a Polygram provides a quick check. Plot should be a bell curve if the data follows normal distribution. Plotting a cumulative probability curve on normal probability paper can perform a sounder method of checking for normalcy. Unless the curve approximates a straight line, a normal distribution should not be used for estimating probabilities.

5.6.1 Testing for Normalcy

A normalcy check can be performed in the following steps:
  i. Rank the data in descending order that is from large too small. If two

or more data have the same value, assign each value a unique rank.

ii. Calculate the plotting position (probability of exceedances) by dividing the rank by (n + 1), where n is the total number of observations. In terms of recurrence interval T, the plotting position is the inverse, $T = 1/(1+n)$

iii. Plot the points on normal probability paper and check if the fitted curve is a straight line.

5.6.2 Log-Normal Distribution

Many hydrologic variables including floods, exhibit a marked skewness, largely because physically they cannot be negative. Whereas normal distribution allows the random variable to range without limit from minus infinity to positive infinity, the log normal has a lower of zero. A **log normal** distribution is a log-transformation that makes the data fit a normal distribution. Because the new value is the log of original value, the mean and standard deviation are in log units. For analysing random variables such as streamflow and precipitation, log normal distribution provides advantage while still preserving most properties of the normal distribution.

5.6.3 Pearson Type III Distribution

The log-Pearson type III distribution is Pearson type III distribution is applied to logarithms of a random variable. If the skew coefficient is zero, the log-Pearson type III is equivalent to log-normal distribution. Log-Pearson type III distribution is recommended for analysing flood flows. It should be noted that for non-normal distributions, frequency factor k corresponds to standard unit z for normal distribution.

Example Problem 5.10

The series of 31 flood flows of Al River are analysed to yield the following:

Parameter	Normal	Log-Normal
Random Variable	$x = Q$ (m³/s)	$y = \log Q$
Mean	4144	3.463
Standard Deviation, s	3311	0.424
Coefficient of Skewness, C_s	1.66	-0.936

Estimate the 50-y flood assuming normal, lognormal distribution and Log-Pearson-type III.

Solution:

50-y Flood-Normal distribution
$$F(> k) = \frac{1}{50} = 0.02, \quad F(k) = 0.5 - 0.02 = 0.48, k = 2.055$$
$$x = \bar{x} + ks = 4144 + 2.055 \times 3311 = 11000 \ m^3/s$$

Log-Normal distribution
$$y = \bar{y} + ky = 3.463 + 2.055 \times 0.424 = 4.334$$
$$Q = 10^y = 10^{4.334} = 21577 = \underline{21600 \ m^3/s}$$

Pearson type III distribution
$$k = (C_s = 2.80, \quad T = 50)$$
$$y = \bar{y} + ky = 4144 + 2.80 \times 3311 = 13414 = 13400 \ m^3/s$$

Log-Pearson type III distribution
$$k = 1.492 (C_s = -1.0, T = 50)$$
$$y = \bar{y} + ky = 3.463 + 1.492 \times 0.424 = 4.096$$
$$Q = 10^y = 10^{4.096} = 12473 = 12500 \ m^3/s$$

Example Problem 5.11

For the flood flow data of the previous example, calculate the return period of a flood of flow exceeding 8000 m³/s assuming normal and lognormal distribution.

Solution:

Normal Distribution
$$k = \frac{(x - \bar{x})}{s} = \frac{(8000 - 4144) \ mm}{3311 \ mm} = 1.165$$
$$F(1.165) = 0.3780,$$
$$P(> x) = 0.5 - 0.3780 = 0.122$$
$$T = \frac{1}{P(> x)} = \frac{1}{0.122} = 8.19 = \underline{8 \ years}$$

Log-normal Distribution
$$k = \frac{(y - \bar{y})}{s} = \frac{(3.903 - 3.463)}{0.424} = 1.04, \quad F(k) = 0.3508$$

$$P(> y) = 0.5 - 0.3508 = 0.1492$$

$$T = \frac{1}{P(> x)} = \frac{1}{0.1492} = 6.70 = \underline{7 \text{ years}}$$

Pearson type III distribution
For $C_S = 1.66, F(> 1.165) = 0.15$

$$T = \frac{1}{P(> x)} = \frac{1}{0.15} = 6.6 = \underline{7 \text{ years}}$$

Log-Pearson type III distribution
For $C_S = , F(> 1.04) = 0.134$

$$T = \frac{1}{P(> x)} = \frac{1}{0.134} = 7.45 = \underline{7 \text{ years}}$$

Discussion Questions

1. Define probability and relate it to the return period.
2. What is a discrete probability distribution and explain its application to hydrologic events?
3. From the general expression of binomial distribution, derive the expression for finding probability of at least one occurrence of an event?
4. Describe main features of Normal distribution and its suitability to analyze hydrologic data.
5. Describe the procedure to check normalcy of a data set.
6. What are the advantages of non-normal distributions over Normal distribution.
7. What is frequency factor?
8. Compare normal distribution with
    a. Log-normal distribution
    b. Pearson type III distribution
9. Differentiate between probability density function and cumulative density function
10. Define the terms: coefficient of variation, variance, kurtosis, and skewness. What characteristic of the distribution, each of these parameters is used to measure?

Practice Problems

Practice Problem 5.1

a) An urn contains 8 red marbles, 7 green marbles and 5 white marbles. What is the probability that a marble selected at random will be either green or white? (12/20)

b) A card is withdrawn from a deck of playing cards. What is the probability that it will be either a face card (Jack, King, Queen) or a Spade? (22/52)

Practice Problem 5.2

In the month of August in Toronto, the chance of getting rainfall on any given day of the month is 20%. An exhibition is being planned during this month that may last for 5 days. What is the probability of having?
   a) All five days are dry (33%)
   b) At least one of five days is wet (67%)
   c) More than one day is wet (26%)

Practice Problem 5.3

What is the probability of a 25-year flood occurring only once in 25 years? (38%)

Practice Problem 5.4

A cofferdam has been built to protect homes in a flood plain area. The cofferdam was built for the 20-y flood. The channel project will require 3 years to complete. Find the probability that

a) The dam will be overtopped at least once during the three-year period. (0.14)

b) The dam will be overtopped only in the third year. (0.045)

Practice Problem 5.5

What return period must a Water Resources Engineer use in her design of a critical underpass drain if she is willing to accept only a 10% risk that flooding will occur in the next five years? (48 years)

Practice Problem 5.6

The average time interval between tornados striking the region of Southern Ontario is approximately 5 years. What is the probability that
   a) No tornado will occur in the next 10 years? (11%)
   b) One tornado will occur in the next 10 years? (17%)
   c) More than one tornado will occur in the next 10 years? (72%)

Practice Problem 5.7

In Algoma district, the mean and standard deviation of annual precipitation respectively are 900 mm and 100 mm. If the annual precipitation of less than 750 mm is considered a dry (drought) year, what is the return period of such an event? (16 y)

Practice Problem 5.8

For southern belt of America 2-year and 10-year rainfall are 1600 mm and 1750 mm respectively. Assuming annual rainfall follows normal distribution, what amount of annual rainfall can be expected once every 25 years? (1800 mm)

Practice Problem 5.9

The 10-year and 25-year floods of Crystal Creek are 65 m³/s and 85 m³/s respectively. Assuming the flood data is normally distributed; calculate the flow of a 100-year flood. (110 m³/s)

Practice Problem 5.10

For the data of Example Problem 5-10 estimate the 100-y flood using normal, Lognormal and Pearson type III distributions. (11900 m³/s, 28200 m³/s, 14000 m³/s)

Practice Problem 5.11

For the data of Example Problem 5-10, assuming log normal distribution, determine the period of a flood exceeding 10000 m³/s. (8 years)

Practice Problem 5.12

The monthly rainfall records of a meteriological station for a year are given in the table below. Work out the arithmetic mean and standard deviation?(11.6 mm, 52.3 mm)

Month	J	F	M	A	M	J	J	A	S	O	N	D
mm	12	10	5	1	2	8	15	25	22	15	12	12

Practice Problem 5.13

From annual rainfall records of past 25 years, the mean is 650 mm and standard deviation is 70 mm. Assuming rainfall data is normally distributed, find the probability that annual rainfall in a given year is:
  a. In the range of 700-800 mm (22%)
  b. At least 700 mm (24%)

Practice Problem 5.14

At a certain meteorological station, probability of receiving rainfall depth of 250 mm or more on a single day is 2.0%. Determine the probability of
  a. Exactly one occurrence in 15 years (23%)
  b. At least once in 25 years. (40%)

Practice Problem 5.15

From the annual series data of Beats River, logarithms of flood flows were analysed and results are as follows:
Mean = 3.60   Std. dev. = 0.143   Coefficient of skewness = 0.043.
Estimate the 100 year and 1000-year flood flows based on
  i. Log Pearson Type III distribution. (9000 m³/s, 12000 m³/s)
  ii. Log Normal distribution (8600 m³/s, 1100 m³/s)

Practice Problem 5.16

A bridge has expected life of 30 years and is designed based on 100-y flood.
  i. What is the risk that bridge would experience larger flood? (26%)
  ii. What return period flood must be used to reduce the risk to 10%? (290 y)

Practice Problem 5.17

The mean, standard deviation and skew of the log-transformed discharges in m³/s for the Sigma River are 2.09, 0.294 and 0.20, respectively. Estimate the 10 years and 100 years flood flows using Log Pearson Type III distribution. (300 m³/s, 620 m³/s)

Practice Problem 5.18

A dam is to be built for a design life period of 50 years. If the desired reliablitiy is 90%, what must be the retun period of flood used to design the dam? If the risk is reduced to 5.0%, find the return period of the design flood? (475 y, 975 y)

Practice Problem 5.19

Analysis of annual flood series yielded a sample mean of 1000 m³/s and standard deviation of 450 m³/s. Estimate the design flood of a structure to provide 90% reliability over 50-y period. Assume data is normally distributed. (2300 m³/s)

Practice Problem 5.20

For a river, based on lognormal distribution 50-y and 100-y flood respectively are 450 m³/s and 600 m³/s. Find the magnitude of 1000-y flood? (1300 m³/s)

Practice Problem 5.21

How long must a gauging station be maintained so that the probability of observing a flood equal or greater than 10-y flood is 80%? (15 y)

Practice Problem 5.22

A maximum one day rainfall of 300 mm or more at a meteriological station shows a return period of 50 years. Determine the probability that
  i. This may happen exactly once in 25 successive years (31%)
  ii. More than once in 25 successive years (40%)

Practice Problem 5.23

Annual precipitation data series is shown in the following table:

Year	1	2	3	4	5	6	7	8	9	10
mm	142	133	148	125	143	153	130	150	147	129

Year	11	12	13	14	15
mm	141	137	171	169	127

  i. Find mean, std. deviation and skewness(143 mm, 13.8 mm, 0.753)
  ii. Assumig that data follows normal distribution, find the probability that in a given year precipitation will be less than 130 mm(17%)
  iii. Probability that in a given year precipitation will be more than 150 mm. (31%)

Practice Problem 5.24

Using lognormal distribution, 25-y and 50-y floods are 420 m³/s and 550 m³/s respectively. What is the magnitude of a 100-y flood? (710 m³/s)

Practice Problem 5.25

What return period of a design storm to be used for the design if the acceptable risk is 20% that storm will occur in the next 25 years? (113 y)

Review Questions

1. It is assumed that peak flood follows lognormal distribution. Mean and standard deviation of the log values of flood peaks are 3.21 and 0.45, respectively. What is the magnitude of a 2-y flood?
   a) 3.21   b) 3.66   c) 1600   d) 4600

2. The probability of getting a Jack or an Ace when dealing a card
   a) 1/13   b) 2/13   c) 3/13   d) 4/13

3. The probability of a 100-y flood occurring in a given year is
   a) 0.1%   b) 10%   c) 1.0%   d) 100%

4. The probability of a flood is 10% and that of a power failure is 3%. Assuming the two events are independent, the probability that both will occur together is
   a) 0.3   b) 0.1   c) 0.003   d) 0.03

5. The probability of a 10-y flood occurring in the second year is
   a) 8%   b) 10%   c) 1%   d) 90%

6. The number of combinations of selecting 3 years out of 4 years is
   a) 4   b) 12   c) 6   d) 18

7. The annual rainfall data is normally distributed with a mean of 900 mm and a standard deviation of 100 mm. What are the chances of receiving rainfall of less than 800 mm in a given year?
   a) 0.34   b) 0.68   c) 0.16   d) 0.84

8. The probability that a 100-y flood will not occur in a given year is
   a) 10%   b) 9%   c) 99%   d) 99.9%

9. The plotting position of a flood with a rank of 3 in a 20-year time series is
   a) 1/13   b) 1/20   c) 3/20   d) 1/7

10. The probability that a 10-y flood will not occur in a 10-year period is
    a) 0.001   b) 0.35   c) 0.10   d) 0.65

11. Which one of the following is a discrete random variable?
    a) Runoff volume
    b) Discharge rate
    c) Annual rainfall
    d) Number of floods

12. Which one of the following assumptions is not valid for Binomial distribution?
   a) Two outcomes per trial
   b) Two trials per experiment
   c) Independent trials
   d) Probability remains same

13. The skew of a distribution measures
   a) Symmetry   b) spread   c) Centre   d) All

14. A 25-year flood will occur _____ in a 100-year period.
   a) Exactly four times
   b) Only once
   c) On an average four times
   d) Only four times

15. The distribution of peak flood is assumed Lognormal. If the mean and standard deviation of the Log of the data values are 3.21 and 0.45 respectively, the 2-year peak discharge is
   a) 3.21   b) 3.66   c) 1622   d) 4571

16. A rainfall event in a region is found to have a return period of 50 years. What are chances that event of this magnitude or larger magnitude will not occur during the next 50 years?
   a) 64%   b) 21%   c) 36%   d) 47%

17. Which of the following relationship will give the probable maximum depth of precipitation over a watershed?
   a) $P = \bar{P} + ks$
   b) $P = ks$
   c) $P = \bar{P}e^{-ks}$
   d) $P = \overline{Pm}$

18. Assuming hydrologic data follows normal distribution, what is the magnitude of a 2-y event?
   a) Std. dev., s   b) Mean +s   c) Mean - s   d) Mean

19. A normal variable has a mean of 4.0 units and standard deviation of 1.0 unit. What is the probability of exceedances of an event equal to 5.0 units?
   a) 68%   b) 16%   c) 34%   d) 84%

20. How much area lies under the standard normal curve between mean and one standard unit?
   a) 95%   b) 68%   c) 34%   d) 16%

21. What is the risk of failure that a 50-y flood will occur at least once in the

next 10 years?
a) 10% b) 18% c) 27% d) 38%

22. Skewness coefficient of normal probability distribution is
    a) <zero b) > Zero c) =Zero d) one

23. Which of the following is a discrete distribution?
    a) Binomial b) Non-normal c) Log-normal d) All

24. Annual precipitation data follows normal distribution, what is the probability of annual precipitation exceeding the population mean?
    a) Nil b) 50% c) 34% d) 99%

25. Annual flood series of n data is arranged in descending order. What is the return period of a flood exceeding magnitude with rank m?
    a) m/n b) m/(n+1) c) (n+1)/m d) n/(m+1)

26. What is the return period a flood that a designer must use in design of dam, if the acceptable risk is 5.0% over a period of 25 years?
    a) 100 y b) 290 y c) 490 d) 990 y

27. A structure is designed based on 100-y flood. What are the chances that flood would not occur in 50 years of design life of the structure?
    a) 99% b) 81% c) 61% d) 55%

28. Standard deviation is
    a) Square of variance
    b) Square root of variance
    c) Square of deviation
    d) Square root of dispersion

29. Coefficient of variation is standard deviation
    a) Squared b) /Mean c) ×Mean d) Cubed

30. For symmetrical distribution, which of the parameter is zero?
    a) Variance b) Std. Deviation c) Avg. Deviation d) Skewness

6 Watershed Characteristics

A **watershed** or a drainage basin is considered the laboratory of hydrologic cycle. It is the **black box** (system) that converts rainfall (input) to runoff (output). For a given storm, the watershed characteristics control the:
- Rate of runoff generation
- Concentration of runoff
- Volume of runoff

All of these characteristics are depicted in the shape of a hydrograph. Thus, key to predicting runoff response from a catchment basin is understanding of the basin itself.

This definition permits the selection of any drainage outlet desired. One can move the drainage outlet up the drainage system or down the drainage system to any location of interest (makes possible the sub-basin studies). By definition, any point on the main drainage system can be selected as the basin outlet. Thus, a basin is defined with respect to the outlet. The physical boundary of a drainage basin is called the **drainage divide**.

The watershed area includes all the points that lie above the elevation of the outlet and within the drainage divide that separates adjacent watersheds. Other terms synonymous with drainage basin are watershed, catchment, basin, river basin, runoff area, and stream basin. Watershed, catchment and basin are most commonly used terms by hydrologists. Watersheds can be classified based on size, mean slope, length, land use, etc. Two hydrologically meaningful criteria are size and land us

6.1 Classification of Watersheds by Size

Three types of watersheds are distinguished according to size:
1. Small size: < 250 km^2
2. Medium size: between 250 km^2 -2500 km^2
3. Large: >2500 km^2

This classification is vague, but the implication is in terms of spatial heterogeneity and dampening (averaging) of hydrological processes. Runoff generation on these watersheds can be considered in two phases: land phase, and channel phase. Each phase has its own storage characteristics.

6.1.1 Large Watersheds

Large watersheds have well-developed channel networks and channel phase, and, thus, channel storage is dominant. Because of large drainage area, they are less sensitive to high-intensity rainfalls of short duration as is the case of small watersheds.

6.1.2 Small Watersheds

In comparison to large watersheds, small watersheds have dominant land phase and overland flow, have relatively less conspicuous channel phase. They are highly sensitive to high-intensity, short-duration rainfalls. Two watersheds of the same size may behave very differently if they do not have similar land and channel phases. Small watersheds are usually least heterogeneous and large watersheds are most homogeneous. As the watershed size increases, storage increases and averaging of hydrologic processes increases as a result. The effect of averaging is to linearize the watershed behavior. On the average, small watersheds are more nonlinear than large watersheds. Small watersheds are, within a given drainage system, represented by upland areas where rainfall and runoff depths are usually greater and an extensive, well-developed channel system is lacking.

6.2 Watersheds Classification by Land Use

Land use defines exploitation of watershed. Accordingly, watersheds can be classified as agricultural, urban, mountainous, forest, desert, coastal or marsh, or mixed; a combination of two or more of the previous classifications. These watersheds behave hydrologically so differently that different branches of hydrology have arisen: -
1. Urban watersheds
2. Agricultural watersheds
3. Forest watersheds
4. Mountainous watersheds
5. Desert watersheds
6. Coastal watersheds
7. Wetland or marsh watersheds

6.2.1 Urban Watersheds

An urban watershed is dominated by buildings, roads, streets, pavements, and parking lots. These features reduce the infiltrating land area and increase imperviousness. Because drainage systems are artificially built, the natural pattern of water flow is substantially altered. For a given rainfall event, interception and depression storage can be significant but infiltration is considerably reduced and so is the case with evaporation. As a result, there is pronounced increase in runoff and pronounced decrease in soil erosion. Thus, an urban watershed is more vulnerable to flooding if the drainage system is inadequate. Depending upon the degree of urbanization, topography, and drainage facility, production of runoff varies for different parts of the watershed. If lakes, ponds and parks are numerous in the watershed, evaporation will be significant and may compensate for reduction in evaporation elsewhere due to impervious land surfaces. Once a watershed is urbanized, its land use is almost fixed, and its hydrologic behaviour changes due to changes in precipitation. If small urbanizing watershed is considered by itself, then runoff peak increases and its time of occurrence decreases with urbanization. This is because as development proceeds, there are more pavements, sidewalks, houses, parking lots, storm sewers, channels, etc., which all decrease infiltration and increase runoff. When an entire complex watershed considered, then all runoff peak may actually be reduced because its roads, bridges, tunnels, etc., can cause impoundments that dampen the runoff hydrograph.

6.2.2 Agricultural Watersheds

An agricultural watershed experiences perhaps the most dynamically significant land-use change. Changing land use and the treatment (cultivated land, fallow, row crop, small grain crop, rotation meadow, rotation, straight row, contoured, grass land, meadows, woods and forests, and gardens) usually lead to increased infiltration, increased erosion, and or decreased runoff. Depression storage is also increased by agricultural operations. When the fields are barren, falling raindrops tend to compact the soil and infiltration is reduced. There is lesser development of streams in agricultural watersheds, for small channels formed by erosion and runoffs are obliterated by tillage operations. The soil texture and structure are altered by regular application of organic and/or inorganic manure. This, in turn, leads to changed infiltration characteristics. Evapotranspiration constitutes the principal loss of water from agricultural point of view.

6.2.3 Forest Watersheds

The hydrological behavior of forest watersheds is quite different from that of agricultural or urban watersheds. Interception is significant, and evapotranspiration is a dominant component of the hydrologic cycle. In forest watersheds, the ground is usually littered with leaves, stems, branches, wood, etc. Consequently, when it rains, the water is held by the trees and the ground cover and has greater opportunity to infiltrate. The subsurface flow becomes dominant and there are times when there is little to no surface runoff. There is greater recharge of groundwater. Because forests resist flow of water, the peak discharge is reduced, although inundation of the ground may be increased. This reduces flooding and flood damage downstream. Due to reduced surface-potential, stream development is much less. Plants and trees provide good protective cover to soil from erosion.

6.2.4 Mountainous Watersheds

The landscape of these watersheds is predominantly mountainous. Because of higher altitudes, such watersheds receive considerable snowfall. By and large, such watersheds have substantial vegetation, such that in some cases, these could be considered as forest watersheds also. Interception is significant. Due to steep gradient and relatively less porous soil, infiltration is less and surface runoff is dominantly high for a given rainfall event. Flash floods are a common occurrence. The areas downstream of the mountains are vulnerable to flooding whenever there is a heavy rainfall in the mountains. Flooding in valleys downstream may be even more severe when there is rain in mountainous on the top of snow. There is little to virtually no change in land use. Erosion is minimal if the mountainous are rocky. Sliding and collapsing of slopes are not uncommon occurrences during periods of heavy precipitation. Due to snow melt, water yield is significant even during spring and summer, which can be used for water supply. Recharge of groundwater is small, and evapotranspiration is considerable.

6.2.5 Desert Watersheds

There is little to virtually no vegetation in desert, watersheds. The soil is mostly sandy and little annual rainfall occurs. Sand dunes and sand mounds are formed by blowing winds. Stream development is minimal. Whenever there is little rainfall, most of it is absorbed by the porous soil, some of it evaporates, and the remaining runs off only to be soaked in during its journey. There is limited opportunity for groundwater recharge due to limited rainfall.

6.2.6 Costal Watersheds

The watersheds in coastal areas may partly be urban and are in dynamic contact with the sea. Their hydrology is considerably influenced by backwater from wave and tidal action. Usually, these watersheds receive high rainfall, mostly of cyclonic type, do not have channel control in flow, and are vulnerable to severe local flooding. Coastal erosion is a continuing problem due to tidal action, and land-use change is common. The water table is high, and saltwater intrusion threatens the health of coastal aquifers, which usually are a source of water supply. The land gradient is small, drainage is slow, and the soil along the coast has a considerable sand component.

6.2.7 Wetland Watersheds

Such lands are almost flat and are comprised of swamps, marshes, water courses, etc. They have rich wildlife and plenty of vegetation. Evaporation is dominant, for water is no limiting factor to satisfy evapotranspiration demand. Rainfall is normally high and infiltration is minimal. Most of the rainfall becomes runoff, which discharges slowly and storage is dominant. Erosion is also minimal, except along the coast. The flood hydrograph peaks gradually and lasts for a long time.

6.3 Watershed Characteristics

6.3.1 Drainage Area

The **drainage area** includes all areas within the vertical projection of the drainage boundary. Due to the effects of sub-surface flow, the watershed divide may not strictly follow the topographic divide. However, for practical purposes, the topographic divide is considered the hydrologic divide.

In general, the larger the catchment area, greater is the runoff volume. Depending on the type and intensity of the storm, only a portion of the area may generate runoff. Some drainage basins contain, within their boundaries, areas that do not contribute runoff to the drainage system. This may include lakes and swamps where drainage infiltrates into the soil.

6.3.2 Basin Shape

A multitude of dimensionless parameters have been proposed to define watershed shape. Some of the commonly used parameters are; form factor, shape factor, elongation ratio, and compactness coefficient. These factors involve some combination of watershed length (L), area (A) and/or perimeter (P). *Length of the watershed is usually defined as the farthest horizontal distance as measured from the outlet.*

6.3.3 Form Factor

A quantitative description of the shape of catchment is provided by the parameter called **form factor**. **Shape factor** is the reciprocal of the form factor. The form factor of elongated watersheds will be relatively smaller. Hence a low form factor describes a catchment with delayed runoff response.

$$Form\ Factor,\ K_F = \frac{A}{L^2}$$

6.3.4 Compact Coefficient

Compact coefficient is the ratio of the perimeter of a watershed to the circumference of a circle whose area is equal to that of the watershed.

$$Compact\ Coefficient, K_C = \frac{P}{2\sqrt{A\pi}} = \frac{0.28P}{\sqrt{A}}$$

The compact coefficient of a watershed approaches unity as the watershed shape approaches that of a circle. The concentration of runoff from drainage basins of equal size is greatly influenced by the distribution of the area with respect to the distance from the outlet. Compact coefficient is an index of the area distribution. Other factors considered constant, the runoff from an elongated watershed (high K_C) will be delayed significantly. The runoff concentration will be faster in case of compact watersheds.

6.3.5 Stream Order

Drainage area may be characterized by the highest order stream/channel. The **first order** streams are those that have no tributaries. The junction of two first order channels form a second order channel. The order of the outlet is the highest for that watershed and the watershed is also described by this order. In relatively homogeneous regions, the basin area and other characteristics are closely correlated with the basin order. Those watersheds with higher order naturally would have quicker response.

6.3.6 Drainage Density

Drainage density, D_d is defined as the total length of drainage channels per unit area. Obviously, it indicates the effectiveness of the basin to drain the area. Drainage basins with high drainage densities indicate quick response. In general, runoff increases as drainage density increases. Numerical values range from as low as 2/km to as high as 800/km. Large scale maps result in greater drainage length because more details are shown.

$$\text{Drainage density}$$
$$D_d = \frac{Total\ length\ of\ all\ channels}{Area\ of\ the\ watershed} = \frac{L_d}{A}$$

Example Problem 6.1

Calculate the compact coefficient of a watershed with a shape approximating a rectangle with the length equal to nine times the width.

Given:

Assuming width is x. $A = 9x^2$ and $P = 20x$

Solution:

$$K_c = \frac{0.28P}{\sqrt{A}} = \frac{0.28 \times 20x}{\sqrt{9x^2}} = 1.86 = \underline{1.9}$$

6.4 Relief Features

The **catchment relief** is the elevation difference between two reference points. Maximum relief is the difference between the highest point in the catchment divide and the lowest point - the catchment outlet.

The **relief ratio** is the ratio of maximum catchment relief to the longest horizontal straight distance measured in a direction parallel to that of the principal watercourse. Relief ratio determines the degree of erosion in a given catchment.

The **hypsometric curve** is a dimensionless curve of elevation versus the catchment area above that elevation.

$$\text{Ordinate:}\ \frac{H_i}{H_{max}} = \frac{Z_i - Z_{min}}{Z_{max} - Z_{min}} \quad \text{Abcissae:}\ \frac{A_i}{A} = \frac{A_i}{\Sigma A_i}$$

Where H_i = Height of ith contour A_i = Area below the ith contour

On the hypsometric curve, outlet of the catchment (Z_{min}) refers to 100% area and 0% of the maximum height. The highest point (Z_{max}) in the divide refers to 0% area and 100% height. A planimeter or other digital device is used to measure the area between two adjacent contours.

The **median elevation** of the catchment is obtained by reading the percentage height corresponding to the 50% area. That is to say, median divides the watershed surface in two equal halves. How the area within a catchment is distributed between contours is of interest when studying the spatial variation of hydrologic variables such as precipitation, vegetative cover and snowfall. Experience shows that precipitation is usually higher at higher elevations.

Example Problem 6.2

From the contour map of catchment of area of 149 km², measurements are made as shown in **Table 6.1**. Develop a hypsometric curve for this catchment.

Solution:

Hypsometric curve is shown in **Figure 6.1**. Median height is read to be 27% of the maximum height or an elevation of 2026 m.

Figure 6.1 Hypsometric Curve (Ex. Prob. 6.2)

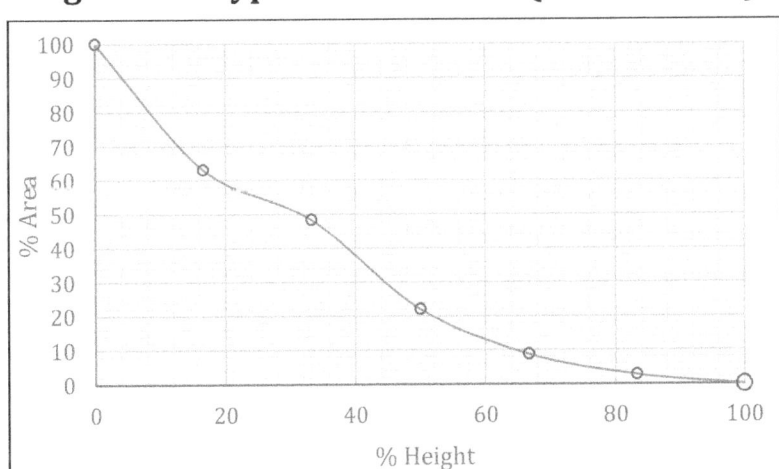

Table 6.1 Hypsometric Curve Data (Ex. Prob. 6.2)

Elevation, m	Height, m	% H	Area, km²	% Area
2010	0	0.0	149	100.0
2020	10	16.7	94	63.1
2030	20	33.3	72	48.3
2040	30	50.0	33	22.1
2050	40	66.7	13	8.7
2060	50	83.3	4	2.7
2070	60	100.0	0	0.0

Example Problem 6.3

The following snow chart and hypsometric data have been measured in a certain catchment. Calculate the catchment snow-water equivalent.

Given:

Elevation, m	1210	1230	1250	1270	1290	1310
Area below, %	0	39	64	81	94	100
Water Equiv., mm	3	4	5	5	7	8

Solution:

Sub-area for a snow course is the difference in the values of cumulative area corresponding to a given snow-course band. As shown in the following spreadsheet, weighted snow water equivalent for each band of area is calculated by multiplying the average values of the water equivalent multiplied by the percent area in the band.

Table 6.2 Worksheet (Ex. Prob. 6.3)

Band	Avg. mm	%Area	Weighted, mm
1	3.5	39	1.37
2	4.5	25	1.13
3	5.0	17	0.85
4	6.0	13	0.78
5	7.5	6	0.45
	Σ =	100	4.57

6.5 Channel Slope/Gradient

Other measures of catchment relief are based on stream and channel characteristics. The longitudinal profile of a channel is a plot of elevation of the channel bed versus horizontal distance. **Channel slope** is the ratio of elevation difference to horizontal distance. As one would expect the channel slope is steeper at the **head end** side and decreases in the downstream direction. The longitudinal profile of streams and rivers are usually concave upward, that is they show a persistent decrease in channel gradient in the downstream direction.

6.5.1 Gross slope (S_1)

Slope of the main channel can be as high as 10% for very steep mountain streams to as low as 5.0×10^{-6} m/m (5.0 mm/km) for some tidal rivers. To express the channel slope as one value, three expressions can be used. **Slope**, S_1 is called the **gross slope**, which is the total drop in elevation divided by the total channel length, L_c.

6.5.2 Mean Slope (S_2)

Mean slope, S_2 is more representative of the channel gradient. It is determined such that the area between the average slope line and the stream profile are equal. Area under the S_2 slope line is area of triangle with height H and length L. calculations of a longitudinal profile are illustrated in **Example Problem 6.4**.

6.5.3 Equivalent Slope (S_3)

S_3 **or equivalent slope** is the most representative and is defined as the slope of a uniform channel that is equivalent in length to the longest watercourse and has the same travel time. To calculate this slope, the channel is divided into n sub-reaches and a slope is calculated for each sub-reach. From the principles of an open channel hydraulics, we know that the time of flow travel is inversely proportional to the square root of the channel slope, thus:

Gross, Mean and Equivalent slope

$$S_1 = \frac{H}{L_c} = \frac{Z_{max} - Z_{min}}{L_c} \qquad S_2 = \frac{H}{L} = \frac{2A}{L^2} \qquad \frac{L_C}{\sqrt{S_3}} = \sum \frac{L_i}{\sqrt{S_i}}$$

Where L_i and S_i represent the length and slope of each sub-reach.

Example Problem 6.4

Given a longitudinal profile with elevations and distances shown in **Table 6.3**. Calculate the gross slope, the mean slope and the equivalent slope.

Solution:

Sample of Calculations (1st reach)

Area and segment slope calculations are shown in **Table 6.3**

$$S_i = \frac{(\Delta Z)_i}{L_i} = \frac{(405-400)m}{5.0 \; km} \times \frac{km}{1000 \; m} \times 100\% = 0.10\%$$

$$\frac{L_i}{\sqrt{S_i}} = \frac{5.0 \; km}{\sqrt{\frac{0.10}{100}}} \times \frac{1000 \; m}{km} = 1.58 \times 10^5 \; m$$

$$A_i = H_i \times L_i = 2.5 \; m \times 5.0 \; km \times \frac{1 km}{1000 \; m} = 1.25 \times 10^{-2} \; km^2$$

Longitudinal profile is shown in **Fig. 6.2**

Table 6.3 Excel Worksheet (Ex. Prob. 6.4)

L	Z	H	L_i	ΔZ	H_i	S_i	$L_i/\sqrt{S_i}$	A_i
km	m	m	km	m	m	%	km	km²
0	400	0.0				0.00		
5	405	5.0	5.0	5.0	2.50	0.10	158.1	0.013
10	425	25.0	5.0	20.0	15.00	0.40	79.1	0.075
15	465	65.0	5.0	40.0	45.00	0.80	55.9	0.225
20	550	150.0	5.0	85.0	107.50	1.70	38.3	0.538
						$\Sigma =$	331.4	0.850

Slope Calculations

$$S_1 = \frac{H_{max}}{L_C} = \frac{150 \; m}{20 \; km} \times \frac{km}{1000m} \times 100\% = 0.7500 = \underline{0.75\%}$$

$$S_2 = \frac{2A}{L_C^2} = \frac{2 \times 0.85 \; km^2}{(20 \; km)^2} \times 100\% = 0.425 = \underline{0.43\%}$$

$$S_3 = \left(\frac{L_C}{\Sigma(L_i/\sqrt{S_i})}\right)^2 = \left(\frac{20 \; km}{331 \; km}\right)^2 = 0.0041 = \underline{0.41\%}$$

Figure 6.2 Longitudinal Profile (Ex. Prob. 6.4)

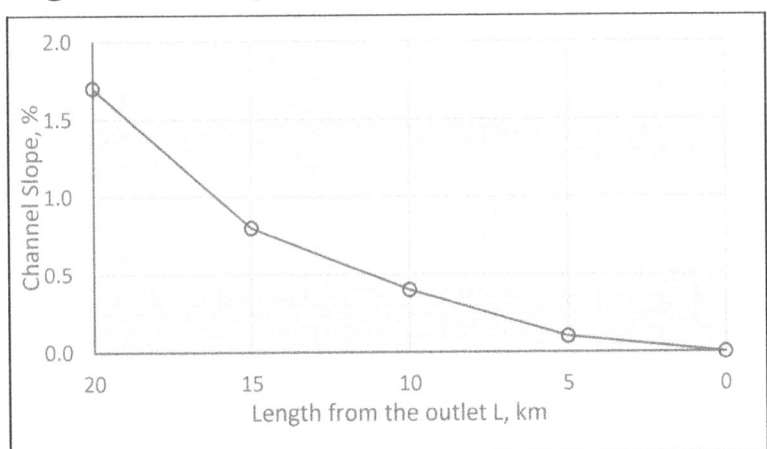

6.6 Basin Slope

Basin slope is a dominant factor in determining the velocity of overland flow. Land slope varies greatly from point to point within the drainage basin. Horton has presented a method of determining the land slope. A modified version of Horton's method involves representing the drainage area by a grid system on its topographic map. The elevation contours are assumed to be at the same contour interval, CI. Each horizontal grid line is measured between its intersection with the watershed boundary, and the total length of grid line segments is obtained. Then the number of intersections of each grid line with the contour lines is obtained and the sum of these intersections, N, is calculated. The same is done for vertical grid lines.

Horizontal Slope, Vertical slope, and Basin slope

$$S_H = \frac{N_H \times CI}{L_H} \qquad S_V = \frac{N_V \times CI}{L_V} \qquad S_B = \frac{(S_H + S_V)}{2}$$

Discussion Questions

1. What are different parameters used to describe relief features of a watershed?
2. Define drainage intensity and how it is related to runoff rate and runoff volume
3. How are watersheds classified based on area. Compare small watersheds with larger watersheds.
4. Classify the watersheds based on land use. Compare the following:
   a. Rural watershed with urban watershed
   b. Agricultural watershed with forest watershed
   c. Mountainous watersheds and coastal watersheds
5. Differentiate between watershed slope and channel slope.
6. Describe three types of slopes used to determine channel gradient.
7. What is a hypsometric curve? Discuss its shape and properties.
8. What are the common parameters to describe the shape of a watershed. How does shape of the watershed influence time distribution of runoff?
9. Wetlands play significant role in regulation of runoff generation from a watershed. Comment.
10. How does stream order affect the time distribution and volume of runoff?

Practice Problems

Practice Problem 6.1
Find compact coefficient of a watershed with the shape of a square. (1.13)

Practice Problem 6.2
The following data have been obtained from the contour map of a catchment with a total area of 135 km². Prepare a hypsometric curve and determine the median elevation. (530 m)

Elevation Z_i, m	510	520	530	540	550	560	570
Area above A_i, km²	135	85	65	30	12	40	

Practice Problem 6.3
Data from snow survey is presented below. Determine the weighted snow water equivalent. (9.8 mm)

Elevation (m)	1000	1500	2000	2500	3000
Area (km²)	0	255	432	519	605
WE (mm)	0	0	8	22	30

Practice Problem 6.4
Given the following longitudinal profile of a river channel, calculate gross slope S_1, mean slope S_2, and equivalent slope S_3.

Distance (km)	0	50	100	150	200	250	300
Elevation (m)	10	30	60	100	150	220	350

($S_1 = 0.113\%$, $S_2 = 0.076\%$, $S_3 = 0.086\%$)

Practice Problem 6.5
The main watercourse is 1.5 km long. The characteristics of two main reaches are given below. Estimate the time of concentration. (50 min)

Reach#	L, m	S, %	R_h, m	n
1	900	0.10	0.50	0.04
2	600	0.30	0.30	0.05

Review Questions

1. Characteristics of watershed does not affect which of the following?
   a) Rate of runoff b) Concentration of runoff
   c) Volume of runoff d) Rainfall rate

2. Based on area, small watersheds have area less than
   a) 50 km² b) 100 km² c) 200 km² d) 250 km²

3. Large watersheds are categorised with area exceeding
   a) 250 km² b) 1000 km² c) 2500 km² d) 5000 km²

4. Which location on the watershed surface has lowest elevation
   a) Centroid b) Outlet c) 50% of area d) 75% of area

5. Which of the following is true about watershed boundary?
   a) Defined by the topography b) Unique for each watershed
   c) Moves with location of outlet d) all

6. Which of the following watersheds are more sensitive to intense storms of small duration?
   Large b) Small c) Forest d) Rural

7. In which of the following type of watersheds natural pattern of drainage is significantly altered?
   a) Urban b) Agricultural c) Rural d) Forest

8. Which of the following falls in the category of land treatment
   a) Row crops b) Cultivated c) Fallow d) All

9. In which of the following type of watersheds flash flooding is more common?
   a) Coastal b) Agricultural c) Mountainous d) Forest

10. Stream pattern is less developed in this type of watersheds.
    a) Medium size b) Agricultural c) Mountainous d) Forest

11. Flood hydrograph from this type of watersheds have smaller and flat peaks and longer time base.
    a) Urban b) Agricultural c) Mountainous d) Forest

12. In which of the following type of watersheds, sub-surface flow is

significant?
a) Urban   b) Agricultural   c) Mountainous   d) Forest

13. For practical purposes, watershed boundary follows
    a) Topographic divide   b) Lowest contour
    c) Stream pattern   d) All

14. Hypsometric curve is a plot of elevation versus
    a) Area above elevation   b) Area below elevation
    c) Length above elevation   d) Length below elevation

15. For a circular watershed, the compact coefficient is
    a) 0   b) 1   c) >1   d) <1

16. What fraction of watershed area falls below the median elevation?
    a) 0%   b) 25%   c) 50%   d) 100%

17. What fraction of watershed area falls below the outlet?
    a) 0%   b) 25%   c) 50%   d) 100%

18. On a hypsometric curve, which point correspond to 0% area?
    a) Watershed outlet   b) Median elevation
    c) Maximum height   d) Minimum height

19. For natural watersheds, the shape of a typical hypsometric curve is
    a) Convex   b) Concave   c) Straight   d) Logarithmic

20. Stream order is highest for the _____ of a watershed.
    a) Watershed outlet   b) Median elevation
    c) First stream in the upper half d) First stream above outlet

21. Which one of the following characteristics is not a measure of the watershed shape?
    a) Elongation ratio   b) Form ratio
    c) Relief ratio   d) All are possible

22. Which of the following type of channel slopes yields more accurate time of travel?
    a) Gross   b) Mean   c) Equivalent   d) Hydraulic

23. Which of the following characteristic of a watershed strongly influences the volume of runoff?
    a) Channel length   b) Basin area   c) Basin slope   d) Basin shape

24. Which measure of watershed characteristics has the dimension of inverse of length?
    a)   Drainage density   b)   Elongation ratio
    c)   Relief ratio   d)   Compact coefficient

25. For a given storm, large peak flows happen in case of
    a)   Low drainage density   b)   High drainage density
    c)   Elongated watershed   d)   Low relief

26. The runoff rate or distribution of runoff is influenced by the
    a)   Drainage density   b)   Shape of the watershed
    c)   Channel slope   d)   All of these

27. Watershed relief refers to
    a)   Drainage density   b)   Elevation difference
    c)   Basin slope   d)   Shape of the watershed

28. When a transparent grid sheet (each grid = 1 cm²) is laid over a watershed map (1:10000), the grid count is 26. The area of the watershed is
    a) 26 ha   b) 2600 m³   c) 26 km²   d) 260 ha

29. Overland flow generation will increase with an increase in
    a)   Basin slope   b)   Channel slope
    c)   Drainage density   d)   Stream order

30. Which of the following type of slope is most representative of channel gradient?
    a)   Gross slope   b)   Mean slope
    c)   Equivalent slope   d)   Basin slope

7 Hydrologic Abstractions

Hydrologic abstractions are the processes acting to reduce total precipitation. In other words, total precipitation less abstraction is **effective precipitation**. Effective precipitation eventually becomes runoff. Thus, the difference between total rainfall and **storm runoff** is the depth abstracted by the catchment. The main processes responsible for abstraction of precipitation are interception, depression storage, detention storage, infiltration and evapotranspiration.

7.1 Interception Storage

Interception storage is the amount of water held on vegetative and other surfaces attached to, but above the watershed surface.
- The water held in interception storage can only leave by evaporation.
- This storage is usually filled during the first part of a rain sequence.
- The maximum amount of interception storage on vegetated areas from an uninterrupted rain is often between 0.5 mm and 4 mm.
- In calculating the response of a watershed to rain it is often possible to make successful allowances for interception by assuming the first few mm of rain will be taken up in interception and thus eliminate it from input to the watershed or initial abstraction. Intervals within the daytime period of a storm during which rain ceases may require additional subtraction for interception when rain resumes.
- *Through fall* is the precipitation that reaches the ground by first passing through vegetative cover.
- The interception losses are very significant in the case of light storms; for heavy storms, interception losses usually make up a small fraction of the total rainfall.

7.2 Depression Storage

Depression storage is water lying in indentations of the watershed surface at elevations at or below the level of the lowest point in the perimeter of the indentation.
- The water held in depression storage can leave by infiltration into the ground or by evaporation.
- The size of depressions involved in this storage varies greatly depending partly on the total watershed extent and includes the scale

of areas from a few m² to many km² in large watersheds in which closed depressions exist.
- Milder is the catchment's relief, greater is the effect of depression storage.
- At the beginning of the storm, depression storage usually plays an active role in abstracting precipitation.
- Depression storage for most catchments is in the range of 10 to 50 mm.
- When developing rainfall-runoff relationships, depression storage is coupled with interception and infiltration (before any runoff begins) and are accounted for as initial abstractions.

7.3 Detention Storage

Detention storage is water that is on the watershed surface and is free to move along a surface flow path to the stream, which provides outflow from the watershed.

- Detention storage is the storage volume, which provides surface runoff after rain, and snowmelt inputs have stopped, and flow recession occurs.
- This storage can be depleted by infiltration and evaporation as well as by surface outflow. Depression and detention storage are significant for overland sheet flow.
- Water present in flowing channels, including any in over bank flood-plain areas, is part of this storage term.
- This storage amount can be related to flow rates in streams during the recession of surface flow rates. In special cases it can be approximated as linear function of such surface flow rates.

7.4 Infiltration

Infiltration is the process of the entry of water into the land surface. Whereas **percolation** is the process of water movement below the ground surface in a vertical direction. If surface conditions are impervious, then the infiltration rate is zero. **Infiltration capacity (f_p)** is the maximum potential rate at which, water can enter into the land surface at a specified point (space) and time.

The major factors affecting the infiltration of water into the soil are initial moisture content, condition of the soil surface, hydraulic conductivity of the soil profile soil texture, soil porosity, degree of swelling of soil colloids, organic matter, vegetative cover, storm duration and viscosity of water.

7.4.1 Infiltration Rate (f)

Infiltration rate is the rate at which water actually is passing downward into the watershed through the watershed surface at a specified location and time.

- The infiltration rate at a point is always less than or equal to the infiltration capacity at that point at the time of observation.
- When the supply rate of water to the watershed surface by rain or snowmelt is less than the infiltration capacity, then the infiltration rate at the point will equal the supply rate.
- Infiltration capacity varies greatly in **time** and **space** over a watershed. For stream and ditch surfaces, roads, impermeable rock outcrops, the infiltration capacity is zero. For areas with some depth of unsaturated soil, or more generally where water movement is into the ground even if the topsoil layer is saturated, the infiltration rate is greater than zero.
- Infiltration rates vary widely, depending on:
    - The condition of land surface, soil structure and soil texture
    - The type and extent of vegetation, storm intensity and duration
    - The antecedent moisture conditions and water temperature

Infiltration at a point can be measured by the use of an infiltrometer. There are two types of infiltrometer: flooding, sprinkler.

7.4.2 Flooding Infiltrometer

A **flooding infiltrometer** can be a single ring infiltrometer or a double ring infiltrometer. A similar arrangement is used to measure infiltration in field irrigation. Metal rings are driven 2 to 5 cm into the ground. The rate, at which water must be supplied to maintain a constant level, typically 5 mm, is taken as a measure of the infiltration rate. Another way is measuring the drop in water depth with time.

An improvement over the single ring infiltrometer is a double ring infiltrometer. In this case, two sets of concentric cylindrical rings of diameters 300 mm and 600 mm are employed. Outer ring is filled with water up to 50 mm to stop the lateral movement of water from the inner ring. Though water level in both the rings is kept the same, measurement of infiltration depth is measured in the inner ring only. In a double ring infiltrometer, infiltration is due to vertical movement only. Hence infiltration measurement can be considered one dimensional. Due to spatial variation, large number of such tests are needed to come up with a reasonable estimate. Except for very small homogeneous areas, this is not very practical. The main disadvantages of flooding-type infiltrometer are:

1. The raindrop-impact effect is not simulated;
2. The driving of tube or rings disturbs the soil structure;
3. The results of a infiltrometer depend to some extent on their size with the larger meters giving fewer rates than the smaller ones; this is due to the border effect.

7.4.3 Sprinkler Infiltrometer

A **sprinkler infiltrometer** also known as rainfall simulator is designed to avoid some of the weaknesses of the flooding infiltrometer. In this case, a simulated rainfall condition is applied over a small plot. The simulated rainfall is continued for as long as necessary to attain an equilibrium runoff condition at the plot outlet. The average infiltration rate is calculated as the difference between the constant rainfall rate and the equilibrium runoff rate. Due to spatial and temporal variations, field measurements are only good for comparative studies. Representative estimates of abstraction due to infiltration are based on rainfall-runoff analysis.

7.4.4 Hydrograph Analysis

Hydrograph analysis can provide more realistic estimates of infiltration capacity for small watersheds with fairly uniform soils. Storm hydrographs for isolated storms are selected. Area under the storm flow hydrograph represents volume of runoff. Knowing the area of watershed, volume of runoff is expressed as runoff depth. Applying the mass balance, precipitation minus runoff represents infiltration. This technique is used to express constant infiltration rate as infiltration index and will be discussed later.

7.4.5 Infiltration Formula

Infiltration rate, f is maximum at the beginning of the storm and gradually decreases as the storm progresses in time. For storms of longer duration, the infiltration rate eventually reaches a constant value, which is referred to as the final or **equilibrium infiltration rate**. Horton (1932) suggested the following exponential equation to model the infiltration process.

Watershed Characteristics

Horton's infiltration equation

$$f = f_c + (f_0 - f_c)e^{-kt}$$

f = instantaneous infiltration rate at time t
f_0, f_c = initial and final infiltration rate
k = rate constant (1/time)

Accumulated or total depth of infiltration after time t can be found by integrating the infiltration equation. This is true only if the rainfall rate exceeds infiltration rate for the time period in question. Cumulative depth can be viewed consisting of two components; constant rate, F_I and variable rate component F_{II}.

Cumulative Infiltration depth

$$F(t) = f_c t + \frac{(f_0 - f_c)(1 - e^{-kt})}{k} = F_I + F_{II}$$

For relatively longer time periods, second term in parentheses becomes negligibly small. Hence in such cases, expression for cumulative depth can be written as follows:

Cumulative depth for longer period

$$F(t) = f_c t + \frac{(f_0 - f_c)}{k}$$

Typical 1-h infiltration for different soils are shown in **Table 7.1**

Table 7.1 Typical Values of f_1 (after 1 hour)

Soil Group	Low (Clays, loam)	Intermediate (loams)	High (Sandy soils)
f_1, mm/h	0.25 - 2.50	2.50 - 12.50	12.50 - 25.0

Example Problem 7.1

Horton's infiltration equation for a particular soil is as follows:

$$f = 12 + 42e^{-t/24} \quad Where \ t = min \ and \ f \ in \ mm/h$$

Applying this expression find infiltration rate and cumulative depth of infiltration at various times and plot the data.

Solution:

k = 2.5 /h or 1/24 = 0.41 /min f_0 = 12 mm/h $f_0 - f_c$ = 42 mm/h

Solution:

Infiltration rate and depths are worked out in an MS Excel worksheet shown in **Table 7.2** and **Fig. 7.1**

Table 7.2 Infiltration Data

Time, min	f, mm/h	F_I	F_{II}	F, mm
0	54.0	0	0.0	0.0
5	46.1	2.5	3.2	5.7
10	39.7	5	5.7	10.7
15	34.5	7.5	7.8	15.3
20	30.3	10	9.5	19.5
25	26.8	12.5	10.9	23.4
30	24.0	15	12.0	27.0
35	21.8	17.5	12.9	30.4
40	19.9	20	13.6	33.6
45	18.4	22.5	14.2	36.7
50	17.2	25	14.7	39.7
55	16.2	27.5	15.1	42.6
60	15.4	30	15.4	45.4
65	14.8	32.5	15.7	48.2
70	14.3	35	15.9	50.9
75	13.8	37.5	16.1	53.6

Figure 7.1 Plot of Infiltration Curves

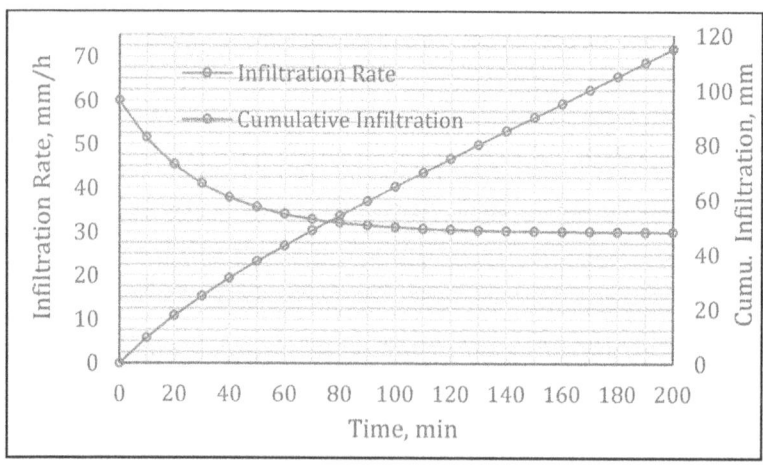

Example Problem 7.2

To determine the infiltration capacity of a soil, data was obtained using a ring infiltrometer. Volume of water added to maintain constant head was observed. Fit Horton type infiltration equation?

Solution:

Infiltration rate is worked out and is shown in column 3 of **Table 7.3**. Data of variable f-fc is plotted, and exponential equation is fitted as shown in **Fig.7.2**. The equation is: f_c = 5.2 mm/h, f_o = 29 mm/h and k = 0.073/min.

Table 7.3 Table of Computations (Ex. Prob. 7.2)

Time, min	mL	Rate f, mm/h	(f-f$_c$) mm/h	Ln(f-fc)
0	0.0	29.00	23.80	3.17
5	105.0	20.07	14.87	2.70
15	69.0	13.19	7.99	2.08
25	50.0	9.56	4.36	1.47
35	39.0	7.45	2.25	0.81
45	33.0	6.31	1.11	0.10
55	30.0	5.73	0.53	-0.63
65	28.0	5.35	0.15	-1.89
75	27.0	5.16		

Figure 7.2 Fitting Exponential Equation

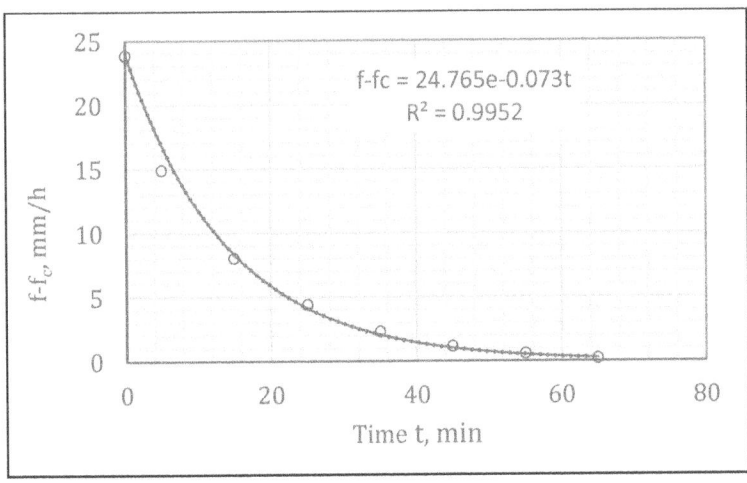

Another way of fitting Horton equation is to plot logarithms of (f-f$_c$) versus time and fitting a linear equation such that intercept is set equal to ln(f$_0$-f$_c$) = ln(23.8) = 3.16 as shown in **Fig. 7.3**. From the straight line is fitted, parameters k = 0.0701/min. which is comparable to the value by the first technique.

Figure 7.3 Fitting Horton Equation

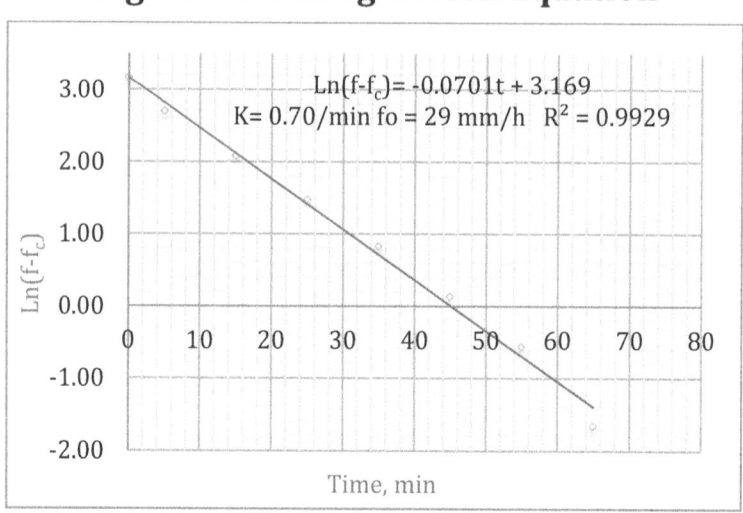

Example Problem 7.3

Estimate the cumulative depth of potential infiltration over a 12-h period. The f$_0$ and f$_c$ respectively are 5 mm/h and 2 mm/h and the rate constant k = 0.8/h.

Given:

f$_0$ = 5.0 mm/h   f$_c$ = 2.0 mm/h   k = 0.8/h   t = 12 h F =?

Solution:

$$F_I = f_c t = \frac{2.0 \text{ mm}}{h} \times 12\ h = 24.0 = 24\ mm$$

$$F_{II} = \frac{(f_0 - f_c)}{k} = \frac{(5-2)\ mm}{h} \times \frac{h}{0.8} = 3.75\ mm$$

$$F(t) = F_I + F_{II} = 24\ mm + 3.75 = 27.75 = \underline{28\ mm}$$

7.4.6 Infiltration Index

Infiltration process is a function of both space and time for a given watershed. For some time, it was thought that the infiltration rate could be observed by taking measurements at various locations on a watershed. To date, this hope has proved illusory and instead of calling it an infiltration rate it is now common to express it as an **infiltration index**, which can be used to calculate storm runoff volume. However, one has to keep in mind that the infiltration index generally assumes that infiltration occurs at some constant or average rate throughout a storm. Consequently, initial rates are underestimated, and final rates are overestimated. It is *more an artefact of calculation than a real physical quantity*. Although, its lower limit for very wet conditions may roughly correspond to the lower limit of the actual infiltration rate averaged over a watershed area.

W-Index

To determine the infiltration index for a given watershed, the amount of storm runoff, R_s from a known storm is estimated by hydrograph analysis. On calculating storm runoff, the infiltration index W is computed. Keep in mind though, W-index represents average rate of infiltration over the duration of the storm. It also includes that period when rainfall intensity is less than infiltration rate and hence no runoff is produced.

W-index
$$W = \frac{(P - R_s - S_S)}{t_D}$$

Where P = total precipitation or rainfall
S_S = Interception and depression storage losses
t_D = total duration of the storm

ф-Index

As compared to W-index, ф-index includes all abstraction or losses including infiltration. It is a rate above which rainfall depth equals storm runoff, what is known as **effective precipitation**. Here, only that time period of storm duration is considered when runoff is produced. This period of rainfall is called effective time period. t_r. Hence, ф-index for a given situation is always greater than W-index. In other words, ф-index can be thought as average rate of abstractions over the duration of effective precipitation.

Phi, φ index

$$\varphi = \frac{(P_f - R_s)}{t_f} = \frac{(P_f - P_e)}{t_f}$$

Where P_f is the total rainfall over t_f hours in which runoff is produced

Example Problem 7.4

A rainfall storm lasting over 20 hours was recorded. The rainfall intensities during each hour of frontal storm are shown in columns 2 of **Table 7.4**. Rainfall and runoff records pertain to Turkey Lake watershed that has drainage area of 10 km². The storm runoff as estimated from the storm flow hydrograph is found to be 310 dam³. Assuming storage losses of 1.5 mm, calculate the φ-index and W-index.

Table 7.4 φ-Index Calculations

t, h	I, mm/h	φ, mm/h	
		5	3.8
1	10.0	10.0	10.0
2	12.5	12.5	12.5
3	5.2	5.2	5.2
4	7.5	7.5	7.5
5	5.7	5.7	5.7
6	2.0		
7	2.0		
8	2.1		
9	2.0		
10	2.5		
11	2.7		
12	4.0		4.0
13	6.0	6.0	6.0
14	7.0	7.0	7.0
15	6.5	6.5	6.5
16	6.0	6.0	6.0
17	2.2		
18	2.0		
19	1.5		
20	2.5		
Σ =	91.9	66.4	70.4
W =		3.8	3.8

Watershed Characteristics

Given:

t = 20 h   A = 10 km², V_Q = 310 dam³   Ss = 1.5 mm,

Solution:

$$R_s = \frac{V_Q}{A} = \frac{310\ dam^3}{10\ km^2} \times \frac{km^2 \cdot mm}{dam^3} = 31.0 = 31\ mm$$

Trial #1 Assume $\phi > 5mm/h$, $P_f = 66.4$ mm, $t_f = 9.0$ h

$$\varphi = \frac{(P_f - R_s)}{t} = \frac{(66.4 - 31)\ mm}{9.0\ h} = 3.93 = 3.9\ mm/h$$

Trial #2   Assume $\phi = 3.9$ mm/h $P_f = 70.4$ mm $t_f = 10$ h

$$\varphi = \frac{(P_f - R_s)}{t_f} = \frac{(70.4 - 31)\ mm}{10\ h} = 3.80 = 3.8\ mm/h$$

$$W = \frac{(P_f - R_s - S_s)}{t_f} = \frac{(70.4 - 31 - 1.5)\ mm}{20\ h} = 1.89 = 1.9\ mm/h$$

Figure 7.4 Infiltration Index (Ex. Prob. 7.4)

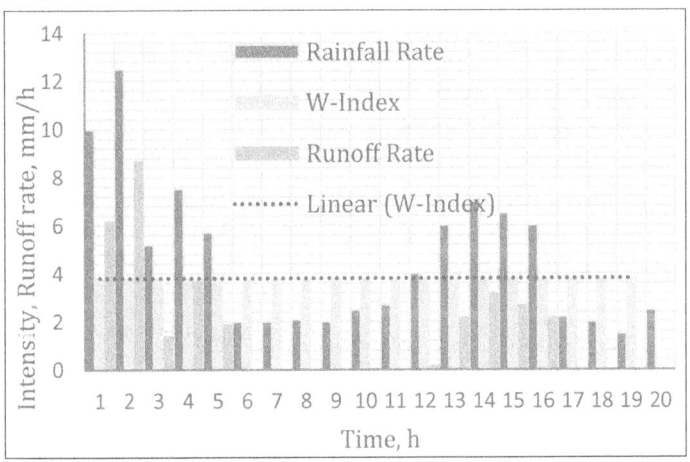

Example Problem 7.5

The following storm fell on Sunny River watershed.

Hour	01	02	03	04
Intensity, mm/h	10.2	12.5	7.5	5.0

The φ-index is estimated to be 6.5 mm/h. Calculate the storm runoff depth.

Sol.

Computations are shown in **Table 7.4** and plot **in Fig. 6.7**. Effective rainfall is 9.7 mm and duration of effective rainfall is 2-h

Table 7.5 Table of Computations (Ex. Prob. 7.5)

Time, h	I, mm/h	φ, mm/h	$R_s = (I-φ) \times t$, mm
01	10.2	6.5	3.7
02	12.5	6.5	6.0
03	4.5	6.5	0.0*
04	5.0	6.5	0.0
			Σ = 9.7

Figure 7.5 Runoff Rate(Ex. Prob. 7.5)

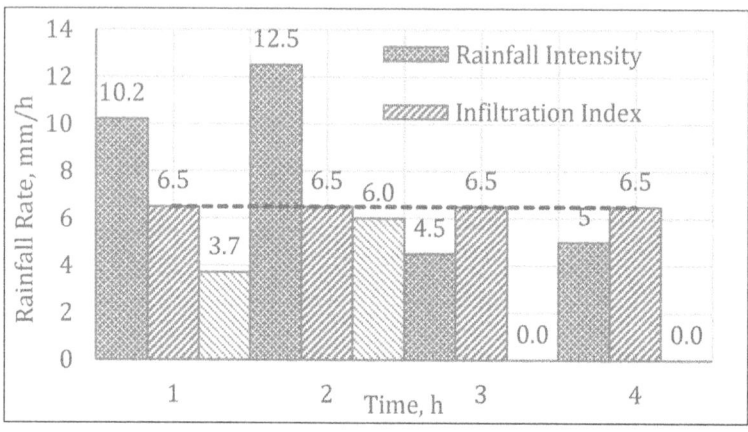

Example Problem 7.6

A rainfall storm fell on a rural watershed of Silver Creek producing rainfall in three consecutive hours shown below:

Hour	01	02	03
Intensity, mm/h	25	55	45

Horton infiltration equation applicable to Silver Creek Is:

$$f = 10 + 45e^{-2t} \; Where \; t = h \; and \; f \; in \; mm/h$$

Estimate storm runoff from this storm.

Solution.

Potential Infiltration rate or infiltration capacity and infiltration depth as given by Horton's equation are shown in **Table 7.5** and **Fig. 7.6**. In the beginning infiltration capacity is greater than the rainfall rate, hence actual infiltration rate must be equal to rainfall rate. There will be no runoff till the time actual infiltration rate is less than rainfall intensity. This is not the time where the potential rate curve meets the rainfall rate curve but sometime after that since in the beginning actual infiltration rate is less than the potential infiltration rate. This point in time can be found by hit and trial method.

Table 7.6 Computations (Ex. Prob. 7.6)

t, min	f, mm/h	F, mm	I, mm/h	f_{act} mm/h	Q_{RS} mm/h	R_S mm	$\sum R_S$ mm
0	55.0	0.0	0	30	0	0	0
5	48.1	4.3	30	30	0	0	0.0
10	42.2	8.0	30	30	0	0	0.0
15	37.3	11.4	30	30	0	0	0.0
20	33.1	14.3	30	30	0	0	0.0
25	29.6	16.9	30	30	0	0	0.0
30	26.6	19.2	30	30	0	0	0.0
35	24.0	21.3	30	30	0	0	0.0
40	21.9	23.2	30	29.6	0.4	0.0	0.0
45	20.0	25.0	30	28.0	2.0	0.1	0.1
50	18.5	26.6	30	26.6	3.4	0.2	0.3
55	17.2	28.1	30	25.2	4.8	0.3	0.7
60	16.1	29.5	30	24.0	6.0	0.4	1.1
90	12.2	36.4	55	18.5	36.5	10.6	11.8
120	10.8	42.1	55	15.2	39.8	19.1	30.8
150	10.3	47.3	45	13.1	31.9	17.9	48.8
180	10.1	52.4	45	11.9	33.1	16.2	65.0

Figure 7.6 Plots of infiltration and rainfall

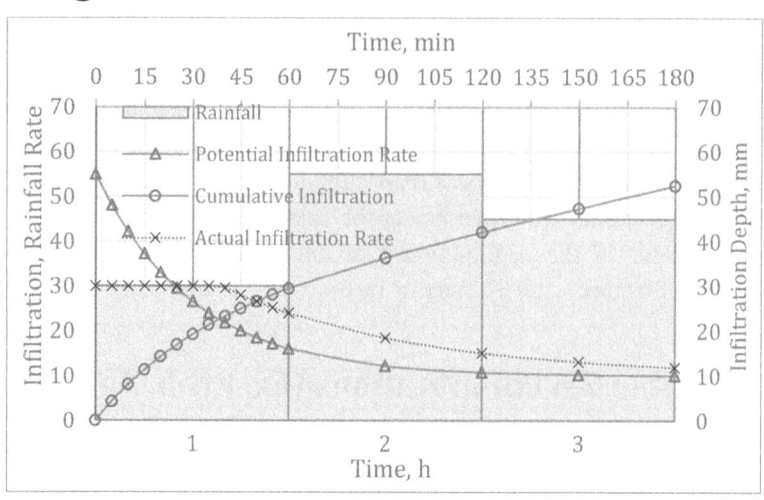

Let us say for the first 30 min, there is no runoff. Thus, actual Infiltration depth for the first 30 min will be then 30×30/60 =15 mm. From **Table 7.5**, this value corresponds to potential infiltration rate at 16 min @ 36 mm/h.> 30 mm/h. This means, runoff begins at t > 30 min. Next trial is for t = 35 min, F = 17.5 mm, which correspond to infiltration rate f = 29 mm/h at t = 25 min. In other words, runoff is delayed by 10 min and starts at time t > 35 min. As shown in **Table 7.6**, storm runoff, Rs = 65 mm.

7.5 Curve Number (CN) Method

Curve number method for estimating storm runoff was developed by US Department of Natural Resources. The CN method assumes that the ratio of actual retention F, to the potential maximum retention S is equal to the ratio of the actual runoff R to the maximum potential runoff that is rainfall less initial abstraction (P-I_a).
Mathematically:

NRCS Curve Number Method

$$\frac{F}{S} = \frac{R_S}{P - I_a} \quad \text{also} \quad F = P - I_a - R_S$$

Where I_a is the initial abstraction (storage before any runoff is produced,
S = maximum potential retention, and
R_S = storm runoff or effective precipitation, P_e

Watershed Characteristics

Combining the two expressions, it follows that storm runoff depth for a given storm can be expressed in terms of maximum retention and initial abstraction as shown below.

$$\frac{P - I_a - R_S}{S} = \frac{R_S}{P - I_a}$$

$$(P - I_a)^2 - R_S(P - I_a) = SR_S$$

Solving for R, we get;

Storm runoff depth
$$R_s = \frac{(P - I_a)^2}{(P - I_a + S)}$$

Potential retention, S refers to the maximum possible retention a watershed surface can have. It is affected by moisture conditions, land use, type of soil and hydrologic conditions. Potential retention is indicated by the curve number as suggested by NRCS.

7.5.1 Initial Abstraction, I_a

Some key points regarding initial abstraction are as follows:

i. Runoff starts after an initial abstraction is satisfied.
ii. If the precipitation is less than or equal to the initial abstraction, the storm runoff depth is zero. $P \leq I_a$, $R_s = 0$
iii. Initial abstraction consists mainly of interception, surface storage and infiltration. Initial abstraction can be expressed as a function of S. Usually, I_a is assumed to be 20% of S as suggested by NRCS. Making this substitution expression for storm runoff depth becomes:

Storm runoff depth (effective precipitation)
$$R_s \text{ or } P_e = \frac{(P - 0.2S)^2}{(P + 0.8S)} \quad \text{when } P > 0.2S$$

iv. Using this equation, the runoff R_s, produced by a given storm, can be found if both P and watershed conditions are known.

7.5.2 Estimation of S

Potential retention, S depends on the watershed characteristics affecting retention. These include soil, vegetation, land use *(SVL complex)* and antecedent soil moisture conditions (AMC). For each **SVL** complex, there is a range of S. The lower limit refers to the wet conditions and the upper limit refers to the dry conditions. NRCS expresses S as a function of what is termed as **curve number, CN**

$$S(mm) = \frac{25400}{CN} - 254$$

The curve number is a measure of **retention** for a given SVL complex and ranges from 0 to 100. In a way, curve number indicates runoff producing potential of a given watershed. Some interpretations of curve number are summarised in **Table 7.6**.

Table 7.7 Curve Number and Storm Runoff

CN	S	R_s	Comment
100	S = 0	R_s = P	Maximum runoff producing conditions
0	S =∞	R_s = 0	No runoff (all the water will be stored)
0<CN<100	S>0	$R_s \geq 0$	There is runoff if P>I_a
0<CN<100	S>0		Relationship between S and N is nonlinear

7.5.3 Determination of Curve Number, N

Curve number parameter is based on the soil cover complex and antecedent moisture conditions or AMC. Soil cover complex factors include land use, treatment or practice, hydrologic condition and more importantly hydrologic soil group.

7.5.4 Hydrologic Soil Group

All soils are classified into four hydrologic groups.

Group A consists of soils of low runoff potential such as deep, well drained sand and gravels with a high rate of transmission.

Group B consists of soils with moderate infiltration rates. They include moderate to well drained soils with moderately fine to moderately coarse textures.

Group C consists of soils with slow infiltration rates, primarily soils having a layer that impedes downward movement of water or soils of moderately fine to fine texture.

Watershed Characteristics

Group D consists of soils of high runoff potential. They are primarily clay soils with a high swelling potential, soils with a permanent high-water table and shallow soils overlying impervious material.

7.5.5 Land Use Treatment

Land use pertains to the watershed cover including every kind of vegetation; litter and mulch; fallow or bare soil; as well as non-agricultural uses such as water surfaces on lakes and swamps; impervious surfaces such as roads, roofs and urban areas. Land treatment mainly applies to agricultural land use. The runoff curve number method distinguishes between cultivated land, grasslands, and woods and forests.

7.5.6 Hydrologic Condition

Hydrologic condition refers to the ability of the watershed surface to produce runoff. A poor condition refers to pasture heavily grazed with sparse vegetation, thus having relatively high runoff producing potential.

7.5.7 Antecedent Moisture Condition (AMC)

Antecedent moisture condition refers to the soil moisture status preceding a storm. The AMC value is intended to reflect the effect of infiltration on both the volume and rate of runoff.

AMC I	Relatively dry conditions
AMC II	Average conditions
AMC III	Wet conditions

Upon selecting the applicable crop cover, treatment and hydrologic conditions, the value of CN is found under the appropriate soil group for AMC II. For dry or wet conditions CN is modified. It is logical to expect low number for dry conditions and high curve number for wet conditions. Potential retention for dry and wet conditions can be calculated using the following relationships:

$$\frac{S_I}{S_{II}} = \frac{S_{II}}{S_{III}} = 2.3$$

7.5.8 Composite CN

When the watershed consists of areas with different curve numbers, the composite curve number can be calculated by using area as a weighting factor.

Composite curve number
$$\overline{CN} = \frac{\Sigma(CN \times A)}{\Sigma A}$$

7.5.9 Storm Runoff

When applying the NRCS Curve Number method, the storm depth needs to be determined. For the design storm of a given duration and frequency, the point rainfall depth is read from **DDF** maps as discussed in Unit 3. A 24-hour storm is typically chosen. For larger watersheds, the point rain depth is modified using the depth area duration (**DAD**) curves. Storm runoff depth, R_S or effective precipitation is then calculated from the storm depth as shown below.

Effective precipitation
$$P_e = R_s = \frac{(P - 0.2S)^2}{(P + 0.8S)} \quad P > I_a$$

Storm runoff depth calculations for a given storm and watershed conditions are illustrated in the following Example Problems.

Example Problem 7.7

Determine the weighted curve number for an urban watershed with a 40% residential (1/4-acre lots), 25% open space, good conditions, 20% commercial and business (85% impervious), and 15% industrial (72% impervious) with corresponding soil groups of C, D, C, and D.

Given:

Soil group = B   Land use = 25% wooded (good condition) 75% pasture (fair condition) P = 100 mm   R =?

Land use	Condition	Soil Group	CN	%Area
Residential	¼ acre	C	83	40
Open space	good	D	80	25
Business	85% impervious	C	94	20
Industrial	72% impervious	D	93	15

Solution:

$$\overline{CN} = \frac{\Sigma(CN \times A)}{\Sigma A} = 0.4 \times 83 + 0.25 \times 80 + 0.2 \times 94 + 0.15 \times 93$$

$$= 85.95 = \underline{86}$$

Example Problem 7.8

A watershed is 25% wooded in good condition and 75% pastures in poor condition. Watershed falls in Soil Group B. Determine the infiltration depth for a storm producing 100 mm of rainfall. Assume AMC II moisture conditions.

Given:

Soil group = B Land use = 25% wooded (good condition) 75% pasture (fair condition) P = 100 mm R =?

Land use	Condition	Soil Group	CN	%Area
Wooded	Good	B	55	25
Pasture	Fair	B	69	75

Solution:

$$\overline{CN} = \frac{\Sigma(CN \times A)}{\Sigma A} = 0.25 \times 55 + 0.75 \times 69 = 65.5$$

$$S_{II} = \frac{25400}{65.5} - 254 = 133.7 = 134 \, mm$$

$$I_a = 0.2S = 0.2 \times 133.7 \, mm = 26.7 = 27 \, mm \, (<100 \, mm)$$

$$R_s = \frac{(P - 0.2S)^2}{P + 0.8S} = \frac{(100 - 0.2 \times 133.7)^2}{100 + 0.8 \times 133.7} = 25.91 = \underline{26 \, mm}$$

$$F = P - R_s = 100 - 25.91 = 74.09 = \underline{74 \, mm}$$

74 mm of rainfall is abstracted.

Example Problem 7.9

A watershed is 25% wooded in good condition and the rest is residential lots, 1/4 acre each. The wooded watershed mainly falls in soil group B. Determine the runoff depth and hence abstractions for a 10-y storm, which produces 12 cm of rainfall. Assume wet soil conditions.

Land use	Condition	Soil Group	CN	%Area
Wooded	Good	B	55	25
Residential	-	B	75	75

Solution:

$$\overline{CN} = \frac{\Sigma(CN \times A)}{\Sigma A} = 0.25 \times 55 + 0.75 \times 75 = 70$$

$$S_{II} = \frac{1000}{N} - 10 = \frac{1000}{70} - 10 = 4.28 \, in \times \frac{25.4 \, mm}{in}$$

$$= 108.8 = 109 \, mm$$

$$S_{III} = \frac{S_{II}}{2.3} = \frac{108.8 \, mm}{2.3} = 47.3 = 47 \, mm$$

$$P_e = \frac{(P - 0.2S)^2}{P + 0.8S} = \frac{(120 - 0.2 \times 47.3)^2}{120 + 0.8 \times 47.3} = 77.4 = \underline{77 \, mm}$$

$$F = P - P_e = 120 - 77.74 = 42.26 = \underline{42 \, mm}$$

42 mm of rainfall is abstracted.

Example Problem 7.10

A design storm was developed in Example Problem 3.12. the storm occurs over a watershed that has a composite curve number of 80. Estimate the storm runoff for 2-h rainfall depth.

Table 7.8 Computations Table (Ex. Prob. 7.10)

Duration	Design Storm, mm		
h	P	R_S	ΔR_S
0	0	0.0	0.0
2	4.9	0.0	0.0
4	10.7	0.0	0.0
6	17.9	1.3	1.2
8	27.6	5.0	3.7
10	43.4	14.2	9.1
12	163.6	117.9	103.8
14	188.7	141.8	23.9
16	200.6	153.2	11.4
18	208.8	161.1	7.9
20	215.2	167.2	6.2
22	220.5	172.4	5.1
24	225.2	176.9	4.5

Given:

Rainfall depths for each 2-h interval are shown in column 2 of **Table 7.8**.

Solution:

Based on curve number method, potential retention is calculated.

$$S_{II} = \frac{25400}{70} - 254 = 133.7 = 108.85 \, mm$$

Since it is a 50 Y storm, wet conditions (AMC III) are assumed

$$S_{III} = \frac{S_{II}}{2.3} = \frac{108.85}{2.3} = 36.78 = 47.329 = 47.3 \, mm$$

$$I_a = 0.2S = 0.2 \times 47.3 \, mm = 26.7 = 9.46 = 9.5 \, mm$$

Plot of rainfall and runoff in each 2-h interval is shown in **Fig. 7.7**

Sample of Calculations (End of 12th hour)

$$R_s = \frac{(P - 0.2S)^2}{P + 0.8S} = \frac{(163.6 - 0.2 \times 47.3)^2}{(163.6 + 0.8 \times 47.3)} = 117.9 = \underline{118 \, mm}$$

$$\Delta R_s = 117.9 - 14.2 = 103.7 = \underline{104 \, mm}$$

For the first 2-h interval, rainfall of 4.9 mm is less than initial abstraction of 9.5, hence no runoff. At the end of 4th hour,

$$R_s = \frac{(P - 0.2S)^2}{P + 0.8S} = \frac{(10.7 - 0.2 \times 47.3)^2}{(10.7 + 0.8 \times 47.3)} = 0.031 \, mm$$

$$\Delta R_s = 0.03 \, mm - 0.0 \, mm = 0.03 \, mm = \underline{0.0 \, mm}$$

Figure 7.7 Storm Runoff Depths (Ex. Prob. 7.10)

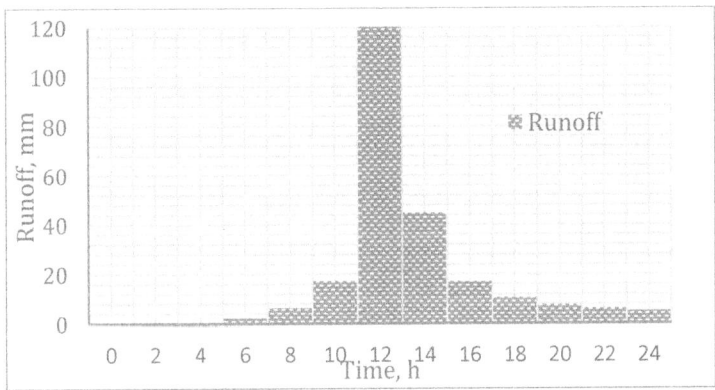

Example Problem 7.11

Rainfall distribution of a 6-h storm is shown in the table below. The runoff curve number CN is known to be 76. Calculate the φ-index?

Time interval, (h)	0-2	2-4	4-6
Intensity, I (mm/h)	10	15	12

Given:

CN = 76   P = 10 × 2 + 15 × 2 + 12 × 2 = 74 mm

Solution:

$$S = \frac{25400}{CN} - 254 = \frac{25400}{76} - 254 = 80.2 \text{ mm}$$

$$P_e = \frac{(P - 0.2S)^2}{P + 0.8S} = \frac{(74 - 0.2 \times 80.2)^2}{74 + 0.8 \times 80.2} = 24.31 = 24 \text{ mm}$$

$$F = P - P_e = 74 - 24 = 50 \text{ mm}$$

Assuming φ is < 10 mm/h

$$2(10 - \varphi) + 2(15 - \varphi) + 2(12 - \varphi) = 24.3$$

$$\varphi = \frac{497}{60} = 8.28 = \underline{8.3 \text{ mm/h}}$$

Effective rainfall in first time interval (0 - 2h)

$$P_e = P - F = 20 \text{ mm} - \frac{8.3 \text{ mm}}{h} \times 2h = 3.4 \text{ mm}$$

Runoff for the other time intervals is calculated in similar fashion.

Time interval, (h)	0-2	2-4	4-6
Rainfall, mm	20	30	24
Effective Rainfall, mm	3.4	13.4	7.4

Example Problem 7.12

For the data of Example **Problem 7.11**, compute the runoff produced in each of the 2-h interval using curve number method.

Solution:

$$R_S(2h) = P_e = \frac{(P - 0.2S)^2}{P + 0.8S} = \frac{(20 - 0.2 \times 80.2)^2}{20 + 0.8 \times 80.2} = 0.186 = 0.19 \text{ mm}$$

$$F = P - R_S = 20 \text{ mm} - 0.19 \text{ mm} = 19.81 = 19.8 \text{ mm}$$

Runoff for the other time intervals is calculated using Excel worksheet and are shown in the following Table.

Time, h	I, mm/h	P, mm	ΣP, mm	ΣR, mm	R, mm	F, mm
0-2	10	20	20	0.2	0.2	19.8
2-4	15	30	50	10.1	9.9	39.9
4-6	12	24	74	24.3	14.2	49.7

As compared to index method, infiltration depth in each time interval is different.

Example Problem 7.13

For the data of the watershed discussed in **Example Problem 7.7**, find the depth of abstraction in each hour of the 3-h storm that produced 22 mm, 80 mm, and 45 mm over three hours.

Solution:

$$S_{II} = \frac{25400}{CN} - 254 = \frac{25400}{86} - 254 = 41.34 = 41 \; mm$$

$$I_a = 0.2S = 0.2 \times 41.34 = 8.26 = 8.3 \; mm$$

$$R_S(1\;h) = P_e = \frac{(P - 0.2S)^2}{P + 0.8S} = \frac{(22 - 0.2 \times 41.34)^2}{20 + 0.8 \times 41.34}$$

$$= 3.42 = 3.4 \; mm$$

$$F = P - R_S = 22 \; mm - 3.42 \; mm = 18.57 = 19 \; mm$$

Runoff for the other time intervals is calculated using MS Excel worksheet shown in **Table 7.9**. A histogram plot of runoff depth is shown in **Fig. 7.8**

Figure 7.8 Rainfall Runoff Histogram

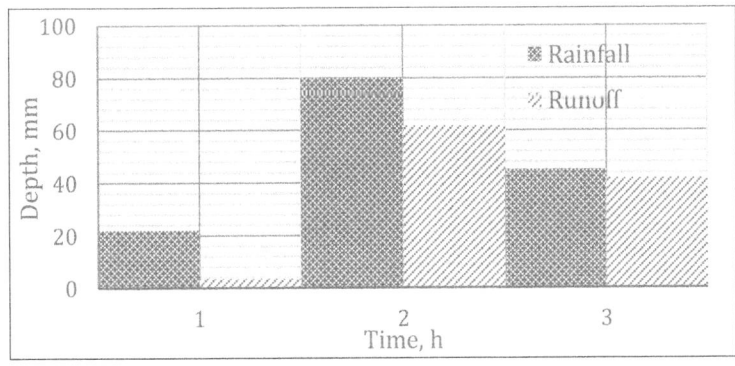

Table 7.9 Computation Ex. Prob. 7.13

Time, h	P, mm	ΣP, mm	ΣR, mm	R, mm	F, mm
0-1	22	22	3.4	3.4	18.6
1-2	80	102	65.0	61.6	37.0
2-3	45	147	106.9	41.8	40.1

7.6 Evaporation and Transpiration

Evaporation and transpiration are hydrologic abstractions. Importance of these abstractions depends on time scale of the hydrologic problem. For relatively short intervals as storm events, these abstractions are small. The bulk of evaporation and transpiration takes place during the time between runoff events, which is usually long.

Evaporation is the process by which water from the watershed surface is transported back to the atmosphere.

Transpiration is the process by which plants transfer water from the root zone to the leaf surface and eventually into the atmosphere.

Evapotranspiration (ET) is the combined effect of direct evaporation and transpiration. Evapotranspiration is an important factor in the water budgeting of a watershed. As it was demonstrated in Unit 1, a 50 to 90% portion of the annual precipitation is returned to the atmosphere. The most important factors affecting evaporation include net solar radiation, vapour pressure difference, temperature, atmospheric pressure, wind velocity and soil type.

Potential evapotranspiration rate (PET) is the ET when soil has sufficient moisture to meet the need of vegetation. PET no longer critically depends on soil and crop factors but essentially depends on the climatic factors.

7.6.1 Measurement of Evaporation

Evaporation is usually measured using devices like evaporation pans and atmometers. An **evaporation pan** is a device designed to measure evaporation by monitoring the loss of water depth during a given time period, usually a day. The rate of evaporation from a pan is not the same as from a lake. **Pan coefficient** is the ratio of pan to **lake evaporation**.

Evaporation from pans is affected by its size, location, material and exposure. Pan coefficient ranges from 0.6 to 0.8.

An **atmometer** is an instrument composed of a porous bulb that draws water from a container. The change in water level is measured and correlated with evaporation.

The effect of climate on evaporation has a substantial impact on water resources development. The planning and design of **storage reservoirs** in arid regions require a detailed evaluation of water loss due to evaporation. In agriculture watersheds, the amount of ET determines the frequency of irrigation.

Example Problem 7.14

On a given day, a rainfall of 2.5 mm is recorded. The drop in water level of class A pan is recorded to be 5.4 mm. Determine the lake evaporation for that day. If the lake surface area is 5.4 km², compute the loss of water in m³/d. Assuming irrigation demand of 30 mm/week, find how many hectares of crop area can be irrigated with the loss of water due to evaporation.

Solution:

$$d_{pan} = 5.4 + 2.5 = 7.9 \; mm$$

$$d_{lake} = C \times d_{pan} = 0.80 \times 7.9 \; mm = 6.32 \; mm/d$$

$$V = d \times A = 6.32 \; \frac{mm}{d} \times 5.4 \; km^2 \times \frac{1000 \; m^3}{km^2 . mm}$$

$$= \underline{3.40 \times 10^4 \; m^3/d}$$

Area irrigated with water lost to ET

$$A = \frac{V}{d} = \frac{3.40 \times 10^4 \; m^3}{d} \times \frac{week}{30 \; mm} \times \frac{7 \; d}{week} \times \frac{ha.mm}{10 \; m^3}$$

$$= 793 = \underline{790 \; ha}$$

7.6.2 Measurement of Evapotranspiration

In agricultural sciences, the term synonymous to evapotranspiration is called **consumptive use**. It differs from evapotranspiration only in that it includes the water used to make the plant tissue. Consumptive use can be measured by tanks and lysimeters.

A **tank** is a watertight container set into the ground. The tank is large enough to simulate natural growing conditions. The tank is mounted on a scale to assist in necessary moisture measurements. ET is determined by measuring the quantity of water necessary to maintain set moisture conditions in the tank. A **lysimeter** is a modified tank with a pervious bottom. This offers an advantage in that excess water is drained. **Consumptive use** is the difference between the amount of water applied to the lysimeter and the amount draining out with a correction for changes in moisture content.

The **plots** are selected under field conditions and provisions are made to measure the runoff from the plot. The underground tile drains collect deep percolation. Water lost as runoff and percolation is subtracted from the water supplied as rain or irrigation. The net difference corrected for soil moisture changes yields the consumptive use. A variation of the field-plot method is the water-balance with inflow-outflow measurements from the drainage basin. There are numerous formulas to determine evapotranspiration. In the absence of any direct measurement, these empirical equations are quite useful. However, sound judgment should be exercised to select the values of empirical constants in the equation.

7.6.3 Determination of Evapotranspiration

Owing to the difficulty in obtaining accurate direct measurement of pan evaporation under field conditions, evaporation is often predicted on the basis of climatological data. The approaches followed are to relate the magnitude and variation of evapotranspiration to one or more climatic factors (temperature, day length, humidity, wind, sunshine etc.). The more commonly used empirical formulae in estimating evapotranspiration are
    a) Blaney-Criddle Method
    b) Thornthwaite Method
    c) Hargreaves" Method

The Blaney-Criddle method is recommended for periods of one month or longer. The Blaney-Criddle method is simple, using measured data on temperature only. It should be noted, however, that this method is not very accurate; it provides a rough estimate or "order of magnitude" only. Especially under "extreme" climatic conditions the Blaney-Criddle method is inaccurate: in windy, dry, sunny areas, the ETo is underestimated (up to some 60 percent), while in calm, humid, clouded areas, the ETo is overestimated (up to some 40 percent).

7.6.4 Blaney Criddle Method

This method requires the use of only two factors, temperature and information of day light hours which is a factor based purely on the latitude of the place. Using Blaney-Criddle approach, potential evapotranspiration can be expressed as follows:

$$ET_0 = 0.46\, p(T + 17.8)$$

Where, ET_0 = potential evapotranspiration, mm of water per day (mean value over the month)
p = monthly percent of total day time hours of the year (**Tab. 7.10**)
T = mean monthly temp. In °C (Average of daily max and minimum values)
The seasonal consumptive use of a crop can be determined from the following relationship

$$ET_C = \Sigma(K_C \times ET_P) = U$$

Where, $ET_C = U$ = seasonal consumptive use of water by the crop for a given month of the growing period
K_C = monthly consumptive use factor of the growing season

The crop factor, Kc, mainly depends on the type of crop, growth stage of the crop, and the climate.

K_c and type of crop

Fully developed maize, with its large leaf area will be able to transpire, and thus use, more water than the reference grass crop: Kc of maize is higher than 1. Cucumber, also fully developed, will use less water than the reference grass crop, thus Kc of cucumber is less than 1.

K_c and the growth stage of the crop

A certain crop will use more water once it is fully developed, compared to a crop which has just recently been planted.

K_c and the climate

The climate influences the duration of total growing period and various stages of growth. In a cool climate, a certain crop will grow slower than in a warm climate.

Table 7.10 Percentage of Annual Daytime Hours

Lat N	Jan	Feb	Mar	Apr	May	Jun	July	Aug	Sept	Oct	Nov	Dec
S	July	Aug	Sept	Oct	Nov	Dec	Jan	Feb	Mar	Apr	May	Jun
60°	.15	.20	.26	.32	.38	.41	.40	.34	.28	.22	.17	.13
55	.17	.21	.26	.32	.36	.39	.38	.33	.28	.23	.18	.16
50	.19	.23	.27	.31	.34	.36	.35	.32	.28	.24	.20	.18
45	.20	.23	.27	.30	.34	.35	.34	.32	.28	.24	.21	.20
40	.22	.24	.27	.30	.32	.34	.33	.31	.28	.25	.22	.21
35	.23	.25	.27	.29	.31	.32	.32	.30	.28	.25	.23	.22
30	.24	.25	.27	.29	.31	.32	.31	.30	.28	.26	.24	.23
25	.24	.26	.27	.29	.30	.31	.31	.29	.28	.26	.25	.24
20	.25	.26	.27	.28	.29	.30	.30	.29	.28	.26	.25	.25
15	.26	.26	.27	.28	.29	.29	.29	.28	.28	.27	.26	.25
10	.26	.27	.27	.28	.28	.29	.29	.28	.28	.27	.26	.26
5	.27	.27	.27	.28	.28	.28	.28	.28	.28	.27	.27	.27
0	.27	.27	.27	.27	.27	.27	.27	.27	.27	.27	.27	.27

Example Problem 7.15

Determine the potential evapotranspiration for various months of the year for a location 15°N. the minimum and maximum temperatures for each month are shown in **Table 7.11**.

Solution:

Data and calculations are shown in **Table 7.11**

Sample of calculations:

For the month of March, p from **Table 7.10** is 0.27

$$\text{Mean } T = \frac{21.8 + 38.0}{2} = 29.9°C$$

$$ET_P = 0.46\, p(T + 17.8) = 0.46 \times 0.27(29.9 + 17.8)$$

$$= 5.924 = 5.92\ mm/d$$

Table 7.11 Calculations of ET_0 (Ex. Prob. 7.14)

Month	Temperature, T °C			p	ET_0, mm/d
	min	max	mean		
Jan	15.5	32.1	23.8	0.26	4.98
Feb	18.8	35.8	27.3	0.26	5.39
Mar	21.8	38.0	29.9	0.27	5.92
Apr	24.5	38.7	31.6	0.28	6.36
May	26.0	39.7	32.9	0.29	6.76
Jun	25.0	39.6	32.3	0.29	6.68
Jul	22.7	32.6	27.7	0.29	6.06
Aug	22.0	30.8	26.4	0.28	5.69
Sep	23.0	31.8	27.4	0.28	5.82
Oct	21.3	34.8	28.1	0.27	5.69
Nov	18.7	35.0	26.9	0.26	5.34
Dec	16.6	32.0	24.3	0.25	4.84
					69.55

7.6.5 Thornthwaite Method

Thornthwaite method assumes of an exponential relationship between mean monthly temperature and mean monthly consumptive use.

Thornwaite method
$$e = 16 \left(\frac{10t}{I}\right)^a$$

Where, e = unadjusted PET (mm per month)
t = mean air temperature (°C)
I = annual or seasonal heat index, the summation of values of monthly heat indices = $\Sigma i = \Sigma(0.2t)^{1.514}$
a = 0.49239 + 0.1792I − 0.000071I²

7.6.6 Hargreaves' Method

Hargreaves, based on his work on data from grass lysimeter, proposed the following relationship to estimate ET,

Hargreaves's Method
$$ET_0 = 0.0135(T + 17.78)SR_i$$

Where, PET = reference crop potential consumptive use
T = mean daily temperature (°C)

SR_i = incident solar radiation in Langley/d, it can be calculated using the following relationship,

$$SR_i = 0.10 SR_0 \sqrt{S\%}$$

Where, S% is the percent possible sunshine hour and SR_o is the clear day solar radiation in Langley/d.

7.6.7 Penman's Equation

Penman's equation for estimating evapotranspiration rate is based on mass and energy balances. It was further modified by Monteith and other researchers. Food and Agricultural Organisation (FAO) of UN outlines detailed procedures for applying the Penman-Monteith equation and empirical factors for particular crops in the estimation PET. The FAO version of the basic equation is shown below.

Reference Evapotranspiration

$$ET_0 = \frac{0.408\Delta(R_n - G) + \lambda(900/(T+273))u_2(e_s - e_a)}{\Delta + \gamma(1 + 0.34u_2)}$$

ET_0 = reference evaporation, mm/d
R_n = net radiation at the crop surface (MJ/m²·d)
G = soil heat flux density (MJ/m²·d)
u_2 = wind speed at 2 m height (m/s)
e_s = saturation vapour pressure (kPa)
e_a = actual vapour pressure
Δ = slope of the vapour pressure curve (kPa/°C)
λ = latent height of vaporization (MJ/kg)
γ = psychrometric constant (kPa/°C)

Discussion Questions

1. Describe flow hydrograph time characteristics?
2. How infiltration indices differ from infiltration rate or capacity?
3. What are main abstractions and how they affect the runoff production for a given storm and watershed characteristics?
4. You have observed some infiltration data and have been asked to fit a Horton type infiltration equation. How would you do it?
5. Derive the equation for accumulative infiltration by integrating Horton's equation. Simplify it for relatively longer time periods.
6. What are various methods of measuring infiltration and discuss limitations of each method?
7. What are the factors on which curve number is based?
8. Compare the terms ET, PET and pan evaporation, lake evaporation. What methods you can use to measure evapotranspiration?
9. Define effective precipitation and ways to estimate it?
10. Describe the NRCS method to determine storm runoff depth?
11. Based on proportionality, derive the following relationship;

$$R_s = \frac{(P - I_a)^2}{(P - I_a + S)}$$

12. Describe the four groups of soils as described in CN method and how they are related to runoff production?
13. If not specified, initial abstraction is assumed to be 20% of potential retention. Under what conditions, a higher value is justified?

Practice Problems

Practice Problem 7.1

The soil in a pond is silt-clay loam with a grass cover. Based on the infiltrometer data, the initial and final rates of infiltration are 47 mm/h and 9.0 mm/h, respectively. If the rate constant k is 0.75 /h, find the depth due to infiltration after one hour. (23 mm)

Practice Problem 7.2

The rainfall intensities during each hour of a storm are as follows:

Hour	1	2	3	4	5	6
Rate, mm/h	10.0	45.0	25.0	5.0	2.5	0.5

Based on the storm hydrograph, storm runoff depth produced by this storm is determined to be 25 mm. Work out the φ-index? (23 mm/h)

Practice Problem 7.3

For Burn Creek Watershed, the φ-index is 4.0 mm/h. Estimate storm runoff depth produced by the storm shown below. (14 mm)

Hour	01	02	03	04
Intensity, mm/h	10.2	12.5	7.5	3.0

Practice Problem 7.4

Determine the storm runoff from a 150-mm rainfall that fell on an agricultural watershed with crops in straight rows, soil group B, poor hydrologic condition and AMC II. (91 mm)

Practice Problem 7.5

A watershed is half wooded in good condition and half residential in 1/4-acre lots. Each part of the watershed has 50% soil group B and 50% soil group C. Determine the runoff volume for a total rainfall of 10 cm. (72 mm)

Practice Problem 7.6

Estimate the value of storm runoff depth from a 2-d storm that produced 25 mm and 55 mm of rainfall, respectively. The average value of curve number was assessed to be 65 (AMCII) and average moisture conditions are assumed before the storm. Determine the storm runoff depth. (0.0 mm, 18 mm)

Practice Problem 7.7

The following rainfall distribution was observed during a 12-h storm. If runoff curve number is 86, find the φ-index? (3.2 mm/h)

Time Interval, h	0-2	2-4	4-6	6-8	8-10	10-12
Intensity, mm/h	5	10	13	18	3	10

Practice Problem 7.8

Over a 5-day period, the total depth of water added to bring the pan water level to the set point is recorded to be 23.6 mm. Assuming pan coefficient of 0.7, determine the volume of water evaporated from a lake having a surface area of 250 ha. (41 ML)

Practice Problem 7.9

A catchment has 40% type B soil and 60% Type C soil. The land cover is half wooded in good condition and half residential consisting of 1/8 acre lots. For a rainfall storm of 160 mm, calculate storm runoff depth. (92 mm)

Practice Problem 7.10

Curve number for a rural watershed is estimated to be 73. Work out the storm runoff depth for a 24-h storm producing 100 mm of rainfall. (38 mm)

Practice Problem 7.11

A 400-ha watershed has predominantly clay soil and CN II is estimated to be 73. Work out direct runoff from a 2-d storm that produced 65 mm and 80 mm of rainfall, respectively. Assume AMC II for the first day. (15 mm, 46 mm)

Practice Problem 7.12

Determine the weighted curve number for a watershed with 40% residential (1/4-acre lots), 25% open space, good condition, 20% business and commercial, and remaining industrial with corresponding soils of group C, D, C, and D. (86)

Practice Problem 7.13

For the watershed in Example Prob. 7.7, find the storm runoff depth expected from a storm that produced 150 mm of rainfall depth? (110 mm)

Practice Problem 7.14

A 255-km² watershed has a composite curve number of 81. Estimate the runoff depth from a 6-h storm described in the following table. (19 mm, 67 mm, 12 mm)

Time Interval, h	0-2	2-4	4-6
Intensity, mm/h	28	36	12

Practice Problem 7.15

For the previous problem data, find the φ-infiltration index and W-infiltration index. Assume losses due to initial abstraction to be 4.0 mm. (9 mm, 8.3 mm)

Practice Problem 7.16

For a specific soil conditions, parameters of the Horton's equation are: f_0 = 35 mm/h, f_c = 6.0 mm/h, and k = 2.0 /h. Find
  i. Infiltration capacity of the soil after 30 min and 60 min? (17 mm/h, 9.9 mm/h)
  ii. Infiltration depth after 30 min and 60 min? (12 mm, 19 mm)

Practice Problem 7.17

Hyetograph of a storm that fell over a basin of area 1050 km² is shown in the table below. Area under the storm hydrograph produced by this storm is computed to be 2.6×10⁷ m³. Based on this information, find Φ-index for this basin? (8.4 mm/h)

Time, h	1	2	3	4	5	6
Intensity, mm/h	7	16	20	14	8	5

Practice Problem 7.18

During an infiltrometer test, initial and final infiltration rates were observed to be 100 mm/h and 10 mm/h respectively. Over 6 hours of the test, a depth of 210 mm of water infiltrated. What is the rate constant of Horton's equation? (0.6/h)

Practice Problem 7.19

The infiltration capacity of a small catchment is given by the following equation.
$$f(t) = 8 + 15\, e^{-0.5t}$$
Where, f is in mm/h and t is in h. Assuming the infiltration to take place at infiltration capacity rates in a storm of 4 h duration, work out the average rate of infiltration over the duration of storm. (15 mm/h)

Practice Problem 7.20

Hyetograph of an isolated storm is presented below:

t, h	1	2	3	4	5
Total rainfall, mm	5.0	16	35	65	77

From the storm flow hydrograph, it was determined that 35 mm of runoff was produced by this storm. Work out the φ-index. (9.3 mm/h)

Practice Problem 7.21

Depth of infiltration in mm of a given soil is described by a power law function shown below:

$$F(t) = 25\, t^{0.65}$$

Where t is in h and F in mm. Find the infiltration capacity after 30 min and 100 min. (21 mm/h, 14 mm/h)

Practice Problem 7.22

A 6-h storm produced 210 mm rainfall. If the catchment has an average CN of 73, find the runoff depth assuming;
a) Dry moisture conditions (51 mm)
b) Normal moisture conditions (130 mm)
c) Wet moisture conditions (160 mm)

Practice Problem 7.23

A catchment soil has Horton infiltration equation parameters: f_o = 100 mm/h, f_c = 20 mm/h, and k = 2.2/min.
a) What rainfall rate would result in ponding from the beginning of the storm.
b) If this rainfall intensity is uniform for a duration of 60 min, what will the total runoff depth be?

Practice Problem 7.24

Rainfall intensity equation for a return period of 25 year is given by the following equation:

$$I = 830/((\Delta t + 33))$$

Where duration, Δt is in min and rainfall intensity in mm/h
Drainage facilities of a catchment falling in this area is to be designed for a rainfall event with a duration of 2.0 h.
a) Determine the rainfall depth (108 mm)
b) Estimate the runoff depth from a catchment which has composite curve number of 79. (55 mm)

Practice Problem 7.25

Rework Practice Problem 7.24, for a storm duration of 1.0 h (30 mm)

Review Questions

1. Which one of the hydrologic abstractions is partly converted to runoff after rainfall ceases?
   a) Interception   b) Depression   c) Detention   d) Evaporation

2. The term through fall refers to
   a) Direct runoff
   b) Rainfall falling on ground
   c) Rainfall intercepted
   d) None of these

3. When rainfall intensity I, is less than infiltration capacity, f_p, which of the following is not true? (f = actual infiltration rate)
   a) R>0   b) $f_p > f$ c) R = 0   d) f = I

4. Infiltration rate is relatively high in
   a) Wet soils
   b) Fine textured
   c) Soils with vegetation
   d) Bare soils

5. Which parameter of the Horton's equation: $f_p = f_0 + (f_0 - f_c) e^{-kt}$ represents the decay rate?
   a) k   b) f_0 c) f_c d) f_p

6. Interception storage does not depend on
   a) Season   b) Crown cover   c) Soil Moisture   d) Rainfall Rate

7. If the depth of storm runoff equals 2.7 cm, rainfall depth is 42 mm, and the rainfall duration is 10 h, the φ-index is
   a) 2.7 mm/h   b) 4.2 mm/h   c) 1.5 cm/h   d) 1.5 mm/h

8. Which of the following terms relates to storm runoff?
   a) Initial abstraction
   b) Effective rainfall
   c) Surface storage
   d) Potential infiltration

9. Which one of the following is not used to measure evapotranspiration?
   a) Infiltrometer   b) Tank   c) Lysimeter   d) Field Plot

10. What amount of water is lost from a lake surface of 15 km² on a day when lake evaporation is measured to be 1.2 mm/d?
    a) 1800 ML   b) 180 ML   c) 18 ML   d) 1.8 ML

11. The typical pan coefficient for the standard US bureau class A is
    a) 0.50　　　　b) 0.60　　　　c) 0.75　　　　d) 0.85

12. Interception losses usually occur
    a) Beginning of storm　　　　b) Towards end of storm
    c) Uniformly distributed　　　d) Middle of the storm

13. A rainfall storm fell on a 550-ha watershed producing an average rainfall intensity of 25 mm/h over a period of 8 h. From the storm flow hydrograph, storm runoff volume is worked out to be 600 dam^3 (ML). The average infiltration rate during the storm is
    a) 5,5 mm/h　　b) 11 mm/h　　c) 16 mm/h　　d) 18 mm/h

14. A watershed has CN of 50. What is the minimum depth of rain that should fall before it produces any storm runoff?
    a) 71 mm　　　b) 61 mm　　　c) 51 mm　　　d) 41 mm

15. For a curve number of 73 for average moisture conditions, what would be the potential retention assuming wet conditions?
    a) 41 mm　　　b) 94 mm　　　c) 120 mm　　　d) 220 mm

16. Assuming wet conditions and curve number of 75, what is the storm runoff depth, if 100 mm of rain fell over a 24 h period?
    a) 34 mm　　　b) 54 mm　　　c) 66 mm　　　d) 76 mm

17. The maximum value of CN for urbanised conditions is
    a) 100　　　　b) 98　　　　c) 95　　　　d) 90

18. Infiltration index is
    a) Actual infiltration rate　　　b) Minimum infiltration rate
    c) Maximum infiltration rate　　d) Average infiltration rate

19. A lysimeter is used to measure
    a) Infiltration　　b) Evaporation　　c) Transpiration　　d) both b and c

20. A 600-ha catchment experienced a uniform intensity rainfall of 20 mm/h for 8-h duration. Assuming an infiltration index of 7.5 mm/h, what is the volume of storm runoff?
    a) 500 ML　　　b) 600 ML　　　c) 750 ML　　　d) 8500 ML

21. Which of the following antecedent moisture conditions indicates high runoff potential?
    a) AMC I b) AMC II c) AMC III d) About same

22. Potential evapotranspiration does not depend on
    a) Soil moisture b) Soil type c) Type of crop d) All

23. Which of the following curve number is not valid?
    a) Zero b) 100 c) 1000 d) None

24. Infiltration capacity of a soil indicates _____ rate of infiltration
    a) Maximum b) Constant c) Average d) Minimum

25. Which of the following formulae is not for computing evaporation or evapotranspiration?
    a) Thornwaite b) Horton c) Penman d) Hargreave

26. Which of the following hydrologic soil group has lowest runoff potential?
    a) A b) B c) C d) D

27. This hydrologic abstraction is relatively insignificant in urban catchments.
    a) Depression Storage b) Detention Storage
    c) Infiltration d) All

28. In majority of the watersheds, minimum curve number is
    a) 10 b) 20 c) 30 d) 50

29. This formula is commonly used for finding consumptive use of crops.
    a) Blaney Criddle b) Thornwaite
    c) Hargreaves d) Penman equation

30. If not specified, which of the following antecedent moisture conditions should be used?
    a) AMC I b) AMC II c) AMC III d) Not matter

8 Flow Hydrograph

A **stream flow hydrograph** at any point on a stream is a plot of discharge rate at the point versus the time. The flow hydrograph is a continuous curve. As we will see later in this unit, it is more useful in hydrology to consider a hydrograph from a certain storm event. A flow hydrograph can be considered a blueprint of the drainage basin. Even for the same storm, no two watersheds will produce exactly the same hydrograph. Much like a fingerprint, a flow hydrograph is an individual characteristic of each watershed.

Figure 8.1 Components of Stream flow

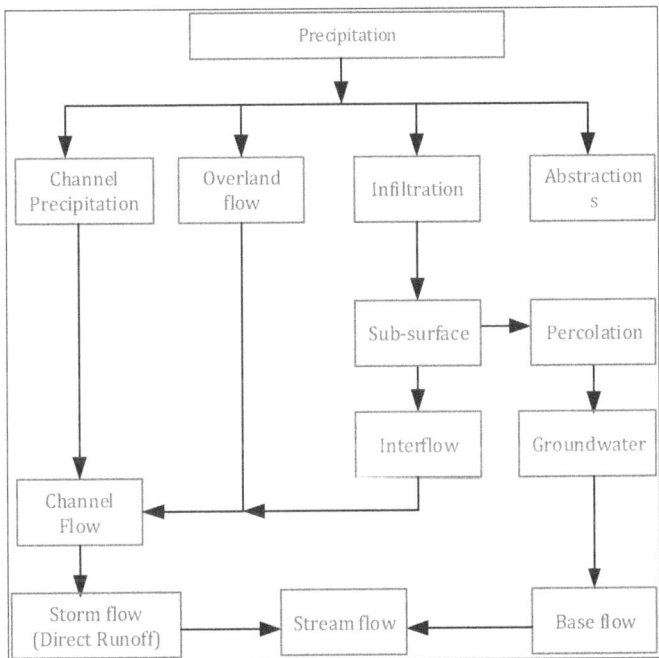

8.1 Components of Stream Flow

The stream as observed at the outlet of the watershed has two main components: **storm flow** and **base flow**. Base flow is the groundwater flow component of the stream flow prior to a given storm. Storm flow relates to the runoff generated due to a specific storm. Total stream flow minus the base flow gives the storm flow. As illustrated in **Figure 8.1** storm flow consists of **overland** flow (surface runoff) and **interflow** (sub-surface runoff).

8.1.1 Surface Runoff

Surface runoff or overland flow is the runoff water that travels over the ground surface to a drainage channel.
- Surface runoff is the result of effective rainfall.
- Surface runoff occurs after most interception storage has been filled, when the rain or snowmelt exceeds the infiltration capacity, and when depression storage along the specified flow path has been filled.
- Precipitation falling on a stream surface becomes surface runoff and therefore is the quickest to reach the outlet.
- Measurements of overland flow in the field are very sparse.
- Surface runoff, being the quickest component of runoff, is the principal contributor to the peak discharge from a storm event.

8.1.2 Interflow

Interflow is the infiltrated water which flows through shallow sub-surface flow routes. Such routes may be the pores of the soil or small channels such as roots and worm passages or sub-surface tile drainage systems. Interflow can occur on forest floors, where leaves and other debris cover the ground.
- The presence of interflow is generally inferred from the absence of observed overland flow during periods when stream flow rates vary widely.
- Interflow may occur during the storm or after the storm has terminated.
- This component lags surface runoff and does not add to the peak flow.
- As an example, water flowing over a paved driveway is overland flow, whereas water seeping out at the lower end of a sloping lawn is primarily interflow.

8.1.3 Base Flow

Base flow is the flow component contributed by the groundwater storage. Groundwater flow is synonymous with base flow.
- The base flow component of runoff is much slower than direct runoff.
- In the absence of any rainfall and snow melt input for long periods of time; this component sustains the stream flow. This is the reason it is called base flow.

- Drainage basins with highly permeable, thick soils usually have a high base flow.
  - A portion of the groundwater-flow component occurs from water infiltrating the banks of the channel during high water levels/flows.

8.2 Hydrograph Shape

A typical runoff hydrograph is shown in **Figure 8.2**. The shape of stream flow hydrograph is determined by watershed and storm characteristics.
  - Low infiltration soils produce high runoff with a high peak.
  - Compact watersheds respond more quickly than elongated watersheds.
  - The greatest effect on the shape of a hydrograph occurs when geology and shape vary with the drainage basin.
  - A storm falling on the lower end of the basin will have a higher peak discharge.
  - Rainfall depth, rate/intensity and distribution (hyetograph) affect the shape of the hydrograph.
  - Urbanization, farming, forest removal, cutting grass, and building roads increase runoff volume as well as rate.
  - Dams and diversions decrease runoff. The flow is regulated by operation of the storage reservoir.

Figure 8.2 Elements of Runoff Hydrograph

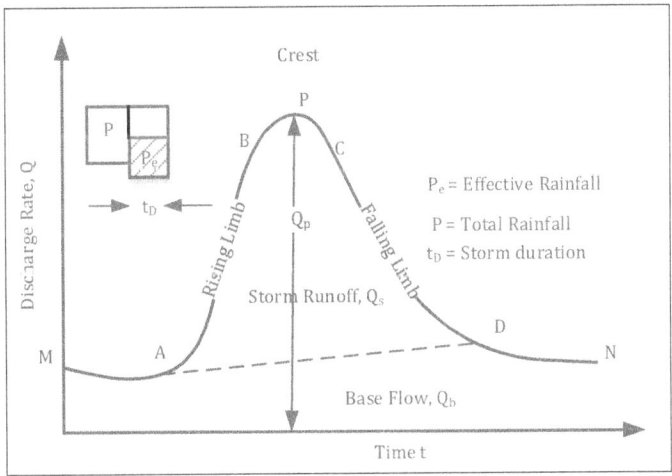

8.2.1 Rising Limb

As shown in **Fig. 8.2**, the elements of a hydrograph are rising limb, crest and recession limb. The **rising limb** graphically represents increasing discharge over time until it reaches peak flow. The steepness of the rising limb is basically controlled by travel time and runoff produced by the storm. The rising limb of a hydrograph is also called concentration curve, represents the increase in discharge due to building up of surface runoff on the catchment and channel.

8.2.2 Crest

Crest is an important element of runoff hydrograph since it contains the peak flow. Peak flow occurs when majority of the area starts contributing to runoff at the outlet. For larger catchments, the peak flow occurs after the cessation of rainfall. Multipeaked complex hydrographs can occur due to overlapping of two or more storms in succession.

8.2.3 Recession Limb

The **recession limb** is the falling limb of the hydrograph and thus has a negative slope. The degree of slope indicates the rate at which water is drained from the basin. Referring to **Fig. 8.2**, recession limb is shown as **decreasing limb** starting from the end of the crest, point of **inflexion** up to the point where groundwater flow begins.

8.3 Hydrograph Time Characteristics

The shape of a hydrograph is measured in terms of time parameters including time to peak, t_p, time of concentration, t_c and lag time, t_L and storm duration, $t_d(\Delta t)$ = Storm duration.

8.3.1 Time to Peak

Referring to **Fig. 8.3**, **time to peak** is the time elapsed from the beginning of the rising limb to the peak discharge. It is primarily determined by such characteristics as length of the main watercourse, drainage density, channel slope and roughness, and infiltration. The time to peak is altered somewhat by the distribution of rainfall over the watershed. For example, the hydrograph of a storm falling on the upper end of a catchment has a longer time to peak. For a given runoff volume, a longer time to peak will produce lower peak flow and vice versa.

Figure 8.3 Hydrograph Time Characteristics

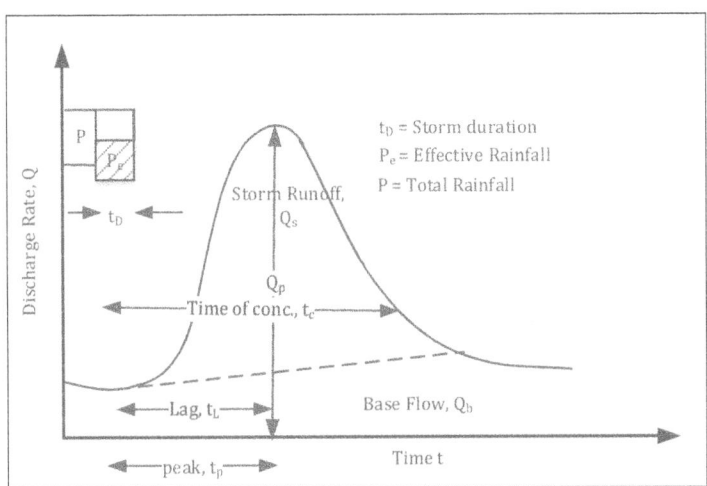

8.3.2 Time of Concentration

The **time of concentration** is the time required for runoff from the most hydraulically remote point to reach the outlet. In other words, it is the time for the runoff to concentrate at the outlet. It implies that the flow rate at the outlet will gradually increase until it reaches the maximum or equilibrium flow rate. If a runoff producing storm lasts at least for a time equal to the time of concentration, each portion of the watershed will start contributing runoff at the outlet of watershed. Except for very small catchments, it is rare for the time of concentration to be attained under natural conditions. Comparing the time of concentration t_c with the effective **storm duration t_D or Δt**, the process of runoff concentration can lead to three distinct types of catchment responses.

i) **Concentrated flow $t_D = t_c$**

In this case, the runoff concentrates at the outlet, reaching its maximum or equilibrium.

ii) **Super Concentrated flow $t_D > t_c$**

Since rainfall continues to occur subsequent flow remains concentrated and equal to the equilibrium value until rainfall stops.

iii) **Sub-concentrated flow $t_D < t_c$**

In this case flow does not reach the equilibrium value. This type of flow is very typical of mid-size and large catchments.

8.3.3 Lag Time

A basic measure of time characteristics is the **lag time** or basin lag. It is the property of a watershed, which is defined as the difference in time between the centre of effective rainfall and the centre of the mass of direct runoff. Because of the difficulty in determining the centre of the mass of direct runoff, the lag time is more commonly defined as the time difference between the centre of effective rainfall and the peak of the direct runoff hydrograph.

Lag time and time to peak
$$t_l = t_p - \Delta t/2 \qquad t_p = \frac{\Delta t}{2} + t_l$$

Time lag is characterized by the ratio of length to the mean velocity of flow. The size and shape of drainage area, slope of the channel and the storm pattern all affect lag time. The U.S. Department of Natural Resources (NRCS) developed an empirical equation to calculate lag time based on curve number. This relationship is shown below.

Lag time (NRCS Equation)
$$t_l = \frac{L^{0.8}(2540 - 23CN)^{0.7}}{14100 CN^{0.7} S_b^{0.5}}$$

t_l = lag time in h L = hydraulic length in m S_b = basin slope m/m

The NRCS relationship is based on data collected from gauged watersheds and is applicable to watersheds with areas of less than 8 km² and curve number falling in the range of 50 to 95. Hydraulic length in this formula is the length from the outlet to the most hydraulically remote point in the watershed.

8.3.4 Time of Concentration Estimation

Several formulas for determining time of concentration are available.

NRCS Lag Equation

Conservation Service further suggested that the basin lag is typically three fifths of the time of concentration. Using this relationship, the time of concentration for a given watershed can be estimated.

$$t_c = \frac{5}{3} t_l = 1.67 t_l$$

This equation can only be valid for conditions of peak discharge when the time of concentration is reached. This is discussed in more detail later on in chapter 9.

Example Problem 8.1

From the topographic map, water boundary is delineated. Area and hydraulic length are estimated to be 620 ha and 4520 m respectively. The soil and vegetation characteristics of the watershed are represented by a CN of 75. The average basin slope is estimated to be 2.6%. Find lag time and time of concentration for this watershed.

Given:

A = 620 ha   L = 4520 m   CN = 75   S = 2.6% = 0.026

Solution:

$$t_l = \frac{L^{0.8}(2540 - 23CN)^{0.7}}{14100 CN^{0.7} S_b^{0.5}} = \frac{4520^{0.8}(2540 - 23 \times 75)^{0.7}}{14100 \times 75^{0.7} \times 0.026^{0.5}}$$

$$= 1.96 = 2.0\ h$$

$$t_c = \frac{5}{3} t_l = \frac{5}{3} \times 1.96 = 3.26 = 3.3\ h$$

Kirpich Formula

Based on experiments on small watersheds, Kirpich developed an empirical equation relating time of concentration with the length of travel and channel gradient. Kirpich formula is applicable for very small agriculture catchments with areas not exceeding 100 ha. For a very rough surface, the Kirpich formula underestimates t_c.

Time of Concentration

$$t_c = \frac{CL^{0.77}}{S^{0.385}} = \frac{CL^{1.15}}{H^{0.385}}$$

Where S is the channel gross slope
C = 0.02 when L, H in m and t_c in min,
C = 0.063 when L, H in km and t_c in h

Hathaway Formula

The Hathaway formula incorporates the roughness of land surface n. Time of concentration is given by:

$$\boxed{t_c = \frac{0.61(Ln)^{0.467}}{S^{0.234}}} \quad \text{Time of concentration}$$

L = length in km   S = slope in m/m t_c = time in h,
n = 0.02(bare land), 0.8 timberland

Example Problem 8.2

Estimate the time of concentration by applying empirical formulas suggested by Kirpich and Hathaway for a catchment with the following characteristics:
L = 1.0 km   S = 1.0%   n = 0.40 (Pasture)

Solution:

Kirpich formula
$$t_c = \frac{0.061 L^{0.77}}{S^{0.385}} = \frac{0.061 \times 1.0^{0.77}}{0.01^{0.385}}$$
$$= 0.359 = \underline{0.36 \ h}$$

Hathaway formula
$$t_c = \frac{0.61(Ln)^{0.467}}{S^{0.234}} = \frac{0.61(1.0 \times 0.4)^{0.467}}{0.01^{0.234}}$$
$$= 1.16 = \underline{1.2 \ h}$$

Steady Flow Formula

To calculate the time of concentration using this method, the main watercourse is divided into sub-reaches. Subsequently, a steady flow formula such as Manning's equation is used to calculate the mean flow velocity and associated travel time through each sub-reach. The concentration time through the reach is the sum of all the sub-reach travel times. This procedure, while practical, is based on several assumptions.

$$\boxed{v = \frac{1}{n} \times R_h^{\frac{2}{3}} \times \sqrt{S} - SI, \quad t_c = t_1 + t_2 + \cdots = \sum \frac{L_i}{v_i}} \quad \text{Time of concentration (Manning's flow equation)}$$

Flow Hydrograph

Manning's equation can also be applied to estimate flow velocities for overland flow. Since flow takes place over wide area in shallow depth, it is safe to assume hydraulic radius equal to depth of flow.

Time of concentration (overland flow)
$$v = \frac{1}{n} \times R_h^{\frac{2}{3}} \times \sqrt{S} = K\sqrt{S} - SI$$

The values of coefficient n, hydraulic radius R_h, and factor K for various land covers are listed in **Table 8.1**

Table 8.1 Coefficients n, K in Manning's Equation

Land Cover		n	R_h, m	K
Forest				
	Dense underbrush	8.0E-01	7.6E-02	2.2E-01
	Light underbrush	4.0E-01	6.7E-02	4.1E-01
	Heavy ground litter	2.0E-01	6.1E-02	7.7E-01
Grass				
	Bermuda grass	4.1E-01	4.6E-02	3.1E-01
	Dense underbrush	2.4E-01	3.7E-02	4.6E-01
	Short	1.5E-01	3.0E-02	6.5E-01
	Rangeland	1.3E-01	1.2E-02	4.1E-01
	Grassed waterway	1.0E-01	3.0E-01	4.5E+00
	Small upland gullies	4.0E-02	1.5E-01	7.1E+00
	Paved area	1.1E-02	1.8E-02	6.3E+00
	Paved area	2.5E-02	6.1E-02	6.2E+00
	Paved gutter	1.1E-02	6.1E-02	1.4E+01

Example Problem 8.3

A stream was surveyed, and its hydraulic characteristics are given below:

Sub-reach	R_h, m	Roughness, n	S, m/m×10⁻⁴	L, m
1 (outlet)	3.00	0.030	3.00	2000
2	0.25	0.035	4.15	2000
3	0.95	0.040	11.25	1500
4	0.70	0.045	11.25	1000
5 Overland flow short grass			50	1000

Calculate the flow velocity using Manning's equation and determine the time of concentration.

Sample of calculations (sub-reach #1):

$$v = \frac{R_h \sqrt{S}}{n} = \frac{(3.0)^{\frac{2}{3}} \times \sqrt{0.0003}}{0.03} = 1.2 \ m/s$$

$$t = \frac{L}{v} = 2000m \times \frac{s}{1.2 \ m} \times \frac{h}{3600 \ s} = 0.463 \ h$$

Table 8.2 Computation Table (Ex. Prob. 8.3)

Reach	R_h, m	n	S, %	L, m	v, m/s	t, h
1	3.00	0.030	0.030	2000	1.201	0.463
2	0.25	0.035	0.041	2000	0.230	2.420
3	0.95	0.040	0.113	1500	0.812	0.513
4	0.70	0.045	0.113	1000	0.589	0.472
5	Overland		5.000	1000	0.145	1.915
			Σ =	7500		5.78

Sub-Reach

Referring to **Table 7.1**, K value for short grass is 0.65, Hence average flow velocity from Manning's equation is;

$$v = K\sqrt{S} = 0.65 \times \sqrt{0.05} = 0.145 \ m/s$$

$$t = \frac{L}{v} = 1000 \ m \times \frac{s}{0.145 \ m} \times \frac{h}{3600 \ s} = 0.463 \ h$$

8.4 Stream Flow Recession

During **recession**, there is no inflow to the drainage basin and all the flow is contributed by surface, sub-surface and groundwater storage. The surface storage is made up of detention and channel storages.

During recession, the discharge rate decreases at a decreasing rate as in the case of a draining bathtub. To drain the same volume, it takes longer the next time. This behaviour is similar to that of a **linear reservoir** in which the discharge is proportional to the amount of storage. Based on the concept of linear reservoir, stream flow recession can be expressed as:

Recession equation

$$\boxed{Q_t = Q_0 e^{-\frac{t}{t_s}} = Q_0 e^{-at} = Q_0 K_r^t}$$

K_r = Recession Constant, $a = 1/t_s$

Flow Hydrograph

Base flow after one-time step (t=1)

$$Q_1 = Q_0 e^{-\frac{1}{t_s}} = Q_0 K_r$$

This would mean, the ratio of successive discharges, i.e., day 1, and day 2 will be equal to the recession constant. That is to say, if the recession constant is 0.80, day 2 discharge would be 80% of discharge on day 1 and so on.

$$K_r = \frac{Q_1}{Q_0} = e^{-\frac{1}{t_s}} \quad or \quad -\ln(K_r) = \frac{1}{t_s} \quad or \quad \ln\left(\frac{1}{k_r}\right) = \frac{1}{t_s}$$

In the above equations, term t_s is called **time of storage**. When $t = t_s$; discharge rate after time equal to time of storage reduces to 37%

Time equal to time of storage

$$\frac{Q_{ts}}{Q_0} = e^{-\frac{t}{t_s}} = e^{-1} = 0.367 = 37\%$$

The last part of recession limb represents the **base flow**. The recession constant can be evaluated by plotting the data points of flow on a given day versus the previous day's flow. The data should fit a straight line and the reciprocal of this slope is recession constant. The recession time constant of the base flow can be used to predict the base flow hydrograph. It may vary with the discharge rate or with the season or both.

Base flow after n time intervals

$$Q_n = Q_0 e^{-\frac{n}{t_s}} = Q_0 (K_r)^n$$

Storage remaining at time t

$$S_t = \int_0^\infty Q_t \, dt = \int_0^\infty Q_0 e^{-\frac{t}{t_s}} dt = Q_t t_s$$

Storage volume released

$$\Delta S = \frac{(Q_t - Q_0)}{\ln K_r} = (Q_0 - Q_t) t_s$$

Example Problem 8.4

On June 1, 1990, the discharge in a stream was measured as 85 m³/s. Another measurement on June 21, 1990, yielded the stream discharge as 42 m³/s. There was no rainfall in the catchment from April 15, 1990. Estimate the recession coefficient

Given:

$Q_1 = 85$ m³/s $\quad K_r = ?$ $\quad Q_{21} = 42$ m³/s

Solution:

$$Q_t = Q_0(K_r)^t \text{ or } \log Q_t = \log Q_0 + t \log K_r$$

$$\log K_r = \frac{1}{t}(\log Q_t - \log Q_0) = \frac{1}{t}\left(\log\left(\frac{Q_t}{Q_0}\right)\right)$$

$$= \frac{1}{20\ d}\log\left(\frac{42}{85}\right) = -0.015$$

$$K_r = A\log(-0.015) = 0.965 = 0.97$$

Example Problem 8.5

The recession constant of Alpha River is found to be 0.90. During the stream flow recession period a flow of 100 m³/s is observed on a certain day. Compute the base flow in the stream after 5 days.

Given:

$Q_0 = 100$ m³/s $\quad K_r = 0.90$ $\quad Q_n = ?$

Solution:

$$Q_n = Q_0(K_r)^n = \frac{100\ m^3}{s} \times (0.90)^5$$

$$= 59.0 = \underline{59\ m^3/s}$$

Example Problem 8.6

Recession flows for Birch River are as follows:

t, d	0	3	6	9	12
Q, m³/s	100	88	77	69	61

Find time of storage and recession flow released in the first six days?

Flow Hydrograph

Solution:

Time, d	0	3	6	9	12	Avg.
Q, m³/s	100	88	77	69	61	
ts, d			23.5	22.5	27.3	24.3	24.4

$$t_s = \frac{t}{\ln(Q_{t-1}/Q_t)} = \frac{3.0\, d}{\ln(100/88)} = 23.46 = 23.5\, d$$

$$\Delta S = (Q_0 - Q_t)t_s = \frac{(100-77)\, m^3}{s} \times 24.4\, d \times \frac{24\, h}{d}$$

$$= 13468 = 1.35 \times 10^5\, m^3$$

Example Problem 8.7

Fit an equation to the data of previous problem and find the values of recession constant and time of storage?

Solution:

As shown in **Figure 8.4**, to fit an equation, Ln(Q) is plotted against time t and straight line is fitted to the equation.

$$Q_t = 99.5 \times e^{-0.0411t}$$

$$K_r = e^{-0.0411} = 0.9597 = 0.96$$

$$t_s = \frac{1}{a} = \frac{h}{0.0411} = 24.3 = 24\, h$$

Figure 8.4 Fitting Equation to Recession Flow Data

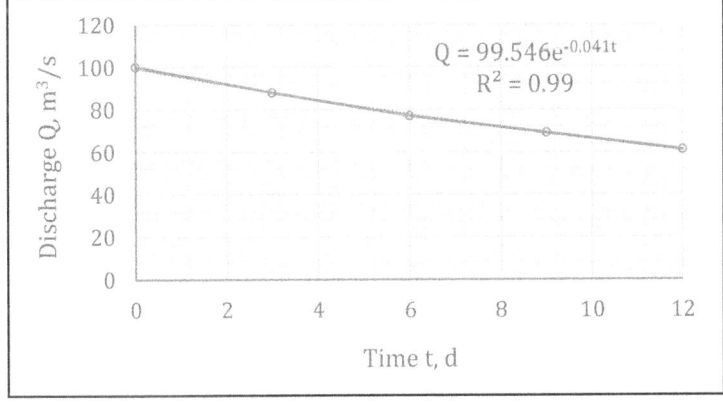

8.4.1 Base Flow Separation

In most cases the stream flow hydrograph is separated into two parts. One part is groundwater (base flow) flow, and the other part is storm runoff that enters the storm quickly after a rainfall event. Base flow component is absent if stream flow before the runoff producing storm is zero, which may be the case for small urban catchments or catchments with deep groundwater table. If base flow is present, which is usually the case in mid-size watersheds, one needs to split stream flow hydrograph in to base flow hydrograph and storm flow hydrograph when studying rain fall runoff relationship.

Straight line Method

Base flow separation is achieved by joining with a straight line from the beginning of direct runoff to a point on the recession limb representing the end of direct runoff. In **Fig 8.5**, line 'a' indicates straight line method. It is easy to visualize the start of direct runoff as indicated by a sharp change, it is rather difficult to pinpoint end of direct runoff. An empirical equation for the time interval in days from peak of direct runoff is:

$$N = 0.83 A^{0.2}$$

Where A is the drainage area in km².

Figure 8.5 Base Flow Separation

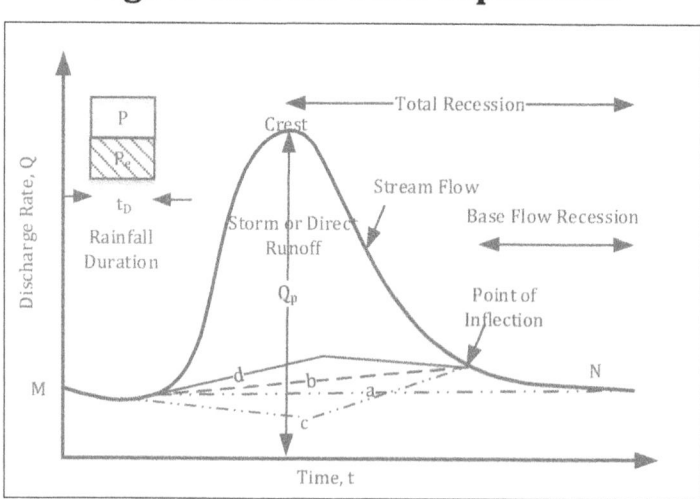

Constant slope Method

In **Fig. 8.5**, this method of base flow separation is indicated by line 'b' indicating increase in base flow during direct runoff generation.

Base Flow Curve Method

As shown by the line 'c' in **Fig. 8.5**, the base flow curve before the commencement of direct runoff is extended up to a point directly under the peak flow. This Point is joined with point of inflexion. This is probably the most widely used method.

Recession Curve Method

Separation of the hydrograph into two components can be done by visual inspection as shown by line 'd' in **Fig. 8.5**. In this case, recession curve is extended backwards towards point of inflexion. This method is more suitable where groundwater contribution is significant.

Example Problem 8.8

A storm produced 41 mm and 29 mm of rainfall in each of the two consecutive 4-h periods. The hydrograph produced due to this storm that fell on catchment of area 31 km² is shown in **Table 8.3 and Fig. 8.6**. Find the storm runoff depth and infiltration index phi.

Solution:

$$N = 0.83(31)^{0.20} = 1.65 \, d = 40 \, h$$

By visual inspection, however, it seems storm runoff begins at zero hour and ends at 48th hour, which gives N value of 48 -12 = 36 h, which seems to be more realistic than 40 h. As shown in **Fig. 8.6**, base flow of 5.0 m³/s is assumed for the entire duration and subtracted from the total flow to yield storm flow values. In the last column of **Table 8.3**, storm runoff volume for each 6-h period equals area of rectangle of width 6 h and length as average of two flows. Total runoff volume is 1490400 m³.

$$R_s = \frac{V_Q}{A} = \frac{1490400 \, m^3}{31 \, km^2} \times \frac{km^2 \cdot mm}{1000 \, m^3}$$

$$= 48.07 = \underline{48.1 \, mm}$$

$$\varphi = \frac{P - R_s}{\Delta t} = \frac{(41 + 29)mm - 48.1 \, mm}{8.0 \, h} = 2.73 = \underline{2.7 \, mm/h}$$

Table 8.3 Flow Hydrograph (Example Prob. 8.7)

t, h	Q, m³/s	Qb, m³/s	Qs, m³/s	Qs, m³/s	VQ, m³
0.00	5.0	5.00	0.00		0
6.00	13.0	5.00	8.00	0.00	86400
12.00	26.0	5.00	21.00	8.00	313200
18.00	21.0	5.00	16.00	21.00	399600
24.00	16.0	5.00	11.00	16.00	291600
30.00	12.0	5.00	7.00	11.00	194400
36.00	9.0	5.00	4.00	7.00	118800
42.00	7.0	5.00	2.00	4.00	64800
48.00	5.0	5.00	0.00	2.00	21600
54.00	5.0	5.00	0.00	0.00	
60.00	4.5	4.50	0.00	0.00	
66.00	4.5	4.50			1490400

Figure 8.6 Base Flow Separation (Ex. Prob. 8.8)

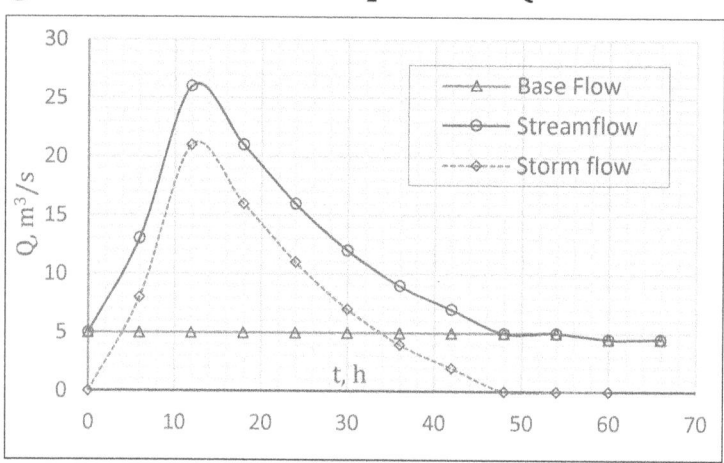

Example Problem 8.9

The hydrograph produced due to this storm that fell on catchment of area 31 km² is shown in **Table 8.4 and Fig. 8.7**. Perform base flow separation by the three methods and determine storm flow for each case.

Table 8.4 Base Flow Separation (Ex. Prob. 8.9)

	Q	Q_{b1}	Q_{b2}	Q_{b3}	Q_{s1}	Q_{s2}	Q_{s3}
1	1600	1600	1600	1600	0	0	0
2	1550	1550	1550	1550	0	0	0
3	5000	1520	1520	3500	3480	3480	1500
4	11300	1500	1500	7200	9800	9800	4100
5	8600	1480	1760	1900	7120	6840	6700
6	6500	1460	2020	1830	5040	4480	4670
7	5000	1440	2280	1760	3560	2720	3240
8	3800	1420	2540	1690	2380	1260	2110
9	2800	1400	2800	1630	1400	0	1170
10	2200	1380	2200	1550	820	0	650
11	1850	1360	1850	1480	490	0	370
12	1600	1340	1600	1420	260	0	180
13	1330	1330	1330	1330	0	0	0
14	1300	1300	1300	1300	0	0	0
15	1280	1280	1280	1280	0	0	0

Sample of calculations:

As shown in Table 8.4 and Fig, 8.7, for the 4th day, Q = 11300 m³/s and base flow estimated by the three methods is 1500, 1500 and 7200 m³/s respectively. Sorm flow for this point accordingly are;

$Q_{s1} = Q - Q_{b1} = 11300 - 1500 = 9800 \ m^3/s$

$Q_{s2} = Q - Q_{b2} = 11300 - 1500 = 9800 \ m^3/s$

$Q_{s3} = Q - Q_{b3} = 11300 - 7200 = 4100 \ m^3/s$

Plot of storm flow hydrographs by the three methods are shown in **Fig. 8.8**

214 *Engineering Hydrology*

Figure 8.7 Base Flow Separation (Ex. Prob. 8.9)

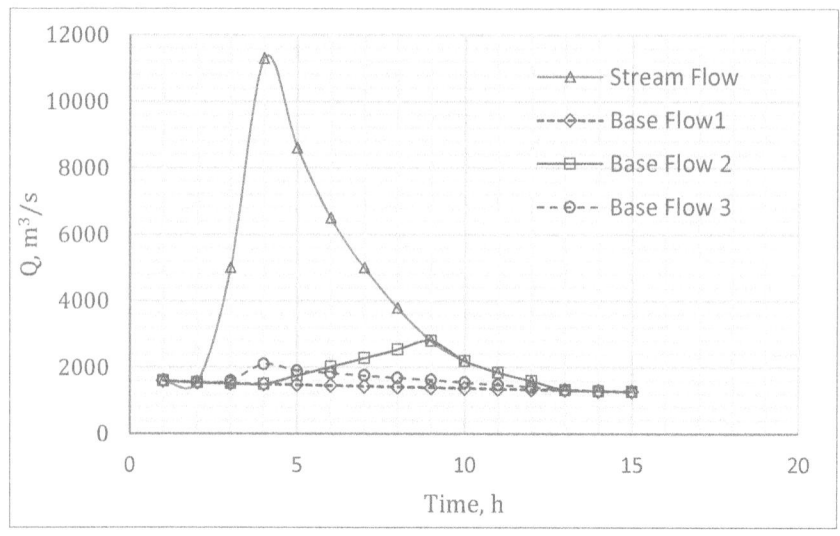

Figure 8.8 Storm Flows (Ex. Prob. 8.9)

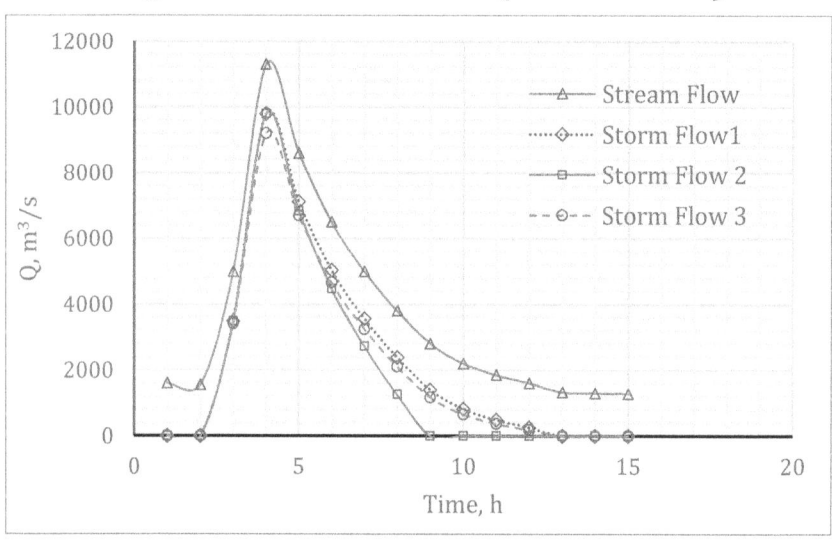

Discussion Questions

1. Define storm flow and discuss the two components it is made up of?
2. What are three types of runoff and factors affecting their generation?
3. Describe how to separate base flow component to produce storm flow hydrograph.
4. Sketch a typical flow hydrograph and label it.
5. List the watershed characteristics that may affect shape of the runoff hydrograph?
6. List the storm characteristics that may affect shape of the runoff hydrograph?
7. What are different parameters used to describe relief features of a watershed?
8. Describe flow hydrograph time characteristics?
9. Define time of concentration and discuss concentrated, super concentrated and sub-concentrated flow and type of watershed conditions they relate to.
10. Sketch a typical flow hydrograph before and after development with significant increase in paved area?
11. What are the basic three elements of a flow hydrograph?
12. Explain why it is justified to apply linear reservoir concept to stream flow recession?
13. Prove that after time equal to time of storage, recession flow reduces to 37% of the previous flow?
14. Compare the terms lag time versus time of concentration. In NRCS formula, what is the mathematical relationship between the two?
15. On a flow hydrograph where is the point of inflexion and what does it indicate?

Practice Problems

Practice Problem 8.1

The main watercourse of a catchment is 1.5 km long. Characteristics of the two main reaches are given below. Estimate the time of concentration. (51 min)

Reach#	L, m	S, %	R_h, m	n
1	900	0.10	0.50	0.04
2	600	0.30	0.30	0.05

Practice Problem 8.2

A watershed is characterized by CN of 75 and an average slope of 2.8%. The distance along the flow path from the outlet to the furthest point on the watershed divide measured from topographic map is 2100 m. Using NRCS lag equation, estimate the lag time and time of concentration. (1.0 h, 1.7 h)

Practice Problem 8.3

For the data of Example Problem 8.1, due to some changes in land use, CN has increased to 82 and hydraulic length is reduced to 4450 m. Determine the new lag time for this watershed. ()

Practice Problem 8.4

The flow path from the sewer inlet to the hydraulically distant point of a park lot is estimated 80 m of gutter flow and 55 m of overland flow through Bermuda grass on a 2.2% slope. Longitudinal slope of the gutter is 1.5%. Determine time of concentration. (21 min)

Practice Problem 8.5

Stream flow in a river is receding and is observed as 280 m³/s on a given day. If the recession constant for this river is 0.88, what was the stream flow in this river 5 days ago, five days after? (530 m³/s, 150 m³/s)

Practice Problem 8.6

For the data of example problem 8.6, find the recession volume released during the last six hours. Also determine recession constant.
(1.35×10⁶ m³, 9.58×10⁻¹)

Practice Problem 8.7

Recession data of ln(Q) versus time in days is regressed using MS Excel and following equation is fitted: $\ln Q = 2.40 - 0.292t$. Find the recession constant? How many days it would take to reduce the base flow to one half? (0.75, 2.4 d)

Practice Problem 8.8

Recession constant of a certain river is 0.92/d. How many days it would take to reduce the base flow to one forth? (17d)

Practice Problem 8.9

A storm produced 35 mm and 25 mm of rainfall in each of the two consecutive 2-h periods. The flow hydrograph produced due to this storm that fell on the catchment of area 32 km² is shown below. Separate base flow and estimate depth of storm runoff and φ-index. (28 mm, 8.1 mm/h)

t, h	0	4	8	12	16	20	24	28	32	36	42
Q, m³/s	5	13	24	20	15	12	9	7	6	5.5	5

Practice Problem 8.10

In the following table, storm flow runoff from a catchment area of 77 km² due to a stom lasting for 4–h is produced. Determine the storm runoff depth and W-index assuming intial storage of 2.5 mm. Rainfall depth received in each of the 2-h period is recorded to be 22 mm and 18 mm.
(17 mm, 5.0 mm/h)

t, h	0	4	8	12	16	20	24	28	32	36
Q, m³/s	0	5	18	21	16	12	9	7	5	0

Review Questions

1. Base flow separation is performed to yield _____ hydrograph.
   a) Streamflow   b) Surface flow   c) Storm flow   d) Interflow

2. Which of the following runoff components is the slowest to reach the outlet?
   a) Baseflow   b) Interflow   c) Storm flow   d) Interflow

3. The recession limb of a flow hydrograph can be expressed as $Q_t = Q_0 \times$
   a) k^t b) e^{kt} c) e^{-kt} d) $e^{k/t}$

4. Which of the following runoff components has greater value of recession constant?
   a) Streamflow   b) Surface flow   c) Storm flow   d) Interflow

5. For a recession constant of 0.50, after a period of 5.0 d, flow will be reduced by a factor of
   a) 5×   b) 10×   c) 25×   d) 32×

6. Storm flow is a combination of
   a) Streamflow, base flow
   b) Surface flow, base flow
   c) Overland flow, interflow
   d) Base flow, interflow

7. Storm flow is streamflow minus
   a) Baseflow   b) Surface flow   c) Overland flow   d) Interflow

8. Rising limb of the storm flow hydrograph is due to
   a) Interflow   b) Base flow   c) Ground flow   d) Overland flow

9. A plot of recession curve on a _____ paper plots a straight line
   a) Log vs log scale
   b) Semi log scale
   c) Arithmetic scale
   d) None of these

10. Which of the following runoff components is the first to reach the outlet?
    a) Base low   b) Ground flow   c) Overland flow   d) Interflow

11. Which part of the flow hydrograph is asymptotic?
    a) Rising   b) Crest   c) Receding   d) Recession

12. Rising limb of a stormflow hydrograph is steeper in case of
    a) Urbanized catchment
    b) Large watershed
    c) Rural catchment
    d) Forested watershed

13. Which part of the flow hydrograph is not affected by the storm characteristics?
    a) Rising
    b) Receding
    c) Recession
    d) All

14. For a certain river, recession constant is known to be 0.92. How many days it would take to reduce the base flow by 10%?
    a) 0.5 d
    b) 1.3 d
    c) 2.7 d
    d) 11 d

15. Inflexion point on the recession side of a hydrograph indicates end of
    a) Interflow
    b) Base flow
    c) Ground flow
    d) Overland flow

16. What are the units of recession constant?
    a) d
    b) 1/d
    c) m·d
    d) Dimensionless

17. Which of the following are the correct units of time of storage?
    a) d
    b) 1/d
    c) m·d
    d) No units

18. Storage at a given time is equal to discharge rate multiplied by
    a) Recession constant
    b) Time of storage
    c) Recession time
    d) Time to peak

19. After a time, equal to time of storage recession flow reduces to
    a) 57%
    b) 42%
    c) 37%
    d) 25%

20. A linear reservoir is the one in which _____ varies linearly with __
    a) Volume, depth
    b) Outflow, storage
    c) Storage, inflow
    d) Storage, time

21. For recession part of the hydrograph, ratio of Q_{t+1}/Q_t equals
    a) Recession constant
    b) Time of storage
    c) Recession time
    d) Log of recession constant

22. In a typical storm flow hydrograph, time to recede equals
    a) Time to peak
    b) Storm duration
    c) Lag time
    d) None of these

23. Which of the following is not a time characteristics of flow hydrograph?
    a) Lag time
    b) Time of concentration
    c) Time to peak
    d) Storm period

24. In which of the following size catchments, time of concentration is usually less than storm duration?
    a) Lake basins
    b) Large watersheds
    c) Medium rural watersheds
    d) Small urban catchments

25. In relatively wide channels, hydraulic radius can be assumed equal to
    a) Perimeter of section
    b) Area of section
    c) Depth of flow
    d) Width of section

26. In majority of the watersheds, which of the following conditions of runoff generation is more common?
    a) Concentrated flow
    b) Super-concentrated flow
    c) Sub-concentrated flow
    d) Almost same

27. Which component of streamflow is called base flow?
    a) Groundwater flow
    b) Interflow
    c) Overland flow
    d) Storm flow

28. Storm flow is also called
    a) Direct Runoff
    b) Surface Runoff
    c) Sub-surface runoff
    d) Delayed Runoff

29. Which type of runoff is the last to reach the outlet of the watershed?
    a) Baseflow
    b) Surface flow
    c) Overland flow
    d) interflow

30. For urban watersheds with relatively short time of concentrations, rainfall falling at a uniform rate will produce peak runoff rate, if the storm lasts for a period equal to
    a) Time of concentration
    b) Lag time
    c) Recession time
    d) a +b

9 Peak Flow Rate

Providing adequate drainage of storm water is one of the many jobs of a Water Resources Engineer. This job has gained new dimensions since the drainage works have changed from primitive ditches to complex networks of curbs, gutters and underground conduits. Simple rules of thumb and crude empirical formulas are generally inadequate. In addition, demands by the society for better environmental control requires that water quality considerations be superimposed on estimates of quantity so that management of total water resource can be affected.

To design a system with sufficient capacity to yield adequate drainage of water, for most of the time, a complete understanding of the rainfall-runoff relationship for a given watershed system is very important. Given such a relationship, it is possible to answer two questions:
1. How much maximum flow can be expected?
2. How often can this amount be exceeded?

A number of design methods for estimating **peak discharge** are available and vary from a rule of thumb approach to macroscopic approach, microscopic approach and continuous simulation. Each method should be applied only after its strengths and limitations are understood. The most popular methods for estimating peak flows are: Rational Method and the NRCS Method. These methods are described in the following sections.

9.1 Peak Flow and Watershed Area

Area is perhaps the most important single parameter governing the rainfall-runoff relationship. This relationship may be developed for a region as runoff data becomes available for a range of watershed areas.

The main advantage of this method is its simplicity. However, what is gained by simplicity is lost in accuracy of prediction. Keeping these limitations in mind, these relationships are good for initial estimates of peak flow or as a general check on another improved design method.

9.2 Rational Method

The most commonly used peak discharge design method is the **Rational Method**, (Emil Kuichling, 1889). A peak flow is associated with certain watershed parameters, such as area, topography, soil texture, vegetation and surface storage, and with the storm characteristics of duration, intensity and frequency. For any consistent system of units, Rational Method may be formulated as:

Rational Formula
$$Q_p = C \times I \times A$$

C = runoff coefficient, proportion of the total rainfall which runs off
I = the maximum rainfall intensity for a duration equal to t_c and for a storm of design return period, T
A = the drainage area

9.2.1 Application

The following information is required for application of Rational Method:

1. Estimate the runoff coefficient C from the knowledge of the watershed characteristics. Using **Table 9.1** or **Table 9.2**, and knowledge of the catchment, value of runoff coefficient is selected. When not sure, it is recommended to select the mid-range.

2. Time of concentration is the time for water to travel from hydraulically remote areas of the watershed to the outlet. The basic foundation of rational formula is that flow is concentrated at the outlet when rainfall occurs at least for a time equal to time of concentration. It is logical since all the area would be able to contribute to runoff at the outlet.

3. For the time of concentration estimated and a selected rainfall frequency, the design rainfall intensity is obtained from IDF curves or equations. Standard drainage systems and small spillways are normally designed for rainfall events of 5-year to 10-year frequency.

4. Compute the peak flow using the rational formula and making appropriate unit conversions

Table 9.1 Typical C Values (Urban Areas)

Description of Area	Runoff Coefficient
Business	
Downtown areas	0.70 - 0.95
Neighborhood areas	0.50 - 0.70
Residential	
Single-family areas	0.30 - 0.50
Multi units, detached	0.40 - 0.60
Multi units, attached	0.60 - 0.75
Residential (suburban)	0.25 - 0.40
Apartment dwelling areas	0.50 - 0.70
Industrial	
Light areas	0.50 - 0.80
Heavy areas	0.60 - 0.90
Parks, cemeteries	0.10 - 0.25
Playgrounds	0.20 - 0.35
Railroad yard areas	0.20 - 0.40
Unimproved areas	0.10 - 0.30
Streets	
Asphaltic	0.70 - 0.95
Concrete	0.80 - 0.95
Brick	0.70 - 0.85
Drives and walks	0.75 - 0.85
Roofs	0.70 - 0.95
Lawns; Sandy Soil:	
Flat, 2%	0.05 - 0.10
Average, 2-7%	0.10 - 0.15
Steep, 7%	0.15 - 0.20
Lawns; Heavy Soil:	
Flat, 2%	0.13 - 0.17
Average, 2-7%	0.18 - 0.22
Steep, 7%	0.25 - 0.3

Table 9.2 Runoff Coefficients for Rural Areas

Vegetation and Topography	Soil Texture		
	Sandy Loam	Silt Loam	Tight Clay
Woodland			
(Flat 0-5% Slope)	0.10	0.30	0.40
Rolling (5-10% Slope)	0.25	0.35	0.50
Hilly (10-30% Slope)	0.30	0.50	0.60
Pasture			
Flat	0.10	0.30	0.40
Rolling	0.16	0.36	0.55
Hilly	0.22	0.42	0.60
Cultivated			
Flat	0.30	0.50	0.60
Rolling	0.40	0.60	0.70
Hilly	0.52	0.72	0.82
Urban Areas			
(Area impervious)	30%	50%	70%
Flat	0.40	0.55	0.65
Rolling	0.50	0.65	0.80

9.2.2 Modifications

Antecedent Moisture Conditions

Modifications to the Rational Method have been proposed in order that coefficient C may account for antecedent moisture conditions. To account for this, a new factor C_a is introduced.

Peak Flow rate

$$Q_p = C \times C_a \times I \times A$$

T	2-10	25	50	100
C_a	1.0	1.10	1.20	1.25

Runoff Concentration with Diffusion

When diffusion is present, recession time increases producing lower peak flow rate. Reducing the runoff coefficient can represent diffusion in the Rational Method.

9.2.3 Areal Weighing of Runoff Coefficients

When a clear pattern of variation in the catchment surface is apparent, an area-weighted runoff coefficient should be used.

$$\bar{C} = \frac{\sum C_i A_i}{\sum A_i} = \frac{\sum C_i A_i}{A}$$

Rational formula for a composite catchment can be written as follows:

$$Q_p = I \times \Sigma(C_i \times A_i)$$

9.2.4 Time of concentration

Time of concentration, t_c is the time for water to travel from hydraulically remote areas of the catchment to the outlet or drain inlet. The estimation of time of concentration can be made by dividing distance of travel by the average flow velocity as found by Manning's flow equation. For small catchments, time of concentration can be estimated by the empirical formula. When the flow is primarily channel flow, Kirpich formula can be used to estimate time of concentration.

Kirpich Formula (channel flow time)

$$t_{ch} = \frac{0.02 L^{0.77}}{S^{0.385}} = \frac{0.02 L^{1.2}}{H^{0.385}}$$

t = time (min), L = length (m) H = drop (m), S = slope (decimal fraction)

For covered surfaces, this value can be modified. For example, for surfaces fully covered with sod, time of concentration will be twice as much and for paved surfaces it would be half of this value.

Kerby Formula

The Kerby formula can be used to calculate overland flow time before it becomes channel flow. Kerby formula incorporates the roughness of land surface N that is similar to Manning's n but larger in value. Time of concentration as overland flow is given by:

Overland flow time
$$t_{ov} = \frac{1.5(LN)^{0.467}}{S^{0.234}}$$

L = length, m S = slope m/m t_{ov} = min N = 0.02 (paved), 0.8 (timberland)

Kirpich and Kerby Formula

In cases when upper part of the reach is overland flow and further down some distance it becomes channel flow, catchment length is divided into two components, overland flow length and channel flow length. Time of concentration is calculated by adding the two components.

$$t_c = t_{ov} + t_{ch}$$

Urban Catchments

In urban catchments, time of concentration would consist of two components, overland flow time usually called **inlet time** to reach inlet and travel time through the drain or gutter called **flow time**. Flow time, t_f is found by estimating flow velocity from Manning's equation. Inlet time is found by using empirical formula as discussed earlier.

Time of concentration
$$t_c = t_i + t_f = \frac{0.02L^{0.77}}{S^{0.385}} + \frac{L}{v}$$

v = flow velocity in m/min, t_i = inlet time, t_f = flow time

9.2.5 Rainfall intensity

For the time of concentration estimated and a selected rainfall frequency, the design rainfall intensity is obtained from a plot of rainfall intensity-duration-frequency, IDF curves or equations. A typical form of the function follows:

Sample IDF function
$$I = \frac{850T^{0.2}}{(D+15)^{0.75}}$$

I = Maximum average Intensity   T = return period   D = Storm duration

Rainfall intensity decreases exponentially with increase in storm duration. Rainfall can occur intensely for shorter durations. On the other hand, for the same duration, rainfall intensity is higher for rare storm that is storm with larger return periods. It is assumed, rainfall intensity of a given frequency would produce the flood of the same frequency. It is usually true for storms with larger return periods. Standard drainage systems and small spillways are normally designed for rainfall events of 5-year to 10-year frequency. Structures like dams are designed based on much larger return periods in the range of 50 to 100 years.

9.2.6 Limitations of Rational Method

Following limitations should be recognized for application of Rational Method.
1. The runoff coefficient C is difficult to establish consistently and objectively particularly for agricultural watersheds where infiltration is highly variable with time and space.
2. The time of concentration t_c is not constant as the formula suggests and may vary with the storm characteristics. It is an extremely difficult parameter to assess meaningfully but plays an important role in the estimate of peak discharge.
3. For rural watersheds, runoff frequency is not equal to the rainfall frequency. Therefore, the Rational Method does not yield runoff estimates of selected frequencies, but runoff amounts that might occur as a result of particular rainfall events of selected frequencies.
4. The rainfall intensity-duration-frequency information is for point rainfall. The probability that such rates will occur uniformly over an area decreases as the area of interest increases.
5. The method is not recommended for use on agricultural drainage basins larger than 500 ha.
6. The value of runoff coefficient C is assumed constant during the progress of an individual storm and also from storm to storm. The estimation of coefficient is based on the degree of imperviousness and infiltration capacity of the drainage surface. But as infiltration capacity will vary with time depending on initial moisture conditions, C must vary. It is for this reason that runoff frequency is not always equal to rainfall frequency.
7. This method yields a point value Q_p and says nothing about the nature of the rest of hydrograph.

In urban watersheds where most of the area is impervious, infiltration does not play a major role in the production of runoff. This is the main reason that the Rational Method has been used more successfully in its application to small urban watersheds.

Example Problem 9.1

Calculate the peak runoff rate from a 3.5 ha parking lot. The time of concentration and runoff coefficient respectively are 20 min and 0.75. The rainfall intensity for 20-min duration is 75 mm/h.

Given:

D = 20 min   I = 75 mm/h   A = 3.0 ha

Solution:

$$Q_p = CIA = 0.75 \times \frac{75 \text{ mm}}{h} \times 3.5 \text{ ha} \times \frac{10 \text{ m}^3}{ha.mm} \times \frac{h}{3600 \text{ s}}$$

$$= 0.546 = \underline{0.55 \text{ m}^3/s}$$

Example Problem 9.2

A roof drain has a maximum flow carrying capacity of 1.25 L/s. Determine how much maximum roof area it can drain without overflowing. Assume the rainfall intensity for a 10-year storm to be 120 mm/h and C = 0.85.

Given:

Q = 1.25 L/s   I = 120 mm/h   A =?

Solution:

$$A = \frac{Q_p}{CI} = \frac{1.25 \text{ L}}{s} \times \frac{1}{0.85} \times \frac{h}{120 \text{ mm}} \times \frac{3600 \text{ s}}{h} \times \frac{mm.m^2}{L}$$

$$= 44.12 = \underline{44 \text{ m}^2}$$

Example Problem 9.3

It is being proposed to develop a 1.5 km² of a drainage area. Pre-development and post-development conditions are shown in **Table 9.3**. Calculate the peak runoff for pre- development conditions using 5-y storm. IDF function is; I (mm/h) = 850 T $^{0.2}$/(D + 15)$^{0.75}$ T = return period D = duration, min

Table 9.3 Data Table (Ex. Prob. 9.3)

Development	Surface	C	D = t_c, h
Pre-development	Natural	0.30	3.0
Post development	Partially paved	0.60	2.0

Peak Flow Rate

Solution:

(Pre-development conditions)

$$I = \frac{850T^{0.2}}{(D+15)^{0.75}} = \frac{850 \times (5.0)^{0.2}}{(180+15)^{0.75}} = 22.47 = 22.5 \; mm/h$$

$$Q_p = CIA = 0.3 \times \frac{22.47 \; mm}{h} \times 1.5 \; km^2 \times \frac{10^3 \; m^3}{km^2.mm} \times \frac{h}{3600 \; s}$$

$$= 2.809 = \underline{2.8 \; m^3/s}$$

Post-development conditions

$$I = \frac{850T^{0.2}}{(D+15)^{0.75}} = \frac{850 \times (5.0)^{0.2}}{(120+15)^{0.75}} = 29.612 = 29.6 \; mm/h$$

$$Q_p = CIA = 0.60 \times \frac{29.612 \; mm}{h} \times 1.5 \; km^2 \times \frac{10^3 \; m^3}{km^2.mm} \times \frac{h}{3600 \; s}$$

$$= 7.402 = \underline{7.4 \; m^3/s}$$

Example Problem 9.4

Compute the 10-y peak flow rate from an agricultural catchment with drainage area of 5.0 ha pasture. The soils are primarily fine-textured soils with rolling topography. Use IDF curves shown in **Fig. 3.7**.

Given:

A = 5.0 ha   T = 10 y   L = 205 m   S = 0.90% = 0.009

Solution:

Time of concentration

$$t_c = \frac{0.02L^{0.77}}{S^{0.385}} = \frac{0.02 \times 205^{0.77}}{0.009^{0.385}} = 7.391 = 7.39 \; min$$

Roughness of sod is relatively high compared to bare earth. Hence, time of concentration is doubled: 7.39×2 = 14.8 = 15 min. For T = 10 years, and duration, of 15 min, I = 160 mm/h (IDF Curves). Further runoff coefficient C = 0.36 for clay and silt loam, rolling topography **(Table 9.1)**

Peak runoff rate

$$Q_p = CIA = 0.36 \times \frac{160 \; mm}{h} \times 5.0 \; ha \times \frac{10 \; m^3}{ha.mm} \times \frac{h}{3600 \; s}$$

$$= \frac{8.0 \times 10^{-1} \; m^3}{s} \times \frac{1000L}{m^3} = 800.0 = \underline{800 \; L/s}$$

Example Problem 9.5

Two adjacent fields of areas of 1-ha and 2-ha contribute runoff to a collector whose capacity is to be determined. It is estimated that in 25 min areas from both the fields start contributing. Rainfall intensity for the 15-y storm is given by the following IDF function:

$$I = \frac{1500}{(D+15)^{0.8}}$$

Given:

$C_1 = 0.35$ $\quad C_2 = 0.65$ $\quad A_1 = 1$ ha $\quad A_2 = 2$ ha

Solution:

$$I = \frac{1500}{(D+15)^{0.8}} = \frac{1500}{(25+15)^{0.8}} = 78.42 = 78.4 \ mm/h$$

$$C = \frac{\Sigma C_i A_i}{\Sigma A_i} = \frac{0.35 \times 1 + 0.65 \times 2}{1+2} = 0.550 = 0.55$$

$$Q_p = CIA = 0.55 \times \frac{78.4 \ mm}{h} \times 3.0 \ ha \times \frac{10 \ m^3}{ha.mm} \times \frac{h}{3600 \ s}$$

$$= \frac{3.56 \times 10^{-2} \ m^3}{s} \times \frac{1000L}{m^3} = 35.6 = 36 \ L/s \quad Or$$

$$Q_p = I \times \Sigma(C_i A_i) = \frac{78.4 \ mm}{h} \times (0.35 \times 1 + 0.65 \times 2) \ ha$$

$$= \frac{129.3 \ ha.mm}{h} \times \frac{10 \ m^3}{ha.mm} \times \frac{1000 \ L}{m^3} \times \frac{h}{3600 \ s} = 35.6 = 36 \ L/s$$

9.2.7 Urban Catchments

Application of the Rational Method to urban catchments (1 < A < 2.5 km²) requires special techniques. Flow varies widely along the length of main channel (sewer) generally small at the upstream and larger at the downstream. In this case, it may be difficult to determine average t_c. An alternative is to apply the Rational Method incrementally. The method requires sb-division of catchment into several sub-areas (**Figure 9.1**).

According to NRCS(Natural Resources Conservation service), water moves through a watershed as sheet flow, shallow concentrated flow, open channel flow or some combination of these before it exits the sewer line. This is called inlet time. Thus, it becomes a case of composite catchment. Various flow paths are tried and the one producing maximum flow is selected.

Figure 9.1 Inlet and Travel Time

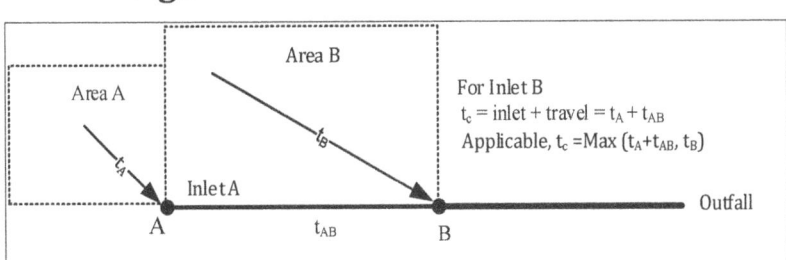

Note: Except for the first inlet, more than one area contributes to runoff.

Referring to **Figure 9.1**, the time of concentration for outlet 1 = inlet time t_A. This is the time taken by the overland flow from area A to reach outlet 1. After calculating the flow at inlet 1, flow velocity in the pipeline is found using Manning's equation. Knowing the flow velocity v_{1-2}, time of travel from 1 to 2, t_{1-2} is calculated. Time of concentration for outlet 2 is equal to inlet time for area A plus travel time from outlet 1 to 2. This process is continued until the peak flow at the outfall is worked out.

Example Problem 9.6

A storm drainage system comprises the four areas as shown below. Determine the 5-y design flow for each section of sewer line.

Figure 9.2 Storm Drainage System (Ex. Prob. 9.6)

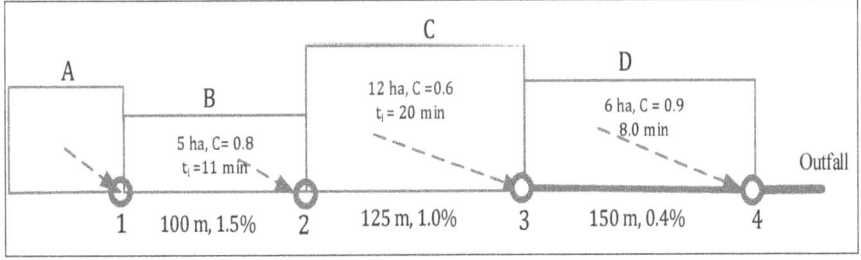

Given:

Catchment	Area A, ha	Coefficient C	Inlet time, min
A	5	0.8	10
B	5	0.8	9
C	12	0.6	20
D	6	0.9	8

Solution:
Computations are shown in **Table 9.4**.

Table 9.4 Table of Computations (Ex. Prob. 9.6)

inlet	C	A	CA	ΣCA	Path	t_i	L, m	m/s	t_f	Tot	I mm/h	Q_p m³/s
1	0.8	5	4	4	A-1	10				10.0	100.0	1.1
2	0.8	5	4	8	A-2	10	100	1.5	1.1	11.1	95.7	2.1
3	0.6	12	7.2	15.2	C-3	20				20.0	71.4	3.0
4	0.9	6	5.4	20.6	C--4	20	150	1.5	1.7	21.7	68.2	3.9

Note: For a given outlet, the longest path is used to calculate time of conc.

Sample of Calculations (Outlet #2)

$$\Sigma C_i A_i = 0.8 \times 5 + 0.8 \times 5 = 8.0 \text{ ha.mm}$$

$$t_c = t_{A-2} = 10 \text{ min} + 100 \text{ m} \times \frac{s}{1.5 \text{ m}} \times \frac{\min}{60 \text{ s}} = 11.11 = 11.1 \text{ min}$$

$$i = \frac{2500}{D+15} = \frac{2500}{11.1+15} = 95.7 \text{ mm/h}$$

$$Q_p = I\Sigma C_i A_i = \frac{95.7 \text{ mm}}{h} \times 8.0 \text{ ha} \times \frac{10 \text{ m}^3}{ha.mm} \times \frac{h}{3600 \text{ s}}$$

$$= 2.10 = \underline{2.1 \text{ m}^3/\text{s}}$$

Example Problem 9.7

Determine 10-y peak flow rate from an urban catchment shown in **Fig. 9.3**. Runoff from both parking lot and park runs as overland flow into s swale running between them. Runoff coefficients C are 0.25 and 0.90 for the paved parking lot and grass park. The IDF equation for the area is given by following equation.

I (mm/h) = $850 T^{0.2}/(D + 10)^{0.75}$ T = return period D = duration in min.

Figure 9.3 Inlet and Travel Time (Ex. Prob. 9.7)

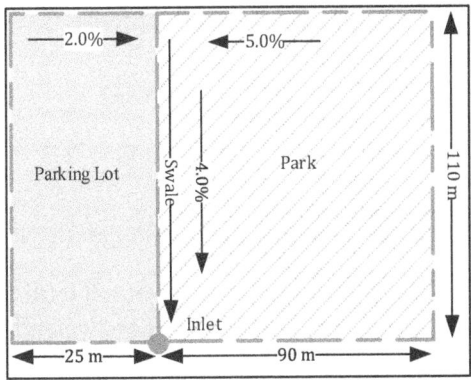

Solution:

Table 9.5 Excel Worksheet (Ex. Prob. 9.7)

Reach	K	S, %	L, m	V, m/s	t, min	t_c, min	C	A	C×A
Park	0.65	3.0	90	0.11	13.32	16.23	0.25	0.99	0.25
Parking	4.5	0.8	25	0.40	1.04	3.95	0.90	0.28	0.25
Swale	6.3	1.0	110	0.63	2.91				
					Max	16.23		Σ =	0.50

Coefficients K as shown in **Table 9.5** for various land covers are read from Table 7.1. Overland flow velocity is obtained by multiplying K with square root of slope as decimal fraction. For example, for green park, sample of calculations are as follows.

Time of travel
$$v = K\sqrt{S} = 0.65 \times \sqrt{0.03} = 0.113 \, m/s$$

$$t = \frac{L}{v} = 90 \, m \times \frac{s}{0.113 \, m} \times \frac{min}{60 \, s} = 13.3 \, min$$

As shown in **Table 9.5**, maximum travel time is from park to inlet.
$t_c = 13.32 \, min + 2.91 \, min = 16.23 = 16 \, min.$

Rainfall intensity
$$I = \frac{850 T^{0.2}}{(D+10)^{0.75}} = \frac{850 \times 10^{0.2}}{(16.2+10)^{0.75}} = 116.3 = 120 \, mm/h$$

Paek runoff rate

$$Q_p = I \times \Sigma(C_i A_i) = \frac{116.3 \, mm}{h} \times 0.50 \, ha$$

$$= \frac{58.16 \, ha.mm}{h} \times \frac{10 \, m^3}{ha.mm} \times \frac{1000 \, L}{m^3} \times \frac{h}{3600 \, s}$$

$$= 161.5 = \underline{160 \, L/s}$$

9.3 Cook's Method

Cook used a different approach to estimate the runoff from small agricultural areas. In this method, the runoff characteristics of a watershed are examined under four categories: relief, infiltration, vegetative cover, and surface storage. Based on observations of peak floods from agricultural areas, numerical values have been assigned to various conditions of above categories by various investigators.

1. The sum (ΣW), of the numerical values assigned to the watershed characteristics is obtained.
2. Runoff curves are then entered with the drainage area and ΣW and the value of peak runoff, P for a 10-year recurrence interval is obtained.
3. This peak runoff, P is then modified for recurrence interval and geomorphic characteristics by the formula:

$$Q_p = P \times R \times F$$

Where Q_P is peak runoff for a specified region and geomorphic location, R is geomorphic rainfall factor (based on longitude and latitude) and F is recurrence interval factor.

9.4 TR-55 Graphical Method

The title **TR-55** comes from technical release number 55 produced by Soil Conservation, now Natural Resources Conservation Service. This method is applicable to small and mid-size catchments and is based on NRCS TR-2-hydraulic computer model. The TR-55 graphical method provides peak flow as a function of unit peak flow that is peak flow per unit area per unit storm depth. The graphs are developed to provide unit peak flow, q_u in $ft^3/s.mile^2$.in (csm/in) as a function of

- Type of the storm distribution Type I, IA, III, IV
- Time of concentration, t_c (0.1 -10 h)
- Initial abstraction to 24-h rain depth ratio, I_a/P

As compared to Rational formula, in this method, concentration time accounts for the runoff concentration and runoff diffusion. In addition, there is a surface storage correction factor F to account for the reduction in peak flow due to ponds and swamps.

Due to the fact that **TR-55 method** considers **runoff diffusion**, it is applicable to mid-size catchments with concentration times of up to 10 h. Typical range for time of concentration is 0.1 - 10 h.

9.4.1 Pervious versus Impervious Area

For urban catchments (developed areas) TR-55 defines two types of areas:(1) Pervious (open space, good condition) (2) Impervious (CN = 98)

For each type of land use, say commercial or residential, CN are based on specific percent of imperviousness. In NRCS Tables, CN values for commercial land use are based on 85% imperviousness. For urban land uses with percent of imperviousness different than those given in the tables, curve number can be computed using a weighted approach. Good condition is used for pervious portion of the area. Unless otherwise stated, CN_{IP} = 98 and CN for the pervious portion for the given soil is based on open space with good cover conditions. For B soil group, pasture in good condition CN = 61. Assuming 85% impervious area, typical for commercial use, weighted N is calculated based on fraction of pervious and impervious area.

$$CN_C = CN_P \times (1-f) + CN_{IP} \times f = 61(1-0.85) + 98 \times 0.85 = 92$$

Table of curve numbers for commercial area for urban land use are based on 85% imperviousness and pervious area with Group B soils. However, suppose the impervious area is different than 85%, say 75%.

$$CN_C = 61(1-0.75) + 98 \times 0.75 = 89$$

This value is less due the fact that fraction of the impervious area is reduced from 85% to 75% and open space area has gone up.

Unconnected Impervious Areas

NRCS further divides in impervious areas into two categories: unconnected and connected. **Connected impervious areas** are those which directly drain into the system or, where run off from the impervious area flows over a pervious area as shallow concentrated flow such as in a grass swale.

Unconnected impervious area is that in which drainage is indirect. In this case, runoff from impervious area flows over pervious area as overland flow or sheet flow, thus increasing the time of concentration.

Correction for unconnectedness

When portion of the impervious areas is below 30 percent and part of it is unconnected, this indicates increased storage and diffusion. This is considered by adjusting the weighted CN further by reducing the percentage of impervious area. If R is the fraction of unconnected impervious area, composite curve number can be found as follows:

Composite curve number
$$CN_C = CN_P \times \left(1 - f(1 - 0.5R)\right) + CN_{IP} \times f(1 - 0.5R)$$
$$CN_C = CN_P \times (1 - f') + CN_{IP} \times f'$$

Where f' is the modified impervious fraction (reduced due to unconnected portion that does not drain directly)

$$f' = f(1 - 0.5R)$$

Curve number for the impervious area is usually taken 98

Example Problem 9.8

It is planned to develop 6.4 ha upland watershed. The developed portion of the area will be residential with 21% impervious and fully connected to the drainage system. The undeveloped portion is forested on soil B in fair condition and has area of 2.8 ha. Determine the weighted CN for the whole catchment?

Solution:

For the developed area, 21% is impervious (CN = 98) and remaining 79% is pervious on B soil, good condition (CN = 61), hence the composite CN for the developed portion is

$$CN = 61(1 - 0.21) + 98 \times 0.21 = 68.7 = 69$$

For the undeveloped portion of 2.8 ha, the land use is forested in fair conditions on B soils (CN = 60). The weighted curve number calculations are shown in **Table 9.6**.

Table 9.6 Weighted Curve Number (Ex. Prob. 9.8)

Land use/cover	A_i, ha	W_i, %	CN_i	$A_i \times CN_i$	$W_i \times CN_i$
Developed	6.4	69.6	68.7	440	48.6
Underdeveloped	2.8	30.4	60	168	18.3
$\Sigma =$	9.2	100		608	66.9

Example Problem 9.9

Determine the weighted curve number for a 32-ha urban watershed that includes 14 ha of commercial land (70% impervious, 15% unconnected, B soil) and 18 ha of residential properties (24% impervious, 90% unconnected B soil).

Given:

Commercial: A = 14 ha   f = 70% R = 15%   B Soil
Residential   A = 18 ha   f = 24% R = 90%   B Soil

Solution:

Commercial portion (1). Out of 70% pervious area, 15% is unconnected, hence modified f is

$$f' = f(1 - 0.5R) = 0.7(1 - 0.5 \times 0.15) = 0.6475 = 0.65$$

For pervious B soil, good condition (CN = 61), hence the composite CN

$$CN_{C1} = CN_P \times (1 - f') + CN_{IP} \times f'$$

$$= 61 \times (1 - 0.6475) + 98 \times 0.0.6475 = 84.96 = 85$$

Residential portion (2)
$$f' = f(1 - 0.5R) = 0.24(1 - 0.5 \times 0.90) = 0.132 = 0.13$$

$$CN_{C2} = CN_P \times (1 - f') + CN_{IP} \times f'$$

$$= 61 \times (1 - 0.132) + 98 \times 0.0.13 = 65.88 = 65.9$$

Area weights
$$W_1 = \frac{14\ ha}{(14 + 18) ha} = 0.4375 = 0.44$$

$$W_2 = \frac{18\ ha}{(14 + 18) ha} = 0.5625 = 0.56$$

Weighted curve number

$$CN_w = \Sigma(CN_{Ci} \times W_i) = 84.96 \times 0.44 + 65.88 \times 0.56$$

$$= 74.23 = 74.2$$

Complete computations are shown in MS Excel worksheet (Table 9.7)

Table 9.7 Weighted Curve Number (Ex. Prob. 9.9)

Land use	A$_i$, ha	f	R	f'	CN$_P$	CN$_{ci}$	W$_i$	W$_i$' CN$_{Ci}$
Commercial	14	0.70	0.15	0.648	61	84.96	0.44	37.2
Residential	18	0.24	0.90	0.132	61	65.88	0.56	37.1
Σ =	32						1.00	74.2

9.5 TR-55 Procedure

1. The first step is to delineate and measure the drainage area contributory to the point of analysis (outlet).

2. Next step is to determine the runoff curve number CN. If the drainage area consists of a variety of subareas in terms of CN, which is more usual, an areal weighted average CN is computed.

3. For the given location, read the 24-h rainfall from DDF or IDF curves. If read as rainfall intensity for 24-h duration, it is converted to depth. For a given region, rainfall depth will be higher for less frequent storms.

4. Knowing the weighted CN value, calculate potential retention S and hence effective precipitation depth.

$$S(mm) = \frac{25400}{N} - 254 \qquad P_e = \frac{(P - 0.2S)^2}{P + 0.8S}$$

5. From step 3 and 4, determine the ratio I_a/P. If less than 0.1 make it 0.1 and if greater than 0.5 make it 0.5

6. Based on the geographical location, select type of rainfall distribution (type I, II, III, IA) and accordingly, choose unit discharge curves.

7. Compute time of concentration, if not given. For overland flow, travel time can be calculated using NRCS formula.

8. For **shallow concentrated flow**, read the flow velocity from graph or using equation $v = k\sqrt{S}$. For defined channel compute flow velocity using Manning's flows equation. Knowing the flow velocity and length of each segment of flow path, travel time for the individual segment can be found.

Peak Flow Rate

9. The values of constants C_0, C_1 and C_2 are read from **Table 9.8** for a given type of storm and ratio of I_a/P and then find K

$$K = C_0 + C_1(\log t_c) + C_2 (\log t_c)^2, \quad q_u = 10^K$$

10. This value of q_u is in ft³/s·mile²·in (csm/in). Multiply by a factor of 0.0044 to express it in units of m³/s·km²·cm.
11. Calculate the peak discharge with $F<1$ as surface storage factor

$$Q_P = q_u \times A \times P_e \times F$$

Example Problem 9.10

Using TR-55 method, find the 100-y flood from a 100-ha basin assuming storm type II, time of concentration = 1.3 h, and 100-Y 24-h rainfall of 5.7 in.

Given:

Weighted CN = 71, Time of conc. = 1.3 h, A = 100 ha = 1.0 km²

Solution:

$$S = \frac{1000}{CN} - 10 = \frac{1000}{71} - 10 = 4.084 = 40.08 \text{ in}$$

$$P_e = \frac{(P - 0.2S)^2}{P + 0.8S} = \frac{(5.7 - 0.2 \times 4.08)^2}{5.7 + 0.8 \times 4.08} = 2.66 \text{ in} = 6.75 \text{ cm}$$

$$\frac{I_a}{P} = \frac{0.83 \text{ in}}{5.7 \text{ in}} = 0.145 = 0.15$$

Table 9.8, storm type II and $I_a/P = 0.15$, $C_0 = 2.53$, $C_1 = -0.617$, $C_2 = -0.152$

$$K = C_0 + C_1(\log t_c) + C_2(\log t_c)^2$$
$$= 2.53 - 0.617(\log 1.3) - 0.152(\log 1.3)^2 = 2.458$$

$$q_u = 10^k = 10^{2.458} = 286.9 = 290 \text{ csm}$$

$$Q_P = q_u \times A \times P_e = \frac{286.9 \times 0.0044 \text{ m}^3}{\text{km}^2.\text{cm}.\text{s}} \times 1.0 \text{ km}^2 \times 6.75 \text{ cm}$$

$$= 8.52 = \underline{8.5 \text{ m}^3/s}$$

Table 9.8 Coefficients for TR-55 Method

Storm Type	I_a/P	C_0	C_1	C_2
I	0.10	2.30550	-0.51429	-0.11750
	0.20	2.23537	-0.50387	-0.08929
	0.25	2.18219	-0.48488	-0.06589
	0.30	2.10624	-0.45695	-0.02835
	0.35	2.00303	-0.40769	0.01983
	0.40	1.87733	-0.32274	0.05754
	0.45	1.76312	-0.15644	0.00453
	0.50	1.67889	-0.06930	0.00000
IA	0.10	2.03250	-0.31583	-0.13748
	0.20	1.91978	-0.28215	-0.07020
	0.25	1.83842	-0.25543	-0.02597
	0.30	1.72657	-0.19826	0.02633
	0.50	1.63417	-0.09100	0.00000
II	0.10	2.55323	-0.61512	-0.16403
	0.30	2.46532	-0.62257	-0.11657
	0.35	2.41896	-0.61594	-0.08820
	0.40	2.36409	-0.59857	-0.05621
	0.45	2.29238	-0.57005	-0.02281
	0.50	2.20282	-0.51599	-0.01259
III	0.10	2.47317	-0.51848	-0.17083
	0.30	2.39628	-0.51202	0.13245
	0.35	2.35477	-0.49735	-0.11985
	0.40	2.30726	-0.46541	-0.11094
	0.45	2.24876	-0.41314	-0.11508
	0.50	2.17772	-0.36803	-0.09525

Example Problem 9.11

Compute the peak runoff rate due to a 100-Y storm falling over a watershed in the coastal area (Type I) having the following characteristics:

Given:

CN = 74   A = 220 ha = 2.2 km² t_c = 1.45 h   Type = I   P= 6.0 in

Solution:

Effective precipitation

$$S = \frac{1000}{74} - 10 = 3.51 \text{ in}$$

$$I_a = 0.2S = 0.2 \times 3.51 \text{ in} = 0.702 \text{ in}$$

$$P_e = \frac{(P - 0.2S)^2}{P + 0.8S} = \frac{(6.0 - 0.2 \times 3.51)^2}{6.0 + 0.8 \times 3.51}$$

$$= 3.18 \text{ in} = 8.1 \text{ cm}$$

$$\frac{I_a}{P} = \frac{0.702 \text{ in}}{6.0 \text{ in}} = 0.12$$

$$K = 2.28 - 0.50(\log 1.45) - 0.11(\log 1.45)^2$$

$$= 2.199 = 2.2$$

Peak flow rate

$$q_u = 10^K = 10^{2.199} = 158 \times 0.0044 = 0.6969 = 0.70 \frac{m^3}{s \cdot km^2 \cdot cm}$$

$$Q_P = q_u \times A \times P_e \times F = \frac{0.697 \, m^3}{km^2 . cm . s} \times 2.2 \, km^2 \times 8.07 \, cm \times 1$$

$$= 12.37 = \underline{12 \, m^3/s}$$

9.6 Triangular Hydrograph

The peak discharge can be calculated by assuming a constant shape of storm flow hydrograph. Assuming a triangular shape, volume of runoff is given by the area of triangle as shown in **Fig. 9.4**. The volume of runoff is also equal to runoff depth multiplied by the area of watershed. By equating these two entities, peak flow can be expressed in terms of runoff depth, area of watershed, and triangular base of the hydrograph.

Figure 9.4 Triangular Flow Hydrograph

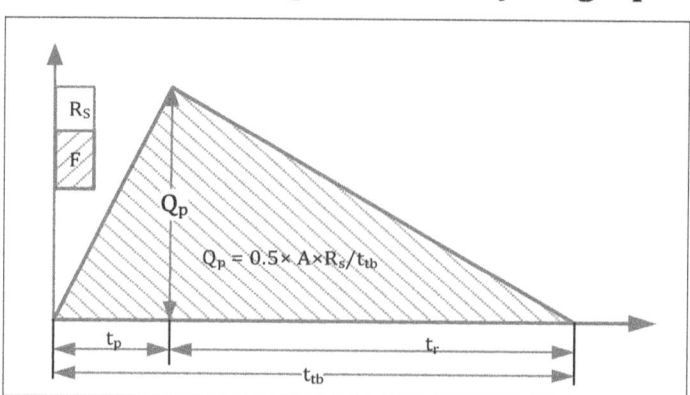

Peak runoff rate (Triangular hydrograph)

$$V_Q = A \times R_S = \frac{1}{2} \times Q_p \times t_{tb} \quad or \quad Q_p = \frac{2A \times R_S}{t_{tb}}$$

R_S = Runoff depth, t_{tb} = Time base of triangular hydrograph
V_Q = Storm runoff volume, A = Area of the watershed

Example Problem 9.12

Calculate the peak flow rate due to an effective rainfall depth of 10 mm. Assume the shape of hydrograph is triangular and time base is 4 times the time to peak flow rate. The drainage area is 100 km² and time to peak flow is estimated to be 6 hours.

Given:

R_s = 10 mm   A = 100 km² t_{tb} = 4×6 h = 24 h

Solution:

Peak runoff rate (triangular hydrograph)

$$Q_p = \frac{2A \times R_S}{t_{tb}} = 2 \times 100 \; km^2 \times 10 \; mm \times \frac{1}{24 \; h}$$

$$= \frac{2000 \; km^2 . mm}{24 \; h} \times \frac{1000 m^3}{km^2 . mm} \times \frac{h}{3600 \; s}$$

$$= 23.14 = \underline{23 \; m^3/s}$$

Peak Flow Rate

Example Problem 9.13

A storm flow hydrograph is approximated by a triangular hydrograph with a time base of 20 h. Find the depth of storm runoff given that peak flow rate is 11 m³/s and area of the watershed is 108 km²?

Given:

$A = 108 \text{ km}^2$ $\quad t_{tb} = 20 \text{ h}$ $\quad Q = 11 \text{ m}^3/\text{s}$ $\quad R_s = ?$

Solution:

$$R_s = \frac{Q_p \times t_{tb}}{2A} = \frac{11 m^3}{s} \times 20 \, h \times \frac{1}{2 \times 108 \, km^2} \times \frac{3600 \, s}{h}$$

$$= \frac{1.018 \, m^3}{km^2} \times \frac{km^2 . mm}{1000 \, m^3}$$

$$= 3.66 = \underline{3.7 \, mm}$$

Example Problem 9.14

Assuming triangular hydrograph shape and base time of 20 h, calculate peak flow produced by a storm falling on a 68 km² watershed and producing 12 mm of effective rainfall.

Given:

$R_s = 12 \text{ mm}$ $\quad A = 68 \text{ km}^2$ $\quad t_{tb} = 20 \text{ h}$

Solution:

$$Q_p = \frac{2A \times R_S}{t_{tb}} = 2 \times 68 \, km^2 \times 12 \, mm \times \frac{1}{20 \, h}$$

$$= \frac{81.6 \, km^2 . mm}{h} \times \frac{1000 \, m^3}{km^2 . mm} \times \frac{h}{3600 \, s}$$

$$= 22.6 = \underline{23 \, m^3/s}$$

Example Problem 9.15

Calculate the peak flow rate due to a 3-h storm producing effective rainfall of 22 mm. Based on NRCS triangular hydrograph shape, the base time is assumed 8/3 times the time to peak flow rate. The drainage area is 8.5 km² and watershed lag time is estimated to be 3.0 h.

Given:

$P_e = R_s = 22$ mm $A = 18$ km² $t_l = 3.0$ h $D = 3.0$ h

Solution:

$$t_{tb} = \frac{8}{3} \times t_p = \frac{8}{3}\left(t_l + \frac{D}{2}\right) = \frac{8}{3}\left(3.0\,h + \frac{3.0\,h}{2}\right) = 12\,h$$

$$Q_p = \frac{2AR_s}{t_{tb}} = 2 \times 18\,km^2 \times 22\,mm \times \frac{1}{12\,h}$$

$$= \frac{66\,km^2.mm}{h} \times \frac{1000\,m^3}{km^2.mm} \times \frac{h}{3600\,s}$$

$$= 18.3 = \underline{18\,m^3/s}$$

Example Problem 9.16

From the topographic map, area and hydraulic length are estimated to be 5.6 km² and 4300 m respectively. The soil and vegetation characteristics of the watershed are represented by a CN of 75. The average basin slope is estimated to be 2.5%. Find lag time for this watershed. Assuming triangular time base to be three times of lag time, determine the peak runoff rate for storm runoff depth of 1.0 cm.

Given:

$A = 5.6$ km² $L = 4300$ m $S_b = 2.5\%$ $R_s = 10$ mm $t_l = ?$ $Q_p = ?$

Solution:

$$t_l = \frac{L^{0.8}(2540 - 23CN)^{0.7}}{14100\,CN^{0.7} S_b^{0.5}} = \frac{4500^{0.8}(2540 - 23 \times 75)^{0.7}}{14100 \times 75^{0.7} \times 0.018^{0.5}}$$

$$= 2.35 = 2.4\,h$$

$$t_{tb} = 3.0 \times t_l = 3.0 \times 2.35\,h$$

$$= 8.81 = 8.8\,h$$

$$Q_p = \frac{2AR_s}{t_{tb}} = 2 \times 5.6\,km^2 \times 10\,mm \times \frac{1}{8.81\,h}$$

$$= \frac{12.7\,km^2.mm}{h} \times \frac{1000\,m^3}{km^2.mm} \times \frac{h}{3600\,s}$$

$$= 3.53 = \underline{3.5\,m^3/s}$$

Discussion Questions

1. Define lag time, time to peak and time to recede. As per NRCS, what is the relationship between lag time and time of concentration
2. What is the rationale behind rational formula?
3. Rational formula is more successful for small urban catchments. Explain?
4. If rationale formula is applied to small rural catchments, what considerations should be made?
5. Describe the procedure for applying rational formula to design storm sewer in urban catchments?
6. For what type of catchments, TR-55 method of finding peak flow is preferred?
7. For urban catchments, how the composite curve number is worked out?
8. Discuss the steps involved in the application of TR-55 method.
9. Assuming triangular shape, the peak flow rate from a certain region is given by the following relationship

$$Q_p = \frac{A \times R_S}{2t_p}$$

Based on this what you can say about the relationship between time to peak and triangular time base?

10. Assuming triangular shape storm flow hydrograph, and recession time 1.67 times the time to peak, derive the relationship:

$$Q_p = \frac{3}{4} \times \frac{A \times R_S}{t_p}$$

Practice Problems

Practice Problem 9.1

Use the Rational formula to find the peak discharge from a 1.5 km² catchment for rainfall rate of 250 mm/h. assume runoff coefficient is 0.75. (78 m³/s)

Practice Problem 9.2

For the IDF function given below, find the peak discharge (T=10y) from a 2.5 km² watershed that is characterised by 25 min of time of concentration and runoff coefficient of 0.65. (67 m³/s)

$$I = \frac{2000}{(D+10)^{0.73}}$$

Practice Problem 9.3

For a 4-ha watershed the runoff coefficient is 0.90 and time of concentration is 20 min. Compute peak discharge for the following two storms.
    a. 55 mm over a duration of 20 min (1.7 m³/s)
    b. 65 mm over a duration of 30 min. (1.3 m³/s)

Practice Problem 9.4

How does the shape of the hydrograph differ in Practice. Problem 9.3

Practice Problem 9.5

Applying rational formula and IDF function of Practice Problem 9.2, determine peak inflow rate to the storm inlet of a 4.5 ha parking lot with runoff coefficient of 0.95. It takes 30 min for all the drainage area to contribute.
    a. Duration of 25 min (1.5 m³/s)
    b. Duration of 60 min (1.1 m³/s)

Practice Problem 9.6

After Repairs of A 3.6 ha Parking Lot, The Runoff coefficient is modified to 0.80 and the time of concentration decreases to 15 min. Assuming maximum rainfall intensity is 100 mm/h for 15-min duration, estimate the peak flow. (0.80 m³/s)

Practice Problem 9.7

A drain has flow carrying capacity of 15 L/s. What is the maximum area it can drain without overflowing. Assume C = 0.95, I = 120 mm/h. (470 m²)?

Practice Problem 9.8

A large circular parking lot with a runoff coefficient of 0.90 and diameter of 120 m is being constructed as overflow parking for a recreation area. All storm water will drain to the centre and carried away by the storm sewer from there. The parking lot will be graded with a slope of 2% towards the centre. Estimate the peak discharge for 10-year storm. (t_c = 4.1 min, I = 147 mm/h, 420 L/s)

$$I = \frac{850 T^{0.2}}{(D + 15)^{0.75}}$$

Practice Problem 9.9

Rework **Ex. Prob. 9.4** assuming the land is cultivated with flat topography and average time of concentration is 15 min. (1.3 m³/s)

Practice Problem 9.10

Calculate the 10-year peak discharge by the Rational Method of a 100-ha composite catchment with the following characteristics. Use the IDF that shown in Practice Problem 9.8. ((11 m³/s)

Area	A, ha	C	t_c, min
I	40	0.6	20
II	60	0.8	60

Practice Problem 9.11

Rework **Ex. Prob. 9.5** assuming C_1 = 0.55 and C_2 = 0.70 (42 L/s)

Practice Problem 9.12

It is planned to develop 6.4 ha upland watershed primarily consisting of soils. The developed portion of the area will be residential with 20% impervious portion. The undeveloped portion is forested on soil B with good cover and has an area of 2.8 ha. Find the weighted CN? (63)

Practice Problem 9.13

Determine the weighted curve number for a 22-ha urban watershed that includes 10 ha of commercial land (70% impervious, 25% unconnected, B soil) and 12 ha of residential properties.
(50% impervious, 80% unconnected B soil). (77)

Practice Problem 9.14

Rainfall intensity for a 50-y storm is as shown in the table below:

Parameter	1	2	3	4	5
Duration, min	15	30	45	60	180
Max. Intensity, mm/h	40	60	75	100	120

Design a storm drain to carry peak flow rate from a 50-y storm falling over 200 ha catchment. The maximum length of travel is 1.0 km with 2.1 m drop in elevation. Assuming runoff coefficient of 15%, What size storm sewer is required without exceeding flow velocity of 3.0 m/s? (2.0 m)

Practice Problem 9.15

An urban catchment of area of 1.2 km² has a pre-development time of concentration of 45 min and runoff coefficient of 0.3. After development, it is estimated that time of concentration would reduce to 30 min and runoff coefficient increase to 0.60. Design storm has maximum intensity of 60 mm/h for 30 min duration and 40 mm/h for 45 min duration. Estimate the design peak flow rate for pre- and post-development? (4.0 m³/s, 12 m³/s)

Practice Problem 9.16

Calculate the peak flow rate due to an effective rainfall depth of 10 mm. Assume the shape of the hydrograph is triangular and base is five times the time to peak flow rate. The drainage area is 100 km² and time to peak is 10 hours. (11 m³/s)

Practice Problem 9.17

A storm fell on a watershed of area 85 km² and produced peak storm flow rate of 24 m³/s with a triangular time base of 35 h. Estimate the storm runoff depth. (18 mm)

Practice Problem 9.18

A 2-h storm dumped 30 mm of rainfall over a watershed of area 64 km² and Φ-index of 10 mm/h. Assuming triangular shape hydrograph with time base of 25 h, determine the peak flow rate. (14 m³/s)

Practice Problem 9.19

Find the 25-y peak flow rate from a 580-ha watershed with average runoff coefficient of 0.60 and with a time of concentration of 2.5 h. IDF for the region is given by the following relationship. ((32 m³/s)

$$I\left(\frac{mm}{h}\right) = \frac{900 T^{0.2}}{(D+15)^{0.77}}$$

Practice Problem 9.20

For the data of **Practice Problem 8.9** determine peak flow rate using TR-55 method. Assume time of concentration of 30 min, Storm type I and 24 h rainfall of 250 mm. (1.2 m³/s)

Practice Problem 9.21

An urban catchment with total area of 1.1 ha consists of a parking lot (Fig. 9.5). It is desired to know the peak flow rate based on a 10-year storm to select the storm sewer to carry the storm runoff. (110 L/s)

$$I = \frac{800 T^{0.2}}{(D+10)^{0.75}}$$

Figure 9.5 Drainage Area (Pr. Prob. 9.21)

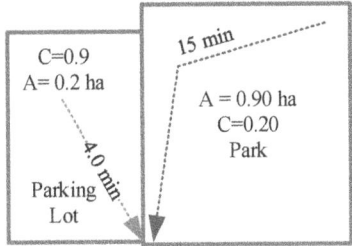

Practice Problem 9.22

For the urban catchment shown in Fig. 9.6, find the peak flow rates at manholes, located at A, B and C. Use the following IDF function. (0.23, 0.65, 0.68 m³/s)

$$I\left(\frac{mm}{h}\right) = \frac{1200}{(D+10)^{0.77}}, D = duration\ in\ min$$

Figure 9.6 Urban Area (Pr. Prob. 8.17)

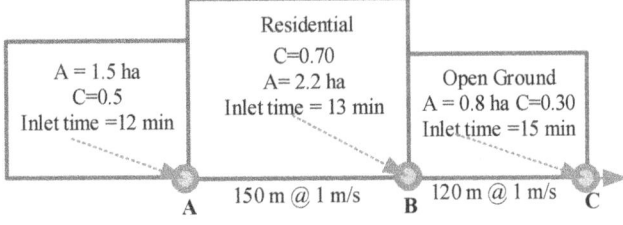

Practice Problem 9.23

Using TR-55 method, compute the peak discharge rate for the following data: weighted curve number of 65, 24-h rainfall for a 100-y storm is 180 mm, storm type II, drainage area is 1.5 km², storage factor = 0.90 and time of concentration of 1.0 h (16 m³/s)

Practice Problem 9.24

A 108 ha semi-urban watershed is characterized by a CN of 80. Hydraulic length and basin slope respectively are 1250 m and 2.2%. Applying the NRCS formula, find the lag time and hence the time to peak runoff rate assuming time to peak is 110% of lag time. Applying NRCS triangular hydrograph formula, determine the peak runoff rate for a storm runoff depth of 1.0 cm. (3.1 m³/s)

Practice Problem 9.25

As shown in **Fig.9.7**, 200 m×150 m parking lot is sloped along its length to drain in to gutter along the downstream edge. the gutter drains into a storm sewer inlet at its centre. The longest route taken by the runoff is 150 m of overland flow across the parking lot and 75 m of gutter with inlet. Applying Manning's equation estimate the time of concentration. Overland flow coefficients K are 6.2 and 14 for parking lot and gutter respectively. (Table 7.1). Determine 25-y peak flow rate using following IDF equation and assuming C = 0.95. (9.2 min, 1.8 m³/s)

$$I\left(\frac{mm}{h}\right) = \frac{2250}{(D+9)^{0.79}}, D = duration\ in\ min$$

Figure 9.7 Parking Lot (Pr. Prob. 8.20)

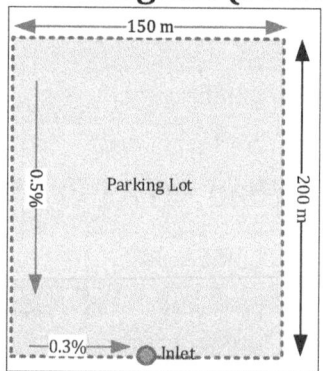

Review Questions

1. The 10-y peak flow (m³/s) versus watershed area (ha) relationship is: $Q_p = 0.15\ A^{0.65}$. What is the peak flow from a catchment with an area of 5.5 km²?
   a) 9.1 m³/s   b) 0.91 m³/s   c) 0.45 m³/s   d) 4.5 m³/s

2. IDF relationship; I (mm/h) = 1350 / (D + 15)$^{0.75}$, where t_D is the storm duration in min. What is the rainfall intensity for a 30-min storm?
   a) 78 mm/h   b) 85 mm/h   c) 60 mm/h   d) 92 mm/h

3. A composite catchment has two sub-areas: 25% with C = 0.75 and the other 75% is undeveloped, C = 0.30. The composite runoff coefficient is
   a) 0.75   b) 0.30   c) 0.41   d) 0.53

4. The time of concentration for a rectangular parking lot is 20 min. In which case would you expect greater runoff?
   a) 110 mm/h for 10 min   b) 45 mm/h for 20 min
   c) 25 mm/h for 1 h   d) 35 mm/h for 30 min

5. What is the peak runoff rate from a 1.2-ha field for rainfall intensity of 120 mm/h? Assume the runoff coefficient is 50%.
   a) 1.2 m³/s   b) 20 m³/s   c) 0.12 m³/s   d) 0.2 m³/s

6. Using the SCS triangular hydrograph (t_b = 2.67 t_p), what is the peak runoff rate from a storm producing 1 cm of runoff and with a time to peak of one hour? The area of the catchment is 100 ha.
   a) 1.1 m³/s   b) 2.1 m³/s   c) 3.1 m³/s   d) 4.1 m³/s

7. A 70-mm storm produces 45 mm of runoff. What is the runoff coefficient?
   a) 0.06   b) 0.45   c) 0.64   d) 1.56

8. The runoff coefficient will be high on _____ soil.
   a) Flat sandy   b) Flat heavy   c) Steep sandy   d) Steep heavy

9. A 100 m² experimental plot is subjected to artificial rain with an intensity of 100 mm/h. Peak runoff rate is measured to be 1.1 L/s. The runoff coefficient is:
   a) 1.0   b) 0.4   c) 0.8   d) 0.5

10. The simplest form of peak discharge formulae is based on
    a) Land use   b) Basin slope   c) Drainage area   d) Flow length

11. The runoff coefficient, as used in the Rational formula, is a function of
    a) Land use   b) Cover   c) Soil group   d) All

12. In designing a drainage outlet, peak flow rate as yielded by the Rational formula is used. If a storm of the same intensity but twice the duration occurs, the resulting peak flow rate will be
    a) Twice as much
    b) Half that of design rate
    c) Same as design rate
    d) Four times as much

13. A watershed with an area of 55 ha has a runoff coefficient of 0.55. A storm with duration >t_c occurs with a rainfall intensity of 60 mm/h. Peak discharge rate is
    a) 50 L/s   b) 60 L/s   c) 70 L/s   d) 80 L/s

14. A rectangular shaped parking lot has inlet time of 25 min. For determining design peak discharge rate, which of the following scenario would be chosen? Assume area contributing is linearly proportional to the duration smaller than time of concentration.
    a) 50 mm/h, 10min duration
    b) 35 mm/h, 15 min duration
    c) 15 mm/h, 25 min duration
    d) 10 mm/h, 60 min duration

15. A triangular direct runoff hydrograph due to a 3-h storm falling over a 250 km² area watershed has a time base of 60. h. Given that direct runoff depth is 6.5 mm, peak flow rate is
    a) 1.4 m³/s   b) 2.3 m³/s   c) 6.9 m³/s   d) 15 m³/s

16. Which of the following is more appropriate value of runoff coefficient for a paved parking lot in an urban area?
    a) 1.0   b) 0.95   c) 0.90   d) 0.85

17. An urban parking lot area is 2200 m². If the maximum rainfall intensity expected is 70 mm/h, what maximum discharge rate should be used to select the size of drain?
    a) 40 L/s   b) 42 L/s   c) 44 L/s   d) 46 L/s

18. Assuming the drainpipe is laid at a gradient so as to provide a flowing full flow velocity of 1.2 m/s, what is the minimum diameter of the drainpipe required to carry a peak flow of 42 L/s?
    a) 200 mm   b) 210 mm   c) 220 mm   d) 230 mm

19. Using the IDF equation: $I = \frac{1500}{(D+15)^{0.8}}$ where D is in min and I in mm/h, what is the rainfall intensity assuming time of concentration of half an hour?
   a) 71 mm/h   b) 92 mm/h   c) 120 mm/h   d) 40 mm/h

20. A culvert is designed for a peak flow Q_p as found using Rational formula. If a storm with twice the intensity but of half the duration occurs, the peak flow will be
   a) Halved   b) Doubled   c) Quadrupled   d) Same

21. A small watershed has drainage area of 80 ha and runoff coefficient of 0.50. Time of concentration is estimated to be 30 min. A storm with rainfall intensity of 50 mm/h occurs for a duration of 45 min. Peak flow rate will be
   a) 1.8 m³/s   b) 2.8 m³/s   c) 4.2 m³/s   d) 5.6 m³/s

22. The land use of a drainage area is 22 ha open(C=0.15), 45 ha residential(C=0.30) and 35 ha commercial(C=0.80). What is the weighted runoff coefficient?
   a) 0.33   b) 0.44   c) 0.55   d) 0.66

23. A partially developed catchment has a runoff coefficient of 0.55. If the peak flow based on rainfall intensity of 60 mm/h is determined to be 12 m³/s, drainage area of the catchment is
   a) 0.16 km²   b) 1.3 km²   c) 12 km²   d) 23 km²

24. A storm dumps 25 mm of rainfall over a catchment of area 12 km². Assuming a triangular hydrograph with a base time period of 15 h, peak flow rate is
   a) 11 m³/s   b) 12 m³/s   c) 13 m³/s   d) 14 m³/s

25. In a triangular hydrograph with time base of 10 h, what is runoff depth produced if the peak runoff rate from a drainage area of 1.5 km² is observed to be 0.5 m³/s?
   a) 2.5 mm   b) 4.5 mm   c) 6.0 mm   d) 9.0 mm

26. What is the appropriate value of curve number for a paved parking lot?
    a) 100   b) 98   c) 90   d) 10

27. Runoff coefficient cannot be
    a) <1   b) 0.98   c) <0   d) >0

28. In tables of curve numbers for urban areas, what percent of area is assumed to be impervious?
    a) 50%   b) 75%   c) 85%   d) 98%

29. For the same storm, which of the following type of urban area will produce maximum runoff rate?
    a) Urban area, 85% impervious, 100% connected
    b) Urban area, 85% impervious, 90% connected
    c) Urban area, 75% impervious, 100% connected
    d) Urban area, 75% impervious, 90% connected

30. For the same storm, which of the following types of urban area will produce maximum runoff rate?
    a) Urban area, 85% impervious, Group B soils
    b) Urban area, 85% impervious, Group C soils
    c) Urban area, 75% impervious, Group B soils
    d) Urban area, 75% impervious, Group C soils

10 Unit Hydrograph

The factors that influence the time distribution of storm runoff include:
- Duration of runoff producing rain
- Distribution of rain
- Infiltration capacity of soil in time and space
- Size and shape of the watershed
- Distribution of stream pattern
- Size, slope, and roughness of stream channels

Most of these factors produce effects, which are difficult to calculate exactly from measurements of watershed and rainstorm patterns. Realizing this difficulty, a common response is to particularize a solution. This means that without defining the ways in which different factors of storms and watersheds react to produce a given result, the integrated effect is estimated in terms of the size of the output. This is a good example of a **black box model** in which case we can determine the output for a known input without knowing what is happening inside the box. This is the approach of time distribution of runoff that is used in the **unit hydrograph** procedure. Sherman first proposed this theory in 1932. Unit hydrograph is a linear model, and the linear assumptions are as follows:
1. The time base of a storm hydrograph depends only on fixed watershed properties and on the duration of runoff production; it is not a function of volume of runoff produced.
2. The hydrograph for runoff produced by rain in two or more-time intervals, adding hydrographs in sequence can create more time periods hydrographs.

The result of these linear assumptions is that the runoff hydrograph for a given **volume** of storm runoff produced in a **known time period** for a given watershed can be calculated by multiplying the flow rate ordinates of a unit hydrograph for that watershed and that time period by the volume of runoff in cm. The term **unit** indicates that the volume of runoff or area under the unit hydrograph is one unit, 1 cm or 1 mm.

The unit hydrograph for a given watershed and time period is called **Y-hour unit hydrograph for watershed X**. Y is not the total time base of the unit hydrograph, but it is the duration of the runoff-producing storm for which this hydrograph can be used. This means that it refers to the hours during the storm in which storm runoff was generated. See **Fig. 10.1**.

Figure 10.1 Unit Hydrograph Definition

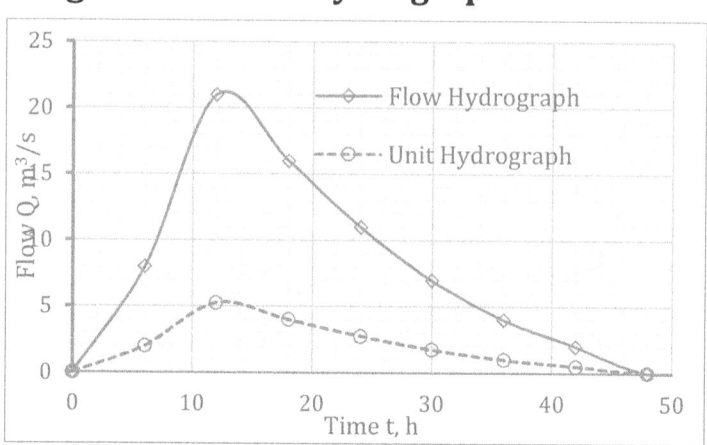

10.1 Derivation of UH

To develop a unit hydrograph, it is desirable to get as many rainfall runoffs records as possible. Preliminary selection of storms to use in deriving a UH for a watershed should be restricted to:
- Isolated storms.
- Storms having uniform distribution of rainfall throughout the period of rainfall excess.
- Storms having uniform spatial distribution over the entire watershed.
- These restrictions place both upper and lower limits on the size of the watershed to be employed. The upper limit is considered to be 25 000 km² and the lower limit is assumed to be 400 ha.
- The preliminary scanning of suitable storms should be restricted to the storms for which:
  - Duration of the rainfall event is 10 to 30% of the lag time.
  - Direct runoff should be in the range of 1-5 cm.
- A suitable number of storms should be analysed to obtain an average of the ordinates for selected unit hydrograph duration.
- The duration of storms should be the same. However, one cannot be too choosy about storm duration. A storm, which is about ±25% of the desired duration, is not rejected.

10.1.1 Procedure for constructing UH

1. For the flow events selected, first base flow separation is accomplished and the volume of **storm runoff** for each event is calculated. Area under the storm flow hydrograph represents volume of runoff. Measurement of area is done using a device or approximating the flow hydrograph with a rectangle or a triangle to perform mathematical calculations.

$$R_s = \frac{V_Q}{A} = \frac{\sum(Q_s \times \Delta t)}{A} \quad \text{Runoff depth}$$

Δt is the time interval between successive flows.

2. A candidate estimate for the unit hydrograph is obtained by dividing the ordinates of the separated storm runoff rate by the storm runoff depth.

$$Q_u(t) = \frac{Q_s(t)}{R_s} \quad \text{UH ordinate}$$

3. Following the same procedure, the unit hydrograph for other storms selected is derived.
4. When these few unit hydrographs have been drawn, there is usually some considerable difference in shape amongst them. This difference is overcome by a few bold strokes of the pencil whereby a smooth curve through the middle of scattered curves is drawn. The volume under this curve is then checked to ensure that the runoff is one unit.
5. As a final step, you need to specify duration of the UH. That is the time interval, Δt in which runoff was produced.
6. Constructing the unit hydrograph in this way produces the integrated effect of runoff resulting from a representative set of equal duration storms. Extreme rainfall intensity is not reflected in the determination.

Example Problem 10.1

A 1-hour storm produces significant rainfall over Black Creek watershed (25 km²). The storm flow rates are listed below. Construct the unit hydrograph.

Given:

A = 25 km²   Δt =1.0 h

t, h	1	2	3	4	5	6	7	8	9	10	11
Q, m³/s	0.87	2.2	12.2	46.9	53.7	32.6	18.6	9.5	5.4	0.9	0.0

Solution:

Storm runoff volume (3rd hour)

$$V_{Q3} = \overline{Q_{s3}} \times \Delta t = \frac{(2.2 + 12.2)m^3}{2\,s} \times 1h \times \frac{3600s}{h}$$

$$= 25920 = 25900\ m^3$$

$$R_s = \frac{\Sigma(Q_s \Delta t)}{A} = \frac{658332\ m^3}{25\ km^2} \times \frac{km^2}{(1000\ m)^2} \times \frac{1000\ mm}{m}$$

$$= 26.33 = 26.3\ mm$$

$$Q_u(3) = \frac{Q_s(3)}{R_s} = \frac{12.2\ m^3}{26.3\ mm.s} \times \frac{10\ mm}{cm}$$

$$= 4.63 = 4.6\ m^3/s.cm$$

Calculations for the remaining unit hydrograph and a plot as generated by MS excel program is shown in **Table 10.1** and **Fig. 10.2**

Figure 10.2 Derivation of Unit Hydrograph

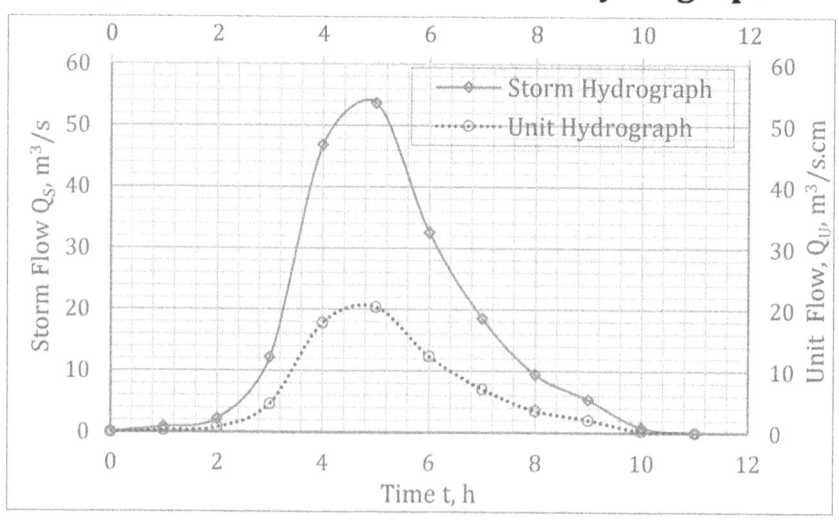

Table 10.1 Computations of UH Ordinates

Time, t	Q_s	Avg. Q_s	V_Q	Q_u	
h	m³/s	m³/s	m³	m³/s.mm	m³/s.cm
0	0.0			0	0
1	0.9	0.44	1566	0.03	0.3
2	2.2	1.54	5526	0.08	0.8
3	12.2	7.20	25920	0.46	4.6
4	46.9	29.55	106380	1.78	17.8
5	53.7	50.30	181080	2.04	20.4
6	32.6	43.15	155340	1.24	12.4
7	18.6	25.60	92160	0.71	7.1
8	9.5	14.05	50580	0.36	3.6
9	5.4	7.45	26820	0.21	2.1
10	0.9	3.15	11340	0.03	0.3
11	0.0	0.45	1620	0	0
	R_s = 26.3	Σ=	658332		

10.2 UH of Other Durations

After a UH hydrograph is constructed for a given duration, it can used to derive a unit hydrograph of another duration by applying the method of superposition or S-curve method.

10.2.1 Method of Superposition

Because a unit hydrograph (UH) is a linear relationship, the principle of superposition can be applied to derive a unit hydrograph of other duration. This is achieved by adding two or more hydrographs lagged by the duration of the storm. For example, to derive a 2-hour UH from a 1-hour UH, lag the two hydrographs by one hour and add the ordinates for any time divided by two. This will give the 2-hour unit hydrograph for that time. The principle of superposition is illustrated in Example Problem 10.2. It is seen that the process of deriving a larger duration UH from a shorter one entails the averaging of ordinates. Therefore, small errors in the ordinates of the short duration UH are smoothed out in deriving the larger duration hydrograph.

Example Problem 10.2

By using the superposition method, derive 3-h UH for Black Creek watershed as described in **Example Problem 10.1**. Also find the 3-h storm hydrograph given that 3-h total effective rainfall is 5.3 cm.

Solution:

Calculations are shown in **Table 10.2**. Plots of 3-h unit hydrograph and 3-h storm hydrograph are shown in **Fig.10.3**

Table 10.2 Computation Table (Ex. Prob. 10.2)

t, h	Q_u, m³/s.cm	Q_1	Q_2	Q_3	Q_u (3-h)	Q_s (3-h)
1	0.3	0.3			0.1	0.5
2	0.8	0.8	0.3		0.4	1.9
3	4.6	4.6	0.8	0.3	1.8	9.5
4*	17.8	17.8	4.6	0.8	7.5	39.6
5	20.4	20.4	17.8	4.6	12.7	67.5
6	12.4	12.4	20.4	17.8	10.9	57.9
7	7.1	7.1	12.4	20.4	6.5	34.5
8	3.6	3.6	7.1	12.4	3.6	18.9
9	2.1	2.1	3.6	7.1	1.9	10.1
10	0.3	0.3	2.1	3.6	0.8	4.2
11	0.0	0.0	0.3	2.1	0.1	0.5
12	0.0	0.0	0.0	0.3	0.0	0.0

Figure 10.3 Plot of 3-h UH and Storm Hydrograph

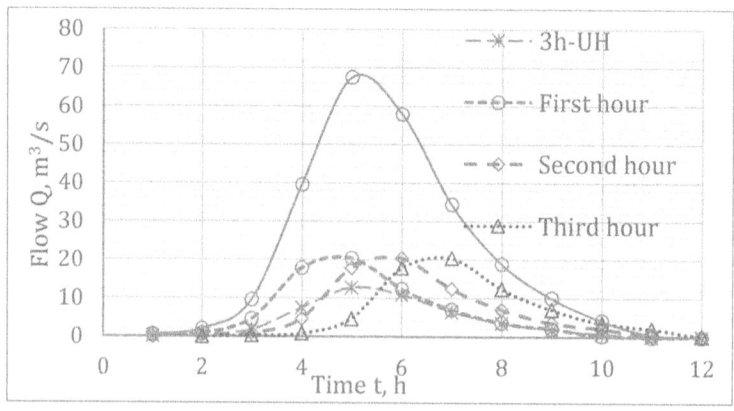

Sample of Calculations (4th hour)

$$Q_u(4) = \frac{\{Q_1(4) + Q_2(4) + Q_3(4)\}}{3}$$

$$= \frac{17.8 + 4.60 + 0.84}{3} = 7.746 = 7.75 \ m^3/s.\,cm$$

$$P_e(3\,h) = 1.2 + 2.85 + 1.25 = 5.30 = 5.3\ cm$$

$$Q_s(4) = \frac{7.75\ m^3}{s.\,cm} \times 5.3\ cm = 41.05 = 41\ m^3/s$$

10.2.2 S-Hydrograph

S-hydrograph method is similar to the method of superposition. An **S-hydrograph** results when a continuous rainfall excess occurs at a constant rate for indefinite period. After the time equal to time base of the unit hydrograph, equilibrium flow rate is reached, and graph looks like the letter S and hence the name S-hydrograph. One advantage of S-hydrograph is that it can be used to derive UH of smaller durations or larger durations. A unit hydrograph with the new duration t_{dn} is obtained by lagging the S-hydrograph by the S-hydrograph of the new duration. In the next step, subtract the two S-hydrographs from one another. As a final step, multiply the resulting hydrograph ordinates by the ratio t_d/t_{dn}.

Example Problem 10.3

The ordinates of a 3-h UH are shown in **Table 10.3**. Develop S- graph and find the equilibrium flow rate.

Solution:

Computations are made using MS excel and are presented in **Table 10.3**. the ordinates of the 3-h are lagged by 3 h and are shown in Columns 3-5.. Ordinates for each hour are added up and listed in Col. 6, which are the ordinates for S hydrograph. The plots of S-curve and the unit hydrographs are shown in **Fig. 10.4**. The equilibrium flow rate is 420 L/s.mm

Sample of Calculations (5th hour)

$$S - Curve(5th\ hour) = 210 + 180 = 390\ L/s.\,mm$$

As shown in Table 10.3, equilibrium value of 420 L/s.mm is achieved in the 8th hour.

Table 10.3 Excel Worksheet (Ex. Prob. 10.3)

Time t, h	3-h UH	UH lagged by 3 h			S-Graph
		L/s.mm			
0	0				0
1	75				75
2	180				180
3	275				275
4	280	75			355
5	210	180			390
6	130	275			405
7	60	280	75		415
8	30	210	180		420
9	15	130	275		420
10	5	60	280	75	420
11	0	30	210	180	420
12		15	130	275	420

Figure 10.4 S-hydrograph (Ex. Prob. 10.3)

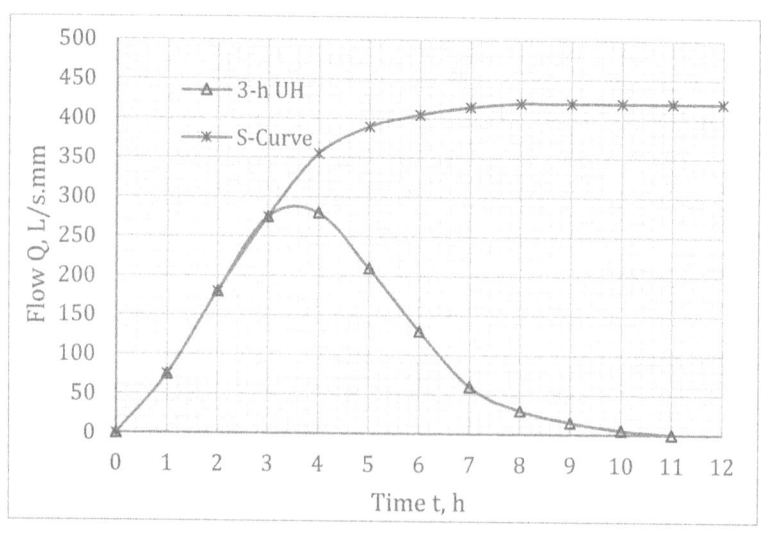

Example Problem 10.4

The ordinates of a 3-h UH S-curve from Example Problem 10.3 are shown in Column 2 of **Table 10.4**. Using S-curve method, develop 1-h(shorter duration) and 4-h(longer duration) unit hydrographs.

Solution:

Computations are made using MS excel program and are presented in **Table 10.4**. With S–curve ordinates offset by 1 h and 4 h, the new durations, are shown in column 3 and 4 respectively. Difference in the S-curve ordinates for both cases are listed in the next two columns. The ordinates of 1-h UH are found by multiplying the difference(Col. 5) by a factor of $t_d/t_{dn} = 3/1 = 3$(and are placed in col.7). Similarly, S-curve ordinates differences for 4 h lag is multiplied by a factor of 3/4 and are shown in the last column of the Table 10.3. Comparing the three unit hydrographs, peak flow rate of 315 L/s.mm is maximum for 1-h unit hydrograph. The peak flow of 266 L/s.mm is minimum for the 4-h unit hydrograph.

The plots of S-curve and the two unit hydrographs are shown in **Fig. 10.5**.

Table 10.4 Excel Worksheet (Ex. Prob. 10.3)

Time	S-curve Offset			Difference		UH	
t, h	0 h	1 h	4 h	1 h	4 h	1-h	4-h
0	0			0	0	0	0
1	75			75	75	225	56
2	180	75		105	180	315	135
3	275	180		95	275	285	206
4	355	275		80	355	240	266
5	390	355	75	35	315	105	236
6	405	390	180	15	225	45	169
7	415	405	275	10	140	30	105
8	420	415	355	5	65	15	49
9	420	420	390	0	30	0	23
10	420	420	405	0	15	0	11
11	420	420	415	0	5	0	4
12	420	420	420	0	0	0	0

Figure 10.5 S-Curve Method (Ex. Prob. 10.4)

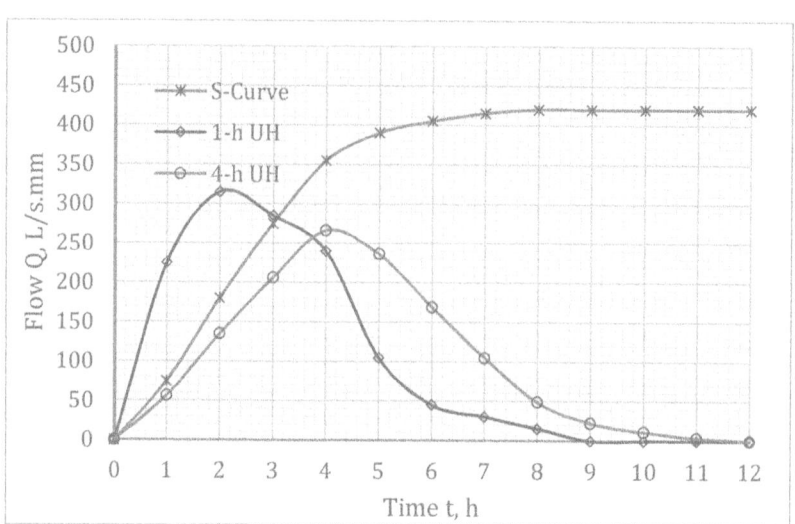

10.3 Application of UH

The **unit hydrograph** with its limitations has many applications in environmental and water resources development. The UH can be used to determine the watershed response due to given input, that is rainfall minus abstractions or effective rainfall. This has immediate applications in flood forecasting and warning. Another important application is in the study of effects of land use changes on flooding and soil erosion.

10.3.1 Prediction of Stormflow

The storm flow or direct runoff hydrograph can be derived by multiplying the UH ordinates by the effective rainfall. However, you need to make sure that the duration of UH is the same as that of runoff producing storm. When the duration of effective precipitation is longer than duration of UH, the precipitation excess P_e is calculated for the same time unit as the unit hydrograph, and storm flow for each time period is calculated. The graphs for individual unit storms are added offsetting them in sequence by one-time unit. This procedure is illustrated in **Example Problem 10.5**. An alternate way is to modify the short duration UH to the greater duration UH by the superposition method.

Unit Hydrograph

To predict storm flow from a given storm, **precipitation excess** P_e or effective rainfall must be known. The CN method can be used if sufficient information is available. An alternative method is to estimate the infiltration index for the drainage area being studied. Subtracting the infiltration index from the precipitation gives the effective precipitation for a given time interval.

Example Problem 10.5

A storm produced 35, 75 and 110 mm of rainfall in each of the three consecutive hours. Assuming a curve number of 80, estimate runoff produced in each hour.

Given:

CN = 80 $\Sigma P(1) = 35$ $\Sigma P(2) = 110$ $\Sigma P(3) = 220$ mm

Solution:

$$S = \frac{25400}{CN} - 254 = \frac{25400}{80} - 254 = 63.5 \; mm$$

$$R_s(3) = \frac{(P - 0.2S)^2}{(P + 0.8S)} = \frac{(220 - 0.2 \times 63.5)^2}{(220 + 0.8 \times 63.5)}$$

$$= 158.7 = 159 \; mm$$

$$R_s(2) = \frac{(P - 0.2S)^2}{(P + 0.8S)} = \frac{(110 - 0.2 \times 63.5)^2}{(110 + 0.8 \times 63.5)}$$

$$= 58.8 = 59 \; mm$$

$$R_s(1) = \frac{(P - 0.2S)^2}{(P + 0.8S)} = \frac{(35 - 0.2 \times 63.5)^2}{(35 + 0.8 \times 63.5)}$$

$$= 5.79 = 5.8 \; mm$$

Individual hour Runoff depth
$R_{s1} = 5.8 \; mm - 0.0 \; mm = 5.8 \; mm$

$R_{s2} = 58.8 - 5.8 \; mm = 53.0 \; mm$

$R_{s3} = 158.7 - 58.8 = 99.9 \; mm$

Example Problem 10.6

Using 1-hour UH for Black Creek in **Example Problem 10.1**, determine the storm flow hydrograph produced by a storm that produced runoff in three consecutive hours. The effective rainfall in each of the 3-h period is: 12.0 mm, 28.5 mm, and 12.5 mm.

Sample of Calculation (07 hour):

$$Q_s(7) = P_e(1)Q_u(7) + P_e(2)Q_u(6) + P_e(3)Q_u(5)$$

$$= 1.2 \times 7.1 + 2.85 \times 12.4 + 1.25 \times 20.4$$

$$= 69.3 = 69 \ m^3/s$$

Plot of storm flow hydrograph is shown in **Fig. 10.6**. Storm hydrograph can also be produced using 3-h unit hydrograph as shown in Example Problem 9-2. Though, it is simple and easy, but it will be accurate if effective precipitation in each hour is about the same.

Table 10.5 Application of UH (Ex. Prob. 10.6)

Time	UH	ER	Runoff rate, m³/s			
t, h	m³/s.cm	P_e, cm	Q_{s1}	Q_{s2}	Q_{s3}	Q_s
0	0	0	0.0			0.0
1	0.3	1.2	0.4			0.4
2	0.8	2.9	1.0	0.9		1.9
3	4.6	1.3	5.5	2.3	0.4	8.2
4	17.8		21.4	13.1	1.0	35.5
5	20.4		24.5	50.7	5.8	81.0
6	12.4		14.9	58.1	22.3	95.3
7	7.1		8.5	35.3	25.5	69.3
8	3.6		4.3	20.2	15.5	40.0
9	2.1		2.5	10.3	8.9	21.7
10	0.3		0.4	6.0	4.5	10.9
11	0		0.0	0.9	2.6	3.5
12	0		0.0	0.0	0.4	0.4
13	0		0.0	0.0	0.0	0.0

Figure 10.6 Flow Hydrograph (Ex. Prob. 10.6)

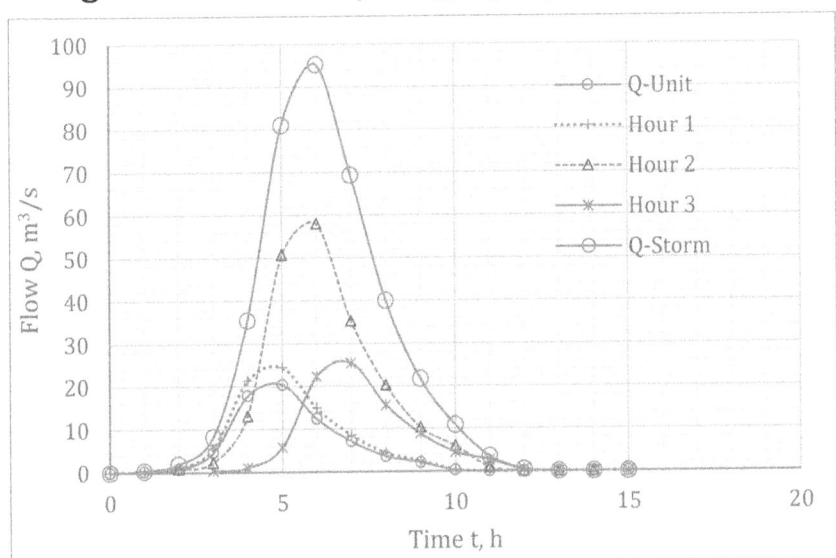

Example Problem 10.7

A 2h-UH of a watershed is shown in the first two columns of **Table 10.4**, Determine the storm flow hydrograph produced by the design storm from Example Problem 3.12. Storm runoff depths for each 2-h interval are shown in column 3 of Table 10.4.

Figure 10.7 Flow Hydrograph (Ex. Prob. 10.7)

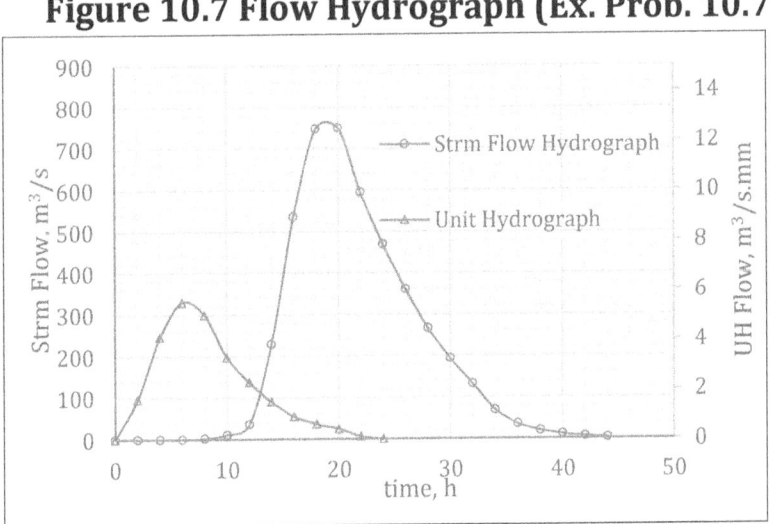

Solution:

Knowing the ordinates of UH, and storm depths, storm hydrograph for each 2-interval is found by multiplication of UH ordinates by the runoff depth and lagging it appropriately. Computations are shown in **Table 10.6** and plot in

Table 10.6 Stormflow Hydrograph (Ex. Prob. 10.7)

h	Q$_U$/mm	R$_S$, mm	\multicolumn{10}{c}{Storm Flow, Q$_S$, m³/s}	Q$_S$ total
0	0	0											0
2	1.6	0											0
4	4.1	0											0
6	5.5	1	0										0
8	5.0	4	2	0									2
10	3.3	9	5	6	0								11
12	2.3	104	7	15	15	0							36
14	1.5	24	6	20	37	166	0						230
16	0.9	11	4	19	50	426	38	0					536
18	0.6	8	3	12	46	571	98	18	0				748
20	0.4	6	2	9	30	519	131	47	13	0			750
22	0.1	5	1	6	21	343	120	63	32	10	0		595
24	0.0	5	1	3	14	239	79	57	43	25	8	0	469
26			0	2	8	156	55	38	40	34	21	7	361
28			0	1	5	93	36	26	26	31	28	18	266
30			0	0	4	62	22	17	18	20	26	25	194
32				0	1	42	14	10	12	14	17	23	132
34					0	10	10	7	7	9	12	15	70
36						0	2	5	5	6	8	10	35
38							0	1	3	4	5	7	19
40								0	1	2	3	4	10
42									0	1	2	3	5
44										0	1	2	2

Unit Hydrograph

Sample of Calculation (07 hour):

Sample calculations for the 10-12 h interval are shown here.

$$Q_s(12) = R_S(6)Q_u(6) + R_S(8)Q_u(4) + R_S(10)Q_u(2)$$
$$= 1.2 \times 5.5 + 3.7 \times 4.1 + 9.1 \times 1.6 = 36.33 = 36 \ m^3/s$$

Note: The figures given in the Table are only shown as whole numbers to fit the table on this page

10.4 Synthetic Unit Hydrograph

When one is faced with the task of estimating peak flows from a watershed for which there is no discharge measurements, there is an overpowering temptation to try to guess what shape a storm runoff hydrograph might have for the watershed. To satisfy this temptation a great number of investigators have tried to relate various measurable properties of watersheds to various properties of the average unit hydrographs derived from measured watersheds. Among the watershed properties most commonly found useful are the watershed shape and length. These are closely related for a given size of watershed so one or the other should be used, but not both. Another common useful property is some measure of stream slope. A third property that has some impact is the lake storage area of watershed.

10.4.1 Snyder Unit Hydrograph

This method relates the lag time to the geometrical characteristics of the watershed. Snyder method uses two parameters C_t and C_p. These parameters are regional parameters, and one can use values of these parameters derived from similar watersheds. The value of C_t depends on basin characteristics and units. In Snyder study, C_t ranged from 1.3 to 1.7. However, study over wide range of regions indicated that C_t may be as low as 0.30 and as high as 6.0. Based on C_t, lag time can be estimated as follows:

Basin lag time
$$t_L = C_t(L \times L_c)^{0.3}$$

t_L = basin lag time in h
L = basin length along the watercourse from outlet to watershed divide in km
L_c = length along watercourse from outlet to a point opposite to centroid, km
C_t = a regional constant representing topographic effects

Other parameter is C_p that primarily depends on storage or retention capacity of watershed and varies from 0.56 to 0.69 as suggested by Snyder. However, values of this parameter ranging from 0.31 to 0.93 have been reported. Most importantly, selection of these coefficients should be made based on unit hydrograph derived in the region.

$$Q_p = \frac{2.8 C_p \times A}{t_L}$$

A = Area of the watershed, km², Q_p = Peak flow in m³/s.cm, C_p = constant

Snyder assumed **standard duration** as 18% (1/5.5) of the lag time. If a non-standard duration is adopted, it affects basin lag time. In this case, t_L is modified and Q_p is worked out based on this value.

$$t_{Lag} = t_L + 0.25 \times (t_D - t_{SD})$$

$$t_{tB} = 72 + 3 \times t_{LR} - Large\ catchments$$

Above equation gives reasonable estimates of the time base for larger watersheds. However, this yields excessively high values for smaller catchments. It has been shown by others that following relationship works better to estimate time base for smaller catchments.

$$t_{tB} = 5 \times (t_{LR} + 0.5 t_{SD}) \quad (Small\ catchments)$$

In sketching the unit hydrograph further, US army Corps of Engineers used width of the unit hydrograph at 50% and 75% of the peak flow. These widths are related to the peak flow as given by following expressions:

Width of unit hydrograph

$$W_{50} = \left(\frac{Q_p}{A}\right)^{-1.08} \quad W_{75} = \frac{W_{50}}{1.75}$$

Example Problem 10.8

Drainage area of a mid-size catchment is 450 km². The basin length is 48 km and the length opposite to centroid is 22 km. Regional Constants C_t is 1.40 and C_p is 0.60. Develop a unit hydrograph for this catchment?

Given:

A = 450 km² L = 48 km, Lc = 22 km, C_t = 1.40, C_p = 0.60

Solution:

$$t_L = C_t (L \times L_c)^{0.3} = 1.40 (48 \times 22)^{0.3} = 11.3 = 11\ h$$

$$D = \Delta t = 0.18 \times t_L = 1.8 \times 11.3\ h = 2.03 = 2.0\ h$$

$$Q_p = \frac{2.8 C_p \times A}{t_L} = \frac{2.8 \times 0.60 \times 450}{11.3} = 66.9 = 67\ m^3/s.cm$$

$$W_{50} = 5.87 \left(\frac{Q_p}{A}\right)^{-1.08} = \left(\frac{66.9}{450}\right)^{-1.08} = 45.9 = 46\ h$$

$$W_{75} = W_{50}/1.75 = 45.9/1.75 = 26\ h$$

$$t_b = 5 \times (t_{LR} + 0.5 t_{SD}) = 5 \times (11.3 + 1) = 61.5 = 62\ h$$

10.4.2 NRCS Dimensionless Hydrograph

Victor Mockus developed one such set of relationships. In this method, the ratio of triangular time base to time to peak is kept at 8/3 and actual time base to time to peak is also kept constant at 5. In addition, it uses a dimensionless hydrograph (Q/Q_p vs t/t_p) to provide a standard unit hydrograph shape. One such shape is the **NRCS dimensionless hydrograph** shown in **Table 10.7** and **Fig. 10.8**.

Table 10.7 NRCS Dimensionless Hydrograph

t/t_p	Q/Q_p	t/t_p	Q/Q_p	t/t_p	Q/Q_p
0.0	0.000	1.1	0.990	2.4	0.147
0.1	0.030	1.2	0.930	2.6	0.107
0.2	0.100	1.3	0.860	2.8	0.077
0.3	0.190	1.4	0.780	3.0	0.055
0.4	0.310	1.5	0.680	3.2	0.040
0.5	0.470	1.6	0.560	3.4	0.029
0.6	0.660	1.7	0.460	3.6	0.021
0.7	0.820	1.8	0.390	3.8	0.015
0.8	0.930	1.9	0.330	4.0	0.011
0.9	0.990	2.0	0.280	4.5	0.005
1.0	1.000	2.2	0.207	5.0	0.000

Figure 10.7 NRCS Dimensionless Flow Hydrograph

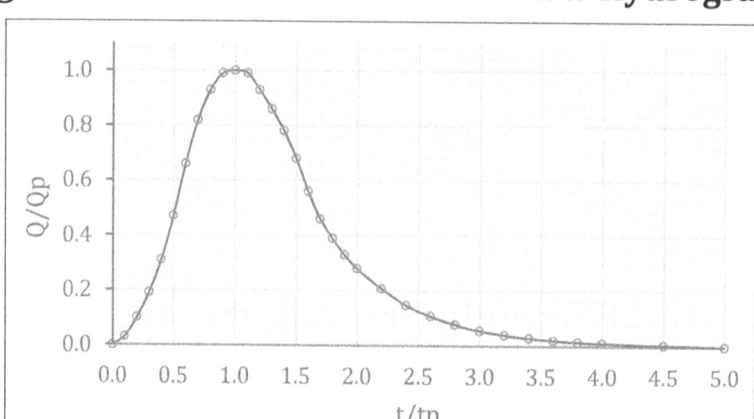

10.4.3 Derivation of UH-NRCS Method

Time to peak flow rate

To be able to use the NRCS dimensionless hydrograph, it is necessary to establish the time scale. Time scale of the UH is established by knowing either the time of concentration t_c or lag time t_L. In the NRCS method the ratio of t_L/t_c is fixed at 0.60 and time to peak runoff rate is assumed to be two thirds of the time of concentration.

Lag Time

NRCS formula for estimating lag time was discussed in chapter 7 and is reproduced here.

Lag time (NRCS)
$$t_l = \frac{L^{0.8}(2540 - 23CN)^{0.7}}{14100 CN^{0.7} S_h^{0.5}}$$

t_l = lag time in h, L = hydraulic length in m, S_b = basin slope m/m

In the NRCS method, the ratio of time to peak flow to lag time is fixed at 1.1. It should be pointed out however that lag time and storm duration are interrelated parameters and can change from storm to storm.

$$t_p = 0.5\Delta t + t_l = 1.1 t_l$$

$$\Delta t = 0.2\, t_p = 0.22 t_l$$

Unit Hydrograph

The above formula yields good results for watersheds up to 15 km². For larger watersheds, time scale is established by determining the time of concentration using Manning's equation.

Time of Concentration

As compared to lag time, time of concentration for a watershed remains relatively constant and can be easily determined. The time of concentration is worked out by dividing the main watercourse into sub-reaches. Assuming uniform flow conditions, flow velocity in each sub-reach is determined using Manning's equation and travel time is found.

$$t_c = t_1 + t_2 + \cdots = \sum \frac{L_i}{v_i}$$

In the NRCS method, lag time is assumed to be 60% of the time of concentration. Knowing t_c, lag time and time scales can be established using the following relationships.

$$t_p = 0.5\Delta t + t_l = 1.1 t_l = 0.67 t_c$$

$$\boxed{\Delta t = 0.2\, t_p = 0.22 t_l = 0.13 t_c}$$

These relationships can be used to construct the curvilinear UH.

Figure 10.8 NRCS Triangular Hydrograph

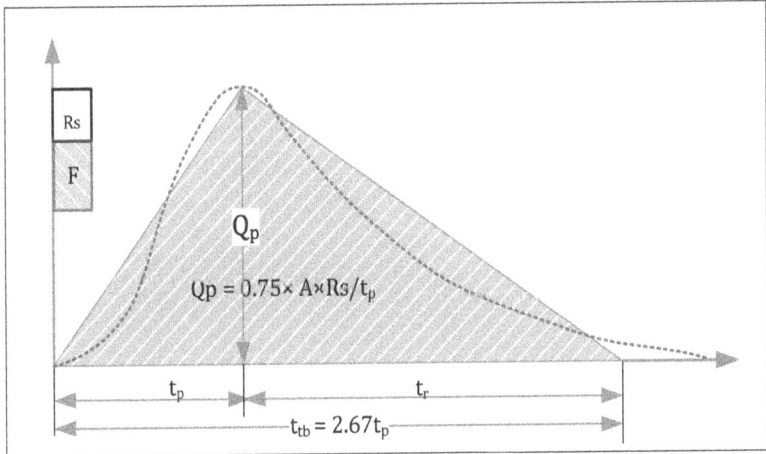

Peak Flow Rate

After finding the time to peak flow t_p, peak flow rate Q_p for the unit hydrograph is found assuming the shape of hydrograph is triangular as shown in **Fig. 10.9**. In the NRCS triangular hydrograph, the time base of the triangular hydrograph is fixed at 8/3 times of time to peak flow, t_p. Further knowing that for UH the runoff depth is unity; peak flow rate for UH is calculated.

Area under Triangular Hydrograph

Area under triangular graph represents runoff flow volume, V_S and mathematically can be expressed as:

$$V_S = R_s \times A = \frac{1}{2} \times t_{tb} \times Q_p$$

$$= \frac{1}{2} \times \frac{8}{3} \times t_p \times Q_p = \frac{4}{3} \times t_p \times Q_p$$

Peak flow NRCS unit hydrograph

$$\boxed{Q_p(UH) = \frac{Q_p}{R_s} = \frac{3}{4} \times \frac{A}{t_p} = \frac{0.75A}{t_p}}$$

On knowing time to peak, peak flow rate of the unit hydrograph is worked out by assuming the triangular shape as shown above. Once both Qp and tp of the unit hydrograph are established, it can be used to complete the curvilinear unit hydrograph by using dimensionless hydrograph.

UH Ordinates

On finding the UH-peak flow rate and time to peak, t_p, ordinates of curvilinear UH are found using dimensionless hydrograph.

$$t = (t/t_p) \times t_p$$

$$Q_u(t) = (Q/Q_p) \times Q_p$$

UH-duration

As a final step, duration of the UH is established as one fifth of time to peak flow.

Example Problem 10.9

Using NRCS Method, derive a synthetic unit hydrograph for the Speed vale watershed. The properties of the watershed are as follows:
Hydraulic length = 2950 m, CN = 67, Basin slope = 0.5%, Area = 1.94 km²

Given:

L = 2950 m   CN = 67 S_b = 0.5%   A = 1.94 km²

Solution:

Lag time
$$t_l = \frac{L^{0.8}(2540 - 23CN)^{0.7}}{14100 CN^{0.7} S_b^{0.5}} = \frac{2950^{0.8}(2540 - 23 \times 67)^{0.7}}{14100 \times 67^{0.7} \times 0.005^{0.5}}$$

$= 3.968 = 4.0\ h$

Time to peak
$t_p = 1.1 t_l = 1.1 \times 4.0\ h = \underline{4.4\ h}$

$\Delta t = 0.2 t_p = 0.2 \times 4.4\ h = 0.88\ h = \underline{1.0\ h}$

UH-Peak flow
$$Q_p(UH) = \frac{0.75 A}{t_p} = \frac{0.75 \times 1.94\ km^2}{4.4\ h}$$

$$= \frac{0.3306\ km^2}{h} \times \frac{1000\ m^3}{km^2.mm} \times \frac{h}{3600\ s} \times \frac{1000\ L}{m^3}$$

$= 91.8 = \underline{92\ L/s.mm}$

Sample of calculations: #4

$t = (t/t_p) \times t_p = 0.6 \times 4.4\ h = 2.64 = 2.6\ h$

$Q = \frac{Q}{Q_p} \times Q_p = 0.66 \times \frac{91.8\ L}{s.mm} = 60.58 = \underline{61\ L/s.mm}$

Computations are shown in **Table 10.8** and plot in **Fig. 10.10**

Table 10.8 NRCS Synthetic Unit Hydrograph

#	t/t_p	Q/Q_p	Time t, h	Q_u (t) L/s.mm
1	0.0	0.00	0.0	0.0
2	0.2	0.10	1.0	9.2
3	0.4	0.31	2.0	28.5
4	0.6	0.66	3.0	60.7
5	0.8	0.93	4.0	85.6
6	1.0	1.00	5.0	92.0
7	1.2	0.93	6.0	85.6
8	1.4	0.78	7.0	71.8
9	1.6	0.56	8.0	51.5
10	1.8	0.39	9.0	35.9
11	2.0	0.28	10.0	25.8
12	2.4	0.15	12.0	13.5
13	2.8	0.08	14.0	7.1
14	3.0	0.06	15.0	5.1
15	3.4	0.03	17.0	2.7
16	3.8	0.02	19.0	1.4
17	4.0	0.01	20.0	1.0
18	4.5	0.01	22.5	0.5
19	5.0	0.00	25.0	0.0

Figure 10.9 NRCS Synthetic UH (Ex. Prob. 10.8)

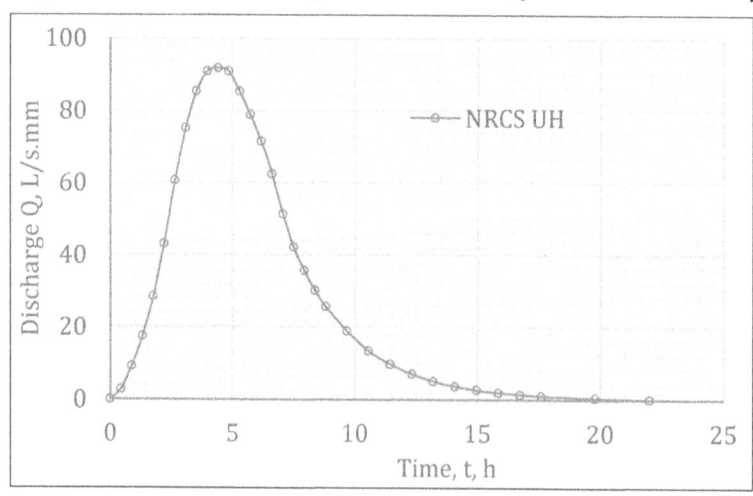

Unit Hydrograph

Example Problem 10.10

The 3-h unit hydrograph is approximated by a triangle with a time base of 75 h and peak runoff rate of 5.6 m³/s.mm. What is the area of watershed?

Given:

$t_{tb} = 75$ h $Q_{u(p)} = 5.6$ m³/s.mm   A =?

Solution:

$$A = \frac{1}{2} \times t_{tb} \times \frac{Q_p}{R_S} = \frac{1}{2} \times 75\,h \times \frac{5.6\,m^3}{s.mm} \times \frac{km^2.mm}{1000\,m^3} \times \frac{3600\,s}{h}$$

$$= 756.0 = \underline{760\,km^2}$$

Example Problem 10.11

Following information is available for the main watercourse of a watershed.

Reach	R_h, m	S, %	L, km	n
1	1.5	0.030	2.0	0.05
2	1.2	0.042	2.0	0.06
3	0.5	0.130	1.5	0.08
4	0.3	0.150	1.0	0.10
5	overland flow 2.0% (0.1 m/s)			

Drainage area of the catchment is 40 km². Estimate the time of concentration using Manning's equation and hence develop a unit hydrograph by NRCS method.

Solution:

Table 10.9 Time of Travel (Ex. Prob. 10.11)

Reach #	R_h m	S %	L km	n -	v m/s	t h
1	1.5	0.030	2.0	0.05	0.45	1.22
2	1.2	0.042	2.0	0.06	0.39	1.44
3	0.5	0.130	1.5	0.08	0.28	1.47
4	0.3	0.150	1.0	0.1	0.17	1.60
5	Overland	2.00	0.5		0.10	1.39
					$\Sigma =$	7.12

Table 10.10 Unit Hydrograph(Ex. Prob. 10.10)

t/t$_p$	Q/Q$_p$	Time t, h	Q$_u$ m^3/s.mm
0.0	0.00	0.0	0.000
0.2	0.10	1.0	0.166
0.4	0.31	2.0	0.515
0.6	0.66	3.0	1.096
0.8	0.93	4.0	1.544
1.0	1.00	5.0	1.660
1.2	0.93	6.0	1.544
1.4	0.78	7.0	1.295
1.6	0.56	8.0	0.930
1.8	0.39	9.0	0.647
2.0	0.28	10.0	0.465
2.2	0.21	11.0	0.344
2.4	0.15	12.0	0.244
2.6	0.11	13.0	0.178
2.8	0.08	14.0	0.128
3.0	0.06	15.0	0.091
3.2	0.04	16.0	0.066
3.4	0.03	17.0	0.048
3.6	0.02	18.0	0.035
3.8	0.02	19.0	0.025
4.0	0.01	20.0	0.018
4.5	0.005	22.5	0.008
5.0	0.000	25.0	0.000

Figure 10.10 Unit Hydrograph(Ex. Prob. 10.10

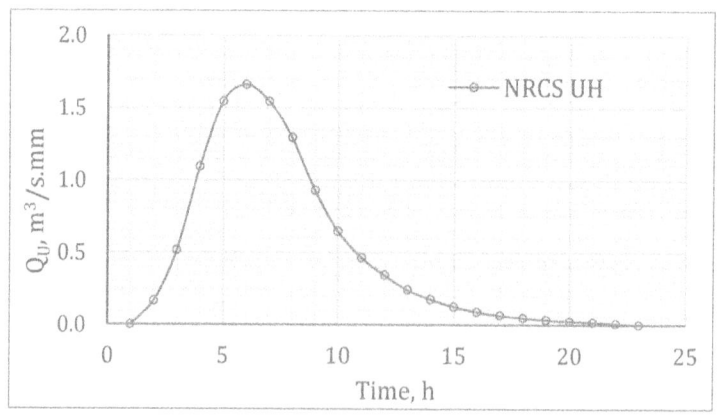

Unit Hydrograph

Sample of Calculations:

$$t_p = 0.67 \times t_c = 0.67 \times 7.12\ h = 4.77h = 5.0\ h\ say$$

$$\Delta t = D = 0.2 t_p = 0.2 \times 4.77\ h = 0.954 = 1.0\ h$$

$$Q_{u(p)} = \frac{0.75A}{t_p} = \frac{0.75 \times 40\ km^2}{5.0\ h} \times \frac{1000\ m^3}{km^2.mm} \times \frac{h}{3600\ s}$$

$$= 1.66 = \underline{1.7\ m^3/s.mm}$$

Example Problem 10.12

For the catchment described in Example Problem 10.9, construct stormflow hydrograph produced due a 3-h storm that produced accumulative rainfall depths 67, 85 mm and 115 mm at the end of the hour. Assume CN of 75 for the catchment.

Given:

CN = 75   ΣP (1) = 67 mm   ΣP (2) = 85 mm   ΣP (3) = 115 mm

Solution:

Maximum abstraction

$$S = \frac{25400}{CN} - 254 = \frac{25400}{75} - 254 = 84.66 = 84.7\ mm$$

Runoff depth at the end of hour

$$R_s(3) = \frac{(P - 0.2S)^2}{(P + 0.8S)} = \frac{(115 - 0.2 \times 84.7)^2}{(115 + 0.8 \times 84.7)} = 52.6 = 53\ mm$$

$$R_s(2) = \frac{(P - 0.2S)^2}{(P + 0.8S)} = \frac{(85 - 0.2 \times 84.7)^2}{(85 + 0.8 \times 84.7)} = 29.64 = 29.6\ mm$$

$$R_s(1) = \frac{(P - 0.2S)^2}{(P + 0.8S)} = \frac{(67 - 0.2 \times 84.7)^2}{(67 + 0.8 \times 84.7)} = 18.60 = 18.6\ mm$$

Individual hour effective precipitation

$$P_e(1) = 18.6\ mm - 0.0\ mm = 18.6\ mm$$

$$P_e(2) = 29.6 - 18.6\ mm = 11.0\ mm$$

$$P_e(3) = 52.6 - 29.6 = 23.0\ mm$$

Sample of Calculations (07 hour):

$$Q_s(7) = P_e(1)Q_u(7) + P_e(2)Q_u(6) + P_e(3)Q_u(5)$$
$$= 18.6 \times 0.129 + 11 \times 0.154 + 23 \times 0. = 7.91 = 7.9 \, m^3/s$$

Table 10.11 Storm Hydrograph(Ex. Prob. 10.12)

t	Q_u (t)	P_e	Q_s, m³/s			
h	m³/s.mm	mm	1	2	3	Total
1	0.017	18.60	0.32	0.00		0.32
2	0.051	11.00	0.95	0.19	0.00	1.14
3	0.110	23.00	2.05	0.56	0.39	3.00
4	0.154		2.86	1.21	1.17	5.25
5	0.166		3.09	1.69	2.53	7.31
6	0.154		2.86	1.83	3.54	8.23
7	0.129		2.40	1.69	3.82	7.91
8	0.093		1.73	1.42	3.54	6.69
9	0.065		1.21	1.02	2.97	5.20
10	0.046		0.86	0.72	2.14	3.71
11	0.034		0.63	0.51	1.50	2.63
12	0.024		0.45	0.37	1.06	1.88
13	0.018		0.33	0.26	0.78	1.38
14	0.013		0.24	0.20	0.55	0.99
15	0.009		0.17	0.14	0.41	0.72
20	0.002		0.04	0.02	0.07	0.13

Figure 10.11 Flow Hydrograph(Ex. Prob. 10.12)

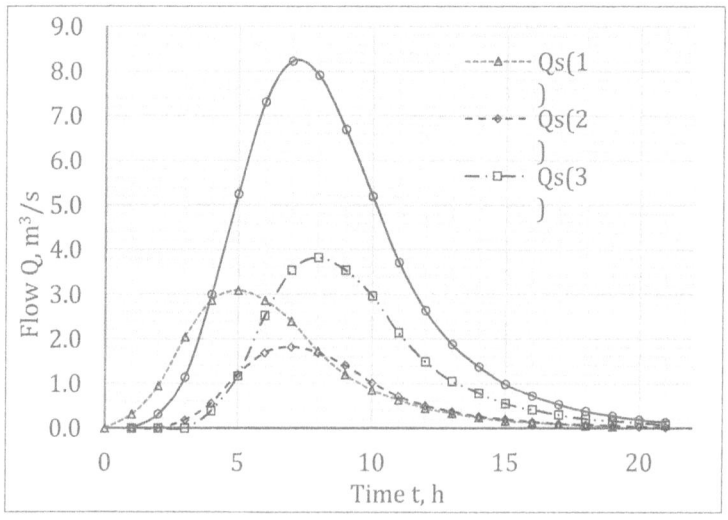

Discussion Questions

1. Explain how depth of runoff is found from the observed storm flow hydrograph.

2. What is unit hydrograph and list the basic assumptions on which it is based?

3. Describe the procedure for deriving a unit hydrograph from a stream flow hydrograph?

4. What is a synthetic unit hydrograph? Describe NRCS method of deriving a unit hydrograph.

5. Describe Snyder method of deriving synthetic unit hydrograph

6. In triangular shape hydrograph, derive the expression for peak Q_u in terms of area, A and time to peak flow, t_p. Assume triangular time base is 8/3 times the time to peak.

7. Assuming triangular shape, the peak flow rate from a certain region is given by the following relationship: $Q_p = \dfrac{A \times R_S}{1.5\, t_p}$, prove that triangular time base is three times the time to peak flow?

8. Compare curvilinear hydrograph and a triangular hydrograph

9. Describe how you can derive a 2-h unit hydrograph from a 1-h unit hydrograph?

10. Describe the use of S-curve.

Practice Problems

Practice Problem 10.1

The storm flow rates produced by a 3-hour storm on Indian river watershed are tabulated below. Drainage area of the watershed is 55 km².

t, h	0	3	6	9	12	15	18	21	24	27	30	33	36
Q_s, m³/s	0	4.0	13	25	17	12	8.0	6.0	4.0	3.0	2.0	1.0	0

a) What is the storm runoff depth? (R_S = 19 mm)
b) Derive the unit hydrograph (peak flow $Q_{U(p)}$ (9h) = 1.3 m³/s.mm)
c) By applying the superposition principle, compute the ordinates of 6-hour UH. ($Q_{U(p)}$ (12 h) = 1.1 m³/s.mm)

Practice Problem 10.2

A storm recorded 75 and 110 mm of rainfall (cumulative) at the end of first and second hour respectively. Assuming a curve number of 75, estimate runoff produced in each of the two hours. (23.6 mm, 25.1 mm)

Hour	8:00	9:00	10:00	11:00
Q_s, m³/s	101	129	131	115

Practice Problem 10.3

The storm flows observed from a storm of 6-h duration that fell on a 500-km² watershed are tabulated below:

h	0	6	12	18	24	30	36	42	48	54	60	66	72
m³/s	0	100	250	200	150	100	70	50	35	25	15	5	0

1. Determine the storm runoff depth? (R_S = 43.2 mm)
2. Find the peak flow of unit hydrograph ($Q_{U(p)}$ (12h) = 5.8 m³/s.mm)

Practice Problem 10.4

A 6-hour storm in September produced a total 6.4 cm of rainfall on Indu River watershed. W-index for the fall season is estimated to be 6.4 mm/h. Using the 6 h unit hydrograph constructed in **Practice Problem 10.1**, compute the peak flow rate. (28 m³/s)

Practice Problem 10.5

Using NRCS Method, derive a synthetic unit hydrograph for the Sunny River watershed. Properties of the watershed are as follows:
Hydraulic length = 2950 m   Curve number = 75
Basin slope = 1.4%   Drainage area = 4.5 km²
Calculate the UH peak runoff rate assuming the CN = 75.
($Q_{u(p)}$ = 4.5 m³/s.cm)

Practice Problem 10.6

The main channel of a catchment of area 2.5-km² is 1500 m long and overland flow length is 420 m. Following information is obtained from the field survey. Determine time of concentration and hence UH by NRCS Method.
(t_c = 90 min, $Q_{u(p)}$ = 0.52 m³/s.mm)

Reach	S, %	R_h, m	n	L, m
1	0.10	0.50	0.04	900
2	0.20	0.30	0.05	600
Overland	v = 0.2 m/s	-		420

Practice Problem 10.7

Using 1-hour UH for Black Creek in **Example Problem 10.1**, determine the storm flow hydrograph produced by a storm beginning at 4 AM. Rainfall intensities and infiltration index for each hour are as follows:

t, hour ending	04	05	06	07	08
I, mm/h	85	22	55	10	21
W, mm/h	30	25	20	15	11

By superposition find storm flow at hour 9, 10, 11 AM (128, 131, 115 m³/s)

Practice Problem 10.8

The ordinates of a 4-h unit hydrograph are given below. Applying the principle of superposition, determine the storm flow hydrograph from a 8-h storm. In successive 4-h durations effective rainfall of 13 and 21 mm were produced respectively. Determine stream flows for 12th, 20th and 40th hour assuming constant base flow rate of 1.5 m³/s. (35 m³/s, 50 m³/s, 5.3 m³/s)

t, h	0	4	8	12	16	20	24	28	32	36	40	44
m³/s.cm	0	2.0	8.0	13	15	13	9	5.2	2.7	1.5	0.5	0

Practice Problem 10.9

The ordinates of a 1-h UH are shown in the table below. From this information, find the area of catchment? (8.6 km²)

t, h	0	1	2	3	4	5	6	7
Q_U, m³/s.cm	0	5.0	8.5	5.5	3.5	1.0	0.5	0

Practice Problem 10.10

The 5-h unit hydrograph of a catchment of area 1100 km² is approximated by a triangle with a time base of 70 h. What is the peak of this UH? (8.7 m³/s.mm)

Practice Problem 10.11

The ordinates of a 4-h UH are approximately triangular in shape with a time base of 48 h and peak flow occurring at 12th hour. Area of the catchment is 230 km². From this information, find the equation of recession limb of the unit hydrograph. (Q_u = 3.55-0.074t)

Practice Problem 10.12

For the data of Practice Problem 10.11 above, using the NRCS dimensionless UH develop the curvilinear unit hydrograph.

h	0	6	12	18	24	30	36	42	48	54	60
m³/s.mm	0	1.3	2.7	1.8	0.76	0.34	0.15	0.067	0.029	0.013	0.0

Practice Problem 10.13

A 6-h UH of a watershed of an area of 450 km² is approximated as a triangle with a time base of 60 h. What is the peak rate of UH? (4.2 m³/s.mm)

Practice Problem 10.14

Applying NRCS method, develop UH for a watershed of an area of 11 km², hydraulic length of 2700 m and basin slope of 0.40%. Assume curve number for the watershed conditions is 65.
(t_l = 4.5 h, t_p = 5.0 h, Δt = 1.0 h, $Q_{u(p)}$ = 0.46 m³/s.mm)

Practice Problem 10.15

For the data of Practice Problem 10.14, using dimensionless NRCS hydrograph, construct 1-h unit hydrogrph.

Practice Problem 10.16

A catchment has drainage area of 400 km². The basin length along the main channel is 35 km and length opposite to the centroid is 10 km. Regional Constants C_t is 1.50 and C_p is 0.70. Develop 3-h UH?
(t_p =8.7 h, D = 3.0 h, t_{pR} = 9.0 h, Q_p = 87 m³/s.cm, t_b =52 h)

Unit Hydrograph

Practice Problem 10.17

The direct runoff hydrograph of a watershed can be approximated as a triangle with base period of 90 h and peak flow of 230 m³/s. Given that the area of watershed is 1850 km², determine the storm depth and peak flow rate of UH. (20 mm, 12 m³/s.mm)

Practice Problem 10.18

A 2-h UH of a catchment can be approximated as a triangle with a time base period of 46 h and peak flow of 14 m³/s.mm. Find area of the catchment? (1160 km²)

Practice Problem 10.19

The Snyder's parameters for a catchment are as follows: C_p = 0.65, C_t = 1.5, L = 25 km, L_c = 12 km. Catchment has a drainage area of 1255 km². Develop a 2-h UH? (t_p =8.3 h, D_s =1.5, D = 2.0 h, t_{pR} = 8.4 h, Q_p = 27 m³/s.mm, t_b =48 h)

Practice Problem 10.20

Applying NRCS method, develop UH for a watershed of an area of 1180 km², hydraulic length of 5.85 km and basin slope of 0.50%. Composite curve number for the watershed conditions is 59.
(t_l = 8.44 h, t_p = 10 h, t_d =Δt = 2.0 h, $Q_{u(p)}$ = 25 m³/s.mm)

Practice Problem 10.21

Develop a 1-h unit hydrograph for a 18 km² watershed characterized by lag time of 4.5 h. Use 1.0-h time step. (t_p = 5.h, $Q_{u(p)}$ = 0.75 m³/s.mm)

Practice Problem 10.22

The triangular shaped storm flow hydrograph given below is representative of a 65 km² watershed. This hydrograph is due to a storm of 1-h duration. Determine storm runoff depth and find peak of unit flow hydrograph for the watershed. (R_s = 10 mm, $Q_{p(u)}$ = 3.0 m³/s.mm)

t, h	0	2	4	6	8	10	12
Q_s, m³/s	0	15	30	23	15	7.5	0

Practice Problem 10.23

Develop complete UH for the watershed in Practice Problem 10.22 using a time step of 1.0 h.

t, h	1	2	3	4	5	6	7	8	9	10	11	12
Q_u, m³/s.mm	0.75	1.5	2.3	3.0	2.6	2.3	1.9	1.5	1.1	0.75	0.38	0

Practice Problem 10.24

A 2-h storm fell on the watershed indicated in Practice Problem 9.22. Effective rainfall respectively are 6.0 mm and 10 mm. Find peak runoff rate. (46 m³/s)

Practice Problem 10.25

1-h unit hydrograph constructed in Practice Problem 10.15 is tabulated below. Flow rate of UH is expressed in m³/s.mm. A 3-h storm fell on this watershed (CN=65) and accumulative rainfall depths for the three consecutive hours are 47, 89 mm and 128 mm. Find peak runoff rate. (

h	1	2	3	4	5	6	7	8	9	10
Q_u	0.046	0.143	0.304	0.428	0.460	0.428	0.329	0.258	0.179	0.129
h	11	12	13	14	15	16	17	18	19	20
Q_u	0.095	0.068	0.049	0.035	0.025	0.018	0.013	0.010	0.007	0.005

Review Questions

1. Area under the storm flow hydrograph of a 55-km² watershed is estimated to be 930 dam³. The storm runoff depth is
   a) 1.7 mm b) 17 mm c) 170 mm d) 190 mm

2. A 2-hour storm produced a runoff depth of 14 mm. The peak runoff rate is 26.5 m³/s. What is the peak flow rate of the UH with 1 cm of runoff?
   a) 0.19 m³/s.cm b) 1.9 m³/s.cm c) 19 m³/s.cm d) 190 m³/s.cm

3. The peak flow rate of a 2-hour UH is found to be 55 m³/s.cm. A 2-hour storm produced 12 mm and 8 mm of runoff in each hour respectively. The peak storm flow produced by this storm is
   a) 110 m³/s b) 110 L/s c) 56 m³/s d) 45 m³/s

4. A 1-hour UH ordinate for the 5th, 6th and 7th hours are respectively 12, 20, 16 m³/s.cm. A 3-h storm produced runoff of 0.5 cm, 0.0 cm and 1.0 cm. Runoff rate for the 7th hour is
   a) 20 m³/s b) 22 m³/s c) 27 m³/s d) 36 m³/s

5. In NRCS triangular hydrograph, the ratio of time base to time to peak is kept at
   a) 3/8 b) 8/3 c) 1/8 d) 2/8

6. The time to peak runoff rate for a given watershed of 100 km² is estimated to be 6 hours. Using NRCS triangular method, the unit hydrograph peak flow rate is
   a) 0.35 m³/s.cm b) 0.70 m³/s.cm c) 70 m³/s.cm d) 35 m³/s.cm

7. According to NRCS method, UH duration is assumed to be what percentage of the time to peak?
   a) 67% b) 33% c) 13% d) 22%

8. A storm flow hydrograph is approximated by a triangle with a base of 20 hours and peak flow (height) of 25 m³/s. Area of the watershed is 90 km². What is the storm runoff depth?
   a) 10 mm b) 15 mm c) 20 mm d) 25 mm

9. An x-hour UH has x hours of
   a) Time base
   b) Time to recede
   c) Time to peak
   d) Effective rainfall duration

10. Which of the following are the correct units of the ordinates of UH?
    a) ha.cm
    b) m³/s
    c) m³/s.cm
    d) m³.mm/s

11. In NRCS synthetic UH, time to peak is _____ times of t_c.
    a) 2/3
    b) 3/2
    c) 5/3
    d) 8/3

12. The time base of a UH depends on which of the following?
    a) Storm duration
    b) Units of discharge rate
    c) Watershed characteristics
    d) All

13. A unit hydrograph represents a storm runoff depth of
    a) 1 mm
    b) 1 in
    c) 1 cm
    d) All

14. The peak flow rate of a 2 h UH as compared to 1 h UH of a given watershed is
    a) Twice
    b) Same
    c) Smaller
    d) Larger

15. Given that peak flow of 6-h unit hydrograph is 5.4 m³/s.mm, what would be the peak flow rate due to a 6-h storm producing 3.50 cm of rainfall? Assume average infiltration rate of 0.50 cm/h.
    a) 2.7 m³/s
    b) 5.4 m³/s
    c) 27 m³/s
    d) 54 m³/s

16. Time to peak flow rate from a 3-h runoff-producing storm falling over a 150-km² watershed is estimated to be 20. h. Assuming NRCS triangular shape, 3-h UH peak flow rate is
    a) 1.6 m³/s
    b) 3.2 m³/s
    c) 4.8 m³/s
    d) 16 m³/s

17. A triangular direct runoff hydrograph due to a 3-h unit hydrograph falling over a 250 km² area watershed has a time base of 60.0 h. and peak flow rate of 12 m³/s. Depth of effective rainfall is
    a) 3.5 mm
    b) 5.2 mm
    c) 6.7 mm
    d) 7.0 mm

18. The word unit in UH refers to one unit of
    a) Storm runoff
    b) Storm duration
    c) Drainage area
    d) Runoff rate

Unit Hydrograph

19. What is the basic assumption in the derivation and application of unit hydrograph?
    a) Liner response to input
    b) Linear time variance
    c) Non-linear response
    d) Non-linear time variance

20. A storm produced 6.0 cm of effective rainfall over 3-h period. Dividing ordinates of storm flow hydrograph by____ yields ____ Unit hydrograph.
    a) 6, 3-h   b) 3, 6-h   c) 3, 3-h   d) 6, 6-h

21. Unit hydrograph is not applicable to larger watersheds exceeding
    a) 50 km²   b) 500 km²   c) 5000 km²   d) 50000 km²

22. The S-curve is the summation of
    a) Unit hydrograph
    b) Effective hyetograph
    c) Storm flow hydrograph
    d) Base flow hydrograph

23. The concept of UH was first proposed by
    a) Darcy   b) Sherman   c) Snyder   d) Horton

24. The time base of a 1-h duration UH as compared to 2-h UH is
    a) Smaller   b) Same   c) Larger   d) Depends

25. Unit hydrograph is the graphical relationship between the time distributions of effective ____ and ____
    a) Rainfall, total runoff
    b) Rainfall, Streamflow
    c) Runoff, Storm runoff
    d) Rainfall, Storm runoff

26. Which of the following methods is used to develop synthetic unit hydrograph?
    a) Snyder   b) Curve Number   c) TR Method   d) Thiessen

27. In NRCS method, to work out the peak flow rate of UH, shape of the hydrograph is assumed to be
    a) Triangular   b) Rectangular   c) Parabolic   d) Hyperbolic

28. Snyder method of developing synthetic UH is more suitable for
    a) Small catchments
    b) Small to mid-size
    c) Large watersheds
    d) All

29. Basin lag is the time from centroid of excess rainfall to _____.
   a) End of storm runoff
   b) End of recession
   c) Time to peak
   d) Inflexion point

30. The time base of dimensionless NRCS unit hydrograph is assumed to be _____ that of time to peak flow.
   a) 4×
   b) 5×
   c) 6×
   d) 7×

11 Flood Routing

After a flow hydrograph at the outlet of a watershed is developed by the methods discussed earlier, next step is to find how this flood would change as it passes through the river channel or the reservoir. As this flood moves down the river, the shape of hydrograph gets modified due to various factors including channel storage, friction, lateral flow additions or withdrawals. When the flood wave passes through a reservoir, its peak is **attenuated,** and the time base is enlarged due to the effects of storage. In case of channel, flood wave is attenuated due to friction if there are no lateral inflows. The addition of lateral inflows can cause reduction in attenuation or even amplification of flood wave.

11.1 Flood Routing Defined

Flood routing is a technique of determining the flood hydrograph at a section of river by utilising the inflow hydrograph at one or more upstream sections. The hydrologic analysis of problems such as flood prediction and protection are based on flood routing. Similarly design of reservoirs and spillways used for flood attenuation includes flood routing. Two broad categories of flood routing are **reservoir routing** and **channel routing**. The difference between these two is that in reservoir routing, the water surface is flat, while in channel routing water surface slope is significant.

11.1.1 Reservoir Routing

In reservoir routing, effects of flood wave as it passes through a reservoir are studied. To perform reservoir routing, it is required to know, elevation storage relationship and variation of outflow with elevation. This type of routing becomes the basis of determining design capacity of spillways and other reservoir structures, and sizing of reservoirs for flood attenuation and other requirements.

11.1.2 Channel Routing

Using the flood hydrograph at an upstream section as input, channel routing is used to predict the flood wave at various sections of the river channel. This information is essential in flood forecasting and flood protection measures.

11.2 Routing Methods

Routing methods can be broadly classified into two categories.
  i. Hydrologic routing
  ii. Hydraulic routing

Hydrologic routing simply employs equation of continuity or mass balance. On the other hand, hydraulic routing employs equation of motion in addition to equation of continuity.

11.2.1 Basic Equations

The passage of flood through a reservoir is unsteady as the flow varies with time. In hydraulic terminology, it is called **gradually varied unsteady flow**. Equation of continuity is based on the principle of mass balance, which dictates that difference in inflow and outflow must be equal to change in storage.

$$\text{Inflow - Outflow = Change in storage or } I - O = \Delta S$$

Where O and I are inflow and outflow volume/depth over a certain time interval Δt in which the change in storage is ΔS. When terms are expressed as flow rates,

$$\bar{I} - \bar{O} = \frac{\Delta S}{\Delta t}$$

Averages can also be expressed in terms of initial and final values.

Continuity equation
$$\left\{\left(\frac{I_1 + I_2}{2}\right) - \left(\frac{O_1 + O_2}{2}\right)\right\} = \frac{S_2 - S_1}{(t_2 - t_1)}$$

The time interval, Δt should be sufficiently short so that variation in inflow and outflow can be assumed linear in that time interval. Further, Δt must be shorter than transit time of the flood wave through the river reach. As such, the above equation can be applied to reservoirs and segments of streams and rivers to estimate changes in storage when inflow and outflow rates are known.

Example Problem 11.1

At a given hour, the inflow and outflow rates from a river reach respectively are 11 m³/s and 16 m³/s. One hour later, the inflow is 15 m³/s, and the

Flood Routing

outflow is 17 m³/s. Determine the change in storage in the reach that occurred during the hour.

Given:

Inflow, m³/s	11	15
Outflow, m³/s	16	17

Solution:

$$S_2 - S_1 = \left\{\left(\frac{I_1 + I_2}{2}\right) - \left(\frac{O_1 + O_2}{2}\right)\right\}(t_2 - t_1)$$

$$= \left\{\left(\frac{11 + 15}{2}\right) - \left(\frac{16 + 17}{2}\right)\right\}\frac{m^3}{s} \times 1.0 h \times \frac{3600 s}{h}$$

$$= -1.26 \times 10^4 = \underline{-1.3 \times 10^4 \ m^3}$$

11.3 Hydrologic Storage Routing

Hydrologic storage routing is also called zero slope routing since the slope of the water surface is practically level. A flood wave I (t) enters the reservoir with an outlet such as spillway at the exit end. The outflow, Q (h) from the reservoir primarily depends on the elevation of water surface, h. Storage in the reservoir is also a function of h such that S = S (h). Further due to passage of flood wave through the river, water level in the reservoir changes with time, h = h (t). Hence both storage and discharge rate change with time. Applying flood routing, variation in S, h and Q can be found. In an uncontrolled spillway, structure like a rectangular weir is provided, the outflow from the reservoir is given by the following equation.

Weir flow equation

$$Q = \frac{2}{3} \times C_d \times L_e \times \sqrt{2gH^3} = Q(h)$$

For reservoir routing following data have to be known:
    i.   Storage volume versus water surface elevation (S vs h)
    ii.   Elevation versus outflow (h vs Q)
    iii. Combining the above two, storage versus outflow (S vs Q)
    iv. Inflow (I) hydrograph, Initial (t = 0) S, I, and Q

There are a variety of methods available for routing of floods through a reservoir. However, all the methods are some modifications of the continuity equation. Reservoir routing is also called **level pool routing** since the water surface is horizontal. One of the methods used is semi graphical.

11.3.1 Modified Puls Method

Terms in the continuity equation can be rearranged as follows:

Modified Continuity equation

$$\left(S_2 + \frac{O_2 \Delta t}{2}\right) = \left(\frac{I_1 + I_2}{2}\right) \Delta t + \left(S_1 - \frac{O_1 \Delta t}{2}\right)$$

In the above equation, initial storage and outflow discharges are known at the start of flood routing. Also, all terms on the right-hand side are known at the beginning of a time step. The terms on the LHS ($S_2 + Q_2\Delta t/2$) can be found for a time step. Since there are two unknowns on the LHS, we need another relationship to solve for both the unknowns viz. S_2 and O_2. Both S and Q are functions of elevation of water surface in the reservoir, whether discharge is controlled through turbines and outlets or goes freely over the spillway. Thus, the term on the LHS is a function of water surface elevation in the reservoir.

$$\left(S_2 + \frac{O_2 \Delta t}{2}\right) = f(h)$$

Since elevation storage and elevation discharge relations are known, the curve of ($S_2 + Q_2\Delta t/2$) versus elevation is constructed. This relationship is used to find the discharge and storage at the end of time interval. To develop this relationship, it is important to select time interval such that linearization of the hydrograph remains a close approximation. For smoothly rising hydrograph, a minimum value of 20% of time to peak should be used.

Computations

Computations for the Puls method are performed as follows:

i. From the known data, plot the curves of storage and discharge versus elevation.

ii. At the start of flood routing, the initial storage and outflow discharge are known.

iii. In the modified continuity equation, all the terms on the RHS are known at the beginning of the time step

$$\left(S_2 + \frac{O_2 \Delta t}{2}\right) = \left(\frac{I_1 + I_2}{2}\right) \Delta t + \left(S_1 - \frac{O_1 \Delta t}{2}\right)$$

iv. Compute the value of ($S_2 + Q_2\Delta t/2$) at the end of time interval

v. Since the relations, S and Q versus h, are known, for the computed value of ($S_2 + Q_2\Delta t/2$), reservoir elevation at the end of time interval

Flood Routing

vi. For the next time step, $(S - Q\Delta t/2) = (S + Q\Delta t/2)$ of previous step $- Q\Delta t$
vii. Procedure is repeated until the entire hydrograph is routed.
viii. Procedure is illustrated in the next example problem

Example Problem 11.2

For a certain reservoir, storage and outflow versus elevation information is shown in **Table 11.1**. A flow hydrograph shown in **Table 11.2** entered the reservoir when the height of water surface was 101.50 m. Route the hydrograph through the reservoir using pulse method.

Solution:

Time to peak flow of inflow hydrograph is 24 h. Time step used for the analysis, $\Delta t = 6.0$ h (25% of time to peak flow). Next step is to prepare storage and discharge versus elevation relationships.

Table 11.1 Computations of Term S+QΔt/2

h	S	Q	S + QΔt/2
m	hm³	m³/s	hm³
101.00	4.550	0.0	4.550
101.50	4.575	15.0	4.737
102.10	4.880	31.0	5.215
102.50	5.284	52.0	5.846
103.00	5.927	86.0	6.856
103.50	6.370	120.0	7.666
103.75	6.527	127.0	7.899
104.00	6.856	140.0	8.368

For starting elevation (101.50 m)

$$S + \frac{Q\Delta t}{2} = 4.575 \ hm^3 + \frac{15.0 \ m^3}{s} \times \frac{6.0 \ h}{2} \times \frac{3600s}{h} \times \frac{hm^3}{100^3 m^3}$$

$$= 4.7370 = 4.74 \ hm^3$$

Computations for the term $(S + Q\Delta t/2)$ are shown in **Table 11.1** using MS excel program. Plot of the storage versus elevation is shown in **Fig 11.1**.

Figure 11.1 Reservoir Outflow versus Elevation

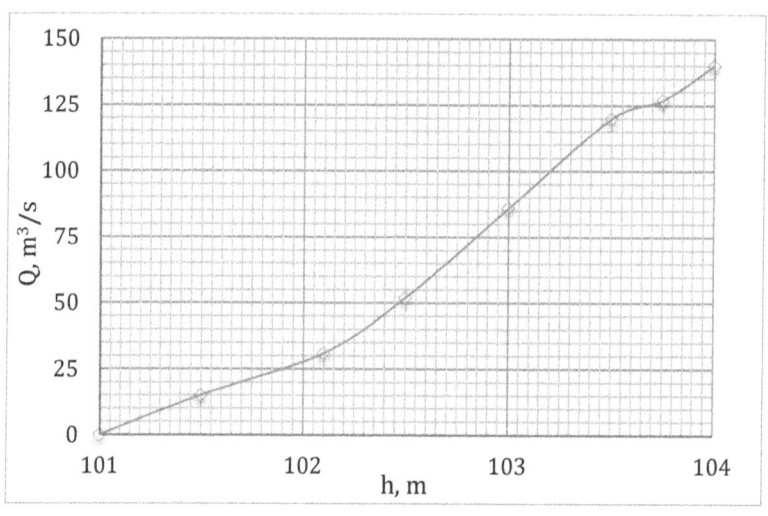

Table 11.2 Excel Worksheet (Ex. Prob. 11.2)

t	I	Avg I	(S-QΔt/2)	(S+QΔt/2)	h	Q
h	m³/s	m³/s	hm³	hm³	m	m³/s
0	12				101.50	15.00
6	22	17.0	4.413	4.780	101.55	16.33
12	57	39.5	4.434	5.281	102.14	33.10
18	85	71.0	4.566	6.099	102.62	60.16
24	70	77.5	4.800	6.474	102.81	73.07
30	52	61.0	4.896	6.213	102.68	62.24
36	41	46.5	4.869	5.873	102.49	51.50
42	33	37.0	4.761	5.560	102.31	42.00
48	21	27.0	4.653	5.236	102.07	30.20
54	15	18.0	4.584	4.972	101.73	22.36
60	14	14.5	4.489	4.803	101.52	15.64
66	12	13.0	4.465	4.746	101.39	11.70
72	11	11.5	4.493	4.741	101.37	11.10

Neet step is to find the starting value of the term

$$S - Q\frac{\Delta t}{2} = 4.575 \; hm^3 - \frac{15.0 \; m^3}{s} \times \frac{6.0 \; h}{2} \times \frac{3600s}{h} \times \frac{hm^3}{100^3 m^3}$$

$$= 4.4130 = 4.41 \; hm^3$$

This calculation is shown in column 4 of **Table 11.2**. Referring to **Fig 11.2**, water level corresponding to 4.78 hm³ is 101.55 m. For water surface elevation of 101.55 m, value of outflow from **Fig 11.1**, is 16 m³/s.

Figure 11.2 (S+Δt/2) vs Elevation(Ex.Prob. 11.2)

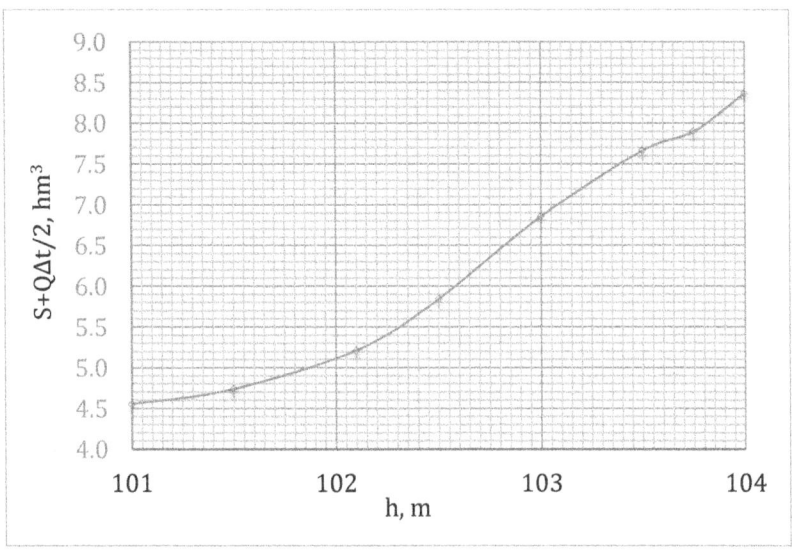

At end of time interval

$$\left(S + \frac{Q\Delta t}{2}\right)_2 = \bar{I} \times \Delta t + \left(S - \frac{Q\Delta t}{2}\right)_2$$

$$= \frac{17 \; m^3}{s} \times 6.0 \; h \times \frac{3600s}{h} \times \frac{hm^3}{100^3 m^3} + 4.41 \; hm^3$$

$$= 4.7802 = 4.78 \; hm^3$$

For next time interval

$$\left(S - Q\frac{\Delta t}{2}\right)_2 = \left(S + \frac{Q\Delta t}{2}\right)_2 - Q_2 \Delta t$$

$$= 4.7802 - \frac{16.0 \, m^3}{s} \times 6.0 \, h \times \frac{3600s}{h} \times \frac{hm^3}{100^3 m^3}$$

$$= 4.434 = 4.43 \, hm^3$$

Procedure is repeated and all computations are shown in excel worksheet shown in **Table 11.2**. Routed outflow hydrograph is shown in **Fig. 11.3**. As seen from the routed hydrograph, peak flow is reduced by about 12 m3/s and peak is lagged by about 6.0 h

Figure 11.3 Routed Hydrograph (Ex. Prob. 11.2)

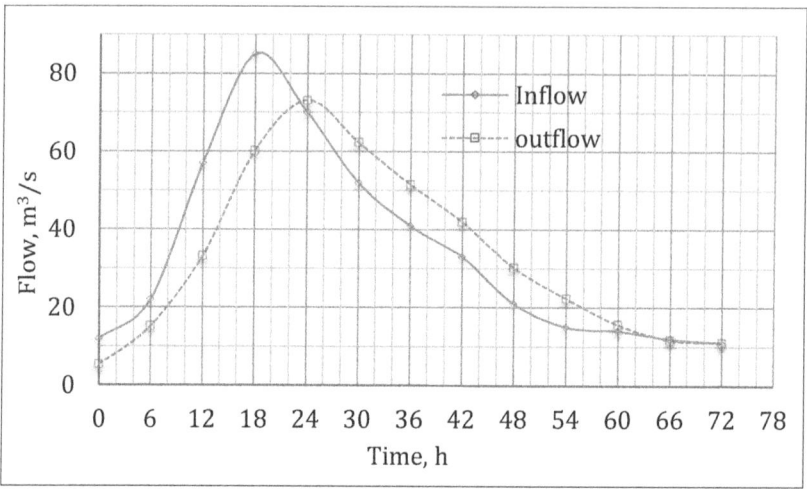

Example Problem 11.3

For a certain reservoir, storage, and outflow versus height above the crest elevation of 100.00 m are described by the following relationships:

$$S(hm^3) = 3.6 + 0.36 h^{0.75} \qquad Q(m^3/s) = 12 \times h^{1.5}$$

A flow hydrograph, data shown in **Table 11.3**, entered the reservoir when the elevation of water surface was 100.50 m. Route the hydrograph through the reservoir using pulse method.

Solution:

A time step Δt of 5.0 h is selected. Based on above relationships, Q, S and (S+QΔt/2) are computed as shown in **Table 11.3**. Plots are shown in **Fig 11.4** and **Fig 11.5**.

Table 11.3 Computations of Term (S+QΔt/2)

Elevation	S	Q	S+QΔt/2
m	hm³	m³/s	hm³
100.00	3.600	0.00	3.600
100.25	3.690	1.50	3.704
100.50	3.780	4.24	3.818
100.75	3.870	7.79	3.940
101.00	3.960	12.00	4.068
101.25	4.050	16.77	4.201
101.50	4.140	22.05	4.338
101.75	4.230	27.78	4.480
102.00	4.320	33.94	4.625
102.25	4.410	40.50	4.775
102.50	4.500	47.43	4.927
102.75	4.590	54.72	5.083
103.00	4.680	62.35	5.241
103.25	4.770	70.31	5.403
103.50	4.860	78.57	5.567
103.75	4.950	87.14	5.734
104.00	5.040	96.00	5.904

Figure 11.4 Reservoir Outflow versus Elevation

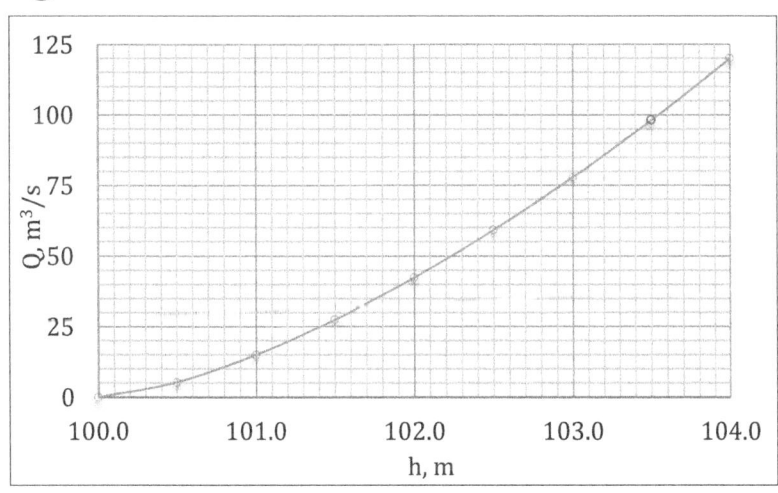

Figure 11.5 (S+QΔt/2) versus Elevation

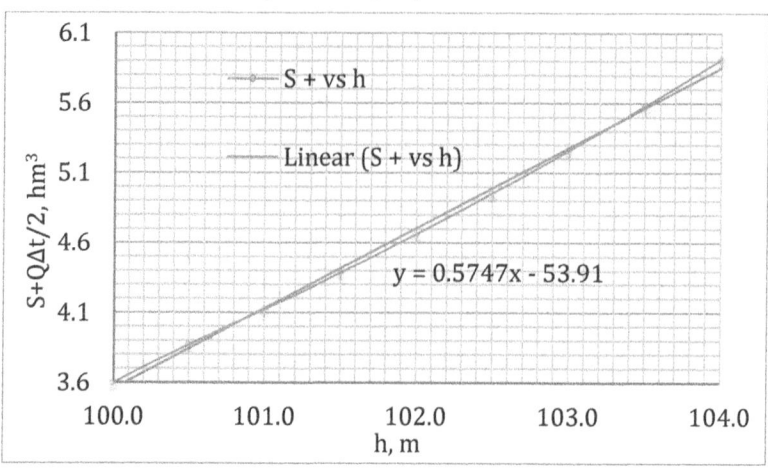

Table 11.4 Excel Worksheet (Ex. Prob. 11.3)

t	I	Avg. I	(S-QΔt/2)	(S+QΔt/2)	h	Q
h	m³/s	m³/s	hm³	hm³	m	m³/s
0	13				100.50	4.24
5	19	16.0	3.741	4.029	100.89	10.13
10	39	29.0	3.847	4.369	101.48	21.56
15	71	55.0	3.981	4.971	102.51	47.83
20	54	62.5	4.110	5.235	102.97	61.37
25	43	48.5	4.130	5.003	102.57	49.43
30	32	37.5	4.113	4.788	102.20	39.16
35	26	29.0	4.083	4.605	101.89	31.06
40	20	23.0	4.046	4.460	101.64	25.10
45	15	17.5	4.008	4.323	101.40	19.88
50	12	13.5	3.966	4.209	101.20	15.82
55	10	11.0	3.924	4.122	101.05	12.97
60	8	9.0	3.888	4.050	100.93	10.76

First time interval

$$S - \frac{Q\Delta t}{2} = 3.78 \; hm^3 - \frac{4.24 \; m^3}{s} \times \frac{5.0 \; h}{2} \times \frac{3600s}{h} \times \frac{hm^3}{100^3 m^3}$$

$$= 3.741 = 3.74 \; hm^3$$

This calculation is shown in column 4 of the excel worksheet of **Table 11.4**. Using the initial value, S+Δt/2 at the end of time interval is calculated.

End of time interval

$$\left(S + \frac{O\Delta t}{2}\right)_2 = \bar{I} \times \Delta t + \left(S - \frac{O\Delta t}{2}\right)_2$$

$$= \frac{16 \, m^3}{s} \times 5.0 \, h \times \frac{3600s}{h} \times \frac{hm^3}{100^3 m^3} + 3.741 \, hm^3$$

$$= 4.029 = 4.03 \, hm^3$$

This calculation is shown in column 5 of the excel worksheet of **Table 11.4**. Referring to **Fig 11.4**, equation of straight line is: y = 0.581x - 54.592. Using this equation, water surface elevation corresponding to 4.03 hm³ is

$$y = \frac{\left\{\left(S + \frac{O\Delta t}{2}\right) + 54.59\right\}}{0.581} = \frac{(4.029 + 54.59)}{0.581} = 100.893 = 100.89 \, m$$

Head over the crust
$$h = y - 100 = 100.893 - 100 = 0.893 = 0.89 \, m$$

$$Q_2 = 12h^{0.75} = 12 \times (0.893)^{0.75} = 11.02 = 11 \, m^3/s$$

Routed outflow hydrograph is shown in **Fig. 11.6**. The routed hydrograph indicates peak flow is reduced by about 10 m³/s and peak is lagged by 5.0 h.

Figure 11.6 Routed Hydrograph (Ex. Prob. 11.3)

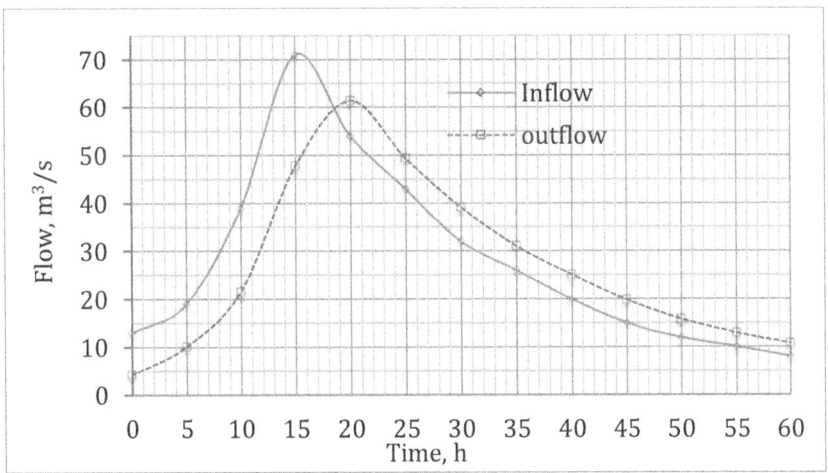

11.3.2 Channel Storage

As the flood waves moves through the channel, water is stored in the channel reach in two ways, prism storage and wedge storage.

Prism Storage

It is the volume of water that would exist if uniform flow occurred at the downstream depth. Saying differently, it is the volume formed by an imaginary plane parallel to the channel bed drawn at the outflow section. At a fixed depth of a downstream section of the reach, prism storage is constant. Prism storage for a given river reach is always positive.

Wedge Storage

It is a wedge like volume formed between the actual water surface and top surface of prism storage. Wedge storage changes from a positive value at an advancing flood to a negative value during a receding flood.

Prism storage is much like a reservoir and can be expressed as function of outflow discharge rate. Wedge storage on the other hand is function of inflow.

$$S_p = f(Q) \quad S_w = f(I)$$

The total storage, S in the river reach thus can be expressed as

Total channel storage
$$\boxed{S = K[xI^m + (1-x)Q^m]}$$

Where, K and x are the coefficients and, m is constant exponent. It has been found that value of the exponent varies from 0.60 for rectangular channels to 1.0 for natural channels.

11.3.3 Muskingum Equation

As discussed above, value of exponent m for natural channel is unity. Storage equation for natural channels is called Muskingum equation.

Muskingum Equation
$$\boxed{S = K[xI + ((1-x)Q)]}$$

Parameter x is known as weighting factor and ranges from 0 to 0.5. It accounts for storage part of the routing. When x = 0, storage is only a function of discharge as in case of linear reservoir. When x = 0.50, both inflow and outflow become equally important in determining storage.

Flood Routing

The coefficient K is known as storage time constant and has dimensions of time. It is a function of channel and flow characteristics. It is approximately equal to the time of travel of flood wave though the reach.

11.3.4 Estimation of K and x

As discussed before, when an inflow flood is routed through a river reach, flood peak is attenuated due to channel storage and is lagged from the inflow peak flow rate. If an inflow outflow hydrograph set is available for a given reach, value of storage can be determined using continuity equation.

To estimate the value of K, a trial value of x is selected and values of the term (xI+(1-x)Q) are made for a series of I and Q. Values of S are plotted against values of xI+(1-x)Q. If the trial value is correct, a straight-line relationship will result. In **Figure 11.7**, relations are shown for three trial values of x. When the chosen value is incorrect, it will yield a looping curve. For the correct value of x relationship, a trend line is fitted and fitted equation is found. Inverse of the slope gives the value of K. For natural channels, the value of x normally falls in the range of 0-0.30.

Example Problem 11.4

The following inflow and discharge hydrograph are observed for a given reach. Estimate the value of K and x as applicable for use in Muskingum equation.

h	0	6	12	18	24	30	36	42	48	54	60	66
I, m³/s	20	80	210	240	215	170	130	90	60	40	28	16
m³/s	20	20	50	150	200	210	185	155	120	85	55	23

Solution:

Using a time interval of 6.0 h, the calculations are made as shown in the excel worksheet in **Table. 11.5**. As shown in **Fig. 11.7**, straight-line relationship for x = 0.30 has a greater coefficient of correlation, yielding equation: y = 0.1013x + 28.

$$K = \frac{1}{(Slope)} = \frac{1}{0.1013} = 9.87 = 9.9/h$$

Figure 11.7 Estimating K of Muskingum Equation

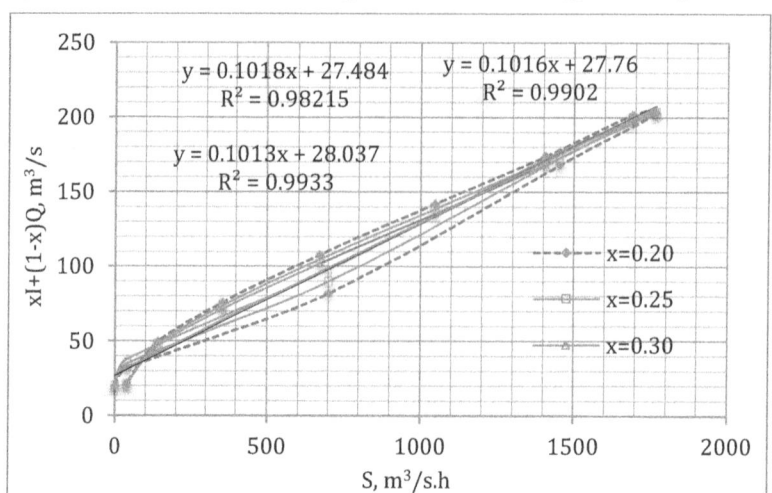

Table 11.5 Excel Worksheet (Ex. Prob. 11.4)

t	I	Q	I-Q	Estimating K and x			xI+(1-x)Q		
				Avg.	ΔS	Σ(ΔS)	X		
							0.20	0.25	0.30
0	20	20	0		0	0	20	20	20
6	80	20	60	30	180	42	32	35	38
12	210	50	160	110	660	702	82	90	98
18	240	150	90	125	750	1452	168	172.5	177
24	215	200	15	52.5	315	1767	203	203.7	204.5
30	170	210	-40	-12.5	-75	1692	202	200	198
36	130	185	-55	-47.5	-285	1407	174	171.2	168.5
42	90	155	-65	-60	-360	1047	142	138.7	135.5
48	60	120	-60	-62.5	-375	672	108	105	102
54	40	85	-45	-52.5	-315	357	76	73.75	71.5
60	28	55	-27	-36	-216	141	49.6	48.25	46.9
66	16	23	-7	-17	-102	39	21.6	21.25	20.9

11.4 Muskingum Method of Routing

Selecting routing time interval Δt, and using Muskingum equation change in storage is given by the following equation:

$$\Delta S = K[x\Delta I + ((1-x)\Delta Q)]$$

Combining this equation with continuity equation, Q_2 is evaluated as;

Flood Routing

$$Q_2 = C_0 I_2 + C_1 I_1 + C_2 Q_1$$

Sum of all the three coefficients must be equal to unity.

$$C_0 + C_1 + C_2 = 0$$

$$C_0 = \frac{-Kx + 0.5\Delta t}{K - Kx + 0.5\Delta t} \quad C_1 = \frac{Kx + 0.5\Delta t}{K - Kx + 0.5\Delta t} \quad C_2 = \frac{K - Kx - 0.5\Delta t}{K - Kx + 0.5\Delta t}$$

If $\Delta t < 2Kx$, the coefficient C_0 will be negative. It is suggested to avoid negative value of coefficients by choosing proper value of Δt.

Example Problem 11.5

Route the following flood hydrograph through a river reach for which $K = 22$ h and $x = 0.25$. Discharge at the beginning is 40 m³/s.

t, h	0	12	24	36	48	60	72	84	96	108	120	132	144
m³/s	40	65	165	250	240	205	170	130	115	85	70	60	54

Solution:

The expression $2Kx = 11$ h, hence $\Delta t = 12$ h is selected
As shown in **Table 10.6**, coefficient C_0, C_1 and C_2 are evaluated as

$C_0 = 0.0222$, $\quad C_1 = 0.5111$ and $C_2 = 0.46667$
For the first time interval, $I_1 = 10$ m³/s, $I_2 = 20$ m³/s and $Q_1 = 40$ m³/s.
Applying the Muskingum equation, Q_2 for the initial time interval is found as follows.

$$Q_2 = C_0 I_2 + C_1 I_1 + C_2 Q_1$$
$$= 0.0222 \times 65 + 0.5111 \times 40 + 0.46667 \times 40$$
$$= 40.55 = 40.6 \, m^3/s$$

Complete calculations are shown in **Table 11.6**. Inflow and outflow hydrographs are shown in **Fig. 11.8**. Peak outflow is 215 and occurs at 60 h compared to flood peak of 250 which occurs at 36 h. Thus, outflow is lagged by 24 h, that is one full day.

Table 11.6 Worksheet (Ex. Prob. 11.5)

K, h	x	Δt, h	Kx	0.5Δt	K-Kx+0.5Δt
22	0.25	12	5.5	6	22.5
$C_0 = 0.0222222$		$C_1 = 0.5111$		$C_2 = 0.466667$	
t	I	C_0I_2	C_1I_1	C_2Q_1	Q
0	40				40.0
12	65	1.4	20.4	18.7	40.6
24	165	3.7	33.2	18.9	55.8
36	250	5.6	84.3	26.0	115.9
48	240	5.3	127.8	54.1	187.2
60	205	4.6	122.7	87.4	214.6
72	170	3.8	104.8	100.1	208.7
84	130	2.9	86.9	97.4	187.2
96	115	2.6	66.4	87.3	156.3
108	85	1.9	58.8	73.0	133.6
120	70	1.6	43.4	62.4	107.4
132	60	1.3	35.8	50.1	87.2
144	54	1.2	30.7	40.7	72.6

Figure 11.8 Routed Hydrograph (Ex. Prob. 11.5)

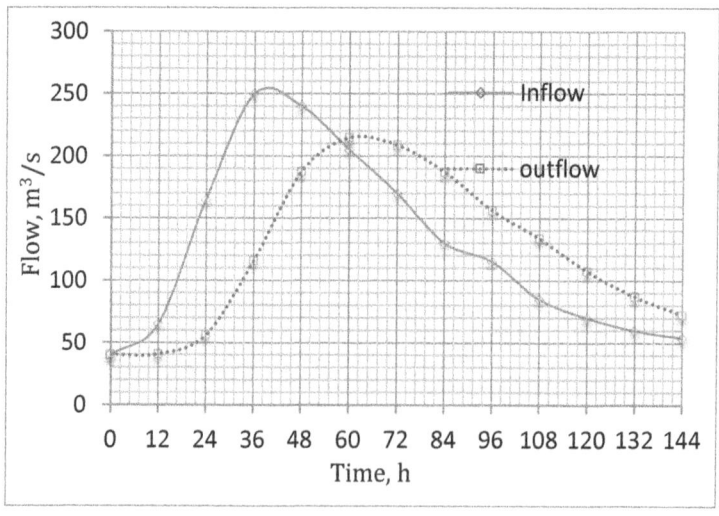

Discussion Questions

1. What are the basic equations used in hydrologic routing and hydraulic routing?
2. Differentiate the following;
   a. Hydraulic routing and hydrologic routing
   b. Level pool routing and channel routing
   c. Prism storage and wedge storage
   d. Gradually varied flow and rapidly varied flow
3. Define routing. Describe different methods of routing.
4. What are the main purposes of flood routing?
5. Describe the stepwise procedure of modified Puls method of reservoir routing?
6. Derive the modified continuity equation used in the Pulse method of reservoir routing
7. Describe a procedure for estimating the values of coefficients K and x of the Muskingum equation?
8. Describe the procedure of channel routing using Muskingum equation?

Practice Problems

Practice Problem 11.1

The storage in a river reach is 8.5 km².mm at a certain time. At this hour, the inflow and outflow are estimated to be 12.5 m³/s and 12.0 m³/s respectively. An hour later, the inflow and outflow increased to 150 m³/s and 12.5 m³/s respectively. Is the storage at the end of the hour greater or less than the initial value? What is the storage at the end of the hour? (Greater, 14 km².mm)

Practice Problem 11.2

An outlet of a reservoir has following discharge head relationship:

h, m	0	0.50	1.0	1.5	2.0
Q, m³/s	0	50	150	350	700

Fit an equation of the form: $Q = ah^b$. (a = 15, n = 0.53)

Practice Problem 11.3

For a Silver Creek reservoir, storage and outflow versus height above the crest elevation of 100.00 m are described by the following relationships:

$$S(hm^3) = 3.6 + 0.36h \qquad Q\left(\frac{m^3}{s}\right) = 12 \times h^{0.75}$$

Compute the expression (S+QΔt/2) using a time interval of 6.0 h and elevation, y ranging from 100 m to 104.0 m. Plot (S+QΔt/2) versus y and fit a linear equation. ((S+QΔt/2) = 0.581y − 54.6)

Practice Problem 11.4

A flood hydrograph shown below entered the Sliver Creek reservoir described in Practice Problem 10.3. Assume water surface elevation at the start of 100.50 m. Route the hydrograph through the reservoir using pulse method. (Peak reduced from 60 to 56 m³/s and lagged by 6.0 h)

Time, h	0	6	12	18	24	30	36	42	48	54	60	66	72
I, m³/s	10	16	34	60	50	38	28	22	16	12	10	8.0	6.0

Practice Problem 11.5

A flood hydrograph shown in the table below entered the Sliver Creek reservoir described in the previous Practice Problem. Assume water surface

Flood Routing

elevation at the start of 100.50 m and use time interval of 5.0 h. Route the hydrograph through the reservoir using pulse method. (Peak 61 m³/s)

Time, h	0	5	20	25	30	40	45	42	50	55	60	65	70
I, m³/s	13	19	39	71	54	43	32	26	20	15	12	10	8.0

Practice Problem 11.6

For a Sagan reservoir, storage and outflow versus height above the crest elevation of 100.00 m are described by the following relationships:

$$S(dm^3) = 3.6 + 18h^{0.75} \qquad Q\left(\frac{m^3}{s}\right) = 10 \times h(m)$$

Route a triangular shaped flood hydrograph with time base of 26 h and peak of 30 m³/s occurring at 6.0 h. Assume zero discharge at the start and use a time interval of 2.0 h. (Peak discharge 29 m³/s and lagged by 2.0 h)

Practice Problem 11.7

As part of storm water management, a detention basin with vertical walls is built. The out flow from the pond is through a large drainage pipe located at the bottom. Head discharge relationship for this spillway and head storage relationship are as follows:

$$S(m^3) = 810h(m) \quad Q\left(\frac{m^3}{s}\right) = 1.93 \times h^{1.71}$$

Route the inflow hydrograph using time interval of 10 min. Assume basin is initially empty. Find peak attenuation and lag time. (1.35 m³/s, 40 min lag)

Time, min	0	10	20	30	40	50	60	70	80	90	100
I, m³/s	0	0.30	0.60	1.0	1.8	2.5	2.7	2.6	2.4	1.7	1.25

min	110	120	130	140	150	160	170	180	190	200
I, m³/s	0.93	0.70	0.52	0.39	0.30	0.22	0.17	0.10	0.05	0.0

Practice Problem 11.8

For the data of **Practice Problem 10.7**, inflow hydrograph is triangular in shape with peak of 1.8 m³/s at 60 min and receding to zero at 180 min. Find peak attenuation and lag time. (0.90 m³/s, 20 min lag)

Practice Problem 11.9

The following inflow and outflow hydrographs were observed in a river reach. Estimate the value of K and x. (x = 0.25, K = 13 h)

Time, h	0	6	12	18	24	30	36	42	48	54	60	66
I, m³/s	5	20	50	50	32	22	15	10	7	5	5	5
Q, m³/s	5	6	12	29	38	35	29	23	17	13	9	7

Practice Problem 11.10

Route the following hydrograph through a river reach for which K = 12 h and x = 0.20. Discharge at the start is 10 m³/s. Find the attenuation of flood peak and lag. (10 m³/s, 12 h)

Time, h	0	6	12	18	24	30	36	42	48	54
I, m³/s	10	20	50	60	55	45	35	27	20	15

Practice Problem 11.11

Route the following flood hydrograph through a river reach for which Muskingum coefficient K = 12 h and x = 0.25. The initial discharge is 45 m³/s. (232 m³/s, 60 h)

h	0	12	24	36	48	60	72	84	96	108	120	132	144
m³/s	50	75	180	290	250	210	180	150	120	90	75	860	50

Practice Problem 11.12

Route the following flood hydrograph through a river reach for which Muskingum coefficient K = 18 h and x = 0.20. The initial discharge is 35 m³/s. (187 m³/s, 5 h)

h	0	10	20	30	40	50	60	70	80	90	100	110	120
m³/s	40	70	130	250	210	170	140	120	100	80	60	40	30

Practice Problem 11.13

Observed data for the inflow and outflow for a Sam River reach is given in the table below. Determine the best value of K and x. (38 h, 0.28)

Time, h	0	6	12	18	24	35
I, m³/s	35	55	92	130	160	140
Q, m³/s	35	30	25	29	41	69

Review Questions

1. The prism storage in a river reach during the passage of flood wave is ____ during ____ phase.
   a) Constant, rising
   b) Negative, rising
   c) Positive, declining phase
   d) Negative, falling phase

2. In Muskingum equation, values of coefficients C_0, C_1, C_2 are such that sum of all three is;
   a) <1
   b) >1
   c) =1
   d) All

3. Hydrologic flood routing use
   a) Equation of continuity only
   b) Equation of motion only
   c) Energy equation only
   d) a, c

4. Hydraulic flood routing use
   a) Equation of continuity only
   b) Equation of motion only
   c) Energy equation only
   d) a,c

5. When a flood hydrograph is routed through a large uncontrolled reservoir, the outflow hydrograph will have
   a) Attenuated peak with shorter time base
   b) Attenuated peak with longer time base
   c) Heightened peak with shorter time base
   d) Heightened peak with longer time base

6. Which of the following methods is a hydrologic channel routing method?
   a) Pulse
   b) Muskingum
   c) Goodrich
   d) Runga Kutta

7. Which of the following methods is not a level pool method of flood routing?
   a) Pulse
   b) Muskingum
   c) Goodrich
   d) Runga Kutta

8. In a linear reservoir, storage varies linearly with
   a) Elevation
   b) Outflow
   c) Inflow
   d) Time

9. In Muskingum method of channel routing, the factor x can have a value in the range of
   a) 0.1-1
   b) 0-1
   c) 1.0-10
   d) 0-0.5

10. In Muskingum method of channel routing, channel storage S =
    a) $K[xI + (1-x)Q]$
    b) $K[xQ + (1-x)I]$
    c) $K[xI - (1-x)Q]$
    d) $K[xQ - (1-x)I]$

11. For natural channels, the factor x in Muskingum equation of flood routing typically falls in the range of
    a) 0-0.3
    b) 0-3
    c) -0.1-0.3
    d) 0-1

12. Total storage in the channel reach, S =
    a) $K[xI^m + (1-x)Q^m]$
    b) $K[xI^m + (1+x)Q^m]$
    c) $K[xI^m - (1+x)Q^m]$
    d) $K[xI^m - (1-x)Q^m]$

13. The value of exponent m in equation for storage in channel reach is
    a) <0
    b) >1
    c) <1
    d) 1

14. The flow in a river reach during flood wave is termed as _____ varied _____ flow
    a) Gradually, steady
    b) Gradually, unsteady
    c) Rapidly, steady
    d) Rapidly, unsteady

15. The wedge storage in a channel reach is a function of _____ discharge.
    a) Inflow
    b) Outflow
    c) Both a, b
    d) None

16. The prism storage in a channel reach is function of
    a) Inflow
    b) Outflow
    c) Both a, b
    d) None

17. In reservoir routing, storage is a function of _____ discharge
    a) Inflow
    b) Outflow
    c) Both a, b
    d) None

18. In Muskingum method of channel routing, outflow discharge Q_2 = _____
    a) $C_0 I_1 + C_1 I_2 + C_2 Q_1$
    b) $C_1 I_1 + C_0 I_2 + C_2 Q_1$
    c) $C_0 I_2 + C_1 Q_1 + C_2 I_1$
    d) $C_0 I_2 + C_1 I_1 + C_2 Q_1$

19. In an uncontrolled spillway, outflow discharge from a reservoir is proportional to
    a) $H^{0.5}$
    b) $H^{1.0}$
    c) $H^{1.5}$
    d) $H^{2.5}$

20. In Muskingum method of channel routing, the coefficient C_0 = 0.048, C_1 = 0.429, hence coefficient C_2 is
    a) 0.477
    b) 0.381
    c) 0.583
    d) 1.477

21. Applying Muskingum method to a channel reach for which K = 12.0 h

Flood Routing

and x = 0.20, and Δt =6.0 h, coefficient C_0 is
a) 0.048　　　　b) 0.429　　　　c) 0.583　　　　d) None

22. Applying Muskingum method to channel reach for which K = 12.0 h, x = 0.20, and Δt =6.0 h, coefficient C_1 is
a) 0.048　　　　b) 0.429　　　　c) 0.583　　　　d) Other

23. If the outflow over the spillway is uncontrolled, the peak of the outflow hydrograph will occur
    a) At the point of intersection of the two hydrographs
    b) Before the point of intersection of the two hydrographs
    c) After the point of intersection of the two hydrographs
    d) All are possible

24. For level pool routing, continuity equation is
    a) $\left(S_2 + \frac{O_2 \Delta t}{2}\right) = \left(\frac{I_1+I_2}{2}\right)\Delta t + \left(S_1 + \frac{O_1 \Delta t}{2}\right)$
    b) $\left(S_2 - \frac{O_2 \Delta t}{2}\right) = \left(\frac{I_1+I_2}{2}\right)\Delta t - \left(S_1 - \frac{O_1 \Delta t}{2}\right)$
    c) $\left(S_2 + \frac{O_2 \Delta t}{2}\right) = \left(\frac{I_1+I_2}{2}\right)\Delta t + \left(S_1 - \frac{O_1 \Delta t}{2}\right)$
    d) $\left(S_2 + \frac{O_2 \Delta t}{2}\right) = \left(\frac{I_1+I_2}{2}\right)\Delta t - \left(S_1 - \frac{O_1 \Delta t}{2}\right)$

25. In level pool routing, peak of the outflow hydrograph must
    a) intersect inflow hydrograph
    b) intersect point of the two hydrographs
    c) lead intersect point of the two hydrographs
    d) coincide with the peak of inflow hydrograph

Appendices

A. Answer Key

#	\multicolumn{11}{c}{Chapter}
	1	2	3	4	5	6	7	8	9	10	11
1	b	b	a	b	c	d	c	c	a	b	a
2	c	d	b	c	b	d	b	a	a	c	c
3	a	a	d	a	b	c	c	c	c	a	a
4	c	c	a.	d	c	b	c	b	a	a	d
5	c	d	c	a	a	d	a	d	d	b	b
6	a	d	c	d	a	b	c	c	b	d	b
7	c	a	b	b	c	a	c	a	c	d	b
8	a	c	c	c	c	d	b	b	d	a	b
9	d	b	b	c	d	c	a	b	b	d	d
10	b	c	c	c	a	b	c	c	c	b	a
11	c	c	b	d	d	d	d	d	d	a	a
12	d	b	c	c	b	d	a	a	c	c	a
13	a	d	c	d	a	a	b	c	a	d	d
14	c	d	a	d	c	a	c	b	b	c	b
15	b	b	c	b	c	b	a	d	d	c	a
16	c	d	d	a	c	c	b	a	b	a	b
17	d	a	b	c	b	a	d	a	b	b	b
18	b	a	b	c	d	c	d	b	b	b	d
19	a	d	b	c	b	a	d	c	a	a	c
20	b	c	d	d	c	a	c	b	d	a	c
21	a	c	a	b	b	c	c	a	d	c	a
22	d	a	a	d	c	c	a	d	a	a	b
23	a	b	c	a	a	b	c	d	b	b	c
24	d	b	c	b	b	a	a	d	c	a	c
25	a	d	b	c	b	b	b	c	c	d	a
26	b	a	c	d	c	d	a	c	b	a	
27	b	b	d	c	c	b	c	a	c	a	
28	b	a	c	a	b	a	d	a	c	c	
29	d	d	b	b	b	a	a	a	c		
30	a	b	b	d	d	c	b	a	b	b	
	1	2	3	4	5	6	7	8	9	10	11

B. Curve Numbers

Sl No.	Landuse	Trestment/practice	Hudrologic condition	Hydrologic soil group			
				A	B	C	D
1	Cultivated	Straight row	.....	76	86	90	93
		Contoured	Poor	70	79	84	88
			Good	65	75	82	86
		Contoured and terraced	Poor	66	74	80	82
				62	71	77	81
			Good	67	75	81	83
		Bunded	Poor	59	69	769	79
			Good	95	95	5	95
		Paddy (rice)	.....				
2	Orchards	With under stony cover	.....	39	53	67	71
		Without under stony cover	.....	41	55	69	73
3	Forest	Dense	....	26	40	58	61
		Open		28	44	60	64
		Shrubs		33	47	64	67
4	Pasture	....	Poor	68	79	86	89
			Fair	49	69	79	84
			Good	39	61	74	80
5	Wasted Land	....	....	71	80	85	88
6	Hard Surface	....	....	77	86	91	93

C. Curve Numbers (Crops)

Cover type	Treatment	Hydrologic condition	Curve numbers for hydrologic soil group			
			A	B	C	D
Fallow	Bare soil	-	77	86	91	94
	Crop residue cover (CR)	Poor	72	81	88	91
		Good	67	78	85	89
Row crops	Straight row (SR)	Poor	70	79	84	88
		Good	65	75	82	86
	Contoured and terraced (C and T)	Poor	66	74	80	82
		Good	62	71	78	81
Small grain	SR	Poor	65	76	84	88
		Good	63	75	83	87
	SR + CR	Poor	64	75	83	86
		Good	60	72	80	84
	C	Poor	63	74	82	85
		Good	61	73	81	84
	C + CR	Poor	62	73	81	85
		Good	60	72	80	83
	C+T	Poor	61	72	79	82
		Good	59	70	78	81
	C+T+CR	Poor	60	71	78	81
		Good	58	69	77	80
Close seeded or broadcast legumes or rotation meadow	SR	Poor	66	77	85	89
		Good	58	72	81	85
	C	Poor	64	75	83	85
		Good	55	69	78	83
	C+T	Poor	63	73	80	83
		Good	51	67	76	80

Fonte: Iowa Storm water Management Manual, 2008.

D. Curve Numbers-Urban

Land-use description	Hydrologic soil group			
	A	B	C	D
Cultivated land[1]: without conservation treatment	72	81	88	91
with conservation treatment	62	71	78	81
Pasture or range land: poor condition	68	79	86	89
good condition	39	61	74	80
Meadow: good condition	30	58	71	78
Wood or forest land: thin stand, poor cover, no mulch	45	66	77	83
good cover[2]	25	55	70	77
Open spaces, lawns, parks, golf courses, cemeteries, etc.				
good condition: grass cover on 75 percent or more of the area	39	61	74	80
fair condition: grass cover on 50 to 75 percent of the area	49	69	79	84
Commercial and business areas (85 percent impervious)	89	92	94	95
Industrial districts (72 percent impervious)	81	88	91	93
Residential[3]:				
Average lot size Average percent impervious[4]				
1/8 acre or less 65	77	85	90	92
1/4 acre 38	61	75	83	87
1/3 acre 30	57	72	81	86
1/2 acre 25	54	70	80	85
1 acre 20	51	68	79	84
Paved parking lots, roofs, driveways, etc.[5]	98	98	98	98
Streets and roads:				
paved with curbs and storm sewers[5]	98	98	98	98
gravel	76	85	89	91
dirt	72	82	87	89

[1] For a more detailed description of agricultural land-use curve numbers, refer to Soil Conservation Service (SCS), 1972, Chap. 9.
[2] Good cover is protected from grazing, litter, and brush cover soil.

E. Normal Distribution Tables

Tables of the Normal Distribution

Probability Content from -oo to Z

Z	0.00	0.01	0.02	0.03	0.04	0.05	0.06	0.07	0.08	0.09
0.0	0.5000	0.5040	0.5080	0.5120	0.5160	0.5199	0.5239	0.5279	0.5319	0.5359
0.1	0.5398	0.5438	0.5478	0.5517	0.5557	0.5596	0.5636	0.5675	0.5714	0.5753
0.2	0.5793	0.5832	0.5871	0.5910	0.5948	0.5987	0.6026	0.6064	0.6103	0.6141
0.3	0.6179	0.6217	0.6255	0.6293	0.6331	0.6368	0.6406	0.6443	0.6480	0.6517
0.4	0.6554	0.6591	0.6628	0.6664	0.6700	0.6736	0.6772	0.6808	0.6844	0.6879
0.5	0.6915	0.6950	0.6985	0.7019	0.7054	0.7088	0.7123	0.7157	0.7190	0.7224
0.6	0.7257	0.7291	0.7324	0.7357	0.7389	0.7422	0.7454	0.7486	0.7517	0.7549
0.7	0.7580	0.7611	0.7642	0.7673	0.7704	0.7734	0.7764	0.7794	0.7823	0.7852
0.8	0.7881	0.7910	0.7939	0.7967	0.7995	0.8023	0.8051	0.8078	0.8106	0.8133
0.9	0.8159	0.8186	0.8212	0.8238	0.8264	0.8289	0.8315	0.8340	0.8365	0.8389
1.0	0.8413	0.8438	0.8461	0.8485	0.8508	0.8531	0.8554	0.8577	0.8599	0.8621
1.1	0.8643	0.8665	0.8686	0.8708	0.8729	0.8749	0.8770	0.8790	0.8810	0.8830
1.2	0.8849	0.8869	0.8888	0.8907	0.8925	0.8944	0.8962	0.8980	0.8997	0.9015
1.3	0.9032	0.9049	0.9066	0.9082	0.9099	0.9115	0.9131	0.9147	0.9162	0.9177
1.4	0.9192	0.9207	0.9222	0.9236	0.9251	0.9265	0.9279	0.9292	0.9306	0.9319
1.5	0.9332	0.9345	0.9357	0.9370	0.9382	0.9394	0.9406	0.9418	0.9429	0.9441
1.6	0.9452	0.9463	0.9474	0.9484	0.9495	0.9505	0.9515	0.9525	0.9535	0.9545
1.7	0.9554	0.9564	0.9573	0.9582	0.9591	0.9599	0.9608	0.9616	0.9625	0.9633
1.8	0.9641	0.9649	0.9656	0.9664	0.9671	0.9678	0.9686	0.9693	0.9699	0.9706
1.9	0.9713	0.9719	0.9726	0.9732	0.9738	0.9744	0.9750	0.9756	0.9761	0.9767
2.0	0.9772	0.9778	0.9783	0.9788	0.9793	0.9798	0.9803	0.9808	0.9812	0.9817
2.1	0.9821	0.9826	0.9830	0.9834	0.9838	0.9842	0.9846	0.9850	0.9854	0.9857
2.2	0.9861	0.9864	0.9868	0.9871	0.9875	0.9878	0.9881	0.9884	0.9887	0.9890
2.3	0.9893	0.9896	0.9898	0.9901	0.9904	0.9906	0.9909	0.9911	0.9913	0.9916
2.4	0.9918	0.9920	0.9922	0.9925	0.9927	0.9929	0.9931	0.9932	0.9934	0.9936
2.5	0.9938	0.9940	0.9941	0.9943	0.9945	0.9946	0.9948	0.9949	0.9951	0.9952
2.6	0.9953	0.9955	0.9956	0.9957	0.9959	0.9960	0.9961	0.9962	0.9963	0.9964
2.7	0.9965	0.9966	0.9967	0.9968	0.9969	0.9970	0.9971	0.9972	0.9973	0.9974
2.8	0.9974	0.9975	0.9976	0.9977	0.9977	0.9978	0.9979	0.9979	0.9980	0.9981
2.9	0.9981	0.9982	0.9982	0.9983	0.9984	0.9984	0.9985	0.9985	0.9986	0.9986
3.0	0.9987	0.9987	0.9987	0.9988	0.9988	0.9989	0.9989	0.9989	0.9990	0.9990

F. Pearson Type III Distribution Table

WEIGHTED SKEW COEFFICIENT Cw	Recurrence Interval In Years							
	1.0101	2	5	10	25	50	100	200
	Percent Chance (>=) = 1-F							
	99	50	20	10	4	2	1	0.5
-0.4	-2.615	0.066	0.855	1.231	1.606	1.834	2.029	2.201
-0.5	-2.686	0.083	0.856	1.216	1.567	1.777	1.955	2.108
-0.6	-2.755	0.099	0.857	1.2	1.528	1.72	1.88	2.016
-0.7	-2.824	0.116	0.857	1.183	1.488	1.663	1.806	1.926
-0.8	-2.891	0.132	0.856	1.166	1.448	1.606	1.733	1.837
-0.9	-2.957	0.148	0.854	1.147	1.407	1.549	1.66	1.749
-1	-3.022	0.164	0.852	1.128	1.366	1.492	1.588	1.664
-1.1	-3.087	0.18	0.848	1.107	1.324	1.435	1.518	1.581
-1.2	-3.149	0.195	0.844	1.086	1.282	1.379	1.449	1.501
-1.3	-3.211	0.21	0.838	1.064	1.24	1.324	1.383	1.424
-1.4	-3.271	0.225	0.832	1.041	1.198	1.27	1.318	1.351
-1.5	-3.33	0.24	0.825	1.018	1.157	1.217	1.256	1.282
-1.6	-3.88	0.254	0.817	0.994	1.116	1.166	1.197	1.216
-1.7	-3.444	0.268	0.808	0.97	1.075	1.116	1.14	1.155
-1.8	-3.499	0.282	0.799	0.945	1.035	1.069	1.087	1.097
-1.9	-3.553	0.294	0.788	0.92	0.996	1.023	1.037	1.044
-2	-3.605	0.307	0.777	0.895	0.959	0.98	0.99	0.995
-2.1	-3.656	0.319	0.765	0.869	0.923	0.939	0.946	0.949
-2.2	-3.705	0.33	0.752	0.844	0.888	0.9	0.905	0.907
-2.3	-3.753	0.341	0.739	0.819	0.855	0.864	0.867	0.869
-2.4	-3.8	0.351	0.725	0.795	0.823	0.83	0.832	0.833
-2.5	-3.845	0.36	0.711	0.711	0.793	0.798	0.799	0.8
-2.6	-3.899	0.368	0.696	0.747	0.764	0.768	0.769	0.769
-2.7	-3.932	0.376	0.681	0.724	0.738	0.74	0.74	0.741
-2.8	-3.973	0.384	0.666	0.702	0.712	0.714	0.714	0.714
-2.9	-4.013	0.39	0.651	0.681	0.683	0.689	0.69	0.69
-3	-4.051	0.396	0.636	0.66	0.666	0.666	0.667	0.667

G. Pearson Type III Distribution Table

Coefficient of skewness γ	Nonexceedance probability (q)								
	0.01	0.2	0.5	0.8	0.9	0.95	0.98	0.99	0.999
	Corresponding return period (T)								
	1.01	1.25	2	5	10	20	50	100	1000
−1.14	Lower limit for coefficient of skewness								
−1.04	−3.0752	−0.7344	0.1550	0.8280	1.1172	1.3310	1.5488	1.6825	2.0164
−1.00	−3.0499	−0.7401	0.1511	0.8305	1.1237	1.3410	1.5627	1.6990	2.0403
−0.80	−2.9189	−0.7683	0.1306	0.8422	1.1566	1.3921	1.6352	1.7857	2.1669
−0.60	−2.7666	−0.7973	0.1056	0.8527	1.1916	1.4492	1.7181	1.8864	2.3178
−0.40	−2.5997	−0.8249	0.0766	0.8605	1.2270	1.5099	1.8093	1.9986	2.4911
−0.20	−2.4221	−0.8496	0.0438	0.8646	1.2614	1.5731	1.9078	2.1221	2.6886
0.00	−2.2394	−0.8699	0.0076	0.8640	1.2934	1.6372	2.0124	2.2559	2.9110
0.20	−2.0579	−0.8845	−0.0308	0.8581	1.3214	1.7002	2.1210	2.3979	3.1575
0.40	−1.8834	−0.8925	−0.0705	0.8463	1.3442	1.7602	2.2310	2.5456	3.4263
0.60	−1.7207	−0.8938	−0.1098	0.8287	1.3606	1.8152	2.3399	2.6959	3.7142
0.80	−1.5726	−0.8885	−0.1477	0.8059	1.3701	1.8637	2.4449	2.8457	4.0171
1.00	−1.4405	−0.8777	−0.1831	0.7785	1.3727	1.9048	2.5439	2.9919	4.3303
1.20	−1.3241	−0.8623	−0.2151	0.7477	1.3688	1.9379	2.6354	3.1321	4.6494
1.40	−1.2225	−0.8435	−0.2436	0.7145	1.3589	1.9630	2.7182	3.2645	4.9701
1.60	−1.1340	−0.8224	−0.2682	0.6799	1.3440	1.9806	2.7919	3.3879	5.2886
1.80	−1.0570	−0.7999	−0.2892	0.6446	1.3249	1.9913	2.8564	3.5015	5.6019
2.00	−0.9899	−0.7769	−0.3069	0.6094	1.3026	1.9957	2.9120	3.6052	5.9078
2.20	−0.9313	−0.7537	−0.3214	0.5749	1.2778	1.9948	2.9593	3.6990	6.2044
2.40	−0.8798	−0.7309	−0.3332	0.5413	1.2512	1.9893	2.9988	3.7834	6.4906
2.60	−0.8343	−0.7088	−0.3426	0.5090	1.2234	1.9799	3.0312	3.8587	6.7657
2.80	−0.7939	−0.6875	−0.3500	0.4782	1.1948	1.9673	3.0573	3.9257	7.0292
3.00	−0.7578	−0.6671	−0.3557	0.4488	1.1660	1.9521	3.0777	3.9850	7.2811
3.20	−0.7255	−0.6476	−0.3598	0.4210	1.1371	1.9348	3.0931	4.0371	7.5215
3.40	−0.6963	−0.6291	−0.3627	0.3947	1.1085	1.9159	3.1041	4.0828	7.7505
3.60	−0.6699	−0.6116	−0.3646	0.3699	1.0802	1.8956	3.1111	4.1225	7.9686
3.80	−0.6459	−0.5951	−0.3656	0.3466	1.0525	1.8743	3.1147	4.1569	8.1760
4.00	−0.6239	−0.5794	−0.3659	0.3246	1.0253	1.8523	3.1153	4.1865	8.3733
4.20	−0.6038	−0.5646	−0.3656	0.3039	0.9989	1.8298	3.1133	4.2117	8.5608
4.40	−0.5852	−0.5506	−0.3648	0.2845	0.9732	1.8070	3.1091	4.2330	8.7392
4.60	−0.5681	−0.5373	−0.3635	0.2662	0.9483	1.7840	3.1028	4.2508	8.9087
4.80	−0.5522	−0.5248	−0.3619	0.2490	0.9241	1.7609	3.0949	4.2653	9.0700
5.00	−0.5374	−0.5129	−0.3601	0.2329	0.9007	1.7378	3.0854	4.2770	9.2233
5.20	−0.5236	−0.5016	−0.3580	0.2177	0.8781	1.7149	3.0747	4.2860	9.3692
5.40	−0.5107	−0.4909	−0.3557	0.2033	0.8563	1.6921	3.0629	4.2927	9.5081
5.60	−0.4987	−0.4808	−0.3533	0.1898	0.8351	1.6696	3.0502	4.2974	9.6402
5.80	−0.4873	−0.4711	−0.3508	0.1771	0.8148	1.6473	3.0366	4.3001	9.7661
6.00	−0.4766	−0.4619	−0.3482	0.1651	0.7951	1.6253	3.0223	4.3011	9.8860
6.20	−0.4666	−0.4532	−0.3455	0.1538	0.7760	1.6037	3.0075	4.3005	10.0003
6.40	−0.4570	−0.4448	−0.3428	0.1430	0.7577	1.5824	2.9921	4.2985	10.1092
6.60	−0.4480	−0.4368	−0.3400	0.1329	0.7400	1.5615	2.9763	4.2953	10.2132
6.80	−0.4395	−0.4292	−0.3373	0.1233	0.7228	1.5409	2.9602	4.2909	10.3123
7.00	−0.4313	−0.4219	−0.3345	0.1142	0.7063	1.5207	2.9439	4.2856	10.4069

H. K coefficient

Flow Type	K
Small Tributary - Permanent or intermittent streams which appear as solid or dashed blue lines on USGS topographic maps.	2.1
Waterway - Any overland flow route which is a well-defined swale by elevation contours, but is not a stream section as defined above.	1.2
Sheet Flow - Any other overland flow path which does not conform to the definition of a waterway.	

K	Land Use / Flow Regime
0.25	Forest with heavy ground litter, hay meadow (overland flow)
0.5	Trash fallow or minimum tillage cultivation; contour or strip cropped; woodland (overland flow)
0.7	Short grass pasture (overland flow)
0.9	Cultivated straight row (overland flow)
1.0	Nearly bare and untilled (overland flow); alluvial fans in western mountain regions
1.5	Grassed waterway
2.0	Paved area (sheet flow); small upland g

Subject Index

A

Adequacy of
rainfall gauge station 40
Agricultural production 20
Alter shield 37
Antecedent moisture
condition 176, 225
Application of
Hydrologic equation 17
Areal mean rainfall 58
Areal weighing of 225
Arithmetic mean 125
Atmometer 184
Average aerial precipitation 62

B

Base flow 198, 199, 208
Base flow
    curve method 212
    separation 211
Basic equations of flood routing 293
Basin
    area 148
    catchment 143
    drainage 14
    lag time 203, 270
    river 5
    shape 148, 154
    slope 154
Bell curve 126
Binomial distribution 121
Binomial process 121
Black box 143
Black box model 256

Blaney Criddle method 186
Bubbler gauge 96
Budget equation 17

C

Catchment relief 149
Central tendency 125
Channel control 96
Channel routing 292
Channel slope 152
Channel storage 303
Chemical gauging 102
Classification of watershed 143
Classification by land use 144
    agricultural 145
    forest 146
    mountainous
    urban 145
Climatic change 25
Closed system 2
Coefficient of
    skewness 126
    variation 39, 126
Cold front 34
Compact coefficient 148
Composite CN 176
Concentrated flow 202
Conditional probability 120
Connected impervious area 231
Constant slope method 212
Consumptive use 184
Continuous variable 124
Convective precipitation 34

Cooks method 235
Correction unconnectedness 237
Crest (hydrograph) 201
Crest gauge 95
Cumulative
    distribution102in
    filtration 164
Current meter 97
Curve number 173,175
Curve number method 173, 175
Cyclonic precipitationb34

D

Decreasing limb 201
Depression storage 160
Depth area duration (DAD) 68
Depth area frequency (DAF) 68
Depth duration frequency 70
Depth rate 13
Desalination of water 24
Detention storage 161
Determination of ET 184,185
Dilution factor 102
Discharge hydrograph 94
Discrete variable 124
Dispersion 126
Distribution of water on earth 4
Double mass curve 47
Drainage area 147
Drainage density 149
Drainage divide 143

E

Earth's water 4
Eddy loss coefficient 106
Effective precipitation168,177
Electromagnetic method 107

Elements of hydrograph 200
Environment restoration 21
Environmental requirement 24
Equilibrium infiltration rate 163
Equivalent slope 152
Errors in measurement 37
Estimation of K and x 304
Estimation of potential
retention (S) 174
Evaporation 183
Evaporation pan 183
Evapotranspiration (ET)
Determination
    Blaney Criddle 186
    Hargreaves method 188
    Thornthwaite 188
    Measurement of 184
Excessive ground water
exploitation 10
Extreme areal mean rainfall 58

F

First order stream 148
Float 97
Float gauge 96
Float type gauge 36
Float velocity 97
Flood routing basic equations 293
Flood routing definition 292
Flood routing/methods 292,293
Flooding infiltrometer 162
Flow hydrograph 93
Flow measuring structure 107
Flow time 227
Frequency factor (K) 127

G

Gauge consistency 46
Gauge site 96
Gradually varied flow 293
Gross slope 152
Ground water management 23

H

Hathway formula 205
Horton's infiltration equation 164
Hydrograph 198
    Analysis 163
    Elements of 200
    Flow time 227
    For individual storms 18
    For larger watersheds 17
    Shape of 200
Hydrologic
    abstraction 160
    budget 16
    condition 176
    cycle 1
    data 12
    equation 17
    routing 293
    soil group 175
    storage 294
    storage routing 293
Hydrological routing 293
Hydrology applications 19
    Agriculture 20
    Design of hydraulic works 20
    Drought mitigation 19
    Flood control 19
    Land conservation 20
Hydrograph shape 200
Hyetograph 58
Hypsometric curve 149

I

Indirect methods 103
Infiltration 161
Equilibrium infiltration 163
Infiltration capacity 161
Infiltration formula 163
Infiltration index 168
Infiltration rate 162
Infiltrometer 17
Inflexion point 201
Initial abstraction 174
Inlet time 227
Intensity duration frequency 71
Inter basin water transfer 22
Interception storage 160
Interflow 199
Isobar 34
Isohyet 62
Isohyet map 62
Isohyetal method 64
Isopluvial 62

K

Kerby formula 226
Kirpich and Kerby formula 227
Kirpich formula 204, 226

L

Lag time 203, 272
Lake evaporation 183
Land use/ treatment 176
Limitations of Rational method 228
Linear reservoir 207
Log normal distribution 132
Lysimeter (modified tank) 185

M

Manning's equation 205
Manning's n 223
Mass conservation 15
Mean deviation 126
Mean, mode, median 125
Mean section method 99
Mean slope 152
Measurement of ET 184
Measurement of flow velocity 97
Measuring points 38
Measuring precipitation 35
Median 125
Median elevation 149
Median height 150
Method of superposition 260
Mid-section method 99
Missing data 42
Modified budget equation 17
Modified impervious fraction 237
Modified pulse method 295
Mount Rose sampler 38
Muskingum equation 303
Muskingum method of routing 305

N

NRCS Curve number (CN)
    method 173
    derivation of UH 273
    dimensionless UH 272
    lag equation 203
    lag time 273
Non normal distribution 131
Non recording stream gauge 95
Normal distribution 126
Normal ratio method 43

NRCS
    Derivation of UH 257
    Dimensionless hydrograph 272
    Lag time 273
    Peak flow rate 275
    Synthetic UH 277
    Time of concentration 274
    Time to peak 273
    TR 55 l method 180
    Triangular hydrograph 274
    Unit hydrograph 275

O

Orographic 34
Ott meter 97
Overland flow 199

P

Precipitation 32
    Convective 34
    Cyclonic 34
    Excess 264
    Forms of 32
    Frontal 34
    Measurement 35
    Orographic 34
    Types 34
Pan coefficient 183
Peak discharge 222
Peak flow rate 273
Pearson skewness 126
Pearson type III distribution 132
Penman equation 189
Percolation 161

Percolation tanks 19
Pervious impervious area 236
Phi index (Φ) index 168
Plots 185
Point area 68
Point depth 68
Point rainfall 39
Population variate (Z) 127
Potential evapotranspiration 183
Potential infiltration 166, 171
Potential retention 174
Precipitation 32
Precipitation excess 264, 266
Prediction of storm flow 265
Price meter 97
Prism storge 303
Probability 119
Probability density function 125,127
Probability distribution 124
Probability function 125
Probability of exceedance 127

Q

Quadrant method 44

R

Radar 37
Rainfall
    Data 39
    Intensity 58, 227
    Types of 34
Rainwater 24
Rating curve 93
Rating curve equation 108
Rating curve parameter 109
Rating table 92

Rational method/formula 223
    Limitations 228
    Modifications 225
Reading gauges 39
Recession 207
Recession curve method 212
Recession limb 201
Recording rain gauge 45
Recording stream gauges 95
Recurrence interval 119
Recycle and reuse of water 24
Reference evapotranspiration 189
Relief features 149
Relief ratio 149
Reservoir routing 292
Reservoir routing methods 293
Return period 119
Rising limb 201
Risk and reliability 121
Routing method 292
Rules of probability 119
Runoff coefficient 225
Runoff diffusion 236
Runoff hydrograph 200
Runoff prediction 39

S

S- Hydrograph 262
Sample variate (Z) 127
Sectional control 96
Shallow concentrated flow 239
Shape factor 113
Slope
    Basin 154
    Gross 152
    Mean 152
    Equivalent 152

Slope area method 103, 104
Small watershed 143
Snow
    Courses 37
    sampler 38
    Surveys/courses 37
Snowpack 37
Snyder unit hydrograph 270
Spatial distribution 62
Specific gravity of snow 38
Sprinkler infiltration/infiltrometer 163
Staff gauge 95
Stage 93, 94
Stage discharge relation 108
Stage hydrograph 93
Standard deviation 126
Standard duration 271
Standard gauge 35
Standard normal curve 125
Standard normal distribution 125, 126
Standardized distribution 126
Standpipe gauge 36
Station average 63
Station average method 43
Steady flow formula 205, 206
Stilling well 96
Storage reservoir 184
Storm drainage system 232
Storm duration 202
Storm eye 62
Storm runoff 175, 177, 258
Straight line method 211
Strategies for freshwater management 11
Stream flow 93
    Components 198
    Hydrograph 198
    Measurement 93

Recession 207
Variation 93
Stream order 148
Streamflow variation 93
Sub concentrated flow 203
Super concentrated flow 203
Surface runoff 199
Surface water resources of India 5
Symmetrical distribution 126
Synthetic storm 78
Synthetic unit hydrograph 270

T

Tank (lysimeter) 185
Temporal distribution 58
Temporal variation 58
Test for normalcy 131
Thiessen's polygon method 63
Threat to biodiversity 10
Time and space scales 14
Time of concentration 202, 226, 272
Time of concentration estimation 203
Time characteristics 201
    Lag time 203
    Time of storage 208
    Time to peak 149
    Time to peak 271
Tipping bucket gauge 36
TR 55 180
TR 55 procedure 239
TR 55, Graphical method 235
Transpiration 183
Travel time through drain 227
Triangular hydrograph area 273
Triangular shaped storm 82

Typical and extreme areal mean rainfalls 58

U

Ultrasonic method 106
Unconnected impervious areas 237
Uneven distribution of water 8
Uniformity of channel section 104
Unit hydrograph 256
    Definition 257
    Derivation 257
    Method of superposition 260
    Of other durations 260
    Procedure for constructing 258
Urban catchments 227, 231

V

Variable
    Discrete 124
    Random 124
Variance 126
Variation in rainfall data 39
Velocity area station method 98

W

Water management 7
    Excessive groundwater exploitation 10
    Fresh water related problems 7
    Strategies for freshwater management 11
    Water conservation 11

Uneven distribution of water 8
Water pollution
    Agriculture 9
    Domestic 9
    Industry 9
    Threat to biodiversity and wetlands 10
Water resources of India 5
    Surface water 5
    Reducing demand 6
    Increasing supply 6
    Conserving water 7
Watershed Characteristics 147
    Drainage area 147
    Basin shape 148
    Form factor 148
    Compact coefficient 148
    Stream order 148
    Drainage density 149
    Desert 146
    Coastal 147
    Relief features 149
    Basin slope 154
    Catchment relief 149
    Channel slope 152
    Equivalent slope 152
    Gross slope 152
    Hypsometric curve 149
    Mean slope 152
    Median elevation 150
    Relief ratio 149
Water Management 21
Water conservation and environment 21
    Water quality 21
    Environment restoration 21
    Dealing with climatic change 25
    Desalination of water 24

Environmental requirement 24
Groundwater management 22
Inter basin water transfer 22
Rainwater 24
Recycle and reuse of water 24
World water resources 3
Water balance 15
Water conservation 11
Water equivalent 36,38
Wedge storage 303
Weighing type gauge 36
Weighted average 63
Weighted CN 238
W-index 168
Wire gauge 95

Z

Zero slope routing 294

Appendices

www.ingramcontent.com/pod-product-compliance
Ingram Content Group UK Ltd.
Pitfield, Milton Keynes, MK11 3LW, UK
UKHW022151230426
12049UKWH00003BA/45